JOYCE
LAIN
KENNEDY'S
CAREER
BOOK

JOYCE LAIN KENNEDY'S CAREER BOOK

THIRD EDITION

Co-authored by Dr. Darryl Laramore

Printed on recyclable paper

VGM Career Horizons
a division of *NTC Publishing Group*
Lincolnwood, Illinois USA

Library of Congress Cataloging-in-Publication Data

Kennedy, Joyce Lain.
    Joyce Lain Kennedy's career book / Joyce Lain Kennedy, Darryl
Laramore. — 3rd ed.
    Includes bibliographical references (p.   ).
    ISBN 0-8442-4526-7. — ISBN 0-8442-4527-5 (pbk. : alk. paper)
    1. Vocational guidance—United States.   2. Career development—
United States.   I. Laramore, Darryl, 1928–   . II. Title.
HF5382 . 5 . U5K46   1997
650 . 14--dc20   96-27793
                                                              CIP

Published by VGM Career Horizons, a division of NTC Publishing Group.
4255 West Touhy Avenue, Lincolnwood (Chicago), IL 60646–1975 U.S.A.
1997, 1993, 1988 by Joyce Lain Kennedy and Darryl Laramore, Ph.D.
Manufactured in the United States of America.

To my late husband, William Alvey Kennedy,
who helped me so much with my career and who
enjoyed so many successes in his
—JLK

and

To my wonderful wife, Joyce Hutchison Laramore,
and my career-wise children, Nina, Christopher, and Megan,
who have made us very proud
—DL

CONTENTS

■ CAREER REWARDS ■

■ MIND-SET AND SUCCESS ■

■ WORK TRENDS ■

■ FUTURE JOBS ■

■ GETTING HELP ■

■ SELF-AWARENESS ■

■ WORK AWARENESS ■

■ RESEARCH ■

■ GOALS ■

■ MAKING DECISIONS ■

■ STUDENT JOBS ■

■ COLLEGE PLANNING ■

■ UNDERGRADUATE ADVANCED STUDY ■

College: How to Make Sure Your Mind Never Returns to Its Original Size ▪ So Your First Choice Turns You Down ▪ Take Good Notes ▪ Read Effectively ▪ When the Grade Disappoints ▪ Tips For Exams ▪ Time Management ▪ The Freshman Blues ▪ Reflection on Liberal Arts ▪ What You Can Do With a Major In . . . ▪ Doubling Your Chances with a Double Major ▪ The Real World: Working Part-Time ▪ Contacts: Your Partners in Success ▪ Get a Head Start on Power Skills ▪ Stop! Think about Graduate or Professional Study ▪ Windows on the World ▪ Business School: Your Golden Passport? ▪ A Law Degree Can Lead Almost Anywhere ▪ Medical School: More Knocks on the Door

■ OTHER EDUCATION ■

Feast on a Banquet of Job-Training Programs ▪ Schools Where Students Pay to Learn Paying Jobs ▪ Public Schools Where Students Train for Jobs ▪ The Two-Year College: Opportunity with Excellence ▪ New Opportunities: Work-Based Learning ▪ Career Training in the Armed Forces ▪ Distance Learning ▪ More Avenues of Education ▪ Ways to Make Good Decisions

■ ADULT JOB SEARCH ■

Your First Full-Time Job: The Art of Getting Hired ▪ Three Broad Categories of Job Seach Skills ▪ Knowing What You Have to Sell ▪ Electronic and Internet Resumes ▪ Knowing Where to Make the Sale ▪ How to Break into Competitive Industries ▪ Liberal Arts Majors: What Can You Do? ▪ Looking for a Job Far Away ▪ Disorganized? Discouraged? Try the Buddy System ▪ Knowing How to Make the Sale ▪ Senior Year Job Search Countdown

■ WINNING ON THE FIRST JOB ■

■ CAREER MANAGEMENT ■

ACKNOWLEDGMENTS

Although many experts read appropriate pages, the chairman of the board is Dr. *Kenneth B. Hoyt*, university distinguished professor of education at Kansas State University. Dr. Hoyt, a living legend in the careers discipline, gave the authors countless hours of truly valuable advice. You have our enduring gratitude.

At Sun Features Inc., *Muriel Turner* worked wonders as the revision project manager for this edition, earning a diamond-studded halo in the process.

To the team at VGM Career Horizons/NTC Publishing Group, we like your corporate culture—it's fun to work in. Special thanks go out to *Bill Pattis*, *Mark Pattis*, *Leonard Fiddle*, *Karen Christoffersen*, *Rosemary Dolinski*, *Amy Yu*, *John Nolan*, *Julie Rigby*, and *Betsy Lancefield*.

Finally a special word of thanks to *Nina Laramore*, whose updating skills lifted the bar. The full list of those who helped prepare the *Career Book* would fell a forest. Our thanks and apologies to any we have omitted.

■ ■ ■ ■

TO THE PARENT

You may be facing your own career concerns—moving up, changing jobs, surviving layoffs—at the same time you are beginning to think about how your child will find his or her way in life.

You are a much bigger factor in your child's successful career launch than you probably realize. In fact, you, the parent, are the *most* influential person in your child's career choice. Years of research in career selection have produced this important, unequivocal finding:

Young people are most influenced by their families—not by their peers, teachers, or counselors. Occupational attitudes are most shaped by what happens at home, not by what happens in classrooms and social settings.

This means you are the number-one resource and power for helping your young person target on a rewarding career and focus on the educational investments that will best lead to that target.

Being number one in anything is a heavy responsibility and the concern you carry for your child's future is justified. The choice of career largely determines how your young adult will live and whether the sum of his or her life will be a plus or minus.

As the authors of the *Career Book*, our purpose is to help you, the parent, meet the challenge of providing young adults with the information they need to make sensible, satisfying decisions about their career and life goals.

What The *Career Book* Can Do For Sons And Daughters, Age 15–25

For young adults, finding answers to these questions is of lifetime importance:

◆ *What do I want to be?*

◆ *What must I do to get what I want?*

◆ *Once launched, how do I move ahead?*

Why do we say these questions are of lifetime importance? Because, in the modern world, job security no longer exists: factories close, government employees are dismissed, whole industries shift to other countries.

True security lies in understanding how to make good career decisions, get training, and find jobs. Once career *strategies* and *processes* are understood, an individual can face the workplace with confidence. In this sense, the *Career Book* is a kind of insurance policy for covering life satisfaction. Whether young people express it in these words or not, that's what they hope the future holds for them.

In an age when work will never again be the same, the *Career Book* guides young adults through the process of making relevant life-satisfaction decisions, for now and later. Specifically, readers learn how to:

◆ Acquire facts about the world of career options

◆ Become more aware of their interests, abilities, and values

◆ Set goals and develop techniques to reach them

◆ Make effective decisions

◆ Involve family and friends in career planning

◆ Make appropriate educational choices

◆ Identify marketable skills

◆ Become an expert job seeker

◆ Nail down success on the job

By providing a young adult with the information to be found in the *Career Book*, you offer an opportunity to reach for true lifetime security and happiness.

the past decade or so. The *Career Book* not only summarizes important changes, but offers suggestions on winning a whole new ballgame in careers.

Because the book deals with developmental issues over a 10-year span (ages 15 to 25), both the sophistication of the text and the learning activities vary, and, in general, show increasing maturity as the guide progresses.

The enormous scope of the *Career Book* invites buffet reading: Your young adult can pick and choose topics that are critical at various stages of life. The format, too, invites dip-in and scoop-out involvement—information comes in concise, quickly absorbed portions. Most segments require no more than a few minutes to read, and most activities take no more than a few minutes to accomplish.

The scope, format, and content of the *Career Book* intend that the guide will have a long shelf life in home libraries. Like the basic cookbook or medical handbook that's consulted again and again, the *Career Book* can be a trusted and valuable reference for use during the years ahead.

Yes, The *Career Book* Is Different

Most guidance books for young people aim at either high-school students preparing for college admission, or at college students seeking careers.

The *Career Book* is for both groups, as well as for students not bound for college.

The *Career Book* ranges from the concerns of untried teens who are just beginning to think about their futures, all the way to those of recent college graduates who are experiencing their early days on their first permanent jobs.

Most guidance books do not clearly report the impact of the breathtaking changes occurring in both national and world economies over

Make Career Planning A Family Affair

Questions parents often ask us resemble these:

◆ *My daughter is a high school senior and she doesn't know what she wants to do. She's interested in so many things she can't decide. Do you have some kind of test that will help her?*

◆ *My son has his mind made up about a major that would never lead to a job. What else can he look into?*

◆ *What do you see as the best careers for the 21st century?*

Parents really want to help, and your help is needed.

But who should turn the steering wheel when young adults plan their careers?

Ultimately, definitive career decisions must be the prerogative of your offspring. It's a mistake to maneuver a young person into a field you wanted, but didn't land in, or to see your young adult as an extension of your own skills package.

On the other hand, your ideas as an adult are likely to be more realistic, seasoned as they are with experience in the real world. This is why it is both your right and your responsibility to exercise leadership in the sense that Gen. George Marshall, who knew a thing or two about it, used the word.

Gen. Marshall described a leader as "a person who exerts an influence and makes you want to do better than you could."

In a Marshall-style leadership role, feel free to help young people gather information about careers; to help in self-discovery by sharing your observations with them about their traits; and, if asked, by helping with such activities as preparing resumes and practicing job interviews.

Read through the *Career Book* and become familiar with its contents. It's not necessary to study these pages like a textbook, but know the sections well enough so that when issues arise, you can locate the pertinent information.

We hope you'll confer regularly with your young person about career planning. We urge you to pay close attention to those sections (5, 6, and 7) that deal with awareness, and which are tailor-made for family conferences.

We also hope you can eliminate sex bias in your thinking about a young person's future career. The *Career Book* is a guide for everyone, male and female.

With nearly half of our workforce already made up of women, statistics project that 9 out of 10 of today's girls will work for 25 to 45 years.

Unless young women, especially, acquire solid skills while they're in school, many will lead humdrum, low-paid job lives. Math, science, and computer courses, for instance, will open a wide range of career options for those who are prepared; many opportunities will be eliminated for those who aren't. That is the word from Joyce Ride—mother of Sally Ride, the nation's first woman astronaut.

Before putting on your Gen. Marshall career leadership hat, why not find out where you stand in your *own* career awareness?

Using one side of a piece of paper, list the careers you consider appropriate for your child. Turn over the paper and list the careers you would want available if you were isolated on a desert island or in space. Now quickly answer the following questions.

1. Do your lists differ?

2. Do you think some careers are important but inappropriate for your child?

3. Are you more interested in seeing your child follow a career satisfying to him or her, or one that will make you proud?

4. Would the list of careers that you think are appropriate for your child be different if his or her sex were different?

5. Do you believe that certain careers are inappropriate for women? What are they and why?

6. Do you consider some careers inappropriate for men? What are they and why?

7. What would your reaction be if your son or daughter chose one of these "inappropriate" careers?

8. Is your knowledge of careers sufficiently up to date so that you feel confident about your choices of "appropriate" and "inappropriate" careers?

9. Would you share your answers to these questions with your son or daughter?

10. Do you think you give your offspring useful advice about how to research a career?

Completing this exercise should help make you aware of your knowledge and attitude about possible career choices for your son or daughter. If you like your responses, fine. If you are not satisfied with your answers, you at least are probably more aware of your own biases and, like the young person who is so important in your life, can learn something from this book.

To People Concerned With Disabilities

The 1990s ushered in a new age for Americans with disabilities, giving those with special challenges their best shot ever at employment.

The lives of 43 million Americans were touched by the 1990 Americans with Disabilities Act in areas ranging from public accommodations and transportation to telecommunications and jobs. Indeed, about one-sixth of the population was affected by the most sweeping civil rights statute since the 1964 Civil Rights Act. The legislation forever changed work in America for both employers and job seekers with disabilities.

As if the breakthrough law itself were not dramatic enough, two more factors encourage differently abled employees to join the workforce.

The first is that the nation needs workers. We are faced with a smaller-sized labor pool of young workers combined with an aging workforce.

The second is that the nation's employers soon will greet a better educated wave of individuals with disabilities for whom adaptability is more than a buzzword. These young adults, who have benefited from the 1975 Education for All Handicapped Children Act, are accustomed to mingling in mainstream activities. Rejecting isolation, the new workplace recruits have higher expectations than earlier generations for their careers.

The 1973 Rehabilitation Act made it illegal in some cases to discriminate against people with disabilities in hiring, firing, and promotion. The Americans with Disabilities Act makes such discrimination unthinkable.

What career choices are open to those who have physical disabilities or other limiting characteristics? *The choices are identical to those for the nondisabled population with one exception: An individual with a disability must look for ways to modify the target occupational choice to accommodate a limitation.*

Because the *Career Book* recognizes that a disability is a single feature—not the whole package—the career guidance information is mainstreamed for the millions of young people with disabilities. Where beneficial, targeted messages are addressed to students with special concerns.

With the imperative of the Americans with Disabilities Act—placing employment within reach of millions who previously were screened out of the workplace—career information takes on new urgency for jobseekers with disabilities.

—JOYCE LAIN KENNEDY
—DARRYL LARAMORE, PhD

■ ■ ■ ■

TO THE COUNSELOR

School Counselors
College and University Counselors
Vocational School Counselors
Private Career Counselors
Career Information Specialists
Librarians
Teachers
Psychologists
Members of the Clergy
Social Workers
Rehabilitation Counselors
—in other words—

Any professional to whom young people turn when they need help in choosing a career direction. This help may be given at any time during the decade of career launch: high school, post secondary education/training, and the first job after graduation.

It's tough to be an adviser, caregiver, and helper.

Dr. Glenn Frank, a former president of the University of Wisconsin, could have been listening to the same young people that you encounter every day when he delivered these thoughts during a baccalaureate address:

I know that all sorts of anxieties haunt your minds, anxieties about the first and further steps in your careers. And these normal anxieties that you would feel even if all skies were cloudless, have, I know, been trebled by the political and economic distraction through which your nation

has been passing as you have pursued your training.

What shall you do with these anxieties?

I want to be honest with you. I do not want to minimize one whit the uncertainties that infest the economic affairs of your time. I do not want to raise in your minds a single hope that will be doomed to die unfulfilled. But I do want to stir in you, if I can, every hope that can be fulfilled.

Stir every hope that can be fulfilled—spoken more than a half century ago, the meaning of these words remains a mission for contemporary advisers across the land.

As counselors, we often speak of the future. That's why it is such an enormous and sometimes overwhelming challenge to stir every hope that can be fulfilled for *each* student or client.

Never Enough Time

Having as our professional goal the purpose of helping people create the best possible future for themselves can be at once satisfying and frustrating. Certainly we would like to give undivided attention to each individual, helping that person conquer life, both in personal and public achievement. What stops us is the myriad of intertwining tasks that are part of our professional responsibility.

Having spent my entire professional life in counseling, I know how it is to frequently feel squeezed in dealing with the time bind of counseling schedules. I know how it is to be forced to devote hours to budgets or college admissions paperwork or participate in curriculum meetings when I feel that I should be helping students by:

◆ Developing strategies and activities to guide young people toward educational and career success

◆ Teaching research techniques to help students meet demands of the 21st century

◆ Assisting counselees to discover their aptitudes, skills, values, and interests.

Time and accessibility. How can we counselors make ourselves available to all who need our guidance on career development and life planning?

We can't. The work schedule of the most dedicated counselor can collapse when the counselor tries to do it all.

Share The Workload

This organized career development plan is a time stretcher to save you hours for your highest priorities.

The *Career Book* contains valuable information for students who are just beginning to think about lifestyles and learning to establish goals, as it does for those ready to enter college, vocational training, the military, or the workforce.

Depending on where the student/client is in the decade of career launch, you can direct the individual to the relevant section, following up as you deem appropriate.

You can choose various levels of interaction. We provide activities that require minimal face-to-face contact between you and the counselee, but allow plenty of opportunity for personal follow-up via a telephone call, hallway conversation, or other brief encounter.

Besides one-on-one counseling, you may use the *Career Book* in small groups as a focus for discussion, or in large classroom learning experiences as a text.

As counselors, you're familiar with much of the career development literature and so we need not belabor the point that the *Career Book* is a comprehensive work tool.

As you read, you will see the *Career Book* takes the reader from self-awareness to decision making to job market packaging, suggesting ways to develop self-confidence, assess values, discover talents, research options, and land the right job.

The *Career Book* can help you be realistic with each counselee as you stir every hope that can be fulfilled.

—DARRYL LARAMORE, PhD

■ ■ ■ ■

TO THE READER

A native American legend tells this story of an orphaned eagle.

A young warrior found a lone eagle egg. Meaning to be helpful, he placed it in the nest of a prairie chicken. The little eagle hatched with his stepbrothers and stepsisters, the prairie chicks.

Growing up friends, they pecked and clucked around the ground together, scratching for worms, insects, and seeds. Eaglethood was one pleasant day after another—with no challenges.

When the eaglet flew, he imitated his prairie chicken family. With a lot of flap and little flight, the eaglet never rose more than a few feet off the ground.

As the years passed the eaglet grew up, matured, and grew old. Scratching the ground one day, the changeling eagle happened to glance up and there in the clouds was the most splendid bird he'd ever seen. He couldn't look away from the magnificent bird as it played tag with the sun. And yet the bird's gorgeous, strong golden wings scarcely seemed to move as it commanded the sky.

"This is the most noble bird I have ever seen," clucked the changeling eagle to the senior prairie chicken. "I wonder what it is."

"Why that's an eagle, the chief of birds," said the senior prairie chicken. "But he's far above you. Keep scratching."

And so our eagle kept scratching the ground. He died never realizing he was not a prairie chicken.

If you want to be a prairie chicken, that's fine. If you'd rather be an eagle, that's good, too. What's most important is that you know what you want and how to get it. If you drift through life not ever really finding out who you are, you are certain to miss the thrill of soaring.

What's In This Book For You?

Readers ranging in age from 15 to 25 will soon have to answer these questions:

♦ *What do you have to do to make things go your way in the 21st century?*

♦ *What do you have to do to be everything you can be?*

We intend to help you figure out the answers to these questions.

Whether you are beginning to develop secret career hopes or already harbor serious ambitions, you need to start now making a plan for living life on your terms.

What you have to do is learn how to plan for the style of your life, realizing that your career choice is the magic that makes it happen.

(Legend source: The Christophers, New York City.)

If you have a disability that is standing in the way of an exciting career, we show you how others overcame such difficulties and how their examples can provide concrete help for dealing with your own.

We ask you to consider whether your ideas are based on racial, ethnic, or sexual stereotypes, and if you are excluding a career that should be high on your options list.

Chapter 8 gives you the most comprehensive crash course in print on researching a career. Extensive career and job market research will help you avoid unpleasant surprises.

Are you aiming too low or expecting too much too soon? In Chapter 9, you learn to set goals that will make you reach and stretch toward your career objective.

Do you have trouble making decisions? The chicken kiev looks good, but so does the fresh fish; you can't decide whether to go to the concert or the movies this weekend; you accepted an invitation to a weekend at the beach, but really want to stay home. Master decision-making skills by following the seven-step formula described in Chapter 10.

Everyone has to start *somewhere* and if you are 15 to 18 years old, begin now to get work experience. Even if you're beyond high school—in college, for instance—Chapter 11 explains the basics of how to find a job you want and how to make the most of the job you land.

(Once you have grasped the principles, you'll find advanced information in later sections.)

Want to go to college? This is a far-reaching decision and Chapter 12 makes the process easier. You will need all the information you can get.

Chapter 13 deals with the college experience, including your choice of major. We suggest you build power skills for the future, and we help you look ahead to graduate and professional education.

Chapter 14 is a round-up of all the ways other than college, including vocational-technical studies and military service, that you can acquire career know-how.

Chapter 15 focuses on your first full-time job, telling how to market yourself effectively in a competitive job market.

In Chapters 16 and 17 you find out how to choose that all-important first job and how to successfully manage it. You also learn how to climb the corporate ladder.

So there you have it—a career book of the widest scope ever. Think of it as a trusted family friend to whom you can turn for answers to career questions. Within its pages, we try to give you the counseling you need to pinpoint, search for, and land the career of your dreams in an age where work will never again be the same.

—JOYCE LAIN KENNEDY
—DARRYL LARAMORE, PhD

■ ■ ■ ■

Why Not Go for Big Career Rewards?

The Career Book *opens with the race for prosperity in a redesigned* economy. The gap is widening between the rich and the poor. To make the playing field more level, readers are urged to become aware of career options and their varying financial rewards.

While it is true that for some career seekers money is the main motivating force, most people believe that money isn't everything. We suggest you consider a range of career satisfactions.

You'll meet one of the richest men in the nation and be inspired by other action-oriented people who jump right in and do, often earning big incomes in the bargain. Next, you'll discover some ways to build wealth, including being your own boss or becoming a topnotch corporate executive.

On a less elevated but more realistic plane, you'll glance at median earnings for typical workers.

You're asked to think about what success truly means to you, and we warn you about the dark side of going after too much too fast.

The section closes with philosophical thoughts on work and a guiding principle to follow when you feel uncertain about a career choice.

Prosperity For Americans: A Wake-Up Call

You'll need a whole new set of charts and economic weather reports to navigate your career in the twenty-first century.

William Bridges, author of *Jobshift: How to Prosper in a Workplace without Jobs*, knows there are doubters, but he is certain: The traditional job, as we know it, is dying.

"The concept of the job itself is a historical artifact from the Industrial Revolution that seems to be coming to an end."

The end won't come all at once, though. "It's more like a rolling wave or a change of seasons," says Bridges, who is also a management consultant and guru to a growing number of career counselors. "It comes gradually and not everywhere at the same time—but before any of us retires, it's going to be gone."

What's replacing the job, according to Bridges, is the "portfolio career," which is less a fixed concept than a way of working, a style of employment that puts the individual's skills and talents to work in a variety of settings. A portfolio career can be a mixture of part-time jobs, or it can be a combination of part-time with temporary, contract, freelance, or consulting work, and even self-employment.

The upheaval in the traditional workplace over the past several years has forced both employers and employment to become more flexible. Companies find themselves creating new categories of jobs, sometimes cutting down on full-time permanent positions and adding more temporary workers, part-timers, job-sharers and outside contractors. The single-task specialist is being edged out by the multifaceted worker who gets sent to where the work is.

According to the Labor Department's Bureau of Labor Statistics, the biggest job growth in recent years has come in industries that typically use more part-time workers, such as the service and retail trades. And the so-called "temporary" industry, although representing less than 2 percent of the nation's total employment, was responsible for 11 percent of the increase in employment.

Forget about the simple pleasures of going to work for a nice company and counting on it to be a nurturing, warm family. Not only is corporate loyalty a thing of the past, but the changing economy is shortchanging many middle-class Americans.

The middle-class—households with earnings of about $20,000 to $60,000 annually—that's where most American workers check in.

"What we are looking at is a permanent proportional decline in the size of the middle class," says economics professor Timothy Smeeding of Syracuse University.

Robert Reich, the Secretary of Labor, agrees. He speaks about the shrinking middle class and the growing income gap between the rich and poor in this country. "The hollowing out of the middle classes has made people deeply insecure, and the American dream is not there for them. They may never do as well as their parents," says Reich. He, however, has long argued that education and retraining are solutions to this problem. Education, he stresses, lifted him out of his own family's financial instability.

According to *Parade's* annual survey of wage earners, the United States is the most economically stratified nation in the industrial world. The latest census bureau figures show that 1993 personal incomes rose for the most affluent 40 percent of households, while the earnings of the less affluent 60 percent fell after inflation.

Government census figures agree that the income spread has become increasingly unequal over the past two decades. The top one-fifth of earners gets almost as much as the other four-fifths put together. That is, the top 20 percent of workers receive 46.6 percent of the pay—nearly one-half of America's payrolls.

Commenting on the shrinking middle class, *Philadelphia Inquirer* investigative reporters

Donald L. Barlett and James B. Steele insist the economy favors the privileged, the powerful, and the influential—at the expense of everyone else.

Describing what happened in the 1980s, they say "Business buccaneers borrowed money to destroy, not to build. They constructed financial houses of cards, then vanished before the cards collapsed." In other words, financial raiders who dismantled companies made fortunes while America's basic industries rotted.

Crossing America for two years, the Pulitzer-prize winning reporters visited 50 cities in 16 states and Mexico. Everywhere they heard tragic reports of once solid manufacturing businesses, building blocks of the traditional high-wage fortress of America, being shut down or moved to cheaper labor areas, including south of the border, where workers are often paid as little as $1.50 an hour.

"It was a litany sounded in city after city, from Hagerstown, Md., to South Bend, Ind.; from Hermann, Mo., to Martell, Calif. Over and over, blue-collar and white-collar workers, mid-level managers—middle class all—talked of businesses that once were, but are no more."

Apart from the workplace chaos generated by the financial manipulations of the 1980s, American workers have another problem: The dollar gap between the American rich and all others is bigger than ever.

The truly rich are not necessarily the same as those with high incomes. Rich means accumulated wealth. The richest 1.6 percent of U.S. adults own nearly 28.5 percent of America's personal wealth, according to the Internal Revenue Service. The IRS suggests that the nation now has well over one million millionaires.

Counted another way—by family wealth rather than by individual wealth—University of California sociologist Maurice Zeitlin says, "The top 10th of the nation's families own 67 cents of every dollar's worth of everything owned by every family in America. Contrast this with what ordinary people own. The families of the bottom half own less than 3 percent of America's wealth. If they're lucky, they have some 'equity' in their home."

Simply put, the chasm between rich and poor has widened over the past decade:

The playing field is not level. This book is intended to make a contribution toward leveling the playing field.

In these pages, we tell you the kinds of things children of affluent and achieving families hear in daily conversation—things that many readers never hear discussed at home or learn in most career guides.

We talk a lot about money as a reward of career status. Happiness at work is more than money. But it is *not less* than money. It takes money to pay for the quality of lifestyle you choose. Of course, for real freedom of choice to exist, first you must know there *are* options and that the options pay differently.

The lower paying options are acceptable to some people who say they prefer meaning to materialism. Perhaps you have read recent articles contrasting the "conspicuous careerism" of the "greedy decade," the 1980s, with the "materialistic downshifting" of the "decency decade," the 1990s. Perhaps you have read that baby boomers are discovering that material possessions didn't get them the satisfaction they expected and so they are returning to simple values, looking for community, family, personal development, and social change.

Not so fast. Career selection fashions come and go but one truth remains—*you have to have a way to pay for the things you want.* And do you really want to suffer in poverty while others swim in luxury mostly because you lack the knowledge cards to play the game? Or to know when your pocket is being picked?

We're not encouraging you to choose financial rewards over career satisfaction or social service. We just want you to have options. All the options. Good options. That's why we begin with the race for prosperity.

We are also telling you that whatever motivates you, it is more important than ever to realize what your skills are and which ones give you the most satisfaction. It is also important to begin at an early age to involve yourself in both paid and volunteer work, in order to utilize those skills and document them. That way you will be able to establish your "portfolio" of marketable skills that you can transfer to a variety of work sites.

■ ■ ■ ■

Success at an Early Age

At 40, William H. Gates III is a multibillionaire. His effort made him the richest man in the world.

As a Harvard sophomore, Gates helped write IBM software, MS-DOS, and it made his fortune. Every IBM and IBM-compatible computer uses it. With Windows 95, Gates can lay indisputable claim to the crown, King of Computing.

In the volatile personal computer/software business, no company has a perpetual lock on leadership. Any wildly successful company becomes a target. Whatever the future brings, Bill Gates' track record is stupendous.

But it is not unique. This is one of history's best times to do great things. Because of the economy's shift from heavy manufacturing to high tech and services, individuals don't always need costly factories and inventories, and they can start new ventures on relatively little money.

Bill Gates is representative of the dynamos that break at warp-speed from the starting gate, leaving the rest of the field far behind. But there are other ways, too. Let's meet other super-achievers and see how they scaled their heights.

■ ■ ■ ■

An Album of Achievers

As you read each achiever's profile, try to guess which of the career rewards the person values highly. Enjoying self-actualization? Making a real contribution to our planet? Having a good time doing the job? Exercising creative expression? Using power? Gaining recognition? Giving service and care to others? Accomplishing organizational achievement? Making pioneering efforts? Being a leader? Or, like Bill Gates, becoming a legendary corporate giant?

Anita Roddick is a new kind of cosmetics queen who markets products in America. She is the environmentally sensitive founder of The Body Shop, a half-billion-dollar British company with shops circling the world. Her shops differ from the usual cosmetics store in their straightforward, no-hype approach. Soaps, gels, shampoos, and other products are made from natural ingredients. Animals are not used to test the products. Roddick's policies include building factories in high-unemployment areas and requiring all employees to devote two hours a week to social work.

Neil Balter of Woodland Hills, Calif., was only 29 when he was honored as one of America's top young entrepreneurs by the Association of Collegiate Entrepreneurs. His California Closet Co., reaping annual revenues of more than $65 million, manufactures closet organizing products. He is a global marketer, selling in the United States and abroad.

Dr. Carmen Hudson-White became a physician at age 41. The African-American one-time welfare mother spent 14 years achieving her goal. Divorced, the amazing woman raised two children while working and putting herself through college and medical school in Chicago. Inevitably money and food ran out at the end of the month. "Looking back," the physician says, "I don't know how we made it."

Dr. Ben Carson is another physician who struggled through racism and poverty to become a renowned surgeon. At the age of 33, the African-American became the the nation's youngest chief of pediatric neurosurgery and he did it at one of the world's most prestigious hospitals, Baltimore's Johns Hopkins. "A lot of the kids I grew up with are dead from drugs and violence," Carson says. The physician credits his mother, Sonya, with helping him find a way up and out. One example: His mom cut his television viewing and required him to read and give her written reports on two books every week.

Jill Davis is a young winemaker at the highly regarded Buena Vista Winery in Sonoma Valley, Calif., where she manages production from harvesting to bottling. Davis' wines have earned more than 80 gold medals. In a business that is mainly male, rising star Davis is one of few women with an enology (winemaking) degree.

Dayton Hyde has launched a crusade to save America's endangered wild horses. On his South Dakota range near Hot Springs there thunders a majestic herd of 300 mustangs that are too old, ill tempered, or ugly to be adopted. The rancher says it's financially tough keeping the horses fed and free. Now over 70, he hopes he'll find a younger sidekick who's good at raising money. The government threatens to take the horses away and warehouse them on a feedlot. "What the Bureau of Land Management doesn't understand is that these horses need freedom," the crusader explains. "All I know is that if they ever come to take these horses back, I'll be lying down in front of the truck."

Ted Waitt 31, is CEO of Gateway 2000, a South Dakota company started nine years ago. It remains the biggest seller of PCs despite fierce competition. Estimated sales in 1994 grew 56 percent, to $1.7 billion and earnings reached $100 million, up 43 percent from the year before.

To get started, he borrowed $10,000 from a bank using his grandmother's certificate of deposit as collateral.

Maralene Downs, an AT&T Bell Laboratories research scientist, was only 27 when she solved a major technical problem that made her a hero of the day. Bell Labs' new optical processor, which uses light rather than electricity, conked out 10 days before its public introduction. Downs suggested using germanium instead of chrome in the equipment and her idea worked like a technical charm.

Lewis Puller Jr. is employed as a lawyer. That's quite an achievement. One of the devastating casualties of the Vietnam War, Puller lost both legs and parts of both hands. Toddy, his heroic wife, supported him during the long road back, which included a bout with excessive drinking and an attempt at suicide. Puller is employed by the Department of Defense where he helps shrink the size of the military. Is this achiever gutsy? In longhand he wrote his riveting memoir. Its title: *Fortunate Son*.

Rebecca Matthias, 40, is President of Mothers Work. Matthias started the company in 1982 when she had trouble finding stylish maternity clothes to wear to her job as a civil engineer. Sensing that a lot of other women had the same problem, she began making and selling upscale maternity clothes for work or a night on the town. In 1994, she opened 51 new stores, raising the total to 11.3; this year she's adding still more. Wall Street analysts estimate Mothers Work will do nearly $56 million in sales in 1996.

Steve Wiggins is CEO of Oxford Health Plans at age 37. Oxford Health Plans, started in 1984, is one of the fastest growing HMOs in the nation. Wiggins, a quiet, blue-eyed Midwesterner who exudes optimism, now expects to do $1 billion earnings in 1996 and Wall Street experts agree. Like so many successful entrepreneurs, Wiggins is driven by a traumatic experience. During the 1970s when he was in high school in Austin, Minnesota, his family's office supply business went bust ."I still remember hanging up the going-out-of-business sign," he says. After that he vowed to be a success.

Perry Barber hops back and forth between Miami and Tokyo because diamonds are her best friend. Baseball diamonds, that is. Barber is a baseball umpire who calls high school, college, professional league, fantasy league, and major league exhibition games. She started out in Little League coaching, where a manager took one look at her, gathered his team, and fled the field. She gets paid for what to her is "almost the most fun a person could have in the world."

Jeffrey Waxman of Princeton, N.J., is a marine biologist who, with his partners in Coastal Environmental Services, helps cities clean up the pollution in lakes and wetlands. They also work for nonprofit groups that defend natural resources, championing causes that are good for the environment. Waxman spends a lot of time in the wild and natural places he loves. "My kids are proud of what I do," says the environmental scientist.

■ ■ ■ ■

Factors in Financial Health

Age
How old you are and how many other people are in your age group is one of the factors that determine financial health. Generations with few members have an edge on large generations because there is less competition for entry-level jobs and, down the road, for management jobs. (Remember, though, that management jobs are likely to come later, rather than sooner, because graduates of the near future still see the baby-boom population bulge standing in their way.)

Those of you born between 1965 and 1975 are in a small generation. Others are at the tail end of a larger group that population experts call the last-wave baby boomers (1956 to 1964). Even if you're a last-wave baby boomer, other factors can overcome your generational "disadvantage." You can make choices that will help boost your affluence, no matter which generation you belong to.

Education
Households headed by college graduates earn two-thirds more than the median for all households. With so many college graduates competing for the best jobs, you will lag behind if you do not obtain a degree or specific job skills.

Occupation
We later cover this topic fully, but do note now that any "wallet roundup" of occupations reveals vast earnings differences. Despite high income for doctors, lawyers, and corporate executives, proprietors of small businesses have a much better chance of becoming millionaires than do professionals and executives.

Marital Status
A study by the University of Michigan's Institute for Social Research says that marriage is more important to your pocketbook than are your education, skills, or attitude toward work. A sample of 5,000 families tracked over 10 years shows that important financial gains and losses are related more to marriage and divorce than

to individual characteristics. In the future, the financial well-being of both men and women will be linked to marital status, as two incomes are becoming increasingly important.

Personal Characteristics

Characteristics of financially successful people include:

◆ Commitment to win

◆ Strong persuasion skills

◆ The ability to look at life as a never-ending series of profitable opportunities—solving problems or adding value to something

◆ Native wit

◆ Ingenuity

◆ Willingness to take risks

◆ Hard work

◆ Excessive energy

◆ Self-confidence

◆ Disciplined mind (intelligence, common sense, and ability to concentrate for long periods)

◆ Extroverted personality that cultivates influential people

◆ Persistence

Just because he had a 14-letter surname and a Teutonic accent that movie makers didn't think would go over with American filmgoers was no reason not to try, says Arnold Schwarzenegger. "I went ahead and did it anyway, thinking I could use all those things to my advantage." Persistence paid off for the Austrian bodybuilder, who has starred in dozens of action films, including "Terminator," "Total Recall," and "True Lies."

Luck

Most wealth watchers say you need luck as well as pluck to make it big. Great wealth occurs when the right person standing on the right street corner hops on the right bus at the right time.

Places

Where you live influences your opportunities. When you're ready to make your move, research the country's hottest growth areas.

Riches: Yesterday, Today

During the 17th and 18th centuries, when our young nation was hungry for most products, the first majestic fortunes were earned by merchants and traders.

As the years rolled on and the age of machines arrived, fortunes developed from other sources. Merchants with seed money and business know-how invested in inventions and the cash rolled in; rarely did the inventors themselves get rich. Textiles, iron, real estate, furs, banking, railroads, and the telegraph were fertile investment fields at that time.

In the late 19th century, steel, mining, oil, mass transit, machinery and equipment, retailing, tobacco, and food processing created super wealth for some.

During World War II, millionaires blossomed from heavy industry and defense contracting; by 1950, new financial giants were springing from aerospace, real estate, mortgage lending, transportation, chemicals, consumer products, and broadcasting.

In the 1980s, leading industries from which the super rich drew their fortunes were oil, real estate, construction, insurance, investment banking, stock brokerage, and private investing. And in the early 1990s fortunes were made in, among other areas, high technology and computers.

Of course, for some the path of entry to stupendous wealth is service to the silver-spoon set followed by marriage. "In each generation," says blue-blood author Nelson Aldrich, Jr., "teachers, horse trainers, gardeners, architects, ski instructors, and even a few gigolos and gold diggers make it."

What about tomorrow's rich—if not famous—people? If you discount the theory that nothing succeeds like inheritance, there are several other schools of thought on acquiring wealth. We'll talk about those next.

Tomorrow's Money Makers

How can you get rich, richer, richest? By following one or a combination of three basic approaches.

The first two pathways to wealth involve owning a business. One approach is the steady-as-you-go school in which you operate a company that satisfies such traditional needs as food, clothing, shelter, and education. You plug along working long hours for many years, saving and investing prudently.

The second approach is the proprietary niche method, in which you have a secret product/process or are one of the nation's few suppliers of a particular item. On the West Coast, a man is raking in money for a metal part used on advertising signs that only he knows how to manufacture. Colonel Sanders had a secret recipe for fried chicken. A man in Missouri became a multimillionaire as one of the few suppliers of police billy clubs and broom handles.

In the third approach, you might be a key employee given stock as part of your compensation. This is the find-fields-on-a-roll strategy. The theory holds that gargantuan fortunes can be made from dealings with embryonic and emerging industries.

How can you know which will be the go-go fields of tomorrow? Science and business magazines regularly report trends to watch. On the next two pages are lists of ideas others have made on how to become a VWP (very wealthy person)—a sampling that is far from complete. The first deals with the here and now. The second is futuristic and speculative, focusing on what *could* develop.

Going Out on Your Own

Starting your own enterprise has always been and continues to be the most promising way to make a great deal of money. Overnight fortunes can happen in one of two ways: by selling stock in your company or by selling out. Fortunes over the long term materialize by profitably operating the company.

Interest in owning your own business is so intense that at least 250 colleges and universities now offer courses in entrepreneurship.

Women, especially, are rushing to run their own shows. For every man who opens a new business, five women start their own companies.

Experts say that between one-third and one-half of all new businesses go belly-up within five years, or remain marginally profitable. Despite the rags-to-rags dark side of entrepreneurship, the ranks of independents are swelling. The number of self-employed now rings in at more than 10 million people—one of every 10 working Americans is on his or her own.

Here's a tip for setting up your own employment. It comes courtesy of Paul Dickson, author of *On Our Own: A Declaration of Independence for the Self-Employed* (Facts on File).

In starting a new business, follow the taxi principle—find out what it costs before you get in. Learn about the special taxes, licenses, and regulations in advance. Double or triple the estimates of time and money it will take you to get off the ground.

Profitable Business Fields for the Here and Now

Here are some industries that market researchers say offer wealth-creating career opportunities.

Genetic engineering. Altering genetic characteristics for a specific purpose is in its infancy but already producing human insulin.

Telecommunications. The marriage of computers to communications has produced local area networks, modems, high-speed video and data traffic, electronic mail, and a host of other wonders.

Robotics. Computer-integrated manufacturing (CIM), of which robotics is a main part, is the best-known industry, but entrepreneurs tomorrow could have robot armies painting houses and cars.

Real estate and finance. Land and processing money never go out of style.

Business services. To avoid creating permanent overhead costs, companies are farming out some specialized duties to small, efficient service companies, such as those that do product design, employee training, stockholder reports, and office relocation.

Importing. Owners of many small import firms benefit from cheap foreign labor and America's rush to buy foreign goods. Electronics and machine parts are especially profitable.

Health and fitness. Americans are spending hundreds of millions of dollars yearly to keep in shape. There's money in sweat.

Child care. Franchising or owning a chain of child-care facilities can be profitable, particularly now that large companies are beginning to offer child-care benefits to female employees with young children.

Corporate Pay Goes Off the Scale

Although starting your own business is a popular way to try for the jackpot, it's not impossible to get rich by working for someone else.

America's chief executive officers are winning soaring salaries—but garnering harsh, resentful criticism.

CEOs in mid-sized firms are receiving total pay averaging $2.1 million, including long-term compensation, says an *Industry Week* magazine survey. CEOs of major firms, such as ITT Corp., are earning $10 million or more annually.

Enough! cry critics. This is obscene. "CEOs are looting U.S. workers," accuses syndicated columnist George Will. "In Japan, the compensation of major CEOs is 17 times that of the

Wealth-Building Industries of the 21st Century

Which unborn industries will eventually become giants is anyone's guess, but Edward Cornish, president of the World Future Society, mentions some possibilities:

Space exploration. It will lead to all kinds of new industries with products made in factories in space.

Air purification. As air gets dirtier, the industry built on the cleaning of air will zoom in importance.

Life extension. As more is understood about the aging process, anti-aging therapies and businesses will sprout.

Underground construction. As surface space grows expensive in large cities and environmental height limits are imposed, a big future industry may lie under our feet.

Personal security. Rising crime, terrorism, and electronic snooping have made people feel increasingly insecure. An armory of security gadgets is growing.

Packaged education. All kinds of educational courses are being put onto audio and video systems, so people can learn whatever they want whenever they want.

averge worker; in France and Germany, 23–25 times; in Britain, 35 times; in America, between 85 and 100-plus times."

In some instances, compensation for top executives has been rising as company earnings fall. A manager in the *Industry Week* survey expresses a popular concern about high pay for low performance. "My company's top exec made $600,000 last year, yet the company had layoffs, wage cuts, and plant closings."

Beyond the money, corporate kingpins enjoy private planes, country club memberships, chauffeured cars, stock options, and more.

As corporate salaries escalate, controversy grows. Are executives really worth millions of dollars a year—sometimes hundreds of times more than their lowest paid employees?

Critics say such wide wage differentials are destructive, causing restlessness in the ranks and affecting an organization's ability to func-

tion effectively. Do you agree? Disagree? Your answer can throw a little light on your interest in being a corporate chieftain.

Money Begets Money in Finance Careers

People who make major financial decisions, who come up with financing innovations, who show other people how to make money, and who shuffle money from one pocket to another can earn incomes in the six figures, even the sevens.

Investment bankers are an example of the astonishing financial rewards possible in moving money around. Despite recent clouds over the glamorous investment banking business, the field is still rich with opportunity for bright, ambitious young people.

Even when investment boom times quiet down, companies often need huge amounts of capital for expansion. One source is the investment banker, who, for a fee, finds funds. The banker may put a cash-lean company in the fast-growth orbit by personally putting up the money, or find a group of high-ticket investors to provide it.

Apart from nepotism and old-boy networks, entry-level investment banking jobs go to MBAs—usually those who come from prestigious graduate schools and have specialized in finance. What investment firms look for is young people who have deal-making talents. What else is required to succeed in this field?

Lynn Gilbert, an executive search consultant in New York City, recruits for investment banking firms. She says you must be a confident risk-taker, thrive on a fast pace, have a strongly competitive personality, and "live" your work.

Any takers?

The Rarified Reaches of Real Estate

Fortunes are made in real estate. Some are relatively small; others are mammoth.

In one recent study by a large real estate company, 71 percent of sales agents cited high earnings potential as the principal lure with flexible schedules and independence of activity in second and third place.

Commercial real estate is incredibly hard work. How would you like to make 400 calls to lease an office building without gaining a single nibble of interest to show for your efforts?

On the other hand, if everything works out, the payoff can be *huge*. Commissions totaling $1 million or more are not unheard of.

Residential real estate agents suffer feast or famine. Most residential agents scrape by or do modestly well. Others—especially those who have found a niche, such as bank foreclosures or

multimillion-dollar estate sales—can buy their own Caribbean island.

Real estate development is another stairway that money stars climb. Developers build residential, industrial, or commercial properties, arranging financing for their visions and ventures. Generally, real estate developers work on OPM—other people's money. Thus, the ability to visualize and to persuade are basic requirements in this work

The new breed of real estate company, say analysts, will operate internationally, dealing with complex financing vehicles, environmental obstacles, and cumbersome political processes.

There are many avenues to a fat bank account in real estate.

More High Flyers

Few people can join the elite corps of athletes and entertainers who earn headlines grabbing multimillion-dollar salaries.

Big name music stars pull in as much as $25 million in a good year. Average pro-league base salaries are in these areas: football, $300,000; basketball, $600,000; baseball, $500,000; hockey, $200,000. Top players earn well over $1 million a year.

Many other Americans compete for less-publicized positions that pay a respectable $100,000 or more annually. A few examples? University presidents, labor union officers, and heads of major welfare organizations such as the American Red Cross. Of course, you can always aim to be the President of the United States and earn $200,000 plus a pleasant assortment of benefits.

What about women? Are there certain fields that seem to offer greener pastures than others? Retailing is the most salary-friendly to female executives, according to a study by the executive search firm Korn/Ferry International. The study shows that women executives at the vice-presidential level or higher in the retail field are receiving average annual salaries exceeding $100,000.

When it comes to salaries for senior women, industrial corporations rank second, but also are in the $100,000-per-year league.

Mark McCormack, the chairman, president, and CEO of International Management Group and author of the bestseller *What They Don't Teach You at Harvard Business School*, has some advice for women:

1. Choose a company, not an industry. Industry averages do not tell the true story. For example, the computer industry is well represented by both men and women. But that doesn't tell you that men tend to occupy the executive suites while women perform piecework on the assembly line

2. Go for high-profile companies. Highly visible companies have highly visible consciences. They care what the world thinks of them. They're sensitive about promoting women. That is one reason why women are moving up at the publishers, broadcasters, and investment banks that make news every day.

3. Avoid fraternities and sororities. At all-male companies, you'll waste a lot of time either being a pioneer or being misunderstood. At the all-female companies, you run the risk of being just a face in the crowd.

4. Working for yourself is the best way to get paid what you're worth.

■ ■ ■ ■

Earnings at a Glance

From the success stories we've described, you'd think American salaries are shooting through the roof. Only for the standouts.

The average income for a full-time U.S. wage and salary worker is less than $22,000.

Listed below are annual salary averages for selected occupations. Because these are averages, many people in each occupation earn higher or lower incomes than the figures shown here.

Numerous factors affect your pay, not the least of which is the profitability of the organization, how long you have held the job, the number of qualified people who would love to have your job, the region of the country, and the industry in which you work.

If you want a general idea of what an occupation's median pay is when you are reading salary information that's several years old, add about 5 percent a year. This approach is not dead accurate, but it's close enough to be useful.

Success Has Many Faces

Dressed in an expensively tailored designer suit, leather attaché case in hand, a confident-looking young woman strides toward a billion-dollar New York skyscraper. Hair squeaky clean and modishly styled, nails manicured and squared, her image plainly says: "I am a woman who matters."

Is *she* successful?

As a member of the sheriff's department, he works with violent street gangs in the barrios of Los Angeles. He dresses like a street person, drives a beater, and often may be seen sitting on a park bench sharing a brown-bag lunch with a gang member. His image says: "I am a man who cares."

Up to $20,000

actor	$7,850
teacher's aide	$12,045
dress maker	$12,100
child care worker	$14,213
nurse's aide	$15,150
bank teller	$16,136
sports instructor	$16,263
file clerk	$17,013
waitperson	$17,075
precision assembler	$18,173
furniture upholsterer	$19,236

$20,000 to $29,999

mayor	$20,236
flight attendant	$21,207
computer operator	$22,193
photographer	$23,300
corrections officer	$25,180
appliance repairer	$26,207
cosmetologist	$27,100
machinist	$27,180
real estate agent	$28,475
truck driver	$28,139
architectural drafter	$29,171

$30,000 to $39,999

paralegal assistant	$30,028
electrician	$30,172
medical secretary	$32,072
drill-press operator	$33,067
respiratory therapist	$34,122
insurance underwriter	$36,131
psychologist (counselor)	$37,000
construction foreman	$37,244
audiologist	$38,058
computer programmer	$38,195
historian	$39,284

$40,000 to $49,999

librarian	$40,071
architect	$40,312
set designer	$41,100
personnel recruiter	$42,164
basketball coach (NCAA)	$43,252
railroad conductor	$44,045
plumber	$45,113
dairy farmer	$45,900
museum curator	$47,161
publication editor	$48,431

$50,000 to $69,999

postal inspector	$50,045
agricultural scientist	$52,213
statistician	$54,219
oceanographer	$56,171
school principal	$57,038
sheet metal worker	$58,138
hotel manager	$61,168
college professor	$62,193
industrial engineer	$64,206
physicist	$67,138
astronomer	$68,077
nuclear engineer	$68,206
veterinarian	$69,197
economist	$69,219

$70,000 and over

actuary	$70,288
chiropractor	$75,823
petroleum engineer	$79,195
stockbroker	$83,453
symphony conductor	$101,900
psychiatrist	$110,134
judge (federal)	$127,041
orthodontist	$193,247
President (U.S.)	$200,000
football player (NFL)	$655,055

Adapted from Les Krantz, Editor, *The National Business Employment Weekly Jobs Rated Almanac* (New York: John Wiley & Sons, 1995).

Is he successful?

What is success? An accomplishment that can be measured by status and material possessions? A state of mind?

In thinking about the meaning of success, consider both viewpoints.

Accomplishments That Can Be Measured

To become rich and famous—it's the American dream. In that dream, people know who you are and what you can make happen. They look up to you, counting how many rungs you've climbed on life's ladder and guessing how many dollars you have in the bank. They know you shop at better stores, drive a foreign car that costs as much as a house, and have live-in help to keep your palace clean.

Perhaps you're a big executive in line for the company presidency, living in the best suburb, with two children in private schools, two VCRs, and your own cabin cruiser.

Perhaps you're a high-tech entrepreneur whose company made $50 million its first year in business.

Perhaps you're a film superstar with homes in three countries and so much celebrity you can't walk down the street without being mobbed.

Or perhaps you haven't quite arrived at a lofty position but are in hot pursuit of all the comforts and luxuries a thriving career can provide.

If you belong to the rich-and-famous school of success, begin your journey by realizing that it's okay to want what you want. Never feel guilty about what is a perfectly natural and healthy ambition.

Success: A State of Mind

In this viewpoint, success is mainly a matter of personal inner fulfillment.

Holding an internal vision of success in no way rules out the possibility of stockpiling a personal fortune, but it does seem to be a characteristic of a special breed of Americans: the helpers, the caregivers.

To understand that not everyone goes for the gold in pursuing success, look at teachers, librarians, social workers, nurses, firefighters, military personnel, members of the clergy, and many, many others.

Test pilot Chuck Yeager was a modestly paid Air Force officer when he became the first flyer to break the sound barrier. The absence of a hefty monetary reward for his feat didn't dim his inner feelings of accomplishment.

For personal rewards, the late career guidance colossus John Crystal suggests asking yourself two questions:

1. *What do I want to accomplish with my life?*

2. *How do I go about achieving my goal?*

If you know what you want to accomplish and realize your goal, that's success.

Success means obtaining your objectives and goals. These may vary from time to time, but you achieve success each time you reach one.

Others may or may not see you as a success, but you have the satisfaction of knowing you are living up to your promise.

Success: Uplinks and Downsides

By now you've figured out what we're driving at. Like beauty, success is in the eye of the beholder. Success is what you think it is, measurable achievement or state of mind.

Personally, we vote for a dose of both. Who wouldn't like to be earning $40,000 a year and living a fairly well-rounded life? On a grander scale, who wouldn't like to be the President of the United States, or a Nobel Peace Prize winner or one of the 10 richest people in the world? It's nice to have prominent spots on life's parade floats.

Face the possibility, though, that you may pay a high psychic price for success if it becomes naked ambition compulsively pursued.

Many young professionals are very serious about measuring their careers and about measuring material success. They have money and power, but some are reporting dissatisfaction, anxiety, and physical problems. Washington psychologist Douglas LaBier believes the trouble stems from conflict caused by compromises and trade-offs that must be made in pursuit of a smashingly successful career.

Conflicts? Compromises? This could mean working long hours at the expense of family and self. It could mean being cunning like a fox at the office to outdistance the competition at all costs. It could mean forgetting about personal attitudes to agree with the boss no matter what.

What do unhappy young careerists tell Dr. LaBier they want?

Fulfillment. That's what everyone wants more of. One sure way to experience it is to know what you want and give chase. Each time you catch up to an objective or a goal, whammo! You're a success! And there's nothing better than a series of successes to put emotional substance in your life.

Please remember the benefits of state-of-mind success, as well as accomplishments that can be measured. It's not a lot of fun being a drudge all of each day.

As San Diego career counselor Maggie Payment says:

At work we are expected to keep our eye on the ball, a shoulder to the wheel, and an ear to the ground, but how can we possibly work in this position?

Success: Win Some, Lose Some

Just as the best football players don't always gain yardage when they have possession of the ball, none of us plays a perfect "success game." We fumble and drop the ball once in a while.

Dwight David Eisenhower was no exception. The five-star general and President of the United States has been called the most successful man of the 20th century.

Even so, Ike occasionally stepped out of bounds in his charge toward greatness.

After being turned down by the Naval Academy, Ike was accepted at West Point. Not a spectacular student, he loved to play football, but a knee injury destroyed his playing career. Ike was crushed. He lost interest in life at West Point, accumulated a mountain of demerits, and graduated with a lackluster ranking of 61st in his class.

When informed by a West Point officer that he would not be recommended for a commission after graduation, Ike practically told the officer to take a hike, that it didn't matter—he might become a South American gaucho instead.

For reasons Eisenhower never understood, a few days later the officer reversed himself and offered the blasé cadet a commission. The rest is history.

Even champions have a few bad quarters during certain periods of their lives.

When Success Means Making the World Better

If you go after all the money, fame, and power you desire, put something back. Make a contribution to the world in some way, little or large. You'll like yourself better. And as achievement expert Samuel A. Cypert says, "Even if you don't subscribe to an organized religion, having faith in something greater than yourself—God, cosmic consciousness, the power of love—will enhance your success by bringing out your highest qualities."

Can Success Make You a Better Person?

One of the world's all-time greatest writers thought so:

> The common idea that success spoils people by making them vain, egotistic, and self-complacent is erroneous; on the contrary it makes them, for the most part, humble, tolerant, and kind. Failure makes people bitter and cruel.
>
> —W. SOMERSET MAUGHAM

Success Can Be Learned

It is natural to want to succeed and as you gather successes about you like a cozy crowd of friends, you will find that success is more fun than failure.

Success begins with wanting to succeed. If others can make it, so can you. The techniques of success can be mastered by those who consciously make the effort.

Author Michael Korda says it well:

> Learn the art of self-motivation. To succeed is to change, to grow, to live. Start living today and begin by taking the first courageous step—the step of deciding now, that you too can be a success!

How Much Others Respect Your Success

Which occupations rate high in prestige and which rate low? Researchers at the University of Southern California and the University of California/Irvine asked nearly 1,200 adults across America to rate the status of various occupations. The results of this research are shown in the next chart.

The occupations were rated on a scale of 0 to 100. The higher the number, the more respected the occupation in this study.

■ ■ ■ ■

Work as a Philosophical Subject

Work is the core of most lives; who you are depends on what you do. Here's a quickie quiz to see how much you know about work.

The Quiz

1. Most people work for money.
   True   False

2. The majority of people like jobs because they need other people.
   True   False

3. Most people gain self-esteem from their jobs.
   True   False

4. Work is activity that produces something of value for the worker and/or other people.
   True   False

5. Work is still work whether it's paid or unpaid.
   True   False

Prestige Index

OCCUPATION	PRESTIGE SCORE	OCCUPATION	PRESTIGE SCORE
accountants	65	fishers	34
actors	58	food servers	28
advertising executives	63	funeral directors	49
airline pilots	73	garbage collectors	28
architects	73	grocery baggers	18
astronauts	80	insurance agents	46
athletes	65	journalists	60
auto mechanics	40	lawyers	75
babysitters	29	letter carriers	47
bakers	35	machinists	47
bank managers	59	managers of fast food	41
bartenders	25	migrant workers	19
biologists	73	musicians (symphony)	59
bus drivers	32	newspaper sellers	19
carpenters	43	nurses (R.N.)	66
car-wash attendants	19	physicians	86
cashiers	33	physicists	74
chemists	73	plumbers	45
city mayors	76	police officers	61
cleaners	23	public relations	49
clergy members	67	real estate agents	48
college presidents	81	salespeople:	
college professors	74	door-to-door	25
computer scientists	74	traveling	40
dentists	72	used car	25
dishwashers	17	secretaries	46
engineers:		street sweepers	19
aeronautical	72	taxi drivers	28
chemical	73	teachers:	
civil	69	elementary	64
mechanical	64	high school	66
envelope stuffers	14	television repairers	39
farm laborers	30	truck drivers	30
fire fighters	53	welders	42

The Answers

All the statements are true. People work basically for three reasons: money, social contact, and self-esteem.

1. "The money is always there but the pockets change," said American writer Gertrude Stein. To get through this life paying for food, clothing, housing, medical care, education, transportation, and a few luxuries, you'll need deep pockets. To many, money also has a symbolic value: It is a way of keeping score.

2. The majority of people are social creatures who dislike being alone. Sociologists say people want human contact for the feeling of belonging or loving. We need other people. We need to chat and interact with them. In a mobile society such as ours—where ties with family and friends may be weakened—the workplace may substitute for the community as we make acquaintances and friends at work.

3. Self-esteem means you feel good about yourself, and a big part of this rests on how you feel about your work. At its best, work is a way of relating to life and others. When you do a poor job, you feel as though you flunked a test. When you do a good job, you feel satisfaction and achievement. Your work defines you as a person. If you're not happy with what you're doing for approximately half your waking hours, you won't be happy with yourself.

4. Work creates value for society, as well as for yourself. Our civilization and standard of living are dependent upon a working society.

5. The efforts of unpaid volunteers and homemakers are valuable to society. Why shouldn't their activities be counted as work merely because money has not changed pockets?

The United States is the most admired nation the world has ever known. Its future depends on its new workers—*you*.

■ ■ ■ ■

Do Something You'd Do for Nothing

In dispensing career-choosing advice, some authors say, "If you can think it, you can do it." Or, "Do what you love and the money will follow."

By urging unshakable belief in yourself, they make a convincing case that you can be anything to which you put your mind.

This is inspiring and motivational advice that can help unlock hidden potential. We agree with it—to a point. We agree that it's wonderful to reach for the stars.

But we don't agree that it is advice that should be taken without qualification. Our concern is what may happen to overreachers when their skills fail to support their aspirations. Their unrealistic expectations set them up to fail and when they do, they may crash psychologically. If you are poor with numbers, it is unlikely you can will yourself into becoming a financial whiz. If you have difficulty with basic writing skills, don't count on becoming a best-selling novelist.

Being able to think doesn't always mean being able to do. And the money doesn't always follow no matter how much you love what you're doing.

Against this background, read the advice we are about to offer with the realization that it is merely a starting point. You may have to make trade-offs as you move toward your career goal. Even idealists know that life's uncertain circumstances may make it necessary to forgo your first choice of a career for one more attainable.

With these qualifiers in mind, light your way with a beacon that has worked for countless career seekers:

Do something you'd do for nothing.

Do something you believe will bring you satisfaction and the kind of pride in achievement that keeps you vitally absorbed in what you're doing. Do something that makes you glad to be alive. Do something you love to be doing.

Do something you'd do for nothing and you will have found a gateway to real and lifelong happiness.

■ ■ ■ ■

CHAPTER
2

A Positive Mind-set Is Essential to Success

Without a positive self-image, ability and hard work may not be enough for future success.

How can you see yourself in the best light? Behavioral experts recommend "conceptualization" to people who have a strong desire to win.

Conceptualization? That's the big word we use to describe the imagery process that begins your career development.

In conceptualizing, you need to imagine who you want to be, what you want to do, where and with whom. A mental dress rehearsal helps you to set the stage for getting what you want in life.

This section calls forward the mind-set you must have to achieve career success and the role that risk taking plays in success.

Program Yourself for Success

To reach the top, you have to feel like a winner and envision yourself as a winner.

People who feel like losers and dim their minds with expectations of loss keep themselves from getting all they want out of life. They create their own negative destinies. No matter how much ability you have, if you do not *fundamentally* believe you have a chance of reaching a particular goal, you won't.

Moreover, some people unknowingly sabotage themselves day after day, year after year. Why? Because deep down they are convinced they are *not worthy* of achieving a goal. They do not value themselves as "okay" people. The reasons for this would require another book, but the point for career climbers is this:

If negative thoughts block the way, any goal is likely to remain beyond your grasp.

Choose to think about winniing, not losing.

For instance, rather than worry, "I'll never get a good job," grab a sheet of paper and write down your sterling qualities. Then think, "It is easy to sell myself to the right employer."

Athletes choose to think about winning, not losing. St. *Louis Post-Dispatch* premier sports writer Bob Broeg says thinking in terms of victory has stood the test of time.

"Athletes, managers, and coaches choose to think winning, not losing," Broeg affirms. "Years ago, player-manager Frank Frisch of St. Louis' famed Gas House Gang snapped, *Finishing second is like playing in the Lollipop League*. More recently, Vince Lombardi, coach of Green Bay's pro football dynasty, said, *Winning is everything*.

"Alabama's Paul (Bear) Bryant, college football's winningest coach, amended Lombardi's cutting comment. *Winning isn't everything*, said The Bear amusedly, *but it sure beats anything else*."

Three wise men, the trio mentioned by Bob Broeg, are typical of sports philosophy as it ex-

ists today. In the words of famed former Chicago Bears coach Mike Ditka:

If you want to do something in life, you better mark it up real high on the board and you better show it to people: This is where I want to be.

Anyone who plays sports knows that a lack of self-confidence can put you on the short end of the score. The famous Notre Dame football coach Knute Rockne is reported to have said:

Show me a good loser and I'll show you a loser. Give me 11 lousy losers and I'll give you a national championship football team.

A strong self-image as a winner is vital to success. Choose to think well of yourself.

Concerning your goal: Remember that somebody has probably done it before and there's little reason why you can't do it now.

■ ■ ■ ■

Winning Starts in Your Head

When we say that achieving success requires you not only to feel like a winner, but also to visualize yourself winning, we are speaking of "conceptualizing" success.

Conceptualizing, to us, is the opening round in career development. Blending fantasy and fact, conceptualizing involves using your imagination to float pictures through your head about what you would like to be doing with your life in the years ahead.

A point of caution: Do not confuse conceptualizing with daydreaming. Both contain an element of fantasy, but daydreaming is *unfocused* imagination. Daydreaming is only wishful thinking, not a commitment to achieving a goal. Unlike daydreaming, conceptualizing is rooted in reality.

Conceptualizing is easy. It is like producing a film in your mind. You imagine a winning script and mentally shoot the physical action. You do it all in your head.

Suppose you want to be a successful home builder. Your script calls for the development of 200 homes on a sunny hillside. Picture yourself in these scenes:

Finding the land; buying it; hiring an architect; ordering cement poured; watching the framing going up; beaming with pleasure when the houses are ready to market; selling the first house; selling the last house; and smiling all the way to the bank.

Here's another example of using conceptualization: On the way to a job interview, imagine yourself in the role of the interviewee and mentally go through the paces of how you want the interview to progress. See yourself entering the interviewer's office, smiling, shaking hands, and making small talk to establish rapport. Concentrate on details as well as the large picture. A detail would be to visualize yourself speaking without your voice cracking. The large picture concludes with a job offer.

That's all there is to it—your mental movie, a form of thought that helps you reach your goal.

The more you conceptualize, the easier it will be to marshal the inner resources you need to be successful.

You can conceptualize any time, any place, including life's idle moments: traffic signals, movie theater lines, elevators, fitness walks, supermarket checkout lines, holding on the telephone.

Words other than conceptualization can be used to describe the imagery process— visualization, mental imagery, and success imagination, for example. Call it what you like, as long as you understand how it works and use the technique to start building your glowing future.

■ ■ ■ ■

Conceptualizing Helps With Risk Taking

Fear of risk, more than any other single trait, binds people to boring lives. No adventure, no hills and valleys, no pains or gains.

Psychologists say that fear of risk is really fear of failing. It is fearing that in the distance between your reach and your grasp, something will go wrong.

Why are you afraid? The culprit is change. Change frames every picture of your life: maturing, studying, working, staying healthy, having relationships, traveling, the weather, technology—everything. Change is ever present and with it comes certain uncertainty—and risk.

Having some fear of risk is reasonable, mature, and expected. A sense of caution when it comes to taking risks shows you are in robust mental health.

Still, we can use conceptualization techniques to desensitize ourselves to a paralyzing fear of risk taking. By mentally role playing risks, we can size them up, become familiar with their range of options, uncover their frightening mysteries, and eventually put the risks into proper perspective.

Train your mind to consciously focus on the "risk of the day." Think it through. Imagine how the risk might work out and how you want it to work out. The more you get into the habit of conceptualizing risk taking, the more comfortable you will feel with taking real-life chances.

Conceptualizing the best that can happen and the worst that can happen puts a risk into focus.

Once you internalize the fact that there is no place on earth where time stands still, or where you can hide from risk, the idea of risk taking becomes less threatening. You'll understand that successful people continually take informed risks.

In your own life, you often do things you are fearful about. Remember when you tried to break the school's high-jump record, or asked someone you really didn't know very well for a date?

While there are no iron-clad certainties where risk is involved, as Henry Ford II is reported to have said.

Nobody can really guarantee the future. The best we can do is size up our chances, calculate the risks involved, estimate our ability to deal with them, and make our plans with confidence.

■ ■ ■ ■

More Ways to Master Risk Taking

Since risks are in the air we breathe, here are eight guidelines to help you deal with them in an informed, logical manner.

1. *Take only necessary risks.* Always ask yourself: "Is this risk necessary?" You may find that you need not assume it.

A classic example of the unnecessary risk is the act of passing another car on a two-lane hill when the driver can't see over the crest. If chance puts an oncoming vehicle into your path, you pay a severe price for taking an unnecessary gamble.

Avoid taking risks that cannot benefit you.

2. *Plan ahead.* F. Lee Bailey, one of America's most prominent lawyers, shares rules he learned as a Navy pilot. In his book, *To Be a Trial Lawyer*

(John Wiley & Sons), he says members of his training class who survived to become aviators thoroughly learned the following rules:

Rule 1
An airplane is a wondrous instrument of motion, and if in your thinking and handling of the controls you stay ahead of it, it will take you from place to place safely and very well.

Rule 2
If you get behind in thinking and handling an airplane, it will surely kill you.

Rule 3
If most of the time you are trying hard just to stay even as you control an airplane, at some point it will get ahead of you—now apply Rule 2.

The point, Bailey explains, is that "thinking ahead and anticipating what may happen next are vital elements of success in many human endeavors. Flying is one of them. Trying lawsuits is another."

Risk taking is still another.

3. *Consider the odds, visualize alternatives.* When you face a risk, develop the habit of calculating the odds for success. Ask yourself: "Are my chances favorable or not so good?"

When you decide the odds are against you, either bypass the risk entirely, or visualize alternative routes of action that could bring similar rewards.

As a simple illustration, suppose you need a jacket and find one you like on sale for $75. The sale ends today. You have no credit cards, but you do have $30 in your wallet and $20 in your checking account. Your paycheck will arrive tomorrow, but it's drawn on an out-of-state bank and your bank's policy is to wait five business days before crediting such checks to customers' accounts.

Should you write a check for the jacket, hoping that somehow the check won't bounce? No. Your check probably will not clear the bank.

There are other ways to handle your problem. You can ask the manager whether the store has a "layaway" plan. If so, will a $10 deposit hold the jacket until your paycheck is credited to your account? Another alternative is to wait until you save sufficient money to buy a jacket that you like.

Always make a rational assessment of your chances, and, when needed, visualize alternatives.

4. Risk only as much as you can afford to lose. How much you can afford to lose is a murky, subjective question that varies with the individual and with the circumstances.

We're not talking about losing the rent money in a poker game, but about going only as far out on a limb as you can while maintaining rational respect for the consequences.

The biggest danger of risk taking is that you may lose sight of how much you realistically can lose. History is rife with instances of people losing more than they could afford in stock deals and greed-based ventures. ("Invest now and double your money in three months.")

A more personal example of risking unwisely is the case of Adrian A., a young executive who wants a job promotion. Her choice of strategy is to look for another job.

Adrian has two choices. She can try to keep her search quiet, fearing her employer will fire her if word gets back, or she can leak the news about her search, hoping her employer will offer her a better position.

The second choice holds the higher risk; is it more than Adrian can afford to lose?

The probable answer is "yes," the risk is too high. Unless her skills are in short supply, Adrian should have another job offer in her pocket before her boss discovers she's on the market.

Otherwise, if the boss gets wind of her search, becomes annoyed, and fires her, Adrian suffers a setback.

While there are plenty of exceptions to every generalization, it's safer to keep quiet about a job hunt when you are employed. To publicize it may cause you to risk more than you can afford to lose.

5. Be sure the reward is worth the risk. A woman in a Midwestern state was arrested for writing $600,000 worth of bad checks. She used the money to buy tickets for the state lottery. She never won a dime.

Most people would say she risked too much for too little. Her action was not "risk-effective."

The size of the reward always should dictate the degree of risk. In the early 1800s, President Thomas Jefferson risked war with France, and conflict with the Congress, by insisting that the United States must have the nearly 830,000 square miles of land between the Mississippi River and the Rocky Mountains, stretching from the Gulf of Mexico to the Canadian border.

Tough talk, courtly diplomacy, and $15 million were required to strike the deal that became known as the Louisiana Purchase. Through it, the United States took title to land that eventually formed all or parts of 15 states.

Jefferson stuck his neck out, but he was playing for historically high stakes.

When in doubt about whether you should go ahead with an idea, remember: The reward must be worth the risk.

6. Leave the dares to fools. As a child, you probably heard the taunt, "I dare you to do it." Walk a high ledge, swim a river, climb a tree.

Perhaps as a child you prided yourself on never turning down a dare. You're not a child anymore. And you must learn to recognize a dare when you hear or see one.

A grown-up version of a dare may sound like this: "You would never tell the boss how you really feel about him," or "You haven't got the nerve to tell that professor what a jerk she is."

Dares are a variety of foolish risks that fools take. Don't fall for them.

7. Take only smart risks. What is known as the "Icarus complex" dramatically illustrates non-thinking actions.

Icarus is the young man in Greek mythology who was told by his father never to soar higher than his parent. Shrugging off Pop's warning, Icarus strapped on wings of feathers held together by wax. As he neared the sun, the wax melted and he plummeted back to earth with a bone-crunching thud. Goodbye, Icarus.

Those who take Icarian risks seem to do so with consistency. They believe they always are on the verge of making it big—"I've got a fabulous deal cooking" or "My friend is going to get me a job in a film studio, any day now." Somehow their ships never seem to come in.

What's wrong? Are they simply unlucky? More likely, the Icarus crowd lives on a diet of constant hope and rare achievements because they make impulse decisions based on few facts.

They never learn that it requires *more than the mere willingness to take a risk* for the risk to pan out.

They got part of the correct message that those who take risks in life achieve the greatest rewards. What they failed to get was the other part of the central idea. Additional factors are in the success equation—such as research, effort, judgment, timing, resources, and follow-through. Impulsive actions based only on wishful thinking are dumb.

Don't emulate Icarus.

8. Bypass risks for egotism. Some people turn risks into failures because their motivations stem from an unusually strong desire to show the world who's pulling the strings. Two illustrations of taking risks for egotism are:

◆ The German dictator whose view of himself and his nation as being invincible led to World War II.

◆ The American president who believed his power was great enough to cover up Watergate.

One final example of the folly of taking a risk that stems from being too sure of yourself: A story is told of the Union Army officer who during the Civil War stood on the front lines and said disparagingly of the Confederate marksmen: "Those idiots couldn't hit the side of a ba. . . ."

▪ ▪ ▪ ▪

The Lighter Side of Risk

Do you know the story about the 250-pound, tough-as-nails Army sergeant who opened a valentine signed by all but a few privates in his platoon?

The sergeant, with no sign of being pleased, shouted, "Okay, all you creeps who signed this card—give me 50 push-ups."

All the "creeps" hit the floor and complied with the order. When they finished, the sergeant bellowed in a voice that could cut steel, "Now, all you chicken livers who were afraid to sign, get down and give me 100 push-ups."

A little risk can be an energy saver.

▪ ▪ ▪ ▪

How Do You Rate on Risk Taking?

Here's an activity to help you get a handle on where you stand when it comes to taking a chance. This is a fun test and there are no right or wrong answers.

Check Your R.T.Q.
(Risk-Taking Quotient)

Circle the letter in front of the choice you probably would make for each situation.

1. **Dating for major social event:**
   A. You would invite a person you enjoy and feel sure would accept your offer.

   B. There's a terrific person you've always had a crush on. You'd love to ask this person but you're not sure he or she would accept and you don't know what kind of an evening you'd have, but you would invite the person anyway.

2. **Buying a car:**
   A. You can afford to buy a two-year-old model that belongs to your friend's father. You know it was well-maintained and would be a good buy. It is a staid model that doesn't fire you with enthusiasm. You would choose this car.

   B. You spot an ad in the newspaper for a flashy four-year-old sports model with 50,000 miles. You look at it and fall in love. It costs $3,000 more than the other car but you might be able to swing it if your parents will loan you some money. The guy who owns it is moving to another job where he will have a company car. The mechanic you take the car to says it appears to be in good shape. You would choose this car.

3. **Getting a job:**
   A. You have been offered a summer job you can do with one hand tied behind your back. It pays $10 an hour. You need the money for next year's tuition and this job would pay just enough to get you through the year with no frills. You would take this job.

   B. You have been offered a summer job you are not certain you can handle. You could build your contacts network be-

cause the job offers exposure to many people. The pay is minimum wage, but you have the chance to earn a $3,000 bonus for high performance. The bonus would make it possible to have money for fun things, rather than just squeak by on a survival standard of living. You would take this job.

4. **Accepting invitation to weekend party:**
   A. You have been invited to a weekend house party with some old friends you know well. You expect the weekend will be pleasant, if bland. You would accept the invitation.

   B. On the same weekend, you have been invited to go white-water rafting with a group you could describe as friendly acquaintances. The group is composed of popular people at your school—it's a group you've secretly wished you could be a part of. The problem is you don't know whether you would have a marvelous time, or would feel out of place. You would accept this invitation.

5. **Choosing a class:**
   A. You need a specific course to complete requirements for your major field of study. One class is taught by a professor you know well. You feel confident that if you work hard, you can pull an A. You would choose this class.

   B. Another class in the same course is taught by an adjunct professor who is a vice president of a large company. The VP has taught the course several times before and previous students say she's a tough taskmaster but fair—and really knows the material. You would have to work yourself ragged to keep up and might not get as high a grade. On the plus side, you probably would learn more current data and make a good contact. You would choose this class.

6. **Keep or quit your job:**
   A. You are 25 years old and unmarried. You have been employed by the same firm for three years and have received several promotions. You like the company and bosses. With continued regular promotions, you should be making $40,000 annually in another five years. You have just been offered a promotion that will pay $27,000. You would accept the promotion and stay with the company.

   B. You are offered a job with a new high technology firm at an annual salary of $31,000. The firm is 2,000 miles away in an area of the country you know little about. The company will pay your moving expenses. The company president says that if all goes well, within five years you could be earning $50,000. You would accept this job offer.

7. **Investing money:**
   A. You have managed to save an extra $2,500. You can invest it in a savings institution for a return of 6 percent. You would know exactly how much money you would earn on your investment each year. You would invest in this institution.

   B. You can invest your $2,500 in a variable rate mutual fund. It is now paying 9 percent interest but because the rate fluctuates with the economy, it could dip well below 6 percent. You would invest in the mutual fund.

8. **Buying rental property:**
   A. You are 25, single, have saved and inherited from a doting aunt a total of $20,000, and need a tax write-off. You have found a house in the suburbs that you could rent to others for enough money to pay the mortgage. It is in a stable neighborhood and in good physical shape. You would buy this property.

   B. You have seen another property in an older city neighborhood that a growing number of young professionals say is a "great investment opportunity." Some have already bought, renovated, and moved into the houses. The house you've seen needs work but you could do much of it yourself. If the neighborhood continues to be upgraded, the potential rent would be much higher than the suburban property. On the other hand, a few naysayers believe the rising potential of the city neighborhood is temporary. You would buy this property.

9. **Going back to school:**
   A. You are 35, married, and have two children. You are successful in your field but have gone as far as you can without an advanced degree. You like your job and don't see that working another 25 years or so would be distasteful at the level you now occupy. You would stay as you are.

   B. In the same circumstances, with your family supporting any decision you make, you decide to quit work for two years, get your advanced degree and hope that it will bring more money and higher-level jobs. Your spouse would have to support the family while you are in school, plus you would have to borrow by taking a second mortgage on your home. If nothing in the job market changes, the payoff could be terrific— but the market could change. You would go back to school.

10. **Deciding when to say "yes":**
    A. You are a new college graduate. You have narrowed potential employers to three companies. The Black Co. is your first choice by far. After that, you rank the Green and White companies equally. You receive an offer from the White Co.

You are asked for an immediate decision. You fear you will lose out on the offer if you wait until you hear from the Black Co. You would accept White's offer.

B. Under the same circumstances, you realize you could ask the people at the White Co. for a few more days to consider the offer. You realize you could call the managers at the Black Co., let it be known that you have another offer and ask if Black has come to a decision about you. You would gamble that you can keep the White Co. on the string and "force" an offer from the Black Co.

Scoring: To repeat, there are no right and wrong answers. This quiz merely helps you to recognize your R.T.Q. Here's how to score:

Give yourself one point for each "A" decision. Give yourself two points for each "B" decision.

If you score 10 points, you like to play it safe. You may want to try to boost your risk-taking comfort level a bit so that you do not miss out on good opportunities.

If you score between 13 and 15, you are willing to take chances, to reach out and grab opportunities as you see them.

If you score between 16 and 20, you are a born risk-taker. Be sure your risk taking is rational rather than emotional.

■ ■ ■ ■

Last Thoughts

Assunta Ng, after leaving Hong Kong at 18, put herself through school and saved $25,000 from a job teaching immigrants in Seattle schools. Ng started the Chinese-language *Chinese Post* newspaper in 1982. Later, she began publishing an English-language version, the *Northwest Asian Weekly*. Now, she is a cultural interpreter and explains immigrant culture to local officials.

David W. Huggins is the founder and CEO of RMS Technologies. RMS does consulting in the data transfer business, mostly to government agencies. Huggins' success took decades, and took him from the military to telecommunications in the private sector. In 1970 he and two partners formed RMS, which today is the fifth largest African-American owned business, according to *Black Enterprise* magazine. "I always wanted to run a business, because I enjoy taking risks. There's nothing like winning," says Huggins.

Outside Forces That May Affect Your Future

This chapter identifies potent career shifts taking place in the United States. Going beyond merely identifying trends, it encourages readers to practice the art of critical analysis in applying trends to themselves. Included are such factors as the myth of the com-ing labor shortage, technology and the middle class, the world marketplace, drug testing, the growth of a contingent workforce, telecommuting, and the emphasis on being a service-producing economy.

The section concludes with advice for readers—whose career years may be riddled with uncertainty—to avoid blind acceptance of forecasts and suggestions.

Watch Hot Trends of the 1990s

As we move through this decade, we see that we are living differently. Communism is history, the cold war is over, baby boomers are graying, and America is still the dominant world power, although Japan and others are narrowing the gap.

Some say the 1990s are the S.O.S. (Save Our Society) decade, the first socially responsible decade devoted to the three "E's"— environment, education, and ethics. Others aren't so sure, saying commercial interests in an era of heightened world competitiveness are taking priority.

What is certain is that there is no shortage of trends that may become major influences in our lives during this decade and beyond. It is increasingly important to look at careers against a backdrop not only of what is happening in the United States, but what is happening across the globe. Here are some big-picture trends and related forecasts.

During the 1950s, we read that by the 21st century everyone would be working thirty hours a week and the rest of their time would be spent at leisure. However, American workers are working longer and longer hours.

Despite jumps in worker productivity and advances in timesaving appliances, Americans continue to lose free time. Actually, they have been losing an hour of leisure time since the 1980s, says a study conducted at Georgia State University.

According to an article, "Navigating by Starlight: Career Guidance From the Class of 1970," which appeared in the August 7, 1995 *Fortune* magazine, there have been other changes and they are likely to continue. Results of a survey sent to the graduating class of 1970 show that 58 percent had worked for four or more employers; 27 percent had been "involuntarily terminated from employment;" 39 percent had been canned at least once; and more than half the men and three out of five women have had more than one distinctly different career. And half of *these* say the change involved significant retraining.

One piece of advice from the author Thomas Stewart is that "The same forces that make income insecure also create one-time chances for wealth. Try to grab them. You know the sign that says, U*se seatbottom cushion for flotation*? You may need to."

Stewart says that another lesson to be learned is, "When the obvious customers for your talents have been found by others, don't discard the skills; take them where no one has imagined going."

Many classmates have become what Eric Vogt, founder of MicroMentor, a producer of multimedia instructional business software, describes as "itinerant knowledge workers." Vogt says, "If you find your passion and dive into it, by God, you get good enough that people pay for some aspect of it."

A 1995 article in the *Annual Review of Institute for Information Studies* described "the nature of work in 2010." According to the author, the old adage was "Them that can't, teach"; whereas the new adage is "Them that learn, can."

When Dr. Kenneth Genova told his colleagues at New York's Mount Sinai Hospital that he was moving to rural Georgia, they thought he was crazy. But the 33-year-old psychiatrist says it was one of the sanest things he ever did.

White-collar urbanites have long accepted pay cuts in exchange for the lower costs of small-town life. The tradeoffs include the loss of the virtual 24-hour access to almost everything. However, fields such as consulting, telecommunications and software development have led to much greater freedom in choosing where to live. Young professionals are finding they can have their white-picket fences and keep their big-city paychecks.

"I thought it would be possible to make the same money, but it was a great surprise and pleasure to make more," Genova says.

"The saving is in the housing and taxes," says Norman Crampton, author of "The 100 Best Small Towns in America," who himself moved from Chicago to Greencastle, Indiana (population, 10,000), five years ago.

Job growth and per capita income for small towns and rural areas have been growing at a faster clip than in metropolitan areas, according to government statistics. Jon Sargent, an economist with the Office of Employment Projections, U.S. Department of Labor, says there are no hard data on white-collar migration, but agrees that the rise of telecommunications technology is changing where and how young professionals live.

"In New York, you go to your job and then you leave it," says Genova. "In a small town, you're a member of the community."

In the book, *Jobshift: How to Prosper in a Workplace Without Jobs*, William Bridges says that there is a qualitative shift going on. "It's not just that fewer of the old-style jobs are left. It's that the work situations encouraged by the new technological and economic realities are not 'jobs' in the traditional sense, and a great deal of what is being done in today's organizations is done by people who do not have a 'real job.' There is no doubt, as the press has started to recognize, America is being 'temped.' Temporary and part-time workers are doing an increasing share of the work in American organizations, and the process has gone farther than most people realize. A confidential Bank of America memo leaked to the press estimated that 'soon only 19 percent of the bank's employees will work full-time.' "

Bridges predicts the demise of the office. "For millions of Americans, the job is at the office. The two entities go together like home and family. But the same technological forces that are making it possible to scatter operations around the world are making it possible to do away with offices to an extent that no one would have dreamed possible just a few years ago."

Bridges continues: "None of the changes of the past decade promises to have so much impact on the workplace and jobs as the re-design of work processes, called reengineering. Reengineering is the systematic work-redesign process that helps organizations make similar savings in time and money, while enhancing quality. When Louisville's Capital Holding Corporation reengineered its back office operations, it found that it could increase its business 25 percent while cutting its staff from 1,900 to 1,100 and expects to go further to 800."

A happy note for Americans as we approach the 21st century: Some analysts say that by the end of the 1990s, the United States likely will have the youngest population of all the major industrial countries. This is partly because of the legal immigration allowed, which gives our population more youth and energy. We "rejuvenate and enrich our talent pool by welcoming new citizens."

When you're ready to watch future trends and consider predictions, read such authors as Marvin J. Cetron and Owen Davies (*Crystal Globe: The Haves and Have-Nots of the New World Order*), John Naisbitt and Patricia Aburdene (*Megatrends 2000*) and Faith Popcorn (*The Popcorn Report*). They'll tell you all about global moves, mood foods, virtual reality supermarkets, light therapy, brain gyms, computer travel, the increase of women in leadership roles, and the triumph of the individual.

■ ■ ■ ■

Trend Watching— What Does It All Mean?

The president of a group of bird watchers once asked a farmer if the bird lovers could roam over his land to pursue their wildlife studies. A little suspicious, the farmer asked for more information. "What exactly is it you want to do?" the farmer questioned.

"We want to watch birds," replied the leader.

Still not satisfied, the farmer tilted his head and asked:

"Watch 'em for what?"

It's the same with trends. You may not always be sure of what you're watching for. In this section, we'll help you to find out. As you read the following sampler of key trends affecting careers, you'll notice examples of the types of questions you should ask yourself. Then we give examples of the answers you might come up with. These are only examples. You might think of other questions and answers that we do not list.

Soon you'll get the hang of figuring out ways that various trends could affect you.

At this point, you should practice your new skill. Every place you see "Q. (your question)" and "A. (your answer)," think about how the trend could impact on your life.

Here are selected trends.

The Expansion of the Third Sector

In *The End of Work: The Decline of the Global Labor Force and the Dawn of the Post-Market Era* (1995), author Jeremy Rifkin describes a third sector—a strong community-based third force in American politics.

This third sector will be expanding as the private sector and the government are downsized. In 1950, tax exempt organizations numbered from 5,000 to 7,000. By 1985, the IRS had processed 45,000 applications for tax exempt status. In 1995, the total combined assets of the non-profit sector were more than $500 billion.

Voluntary organizations exist in most foreign countries, but they are the most developed in the United States. "The economist and educator Max Learner once observed that through their affiliations with volunteer organizations Americans hope to overcome their sense of personal isolation and alienation and become part of a real community," writes Rifkin.

In 1994 the Clinton administration created the Non-Profit Liaison Network, which "will work with the non-profit sector on common goals." President Reagan also recognized the power of the third sector and made volunteerism a key theme of his administration, and President Bush in his "Points of Light" speech stressed the importance of the volunteer sector.

Non-profit organizations need paid managers, fund raisers, accountants, lawyers, marketing professionals, computer experts, and other qualified staff. For this reason, today's young people should strongly consider the third sector, not only as a career option but as a way to receive life satisfaction that paying jobs may not provide.

Women Shake Up the Working World

The tidal wave of women leaving home for a job is the single most important change that has happened in the American labor market. Women now make up 45 percent of the workforce; by the year 2000, their share will increase to 47 percent. In less than a generation the size of the female labor force has more than doubled. More than half of mothers with children one year old or younger are in the labor force.

But lately the number of women entering the labor force has slowed and the birth rate is rising. This may mean a shift back to families and children. Or it may be a temporary trend—most families find it hard to live on one salary.

Analysis

Q. (For females) Should I plan on working rather than staying home to raise a family?

A. Yes. I have aptitudes, interests, and talents that go beyond homemaking. I may change my mind and not work, but then again, my husband could become disabled or die and I would need to support my family. My counselor says a study shows that 20 percent of working women are separated, divorced, or widowed, and 25 percent are single. That means nearly half are supporting themselves.

Q. (For males) Would having a working wife—rather than one who is a full-time homemaker—change my life or career?

A. Yes. A working wife obviously would give us two incomes and we could afford more luxuries. If my wife or I were offered a good job in a distant city, we would have a tough decision to make about whether to relocate. If we had children, I might have to take time off from work to share duties such as taking them to the doctor.

Analysis

Q. If the people are right who say that "Middle America" is about to become extinct, what can I do to protect myself? I may not rise to top management levels, but I don't want to be a laborer either. Maybe I should go into computers, even though this field is not one that greatly interests me. What should I do?

A. I'll compromise. I'll choose a field that's interesting, but I'll also learn to use a computer. My counselor says many jobs will require computer skills.

Business Goes International

Our economy is becoming more international because nations depend on each other for materials, technology, capital, labor, imports, exports—the full range of economic factors. Jobs go to the nations offering the cheapest workers capable of doing the required task.

The Middle Class: An Endangered Species?

Some observers declare that America is quickly losing its middle class. They say that many jobs have been "dumbed-down," meaning you can make a job so simple that anyone can do it. This analysis holds that soon there will be more low-end jobs for high school dropouts and more jobs at the upper end for college graduates, with fewer jobs in the middle. A sketch of job levels and incomes would be shaped like an hourglass.

Others disagree, arguing that the income of the middle class has remained more or less stable.

Analysis

Q. I want to be a manager. Will I work overseas?

A. After checking out this question in my school media center, I discovered that employers tend to hire citizens of the country in which the work is done. I probably couldn't get hired to work overseas unless I had a special ability. I haven't decided whether to major in international business—I want to interview several graduates of international business programs before I make that decision.

Q. Should I major in a foreign language?

A. I was thinking about it until I found out that the only jobs for which foreign language is the number one qualification are in teaching, translating, and interpreting. Instead, I'll minor in a foreign language, or become fluent in one. That way my bilingual ability will be a plus in whatever field I choose. I hear that Japanese, Chinese, Russian, or Spanish would be a good choice.

Most U.S. Job Growth Is in Service Industries

Jobs for Americans will continue to shift from goods-producing industries (manufacturing, mining, construction, and agriculture) to the service-producing sector (transportation, trade, finance, services, and government). The Bureau of Labor Statistics predicts that virtually all U.S. job growth between now and the 21st century will be in the service-producing sector, which already accounts for nearly three-quarters of all American employment. The United States is not unique. Other major industrial nations are headed toward a service-producing economy too. Service-producing sectors now account for more than 6 out of 10 jobs in France and Japan.

Analysis

Q. Should I avoid a career in manufacturing?

A. Not necessarily. U.S. manufacturing industries have cut back to a leaner, more efficient

industrial base that offers good jobs. What I will do is look for a well-managed company in an industry that appeals to me—if I decide manufacturing is where my heart is.

The Age of Consolidation

It started in the 1980s during dealmaking that left airlines, tires, and appliances in the hands of a diminished number of companies. Fewer and bigger companies are now being pushed on by ferocious foreign competition, a soft U.S. economy, and rising research and development costs. The consolidation wave is moving into banking, insurance, pharmaceuticals, retailing, commercial real estate, and even such young industries as software and biotechnology. As companies get larger and leaner, they shed workers—hundreds of thousands were laid off during recent years.

Analysis

Q. (your question) _____

_____

A. (your answer) _____

_____

_____

_____

Now you have seen five trends with sample questions and answers. From here on, you supply the questions and you supply the answers. How can these trends affect your career?
THINK!S T R E T C H!ANALYZE!

High Tech: Fast Growth, Few Jobs

Many career seekers see high technology as the wave to catch. But, relatively speaking, there won't be many high-tech jobs. New high-tech industries will account for only a fraction of total U.S. employment by the end of the century. Remember, high tech depends on automation and automation replaces human labor. *Those who catch the high-tech wave will have solid training in science or engineering as a base to which management or other skills are added.* All the headlines for new jobs— gene broker, laser engineer, local network technician, robotic mining supervisor, hypersonic pilot, moon base ranger—should not hide the fact that we still will need good repairers, clerks, doctors, teachers, and other familiar workers.

Analysis

Q. (your question) _____

_____

A. (your answer) _____

_____

_____

_____

Jobs Will Change

Young people will work in industries and occupations markedly different from those in which their parents are working today. Some forecasters say our factories will nearly disappear and that jobs of the future will be dull and low paying. Others claim that new industries and opportunities will spring up to replace those lost.

It is impossible to know precisely where we are heading, but there's little argument about one aspect: *The nature of work will change.* It is not so much that jobs are becoming high tech, but that technology will alter how most jobs are performed. In the future, a house painter may use a robot for routine spraying. Auto mechanics already consult computers to diagnose car troubles. Bank tellers leave routine transactions to teller machines while they use their own judgment in deciding whether a payroll check is a forgery.

Analysis

Q. (your question) _____

_____

A. (your answer) _____

_____

_____

_____

_____

Talk of a Leisure Society Is Overworked

Despite a lot of talk about an upcoming leisure society where machines do the work and people aren't bothered by blue Mondays, Americans in the decades ahead are likely to be very interested in careers.

Work and its rewards appear to be in the human genes. A Department of Labor survey reports that most workers, if given a choice for change, would rather work more hours and make more money. A preference for a shorter workweek was expressed by only 6 percent of men and 9 percent of women. Even among higher-paid workers, only about 10 percent of men and 20 percent of women were willing to trade hours of work—and the income linked to them—for additional leisure. George Bernard Shaw observed, "Perpetual holiday is a good working definition of hell." Was he right?

Suppose you don't really have a choice. The human need to do—to achieve—to know that one's work is important, may be denied to increasing numbers of workers who are forced to take jobs with an "assembly line" or "fast-food" approach. What then? Does this mean that workers who fail to find satisfaction at their place of employment must turn to leisure hours for a sense of self-fulfillment?

Analysis

Q. (your question) _____

_____

A. (your answer) _____

_____

_____

_____

The Hunt for New Workers

Contrary to earlier predictions, the nation's labor force in 2000 will not be so dramatically different than today's. This is the word from a number of new major studies.

The workforce will become more diverse, but white native males will still play an important role, making up nearly 32 percent of newcomers to the workforce this decade.

The percentage of all males will drop from 55 percent to 53 percent, while the percentage

of women will rise from 45 percent to 47 percent. The percentage of whites (men and women) will decrease from 86 percent to 84 percent, while the percentage of African-Americans will grow from 11 percent to 12 percent.

Even if the overall picture doesn't do a flip-flop, large numbers of people are involved. Assuming the workforce in 2000 totals 141 million people, even a 1 percent increase or decrease means 1.4 million individuals.

Analysis

Q. (your question) _____

_____

A. (your answer) _____

_____

_____

_____

When Robots Apply for Jobs

Robots look nothing like the cuddlesome humanoids of the movies. Typically they are gawky mechanical arms with rotating and clutching devices, doing such routine duties as spray painting or spot welding. The robotics industry in America hasn't moved as quickly as expected, and an increasing share of the robotics market is going to Japanese and some European producers. Robots are expensive. Robots will become more sophisticated. Robots will become widely used as companies seek ways to boost productivity. Estimates vary as to how many human workers robots will replace. Some estimates say that robots, CAD/CAM, and flexible manufacturing complexes can cut a company's workforce by up to one-third.

Others say that industry can't come up with the many billions of dollars required to convert to robotics.

The timetable is in doubt, but it seems likely that robots and artificial intelligence systems eventually will cut deeply into the human workforce.

Analysis

Q. (your question) _____

_____

A. (your answer) _____

_____

_____

_____

easy-fire deal when they accept employment. Floaters rarely get fringe benefits—no health, no pension, no unemployment insurance.

Two decades ago, part-timers made up about 15 percent of the workforce. Today, including "temps" and independent contractors, contingent workers account for more than 25 percent. The two figures aren't exactly comparable but you can see which way the wind is blowing.

Analysis

Q. (your question) _____

_____

A. (your answer) _____

_____

_____

_____

Contingent Workforce Is Growing

Americans who move from project to project, or whose regular jobs do not fill an entire week, are *contingent* or *floating* workers. Some are part-time or project workers by choice. But others are left out in the cold when it comes to finding full-time permanent employment.

Contingent workers are the human equivalent of the inventory-control system known as "just in time." Nuts and bolts, for example, now are brought into factories the day they are called for on the assembly line. This saves companies the expense of warehousing the parts until they are needed.

Similarly, almost any type of worker, from secretary to technician to executive, can be hired as needed, then ushered out when business slows, with no severance benefits or help in finding a new job. They understand the easy-hire,

Secondary Labor Market Is Ghetto for Young Workers

Of particular interest to women and men in their teens and early 20s is the fact that large numbers of them are mired in what is termed the secondary labor market. These people are part of the contingent workforce.

To explain: The primary labor market consists of jobs offering opportunity for advancement and for employer training. By contrast, the secondary labor market is made up of jobs that pay little, offer no fringe benefits, demand few skills, lack employment stability, and are void of advancement opportunities.

Many young people who do not go on to formal education/training beyond high school find themselves stuck in the secondary labor market. In essence the labor market is "baby-sitting" young people in low-end jobs. They may or may not escape from these bottom-feeding jobs at about age 25, when employers view them as "seasoned" enough to justify investing money in training them for better jobs.

Analysis

Q. (your question) _____

_____

A. (your answer) _____

_____

_____

_____

Technology Is Reinventing the Workplace

Are you ready for glasers (nuclear lasers) that rocket an almost infinite number of messages around the world by satellite? Fifth-generation computers with artificial intelligence? New biological tools that grow human insulin in the laboratory? Technological change—often involving the use of microprocessors, information technology, computer-controlled offices, and genetic engineering—is on the upswing. All these technological advances won't make the human worker obsolete. But rapid turnover—with some people changing jobs five or six times during their worklives—and the remaking of industries will require workers to adjust more quickly and more often.

Analysis

Q. (your question) _____

_____

A. (your answer) _____

_____

_____

_____

_____

Working at Home

The Information Age allows some people to work at home in new ways—but the home-based workplace may be oversold. The fact is, there is no official count on how many people only work at home compared to those who occasionally bring work home from the office.

People who communicate with their offices by personal computer, modem, and fax machines may be called "telecommuters." Tele-commuting appeals particularly to people who have child-care problems, although we're finding out that parents can't concentrate on work and watch kids at the same time. It also appeals to people with physical mobility limitations or aversions to downtown congestion.

A big downside to working at home is that it can be lonely, giving workers a sense of isolation. Workers who are out of sight and out of mind may be passed over for promotion. Employers complain about the lack of control over home workers, many of whom are professionals, not administrative or clerical workers.

Opinion is divided about how many people will work at home in the future.

Analysis

Q. (your question) _____

_____

A. (your answer) _____

_____

_____

_____

Analysis

Q. (your question) _____

_____

A. (your answer) _____

_____

_____

_____

Job Sharing and Flextime Gain

In job sharing, two employees share one full-time job. Flextime or flexible scheduling plans offer a two-part work schedule; the main part consists of a "core time" when all employees must be at work. The beginning and end of each workday is a flexible period when they can choose their own arrival and departure times.

About half of companies recently surveyed by the Conference Board offer flextime hours. In other alternative work schedules, 36 percent offered a four-day, 40-hour workweek, and 22 percent offered job sharing. Just a decade ago, job sharing was almost unknown and a mere 16 percent of companies offered flextime.

But while alternative work schedules are a rose garden for many, thorns are beginning to appear. Job sharers may try to cram a week's work into half a week's hours. When work becomes less of a priority, workers often miss promotions. Bosses may not realize that a person who works four days a week is too tired to come in on Friday to handle an emergency. It seems that a flexible schedule is making some peoples' lives even more frenzied.

The Work and Family Connection

More and more companies are offering day-care benefits for employees' children—and sometimes for elderly parents who cannot remain alone all day. Companies may reimburse employees for day-care costs, provide care centers on the work site, or, at the least, establish information and referral programs and offer flexible work schedules. The number of large companies offering day-care benefits has grown in recent years.

Corporate America seems to be coming around to the realization that when work and family responsibilities collide the results can be detrimental to all. Absenteeism and tardiness rise. Productivity and performance fall. Morale gets a migraine. Profits sag.

Analysis

Q. (your question) _____

_____

A. (your answer) _____

_____

_____

_____

_____

The Dual-Career Couple Is the Norm

It's two for the money in America. Nearly 50 percent of married couples have two incomes, up from half that number three decades ago. The figure will jump even higher as more and more women hit the job market running. This trend can give workers more flexibility to make job and career moves, because one breadwinner can pay the bills for a period of time.

Analysis

Q. (your question) _____

_____

A. (your answer) _____

_____

_____

_____

A Crisis in Workplace Literacy

An insurance clerk paid $2,200 on a dental claim that should have been only $22.00. Why? The clerk didn't understand what a decimal point means.

A plant worker, unable to read the assembly instructions, nearly killed several co-workers by fitting the wrong heavy piece of equipment onto a machine.

Illiterates like these are worrying employers, who express concern that up to one-third of today's workers will be unable to read well enough to qualify for entry-level jobs. Almost half of the firms in a recent survey say that between 15 percent and 35 percent of their current employees aren't capable of handling more complex tasks; about 10 percent say that up to half of their current workers do not have the skills needed for promotion.

Analysis

Q. (your question) _____

_____

A. (your answer) _____

_____

_____

_____

Harassment's Legacy for Equality in the Workplace

The national uproar over Clarence Thomas, Anita Hill, and sexual harassment has caused women across the nation to break their silence on the sensitive issue of sexual harassment, an issue that cuts to the very soul of gender discrimination. The Civil Rights Act of 1991 made it easier for women to win limited financial awards for intentional bias, including sexual harassment. Companies have become far more aware of the issue. Will the events of the early 1990s change the workplace environment for women in the future? For better? For worse? Analyze.

Analysis

Q. (your question) _____

_____

A. (your answer) _____

_____

_____

_____

Unions Fighting Back

By the year 2000 unions may claim less than 10 percent of the nation's workers—if the long membership slide continues. Although unions are shadows of their earlier selves (in 1983 they claimed 20 percent of the workforce), they are fighting back with new recruiting and member benefit efforts. In tapping the huge pool of unskilled, foreign-born laborers, for example, unions host job-search seminars, English lessons, and counseling.

At the upper end of the worker scale, several polls show renewed approval of unions among professional and white-collar workers. As one pollster says, "Apparently they are joining blue-collar workers in seeing themselves as just cogs on a larger wheel, less able as individuals to exert the kind of control they wish to have over their own lifestyles."

The shift away from heavy manufacturing—the former mainstay of unions—to white-collar and technical jobs in service industries means that unions probably never will be invited to as

many employment parties as they once were. But the labor groups remain powerful in government, transportation, communications, public utilities, construction, and mining.

Analysis

Q. (your question) _____

_____

A. (your answer) _____

_____

_____

_____

Appetites Grow for Cafeteria-Style Benefits

More companies are beginning to offer employee fringe benefits on the cafeteria plan. This permits employees to use benefits credits as they wish. They can, for instance, choose to take college courses at the expense of retirement benefits, or health insurance over extra vacation days. Overall, including legally required benefits like social security payments, the cost of employee benefit payments averages nearly 38 percent of payroll, or roughly $12,000 per year per employee as of the beginning of this decade.

To make a fast calculation of whether the benefits in a job offer are good, see if they add up to one-third of your salary offer. This is only a rule of thumb; actual cases vary considerably.

Analysis

Q. (your question) _____

_____

A. (your answer) _____

_____

_____

_____

Companies Get Tough on Drugs

At no time in the past have illegal drugs in the workplace posed so menacing a danger to the American economy. Their presence on the job is diluting the energy, integrity, and reliability of the American labor force, just as competition from foreign enterprise grows more threatening. The epidemic of drug abuse is so tragic that many companies say they no longer can overlook it and are instituting get-tough policies to cope with the problem.

Despite continuing legal challenges over privacy, a Conference Board study shows that more than half of companies surveyed in a broad range of industries now test job applicants and/or employees for substance abuse, or are about to implement these programs. Employers tend to reject job applicants when evidence of drug use is found. Most companies that test employees operate rehabilitation programs instead of firing abusers and training replacements.

Analysis

Q. (your question) _____

_____

A. (your answer) _____

_____

_____

_____

Lifelong Learning Is a New Reality

If a motto were emblazoned on the family crests of tomorrow's workers, it appropriately could be one suggested by leading careers authority Kenneth B. Hoyt: "Always a commencement, never a graduation." That is, tomorrow will hold lots of beginnings, but workers will never be finished learning. Figuratively speaking, graduation day will never come. Lifelong education and training has been recommended for years. What's new, urgent, and real about the idea is the threat of obsolescence caused by technology. Workers who decide they've learned it once and once is enough will find themselves in deep trouble in the job market.

Analysis

Q. (your question) _____

_____

A. (your answer) _____

_____

_____

_____

_____

A Job Is Not Forever

Downsizing, layoffs, hiring freezes, and corporate mergers have been killing jobs left and right throughout the last decade. Many economists believe more of the same is ahead.

More and more young professionals and managers are becoming advocates of loyalty to oneself. That's because companies are no longer doing handsprings to encourage corporate loyalty as they strip away layers of bureaucracy. They're firing hundreds of thousands of employees who mistakenly thought that as long as they worked hard and kept their noses clean, their future was safe in the hands of their organizations. Seniority is no longer a guarantee of job security, much less of promotion and advancement. Only diamonds are forever.

Analysis

Q. (your question) _____

_____

A. (your answer) _____

_____

_____

_____

_____

■ ■ ■ ■

Can You Trust The Experts?

Even experts don't always make the right calls. In their fascinating book, *The Experts Speak* (Pantheon Books), Christopher Cerf and Victor Navasky cite examples of the most astounding miscalculations, egregious prognostications, and just plain foul-ups. Among their treasures are these gems:

◆ No one knows more about this mountain [Mount St. Helens] than Harry. And it don't dare blow up on him. This [gol-danged] mountain won't blow.

—Harry Truman (83-year-old owner of a lodge near Washington State's Mount St. Helens) commenting on predictions that the long-dormant volcano was about to erupt, 1980. Harry made a decision not to evacuate. A few days later, Mount St. Helens erupted, killing, among others, Harry Truman and his 16 cats.

◆ God himself could not sink this ship.

—*Titanic* deckhand, responding to a passenger's question, "Is this ship really unsinkable?" Southampton, England, April 10, 1912. The deckhand had decided to believe and repeat assurances from the ship's designers. At 20 minutes to midnight on April 14, 1912, the Titanic struck an iceberg and sank, drowning 1,500 of her passengers and crew.

◆ For [heaven's] sake go down to reception and get rid of a lunatic who's down there. He says he's got a machine for seeing by wireless! Watch him—he may have a razor on him.

—Editor of the *Daily Express*, London, deciding not to see and interview John Logie Baird (the inventor of television), 1925.

◆ The horse is here to stay, but the automobile is only a novelty—a fad.

—President of the Michigan Savings Bank, advising Horace Rackham (Henry Ford's lawyer) not to invest in the Ford Motor Company, 1903. Rackham made his own decision. He disregarded his banker's advice and bought $5,000 worth of Ford stock. When he sold his shares several years later, they were worth $12.5 million. We have no record of what the banker said when he realized he missed an opportunity to invest and earn millions of dollars himself.

◆ The Hawaiian Islands are over-protected; the entire Japanese fleet and air force could not seriously threaten Oahu [Pearl Harbor].

—Captain William T. Pulleston (former Chief of U.S. Naval Intelligence), August 1941. Apparently the U.S. government decided Pulleston was correct. At 7:55 A.M. on December 7, 1941, Japanese carrier-based planes attacked Pearl Harbor, destroying or severely damaging 188 aircraft and 8 of the Pacific fleet's 9 battleships.

History is spotted with such blue-ribbon bloopers. We encourage using experts to *help* make decisions, but, remember, the ultimate responsibility for making decisions that affect your life is yours.

■ ■ ■ ■

Can You Trust The Forecasts?

Whatever happened to the Information Age?

Just a few years ago we heard a lot about the cashless society and the paperless office. An insurance giant even had a campaign slogan, "Paper Free in '83." Other predictions for the Information Age were abundant.

Among them: electronic home shopping, electronic libraries, personal computers on every desk, home computers on every hearth, electronic or E-mail, video phones, video conferencing, smart buildings with talking elevators, and home banking with fiber-optics bill paying.

While many of these things became realities, much of the new Information Age forecasting turned out to be wishful thinking. With fax machines and copiers so readily available, there's more paper in offices now than ever in history. Other high-tech gizmos for home and office are readily available but underused. Why? People have either found them too costly to buy or too difficult to deal with.

The Information Age has been slower in arriving than early forecasters of techno-hype anticipated. But *make no mistake—it's well on the way*. Even if you're not a techie, what does this mean for your career?

■ ■ ■ ■

Player Pianos, Rock Bands, and Advice for Tomorrow

Player Piano is a novel written decades ago by Kurt Vonnegut, Jr. He uses the instrument as a metaphor for one vision of America's high-tech, machine-driven future.

The view is not a happy one. Only a thin tier of technical superchiefs are employed to manage society's needs. Everyone other than the well-educated managers and engineers is surplus.

No one starves, but happiness is a forgotten human condition. The elite managerial-technical corps grow bored with machines. The others grow bored with make-work.

Player Piano's world is safe, sterile, stultifying—and essentially lacking in career opportunities.

In real life, one camp of experts sees the future with essentially a player-piano view: a superb education for the elite few at the top and not much beyond high school for the masses.

By contrast, another camp of experts says there'll be rock bands of live musicians belting out tunes in the workplace. They remind us that America grew from an agricultural society to a mechanical society, and is now becoming a computerized society. The rock-band people say that the computerized society will not replace the mechanical society overnight. Probably it will not replace it completely any more than the mechanical society replaced the agricultural society completely.

Many occupations we know today existed 50 years ago—salesperson, lawyer, secretary, to name several. Many occupations we know today are likely to exist 50 years from now. The job duties change, but not the basic function.

The rock-band camp argues that change will come only gradually to American workers because—and this is important—*we do not live in a linear world*.

Trends do not unfold in a straight line. We take a step or two forward, then follow with a step or two backward. Cable TV started off with a rush of glowing projections, then slowed because the costs were crushing; birth rates peak and fall; Democrats and Republicans alternate political control. We do not live in a linear world.

There is no doubt that change is more rapid than ever before in history, but it's also likely that the great bulk of jobs in the United States will continue to be conventional, although updated.

Now that you know about player pianos and rock bands, here's advice for those who want a harmonious future.

◆ Master the basic principles of your discipline. Unless you know them well enough to innovate, you may find yourself replaced by a machine. Computers can solve routine problems.

◆ Keep abreast of changes in your field on a regular basis. Consider making a written record of the changes you think are likely, describing how you think they may affect your career.

◆ Be ready to make at least one major career change in your working life. Expect that you may have to take sabbaticals (learning vacations) for reeducation several times throughout your lifespan.

◆ Become a skilled job hunter. In good times and bad, jobs open each year.

■ ■ ■ ■

Baron Rothschild was a famous financier. He once observed that only two men in Europe really understood trends in the gold market. One was with the Bank of England. The other was with the Bank of France.

"Unfortunately," Baron Rothschild said, "they disagree."

That's often true of experts; nevertheless, informed views can cause you to focus on points you might otherwise miss. Being informed is a good way to break into tomorrow's most lucrative and rewarding fields. Careers tomorrow are what we look at next.

CHAPTER
4

Toward Tomorrow's Careers

What a difference a decade makes! The first edition of this work straightforwardly dealt with the authors' evaluation of how key career fields were likely to perform.

Times have changed so dramatically during the past 10 years that the occupational sampler in this edition offers fewer specific occupations and more overview data than that found in earlier editions. It also includes a new listing of occupations classified by the education and training each requires.

This chapter is very helpful because it gives you an idea of the kinds of information you can acquire for career decision-making purposes. View the following pages only as a beginning to your research efforts. Scope out fields of interest in far greater detail as suggested in Chapter 8. Remember, too, that VGM Career Horizons publishes the widest variety of career books available on the market today—so check your local bookstores or libraries for more in-depth information on the field of your choice.

Careers: Looking to the Future

This informal rundown highlights interesting points and trends in the job market. After reading it, you'll have a good idea of the big picture in work. The section is not designed to be a comparative text contrasting features of one occupation with another. You learn to do that in later pages describing research techniques.

The old career track? History. It's been replaced by a new focus on "employability" rather then "employment." By skill-based jobs rather than lifetime jobs. By career self-reliance rather than career dependency.

Unimagined changes are taking place in workplaces today, fueled by racing technology and global competition for work.

Companies are telling new employees not to expect long-term employment.

Companies are telling new employees that they are expected to be immediately productive—to have skills to make the jobs hum from Day One.

Companies are telling new employees not that they are a part of one big happy family, but that employees must look to their own futures without the companies as a safety net.

Why are all these unsettling changes happening? These changes have caused more than 43 million jobs to be erased in the United States since 1979. They have caused the greatest job insecurity since the Great Depression of the 1930s. They are demanding that the very notion of employment be redefined.

In one view, we are in the middle of the fourth workplace revolution—a computer revolution—where in the foreseeable future, perhaps 20 years, we'll have 50 percent or higher unemployment because work will be handled by computers and lower-paid workers overseas.

The first workplace revolution was agricultural, when humans became farmers rather than nomadic hunters and gatherers. The second revolution was the industrial revolution, when steam power and its mechanization made factories a place to work. The third revolution was when manufacturing gave way to a service economy providing services rather than goods.

How far away are we really from a time when half the population won't be working? No one knows for sure, but researchers point out that the first revolution took millions of years, the second 10,000 years, the third 100 years, and the fourth is expected to take only 20 years.

Even if the prediction of a 20-year timetable turns out to be dramatically wrong, it seems clear the planet is turning into two kinds of places. At one end of the spectrum is an information-rich class that controls and manages the high-tech global economy. At the other end of the spectrum is an information-poor class that has very little hope for meaningful jobs in an increasingly automated world.

Some observers believe we already have more people ready and willing to work than there are available openings because technological developments have drastically reduced the need for farmers and factory workers. These workers held two thirds of the jobs in the United States in the 1920s. Others aren't so sure we have too many people to be employed, correctly pointing out that lots of useful work needs doing, from conquering deadly diseases, to repairing wrecked environments, to caring for needy children, and more.

Does all this technological change mean you must be a technical genius to handle all the computerization as the future races closer every day? Not at all. But if you want to make sure you don't imprison yourself in the information-poor class, you *must* become computer literate.

You must accept responsibility for changing jobs as often as needed because your career will likely outlast most jobs you take.

You should get comfortable with the idea that the skills you bring to the workplace are what stand between you and failure. Constant retraining is essential to keep you from becoming increasingly less qualified for your jobs. You'll be responsible for most of the retraining, whether it's taken in your locale or by distance education on the Internet.

Growth potential is only one of the characteristics that should count in your career choice, but do keep an eye out for healthy industries that are expected to grow fast enough to create new job openings and expanding opportunities for promotion.

And keep watch for occupations in which you can move your skills from one kind of work to another—in case you have to move quickly and unexpectedly to a new line of work.

Based on both government and private reports, here is a sampling of the occupational outlook.

■ ■ ■ ■

Farms are becoming larger and larger. From a pre-World War II peak of 6.5 million farms to a little more than 2 million today, farming is a changed business. By 2000, farms taking in more than $250,000 annually may account for as much as 90 percent of the nation's farm output, according to a government analysis.

What this means is that it will be nearly impossible for young people to become farmers from scratch. More new farmers will become hired hands than farm owners. The long-term jitters come from having exported our crop know-how to South America and other countries, now competitors in the world marketplace. Water shortages and poor land quality add to farmers' increasing concerns.

A Bright Side

Breakthroughs in biotechnology have resulted in the development of plants and animals which are genetically engineered to be stronger, more resistant to disease, and better producers. These developments have revolutionized agriculture, opening new areas in the field, such as the growth and harvesting of new plants raised for the processing of new drugs or products; agriculture now goes beyond the production of food.

Agriculture

You don't have to own a farm to work in agriculture. Sometimes called agribusiness, agriculture is not limited to farming and raising livestock. Experts project that the largest unfilled demand for agriculture graduates will be in marketing, merchandising, and technical sales rather than in production. A couple of million people work in agriculture—altogether a solid industry, but one with planet-size problems fraught with aggressive change.

Valleys Are Greener

A recent financial crisis in which heartbroken farmers lost their land after generations of working the soil appears to have eased. Some people say American agriculture is better than it's been in 15 years.

But if money is your highest priority and you don't inherit land, farming may be a sucker bet. You are busy from morn' till night: growing grain, raising livestock, haggling with banks, doing paperwork, and fixing the combine.

On the other side of the dell, you can count as rewards the opportunity for self-determination and to make a valuable contribution to end hunger. If you get in on the biotech side, you can experience firsthand the thrill of developing cutting-edge products and new lifesaving drugs. And there's always the chance you can become a big farmer and wealthy.

A wild card is what will happen as the globe's nations get cozier. Farm policy will be a hot trade issue and voices are calling for all trade subsidies to end by 2000.

A Bumper Crop of Careers

Larger farms will spur the growth of new farm services to meet their needs—financial counseling, management, consulting services. With the dawn of the biotech farm, animal healthcare companies will hire staff to help farmers solve their problems of decline. **Computer personnel** will specialize in farm systems. **Market advisers** and **crop brokers** will devise marketing strategies.

Agricultural engineers will automate the farm scene. Courses in tractor design and tillage systems are vanishing from ag engineering curriculum, replaced by such electives as wastewater management, pollution streams, computer modeling, or wind erosion.

Agricultural scientists help shift farming away from chemical herbicides and pesticides toward a "land ethic approach."

Many college students haven't yet gotten the word about the full range of agricultural careers, such as aquaculture, genetic engineering, business brokering, and plant science.

Agriculture, from seed to supermarket shelf, has become a sophisticated industry offering lots of good jobs other than watching the corn grow.

■ ■ ■ ■

Business & Office

It's glad tidings for the broad managerial and professional occupational categories—they're likely to increase faster than average. But for some white-collar workers, office automation is throwing jolts and slowing growth, perhaps to a standstill.

Management Jobs

If you want the opportunity to make lots of money, consider management. General managers and top executives are among the highest paid workers. However, competition is fierce and income varies greatly according to responsibility, experience, and size and type of firm.

Competition and money problems have caused middle managerial ranks to be cut drastically in the last decade. Millions of managers are "on the beach." Many older managers have taken lower-paying jobs.

Even so, management jobs are among the very best in the job market. A large number of tomorrow's most attractive management opportunities will be found in small- to medium-size companies, particularly service firms. Entrepreneurship will continue to be a fast-track choice for young people who tire of waiting for crowded management ranks to open.

To maximize your chances in a management job, stick to functions that make money or products, or cut costs. Keep your eye on the global nature of business today. Experience in international economics, marketing, or information systems, or knowledge of several different disciplines will increase your marketability and competitive edge. Most importantly, management requires motivation, excellent personal and analytical skills, and sound intuition in the case of insufficient information. With the competition for management jobs today, you have to be the very best to succeed.

Who <u>Are</u> All These People?

If you're uncertain what some of the jobs we mention in this section involve, remember to ask your school counselor, career center technician, or librarian for occupational materials that describe the nature of the work. A basic guide is the U.S. Labor Department's *Occupational Outlook Handbook*, which comes out every two years.

Occupational Outlook Handbook Online

The *Occupational Outlook Handbook*, after 50 years in printed form, is now available online for free. It describes nearly 90 percent of the jobs and career fields in the United States. A great place to go career shopping, the *Handbook* is now easier to access than ever.

Projections: 2005
A Quick Look at the Job Picture in the Early 21st Century

Employment growth over the 1994–2005 period will differ in many ways from that of the previous eleven years. The service-producing sector is increasing in size, with a large number of jobs being generated by the "graying" of America. Technological innovations, corporate restructuring, and the increasing globalization of the economy are all affecting the structure of the job market. Manufacturing jobs are decreasing, for example, and employment in health and human services is increasing sharply.

Education will play an even bigger role in the workplace than previously. Generally speaking, the more education a person has, the more he or she can expect to earn. Conversely, high school dropouts can expect to remain mired in low-paying jobs with minimal opportunities for professional advancement.

The following chart, developed by the U.S. Department of Labors Bureau of Labor Statistics, is a good way to look at what experts think will happen to various occupations. The chart list numbers in thousands—"200" means "200,000."

The column titled *Employment* shows how many people are more or less currently (as of 1994) employed and how many are likely to be employed in the year 2005. The column titled *Employment change* for the same time period shows the percentage of growth and the actual number. If a figure has a minus sign in front of it, the occupation is shrinking, not growing. The column titled *Total job openings due to growth and net replacements* identifies the numbers of jobs over the 10 year period (not for each year). A rule of thumb says that two-thirds of job openings occur because of replacement, and one-third due to growth. The column titled *Earning quartile* gives you an idea of the pay. The highest paying jobs are "1." The final column, *Most significant source of training*, indicates how much study is needed to do the job. "O-J-T" means on-job-training.

Occupation	Employment		Employment change, 1994-2005		Total job openings due to growth and net replacements, 1994-2005	Earnings quartile	Most significant source of traning
	1994	Projected, 2005	Percent	Number			
Total, all occupations	127,014	144,708	14	17,694	49,631		
Executive, administrative, and managerial occupations	12,903	15,071	17	2,168	4,844		
Managerial and administrative occupations	9,058	10,575	17	1,517	3,467		
Administrative services managers	279	307	10	28	87	1	Work experience, plus degree
Communication, transportation, and utilities operations managers	154	135	-12	-19	32	1	Work experience, plus degree
Construction managers	197	253	28	56	97	1	Bachelor's degree
Education administrators	393	459	17	66	176	1	Work experience, plus degree
Engineering, mathematical, and natural science managers	337	432	28	95	165	1	Work experience, plus degree
Financial managers	768	950	24	182	324	1	Work experience, plus degree
Food service and lodging managers	579	771	33	192	313	3	Work experience
Funeral directors and morticians	26	29	11	3	8	1	Long-term O-J-T
General managers and top executives	3,046	3,512	15	466	1,104	1	Work experience, plus degree
Government chief executives and legislators	91	94	4	4	26	1	Work experience, plus degree
Industrial production managers	206	191	-7	-15	43	1	Bachelor's degree
Marketing, advertising, and public relations managers	461	575	25	114	211	1	Work experience, plus degree
Personnel, training, and labor relations managers	206	252	22	46	104	1	Work experience, plus degree
Property and real estate managers	261	298	14	37	81	2	Bachelor's degree
Purchasing managers	226	235	4	9	55	1	Work experience, plus degree
All other managers and administrators	1,829	2,081	14	252	639	1	Work experience, plus degree
Management support occupations	3,845	4,496	17	651	1,377		
Accountants and auditors	962	1,083	13	121	312	1	Bachelor's degree
Budget analysts	66	74	12	8	19	1	Bachelor's degree
Claims examiners, property and casualty insurance	56	65	15	9	14	2	Bachelor's degree
Construction and building inspectors	64	79	22	14	28	1	Work experience
Cost estimators	179	210	17	31	48	2	Work experience
Credit analysts	39	48	24	9	16	1	Bachelor's degree
Employment interviewers, private or public employment service	77	104	36	27	43	1	Bachelor's degree
Inspectors and compliance officers, except construction	157	175	12	18	50	1	Work experience
Loan officers and counselors	214	264	23	50	85	1	Bachelor's degree
Management analysts	231	312	35	82	109	1	Masters's degree
Personnel, training, and labor relations specialists	307	374	22	67	129	1	Bachelor's degree
Purchasing agents, except wholesale, retail, and farm products	215	226	5	12	64	1	Bachelor's degree
Tax examiners, collectors, and revenue agents	63	63	0	0	14	1	Bachelor's degree
Underwriters	96	103	7	7	25	1	Bachelor's degree
Wholesale and retail buyers, except farm products	180	178	-2	-3	50	2	Bachelor's degree
All other management support workers	940	1,138	21	198	371	1	Bachelor's degree
Professional specialty occupations	17,314	22,387	29	5,073	8,376		
Engineers	1,327	1,573	19	246	581		
Aeronautical and astronautical engineers	56	59	6	3	16	1	Bachelor's degree
Chemical engineers	50	57	13	7	21	1	Bachelor's degree
Civil engineers, including traffic engineers	184	219	19	34	90	1	Bachelor's degree
Electrical and electronics engineers	349	417	20	69	157	1	Bachelor's degree
Industrial engineers, except safety engineers	115	131	13	15	47	1	Bachelor's degree
Mechanical engineers	231	276	19	45	98	1	Bachelor's degree
Metallurgists and metallurgical, ceramic, and materials engineers	19	20	5	1	6	1	Bachelor's degree
Mining engineers, including mine safety engineers	3	3	-18	-1	1	1	Bachelor's degree
Nuclear engineers	15	15	4	1	5	1	Bachelor's degree
Petroleum engineers	14	11	-21	-3	4	1	Bachelor's degree
All other engineers	292	367	26	75	136	1	Bachelor's degree

Occupation	Employment		Employment change, 1994-2005		Total job openings due to growth and net replacements, 1994-2005	Earnings quartile	Most significant source of traning
	1994	Projected, 2005	Percent	Number			
Architects and surveyors	200	215	7	14	70		
Architects, except landscape and marine	91	106	17	15	35	1	Bachelor's degree
Landscape architects	14	16	17	2	5	1	Bachelor's degree
Surveyors	96	92	-3	-3	30	2	Postsecondary vocational training
Life scientists	186	230	24	44	94		
Agricultural and food scientists	26	31	19	5	12	1	Bachelor's degree
Biological scientists	82	103	25	21	43	1	Doctor's degree
Foresters and conservation scientists	41	49	18	8	18	1	Bachelor's degree
Medical scientists	36	47	31	11	21	1	Doctor's degree
All other life scientists	1	1	1	0	0	1	Doctor's degree
Computer, mathematical, and operations research occupations	917	1,696	85	779	863		
Actuaries	17	18	4	1	4	1	Bachelor's degree
Computer systems analysts, engineers, and scientists	828	1,583	91	755	819		
Computer engineers and scientists	345	655	90	310	338		
Computer engineers	195	372	90	177	191	1	Bachelor's degree
All other computer scientists	149	283	89	134	147	1	Bachelor's degree
Systems analysts	483	928	92	445	481	1	Bachelor's degree
Statisticians	14	15	3	0	3	1	Bachelor's degree
Mathematicians and all other mathematical scientists	14	15	5	1	3	1	Doctor's degree
Operations research analysts	44	67	50	22	35	1	Masters's degree
Physical scientists	209	250	19	41	104		
Chemists	97	115	19	18	45	1	Bachelor's degree
Geologists, geophysicists, and oceanographers	46	54	17	8	24	1	Bachelor's degree
Meteorologists	7	7	7	0	2	1	Bachelor's degree
Physicists and astronomers	20	18	-9	-2	5	1	Doctor's degree
All other physical scientists	40	56	41	16	27	1	Bachelor's degree
Social scientists	259	318	23	59	103		
Economists	48	59	25	12	30	1	Bachelor's degree
Psychologists	144	177	23	33	45	1	Masters's degree
Urban and regional planners	29	35	24	7	13	1	Masters's degree
All other social scientists	38	45	19	7	15	1	Masters's degree
Social, recreational, and religious workers	1,387	1,924	39	536	810		
Clergy	195	234	20	38	77	2	First professional degree
Directors, religious activities and education	81	96	19	15	31	2	Bachelor's degree
Human services workers	168	293	75	125	170	4	Moderate-term O-J-T
Recreation workers	222	266	20	45	86	2	Bachelor's degree
Residential counselors	165	290	76	126	158	1	Bachelor's degree
Social workers	557	744	34	187	288	2	Bachelor's degree
Lawyers and judicial workers	735	918	25	183	279		
Judges, magistrates, and other judicial workers	79	79	1	1	11	1	Work experience, plus degree
Lawyers	656	839	28	183	268	1	First professional degree
Teachers, librarians, and counselors	6,246	7,849	26	1,603	2,886		
Teachers, preschool and kindergarten	462	602	30	140	215	3	Bachelor's degree
Teachers, elementary	1,419	1,639	16	220	511	1	Bachelor's degree
Teachers, secondary school	1,340	1,726	29	386	782	1	Bachelor's degree
Teachers, special education	388	593	53	206	262	1	Bachelor's degree
College and university faculty	823	972	18	150	395	1	Doctor's degree
Other teachers and instructors	886	1,151	30	265	331		
Farm and home management advisors	14	14	-1	0	1	2	Bachelor's degree
Instructors and coaches, sports and physical training	282	381	35	98	119	2	Moderate-term O-J-T
Adult and vocational education teachers	590	757	28	167	211		
Instructors, adult (nonvocational) education	290	376	29	85	107	2	Work experience
Teachers and instructors, vocational education and training	299	381	27	81	104	2	Work experience
All other teachers and instructors	596	769	29	173	251	1	Masters's degree
Librarians, archivists, curators, and related workers	168	182	8	14	56		
Curators, archivists, museum technicians, and restorers	19	23	19	4	9	1	Masters's degree
Librarians, professional	148	159	7	10	47	1	Masters's degree
Counselors	165	215	31	50	83	1	Masters's degree
Health diagnosing occupations	850	1,003	18	153	312		
Chiropractors	42	54	29	12	20	1	First professional degree

Occupation	Employment		Employment change, 1994-2005		Total job openings due to growth and net replacements, 1994-2005	Earnings quartile	Most significant source of traning
	1994	Projected, 2005	Percent	Number			
Dentists	164	173	5	9	54	1	First professional degree
Optometrists	37	42	12	4	12	1	First professional degree
Physicians	539	659	22	120	205	1	First professional degree
Podiatrists	13	15	15	2	5	1	First professional degree
Veterinarians and veterinary inspectors	56	62	11	6	17	1	First professional degree
Health assessment and treating occupations	2,563	3,294	29	731	1,101		
Dietitians and nutritionists	53	63	19	10	24	2	Bachelor's degree
Pharmacists	168	196	17	28	54	1	Bachelor's degree
Physician assistants	56	69	23	13	22	1	Bachelor's degree
Registered nurses	1,906	2,379	25	473	740	1	Associate degree
Therapists	380	586	54	207	262		
Occupational therapists	54	93	72	39	47	1	Bachelor's degree
Physical therapists	102	183	80	81	96	1	Bachelor's degree
Recreational therapists	31	37	22	7	11	1	Bachelor's degree
Respiratory therapists	73	99	36	26	37	1	Associate degree
Speech-language pathologists and audiologists	85	125	46	39	52	1	Masters's degree
All other therapists	36	50	39	14	19	1	Bachelor's degree
Writers, artists, and entertainers	1,612	1,975	22	363	680		
Artists and commercial artists	273	336	23	64	117	2	Work experience, plus degree
Athletes, coaches, umpires, and related workers	38	46	20	8	19	2	Long-term O-J-T
Dancers and choreographers	24	30	24	6	11	2	Postsecondary vocational training
Designers	301	384	28	84	130		
Designers, except interior designers	238	314	32	76	113	1	Bachelor's degree
Interior designers	63	70	12	8	17	1	Bachelor's degree
Musicians	256	317	24	62	105	3	Long-term O-J-T
Photographers and camera operators	139	172	24	34	61		
Camera operators, television, motion picture, video	18	19	6	1	5	2	Moderate-term O-J-T
Photographers	121	153	27	32	57	2	Moderate-term O-J-T
Producers, directors, actors, and entertainers	93	121	30	28	47	2	Long-term O-J-T
Public relations specialists and publicity writers	107	128	20	21	44	2	Bachelor's degree
Radio and TV announcers and newscasters	50	51	1	0	21	2	Long-term O-J-T
Reporters and correspondents	59	57	-4	-2	13	1	Bachelor's degree
Writers and editors, including technical writers	272	332	22	59	111	1	Bachelor's degree
All other professional workers	822	1,142	39	319	494	2	Bachelor's degree
Technicians and related support occupations	4,439	5,316	20	876	1,798		
Health technicians and technologists	2,197	2,815	28	618	1,024		
Cardiology technologists	14	17	22	3	6	3	Associate degree
Clinical laboratory technologists and technicians	274	307	12	33	86	2	Bachelor's degree
Dental hygienists	127	180	42	53	74	2	Associate degree
Electroneurodiagnostic technologists	6	8	28	2	3	3	Moderate-term O-J-T
EKG technicians	16	11	-30	-5	3	3	Moderate-term O-J-T
Emergency medical technicians	138	187	36	49	72	3	Postsecondary vocational training
Licensed practical nurses	702	899	28	197	341	2	Postsecondary vocational training
Medical records technicians	81	126	56	45	59	2	Associate degree
Nuclear medicine technologists	13	16	26	3	5	2	Associate degree
Opticians, dispensing and measuring	63	76	21	13	28	3	Long-term O-J-T
Pharmacy technicians	81	101	24	20	33	3	Moderate-term O-J-T
Psychiatric technicians	72	80	11	8	18	4	Associate degree
Radiologic technologists and technicians	167	226	35	59	82	2	Associate degree
Surgical technologists	46	65	43	19	27	3	Postsecondary vocational training
Veterinary technicians and tehnologists	22	26	18	4	8	2	Associate degree
All other health professionals and paraprofessionals	374	488	30	114	179	2	Associate degree
Engineering and science technicians and technologists	1,220	1,312	8	92	357		
Engineering technicians	685	746	9	61	207		
Electrical and electronic technicians and technologists	314	349	11	35	108	1	Associate degree
All other engineering technicians and technologists	371	397	7	26	99	2	Associate degree

Occupation	Employment		Employment change, 1994-2005		Total job openings due to growth and net replacements, 1994-2005	Earnings quartile	Most significant source of traning
	1994	Projected, 2005	Percent	Number			
Drafters	304	304	0	1	70	2	Postsecondary vocational training
Science and mathematics technicians	231	262	13	31	79	2	Associate degree
Technicians, except health and engineering and science	1,023	1,189	16	167	418		
Aircraft pilots and flight engineers	91	97	8	7	32	1	Long-term O-J-T
Air traffic controllers and airplane dispatchers	29	29	0	0	6	1	Long-term O-J-T
Broadcast technicians	42	40	-4	-2	9	1	Postsecondary vocational training
Computer programmers	537	601	12	65	228	1	Bachelor's degree
Legal assistants and technicians, except clerical	219	301	38	82	103		
Paralegals	110	175	58	64	74	2	Associate degree
Title examiners and searchers	28	28	0	0	3	2	Moderate-term O-J-T
All other legal assistants, including law clerks	80	98	22	18	27	1	Associate degree
Programmers, numerical, tool, and process control	7	6	-9	-1	2	1	Work experience
Technical assistants, library	75	91	21	16	32	2	Short-term O-J-T
All other technicians	24	24	0	0	5	2	Moderate-term O-J-T
Marketing and sales occupations	13,990	16,502	18	2,512	6,706		
Cashiers	3,005	3,567	19	562	1,772	4	Short-term O-J-T
Counter and rental clerks	341	451	32	109	203	4	Short-term O-J-T
Insurance sales workers	418	436	4	18	88	1	Long-term O-J-T
Marketing and sales worker supervisors	2,293	2,673	17	380	788	2	Work experience
Real estate agents, brokers, and appraisers	374	407	9	33	113		
Brokers, real estate	67	75	12	8	22	1	Work experience
Real estate appraisers	47	53	13	6	16	1	Work experience
Sales agents, real estate	260	279	7	19	75	1	Postsecondary vocational training
Salespersons, retail	3,842	4,374	14	532	1,821	3	Short-term O-J-T
Securities and financial services sales workers	246	335	37	90	126	1	Long-term O-J-T
Travel agents	122	150	23	28	55	3	Postsecondary vocational training
All other sales and related workers	3,349	4,109	23	760	1,741	2	Moderate-term O-J-T
Administrative support occupations, including clerical	23,178	24,172	4	994	6,991		
Adjusters, investigators, and collectors	1,229	1,507	23	277	399		
Adjustment clerks	373	521	40	148	175	3	Short-term O-J-T
Bill and account collectors	250	342	36	91	112	3	Short-term O-J-T
Insurance claims and policy processing occupations	461	495	8	35	92		
Insurance adjusters, examiners, and investigators	162	192	19	30	45	2	Long-term O-J-T
Insurance claims clerks	119	135	13	16	27	2	Moderate-term O-J-T
Insurance policy processing clerks	179	168	-6	-12	20	3	Moderate-term O-J-T
Welfare eligibility workers and interviewers	104	108	4	4	16	2	Moderate-term O-J-T
All other adjusters and investigators	41	40	-1	0	4	2	Moderate-term O-J-T
Communications equipment operators	319	266	-17	-53	83		
Telephone operators	310	260	-16	-50	81		
Central office operators	48	14	-70	-34	12	3	Moderate-term O-J-T
Directory assistance operators	33	10	-70	-24	8	3	Moderate-term O-J-T
Switchboard operators	228	236	3	7	62	3	Short-term O-J-T
All other communications equipment operators	9	6	-31	-3	2	3	Moderate-term O-J-T
Computer operators and peripheral equipment operators	289	175	-39	-114	62		
Computer operators, except peripheral equipment	259	162	-38	-98	56	3	Moderate-term O-J-T
Peripheral EDP equipment operators	30	13	-55	-16	6	3	Moderate-term O-J-T
Information clerks	1,477	1,832	24	355	699		
Hotel desk clerks	136	163	20	27	84	3	Short-term O-J-T
Interviewing clerks, except personnel and social welfare	69	83	20	14	36	3	Short-term O-J-T
New accounts clerks, banking	114	116	2	2	40	3	Work experience
Receptionists and information clerks	1,019	1,337	31	318	508	4	Short-term O-J-T
Reservation and transportation ticket agents and travel clerks	139	133	-4	-6	31	3	Short-term O-J-T
Mail clerks and messengers	260	256	-1	-4	70		
Mail clerks, except mail machine operators and postal service	127	116	-8	-10	35	4	Short-term O-J-T
Messengers	133	140	5	7	35	3	Short-term O-J-T

Occupation	Employment		Employment change, 1994-2005		Total job openings due to growth and net replacements, 1994-2005	Earnings quartile	Most significant source of traning
	1994	Projected, 2005	Percent	Number			
Postal clerks and mail carriers	474	481	1	7	126		
Postal mail carriers	320	320	0	-1	85	1	Short-term O-J-T
Postal service clerks	154	161	5	7	41	1	Short-term O-J-T
Material recording, scheduling, dispatching, and distributing occupations	3,556	3,688	4	132	863		
Dispatchers	224	258	15	34	65		
Dispatchers, except police, fire, and ambulance	141	168	19	27	46	3	Moderate-term O-J-T
Dispatchers, police, fire, and ambulance	83	80	8	7	18	3	Moderate-term O-J-T
Meter readers, utilities	57	46	-19	-11	13	3	Short-term O-J-T
Order fillers, wholesale and retail sales	215	231	8	16	63	2	Short-term O-J-T
Procurement clerks	57	52	-9	-5	13	3	Short-term O-J-T
Production, planning, and expediting clerks	239	251	5	12	56	2	Short-term O-J-T
Stock clerks	1,759	1,800	2	41	443	3	Short-term O-J-T
Traffic, shipping, and receiving clerks	798	827	4	29	150	3	Short-term O-J-T
Weighers, measurers, checkers, and samplers, recordkeeping	45	46	3	1	12	3	Short-term O-J-T
All other material recording, scheduling, and distribution workers	161	177	10	16	47	3	Short-term O-J-T
Records processing occupations	3,733	3,438	-8	-294	877		
Advertising clerks	17	18	5	1	5	2	Short-term O-J-T
Brokerage clerks	73	73	1	1	9	3	Short-term O-J-T
Correspondence clerks	29	27	-8	-2	6	2	Short-term O-J-T
File clerks	278	236	-15	-42	102	4	Short-term O-J-T
Financial records processing occupations	2,757	2,506	-9	-250	573		
Billing, cost, and rate clerks	323	328	2	5	98	2	Short-term O-J-T
Billing, posting, and calculating machine operators	96	32	-67	-64	40	2	Short-term O-J-T
Bookkeeping, accounting, and auditing clerks	2,181	2,003	-8	-178	400	3	Moderate-term O-J-T
Payroll and timekeeping clerks	157	144	-9	-14	35	3	Short-term O-J-T
Library assistants and bookmobile drivers	121	127	5	7	57	3	Short-term O-J-T
Order clerks, materials, merchandise, and service	310	337	9	27	95	2	Short-term O-J-T
Personnel clerks, except payroll and timekeeping	123	98	-21	-26	27	2	Short-term O-J-T
Statement clerks	25	16	-38	-9	3	3	Short-term O-J-T
Secretaries, stenographers, and typists	4,100	4,276	4	175	1,230		
Secretaries	3,349	3,739	12	390	1,102		
Legal secretaries	281	350	24	68	128	3	Postsecondary vocational training
Medical secretaries	226	281	24	55	103	3	Postsecondary vocational training
Secretaries, except legal and medical	2,842	3,109	9	267	871	3	Postsecondary vocational training
Stenographers	105	102	-3	-3	22	3	Postsecondary vocational training
Typists and word processors	646	434	-33	-212	106	3	Moderate-term O-J-T
Other clerical and administrative support workers	7,740	8,253	7	513	2,582		
Bank tellers	559	407	-27	-152	244	4	Short-term O-J-T
Clerical supervisors and managers	1,340	1,600	19	261	613	2	Work experience
Court clerks	51	59	15	8	12	2	Short-term O-J-T
Credit authorizers, credit checkers, and loan and credit clerks	258	267	4	9	49		
Credit authorizers	15	19	24	4	5	2	Short-term O-J-T
Credit checkers	40	35	-14	-6	3	3	Short-term O-J-T
Loan and credit clerks	187	196	5	10	37	3	Short-term O-J-T
Loan interviewers	16	17	10	2	4	3	Short-term O-J-T
Customer service representatives, utilities	150	179	19	29	61	2	Short-term O-J-T
Data entry keyers, except composing	395	370	-6	-25	17	3	Postsecondary vocational training
Data entry keyers, composing	19	6	-67	-13	1	3	Postsecondary vocational training
Duplicating, mail, and other office machine operators	222	166	-25	-56	99	2	Short-term O-J-T
General office clerks	2,946	3,071	4	126	908	3	Short-term O-J-T
Municipal clerks	22	21	-3	-1	2	2	Short-term O-J-T
Proofreaders and copy markers	26	20	-20	-5	7	3	Short-term O-J-T
Real estate clerks	24	25	5	1	8	3	Short-term O-J-T
Statistical clerks	75	68	-10	-7	11	3	Moderate-term O-J-T
Teacher adies and educational assistants	932	1,296	39	364	480	4	Short-term O-J-T

Occupation	Employment		Employment change, 1994-2005		Total job openings due to growth and net replacements, 1994-2005	Earnings quartile	Most significant source of traning
	1994	Projected, 2005	Percent	Number			
All other clerical and administrative support workers	721	698	-3	-23	69	2	Short-term O-J-T
Service occupations	20,239	24,832	23	4,593	9,813		
Cleaning and building service occupations, except private household	3,450	4,071	18	621	1,293		
Institutional cleaning supervisors	125	147	18	22	58	3	Work experience
Janitors and cleaners, including maids and housekeeping cleaners	3,043	3,602	18	559	1,140	4	Short-term O-J-T
Pest controllers and assistants	56	76	36	20	31	4	Moderate-term O-J-T
All other cleaning and building service workers	226	245	8	19	63	4	Short-term O-J-T
Food preparation and service occupations	7,964	9,057	14	1,093	3,498		
Chefs, cooks, and other kitchen workers	3,237	3,739	16	502	1,102		
Cooks, except short order	1,286	1,492	16	206	524		
Bakers, bread and pastry	170	230	35	60	102	4	Moderate-term O-J-T
Cooks, institution or cafeteria	412	435	6	23	125	4	Long-term O-J-T
Cooks, restaurant	704	827	17	123	297	4	Long-term O-J-T
Cooks, short order and fast food	760	869	14	109	297	4	Short-term O-J-T
Food preparation workers	1,190	1,378	16	187	282	4	Short-term O-J-T
Food and beverage service occupations	4,514	5,051	12	537	2,263		
Bartenders	373	347	-7	-25	138	4	Short-term O-J-T
Dining room and cafeteria attendants and bar helpers	416	416	0	0	157	4	Short-term O-J-T
Food counter, fountain, and related workers .	1,630	1,669	2	40	463	4	Short-term O-J-T
Hosts and hostesses, restaurant, lounge, or coffee shop	248	292	18	44	114	3	Short-term O-J-T
Waiters and waitresses	1,847	2,326	26	479	1,390	4	Short-term O-J-T
All other food preparation and service workers .	213	267	25	54	132	4	Short-term O-J-T
Health service occupations	2,086	2,846	36	759	1,131		
Ambulance drivers and attendants, except EMTs	18	21	15	3	8	4	Short-term O-J-T
Dental assistants	190	269	42	79	137	3	Moderate-term O-J-T
Medical assistants	206	327	59	121	155	3	Moderate-term O-J-T
Nursing aides and psychiatric aides	1,370	1,770	29	400	594		
Nursing aides, orderlies, and attendants	1,265	1,652	31	387	566	4	Short-term O-J-T
Psychiatric aides	105	118	12	13	28	4	Short-term O-J-T
Occupational therapy assistants and aides	16	29	82	13	16	3	Moderate-term O-J-T
Pharmacy assistants	52	64	23	12	22	3	Short-term O-J-T
Physical and corrective therapy assistants and aides	78	142	83	64	87	4	Moderate-term O-J-T
All other health service workers	157	224	43	67	112	4	Short-term O-J-T
Personal service occupations	2,530	3,719	47	1,189	1,670		
Amusement and recreation attendants	267	406	52	139	211	3	Short-term O-J-T
Baggage porters and bellhops	35	44	26	9	16	4	Short-term O-J-T
Barbers	64	60	-6	-4	20	4	Postsecondary vocational training
Child care workers	757	1,005	33	248	321	4	Short-term O-J-T
Cosmetologists and related workers	645	754	17	109	273		
Hairdressers, hairstylists, and cosmetolgists	595	677	14	82	233	4	Postsecondary vocational training
Manicurists	38	64	69	26	36	4	Postsecondary vocational training
Shampooers	12	13	8	1	4	4	Short-term O-J-T
Flight attendants	105	135	28	30	49	2	Long-term O-J-T
Homemaker-home health aides	598	1,238	107	640	747		
Home health aides	420	848	102	428	488	4	Short-term O-J-T
Personal and home care aides	179	391	119	212	259	4	Short-term O-J-T
Ushers, lobby attendants, and ticket takers	59	77	29	17	33	3	Short-term O-J-T
Private household workers	808	682	-16	-126	245		
Child care workers, private household	283	278	-2	-5	139	4	Short-term O-J-T
Cleaners and servants, private household	496	387	-22	-108	100	4	Short-term O-J-T
Cooks, private household	9	5	-49	-4	2	4	Moderate-term O-J-T
Housekeepers and butlers	20	12	-37	-7	4	4	Moderate-term O-J-T
Protective service occupations	2,381	3,199	34	818	1,514		
Firefighting occupations	284	328	16	44	169		
Fire fighters	219	258	18	40	138	1	Long-term O-J-T
Fire fighting and prevention supervisors	52	56	7	4	24	1	Work experience

Occupation	Employment		Employment change, 1994-2005		Total job openings due to growth and net replacements, 1994-2005	Earnings quartile	Most significant source of traning
	1994	Projected, 2005	Percent	Number			
Fire inspection occupations	13	14	7	1	6	1	Work experience
Law enforcement occupations	992	1,316	33	324	610		
Correction officers	310	468	51	158	194	2	Long-term O-J-T
Police and detectives	682	848	24	166	416		
Police and detective supervisors	87	93	7	6	45	1	Work experience
Police detectives and investigators	66	80	20	13	40	1	Work experience
Police patrol officers	400	511	28	112	271	1	Long-term O-J-T
Sheriffs and deputy sheriffs	86	110	29	25	42	2	Long-term O-J-T
Other law enforcement occupations	43	54	25	11	19	2	Moderate-term O-J-T
Other protective service workers	1,106	1,554	41	449	735		
Detectives, except public	55	79	44	24	35	3	Moderate-term O-J-T
Guards	867	1,282	48	415	580	3	Short-term O-J-T
Crossing guards	58	60	3	2	17	3	Short-term O-J-T
All other protective service workers	126	133	6	8	104	4	Short-term O-J-T
All other service workers	1,020	1,259	23	240	462	3	Work experience
Agriculture, forestry, fishing, and related occupations	3,762	3,650	-3	-112	988		
Animal breeders and trainers	16	15	-5	-1	3	1	Bachelor's degree
Animal caretakers, except farm	125	158	26	33	62	4	Short-term O-J-T
Farm workers	906	870	-4	-36	263	4	Short-term O-J-T
Gardening, nursery, and greenhouse and lawn service occupations	844	986	17	142	271		
Gardeners and groundskeepers, except farm	569	623	9	54	128	4	Short-term O-J-T
Lawn maintenance workers	96	127	32	31	43	4	Short-term O-J-T
Lawn service managers	36	47	33	12	18	3	Work experience
Nursery and greenhouse managers	19	26	37	7	11	3	Work experience
Nursery workers	83	109	31	26	50	4	Short-term O-J-T
Pruners	26	34	32	8	14	4	Short-term O-J-T
Sprayers/applicators	15	20	32	5	7	4	Moderate-term O-J-T
Farm operators and managers	1,327	1,050	-21	-277	221		
Farmers	1,276	1,003	-21	-273	211	4	Long-term O-J-T
Farm managers	51	46	-9	-5	10	4	Work experience, plus degree
Fishers, hunters, and trappers	49	47	-4	-2	11		
Captains and other officers, fishing vessels	7	6	-11	-1	2	2	Work experience
Fishers, hunters, and trappers	42	41	-3	-1	9	2	Short-term O-J-T
Forestry and logging occupations	124	118	-5	-6	34		
Forest and conservation workers	42	42	1	1	12	3	Short-term O-J-T
Timber cutting and logging occupations	82	76	-8	-7	22		
Fallers and buckers	29	27	-9	-3	8	3	Short-term O-J-T
Logging tractor operators	20	20	-1	0	4	2	Short-term O-J-T
Log handling equipment operators	16	15	-9	-1	5	3	Short-term O-J-T
All other timber cutting and related logging workers	17	15	-13	-2	5	3	Short-term O-J-T
Supervisors, farming, forestry, and agricultural related occupations	85	91	7	6	22	3	Work experience
Veterinary assistants	31	37	19	6	13	4	Short-term O-J-T
All other agricultural, forestry, fishing, and related workers	255	278	9	23	87	4	Short-term O-J-T
Precision production, craft, and repair occupations		14,047	14,880	6	833	4,489	
Blue-collar worker supervisors	1,884	1,894	1	11	480	1	Work experience
Construction trades	3,616	3,956	9	340	1,183		
Bricklayers and stone masons	147	162	10	15	43	2	Long-term O-J-T
Carpenters	992	1,074	8	82	290	2	Long-term O-J-T
Carpet installers	66	72	9	6	28	3	Moderate-term O-J-T
Ceiling tile installers and acoustical carpenters	16	14	-10	-2	3	2	Moderate-term O-J-T
Concrete and terrazzo finishers	126	141	12	15	41	3	Long-term O-J-T
Drywall installers and finishers	133	143	7	9	50	2	Moderate-term O-J-T
Electricians	528	554	5	25	152	2	Long-term O-J-T
Glaziers	34	34	2	1	9	2	Long-term O-J-T
Hard tile setters	27	28	1	0	7	2	Long-term O-J-T
Highway maintenance workers	167	182	9	15	62	3	Short-term O-J-T
Insulation workers	64	77	20	13	34	2	Moderate-term O-J-T
Painters and paperhangers, construction and maintenance	439	509	16	70	174	2	Moderate-term O-J-T
Paving, surfacing, and tamping equipment operators	73	93	26	19	37	2	Moderate-term O-J-T

Occupation	Employment		Employment change, 1994-2005		Total job openings due to growth and net replacements, 1994-2005	Earnings quartile	Most significant source of traning
	1994	Projected, 2005	Percent	Number			
Pipelayers and pipelaying fitters	57	63	12	7	23	3	Moderate-term O-J-T
Plasterers	30	33	11	3	11	2	Long-term O-J-T
Plumbers, pipefitters, and steamfitters	375	390	4	15	92	2	Long-term O-J-T
Roofers	126	143	13	17	42	3	Moderate-term O-J-T
Structural and reinforcing metal workers	61	64	5	3	19	2	Long-term O-J-T
All other construction trades workers	155	181	17	26	68	3	Moderate-term O-J-T
Extractive and related workers, including blasters	220	204	-7	-16	59		
Oil and gas extraction occupations	66	39	-41	-27	12		
Roustabouts	28	13	-55	-16	5	1	Short-term O-J-T
All other oil and gas extraction occupations	38	26	-30	-11	7	1	Moderate-term O-J-T
Mining, quarrying, and tunneling occupations	18	12	-34	-6	3	1	Long-term O-J-T
All other extraction and related workers	136	153	12	17	43	1	Moderate-term O-J-T
Mechanics, installers, and repairers	5,012	5,586	11	574	1,950		
Communications equipment mechanics, installers, and repairers	118	78	-34	-41	26		
Central office and PBX installers and repairers	84	51	-39	-33	17	1	Postsecondaryvocational training
Radio mechanics	7	6	-16	-1	2	2	Postsecondary vocational training
All other communications equipment mechanics, installers, and repairers	27	20	-25	-7	6	1	Postsecondaryvocational training
Electrical and electronic equipment mechanics, installers, and repairers	554	555	0	1	175		
Data processing equipment repairers	75	104	38	29	49	2	Postsecondaryvocational training
Electrical powerline installers and repairers	112	123	10	11	37	1	Long-term O-J-T
Electronic home entertainment equipment repairers	34	30	-10	-3	9	2	Postsecondary vocational training
Electronics repairers, commercial and industrial equipment	66	68	2	1	20	2	Postsecondary vocational training
Station installers and repairers, telephone	37	11	-70	-26	7	1	Postsecondary vocational training
Telephone and cable TV line installers and repairers	191	181	-5	-9	43	1	Long-term O-J-T
All other electrical and electronic equipment mechanics, installers, and repairers	39	38	-3	-1	10	2	Postsecondary vocational training
Machinery and related mechanics, installers, and repairers	1,815	2,072	14	258	700		
Industrial machinery mechanics	464	502	8	38	173	2	Long-term O-J-T
Maintenance repairers, general utility	1,273	1,505	18	231	508	2	Long-term O-J-T
Millwrights	77	66	-15	-11	20	1	Long-term O-J-T
Vehicle and mobile equipment mechanics and repairers	1,502	1,736	16	234	655		
Aircraft mechanics, including engine specialists	119	134	13	15	49		
Aircraft engine specialists	23	25	8	2	8	1	Postsecondary vocational training
Aircraft mechanics	96	109	14	13	40	1	Postsecondary vocational training
Automotive body and related repairers	209	243	17	35	92	2	Long-term O-J-T
Automotive mechanics	736	862	17	126	347	2	Long-term O-J-T
Bus and truck mechanics and diesel engine specialists	250	293	17	42	100	2	Long-term O-J-T
Farm equipment mechanics	41	47	14	6	17	2	Long-term O-J-T
Mobile heavy equipment mechanics	101	110	9	9	37	2	Long-term O-J-T
Motorcycle, boat, and small engine mechanics	46	48	4	2	14		
Motorcycle repairers	11	12	4	0	4	2	Long-term O-J-T
Small engine specialists	35	36	4	1	11	2	Long-term O-J-T
Other mechanics, installers, and repairers	1,023	1,145	12	122	394		
Bicycle repairers	40	44	10	4	13	2	Moderate-term O-J-T
Camera and photographic equipment repairers	11	12	9	1	4	2	Moderate-term O-J-T
Coin and vending machine servicers and repairers	19	17	-14	-3	4	2	Long-term O-J-T
Electric meter installers and repairers	12	10	-18	-2	3	2	Long-term O-J-T

Occupation	Employment		Employment change, 1994-2005		Total job openings due to growth and net replacements, 1994-2005	Earnings quartile	Most significant source of traning
	1994	Projected, 2005	Percent	Number			
Electromedical and biomedical equipment repairers	10	11	17	2	4	2	Long-term O-J-T
Elevator installers and repairers	24	28	15	4	10	2	Long-term O-J-T
Heat, air conditioning, and refrigeration mechanics and installers	233	299	29	66	125	2	Long-term O-J-T
Home appliance and power tool repairers	70	66	-6	-4	19	1	Long-term O-J-T
Locksmiths and safe repairers	20	21	10	2	7	2	Moderate-term O-J-T
Musical instrument repairers and tuners	10	11	15	1	4	2	Long-term O-J-T
Office machine and cash register servicers	59	63	6	4	29	2	Long-term O-J-T
Precision instrument repairers	40	40	0	0	10	2	Long-term O-J-T
Riggers	11	11	-4	0	2	2	Long-term O-J-T
Tire repairers and changers	89	95	7	6	42	4	Short-term O-J-T
Watchmakers	6	5	-15	-1	2	2	Long-term O-J-T
All other mechanics, installers, and repairers	371	412	11	42	116	2	Long-term O-J-T
Production occupations, precision	2,986	2,906	-3	-80	730		
Assemblers, precision	324	315	-3	-9	91		
Aircraft assemblers, precision	20	19	-8	-2	4	2	Work experience
Electrical and electronic equipment a semblers, precision	144	127	-12	-17	36	3	Work experience
Electromechanical equipment assemblers, precision	47	44	-6	-3	12	3	Work experience
Fitters, structural metal, precision	14	9	-35	-5	3	2	Work experience
Machine builders and other precision machine assemblers	58	65	11	6	18	2	Work experience
All other precision assemblers	40	50	26	11	18	2	Work experience
Food workers, precision	292	282	-4	-11	81		
Bakers, manufacturing	36	40	12	4	12	3	Moderate-term O-J-T
Butchers and meatcutters	219	202	-8	-17	58	3	Long-term O-J-T
All other precision food and tobacco workers	38	39	4	2	11	3	Long-term O-J-T
Inspectors, testers, and graders, precision	654	629	-4	-25	138	2	Work experience
Metal workers, precision	885	824	-7	-61	190		
Boilermakers	20	19	-4	-1	4	2	Long-term O-J-T
Jewelers and silversmiths	30	32	6	2	8	2	Long-term O-J-T
Machinists	369	349	-5	-20	79	2	Long-term O-J-T
Sheet metal workers and duct installers	222	205	-8	-17	45	2	Moderate-term O-J-T
Shipfitters	12	11	-10	-1	2	2	Long-term O-J-T
Tool and die makers	142	127	-11	-15	34	1	Long-term O-J-T
All other precision metal workers	90	82	-9	-8	18	2	Long-term O-J-T
Printing workers, precision	150	157	4	7	53		
Bookbinders	6	6	-4	0	1	3	Moderate-term O-J-T
Prepress printing workers, precision	131	132	1	1	43		
Compositors and typesetters, precision	11	8	-23	-2	2	2	Long-term O-J-T
Job printers	14	11	-27	-4	3	2	Long-term O-J-T
Paste-up workers	22	16	-28	-6	4	2	Long-term O-J-T
Electronic pagination systems workers	18	33	83	15	19	2	Long-term O-J-T
Photoengravers	7	5	-20	-1	1	2	Long-term O-J-T
Camera operators	15	14	-6	-1	3	2	Long-term O-J-T
Strippers, printing	31	34	9	3	9	2	Long-term O-J-T
Platemakers	13	11	-15	-2	2	2	Long-term O-J-T
All other printing workers, precision	13	19	44	6	8	2	Long-term O-J-T
Textile, apparel, and furnishings workers, precision	240	219	-9	-21	40		
Custom tailors and sewers	84	63	-25	-21	10	4	Work experience
Patternmakers and layout workers, fabric and apparel	17	23	31	5	7	4	Long-term O-J-T
Shoe and leather workers and repairers, precision	24	17	-28	-7	2	4	Long-term O-J-T
Upholsterers	63	64	1	1	9	4	Long-term O-J-T
All other precision textile, apparel, and furnishings workers	51	51	0	0	11	4	Long-term O-J-T
Woodworkers, precision	241	277	15	36	86		
Cabinetmakers and bench carpenters	131	151	15	20	45	3	Long-term O-J-T
Furniture finishers	38	40	6	2	12	3	Long-term O-J-T
Wood machinists	50	59	19	10	19	3	Long-term O-J-T
All other precision woodworkers	22	26	19	4	10	3	Long-term O-J-T
Other precision workers	199	204	2	5	52		
Dental laboratory technicians, precision	49	47	-5	-2	11	3	Long-term O-J-T
Optical goods workers, precision	19	22	12	2	7	3	Long-term O-J-T

Occupation	Employment		Employment change, 1994-2005		Total job openings due to growth and net replacements, 1994-2005	Earnings quartile	Most significant source of traning
	1994	Projected, 2005	Percent	Number			
Photographic process workers, precision	14	16	15	2	6	4	Long-term O-J-T
All other precision workers	117	119	2	3	28	3	Long-term O-J-T
Plant and system occupations	330	334	1	4	87		Long-term O-J-T
Chemical plant and system operators	37	36	-3	-1	8	1	Long-term O-J-T
Electric power generating plant operators, distributors, and dispatchers	43	42	-3	-1	10		
Power distributors and dispatchers	18	15	-14	-2	4	1	Long-term O-J-T
Power generating and reactor plant operators	26	26	4	1	6	1	Long-term O-J-T
Gas and petroleum plant and system occupations	31	28	-10	-3	7	1	Long-term O-J-T
Stationary engineers	30	27	-10	-3	7	1	Long-term O-J-T
Water and liquid waste treatment plant and system operators	95	104	9	9	30	1	Long-term O-J-T
All other plant and system operators	93	97	5	4	25	1	Long-term O-J-T
Operators, fabricators, and laborers	17,142	17,898	4	757	5,626		
Machine setters, set-up operators, operators, and tenders	4,779	4,505	-6	-274	1,353		
Numerical control machine tool operators and tenders, metal and plastic	75	94	26	20	34	3	Moderate-term O-J-T
Combination machine tool setters, set-up operators, operators, and tenders	106	123	16	17	38	2	Moderate-term O-J-T
Machine tool cut and form setters, operators, and tenders, metal and plastic	709	593	-16	-116	175		
Drilling and boring machine tool setters and set-up operators, metal and plastic	45	30	-35	-16	9	3	Moderate-term O-J-T
Grinding machine setters and set-up operators, metal and plastic	64	52	-18	-12	13	3	Moderate-term O-J-T
Lathe and turning machine tool setters and set-up operators, metal and plastic	71	50	-31	-22	14	3	Moderate-term O-J-T
Machine forming operators and tenders, metal and plastic	171	151	-11	-19	58	3	Moderate-term O-JT
Machine tool cutting operators and tenders, metal and plastic	119	85	-29	-34	23	3	Moderate-term O-J-T
Punching machine setters and set-up operators, metal and plastic	48	37	-21	-10	12	3	Moderate-term O-J-T
All other machine tool cutting and forming etc.	191	188	-1	-2	46	3	Moderate-term O-J-T
Metal fabricating machine setters, operators, and related workers	157	138	-12	-19	39		
Metal fabricators, structural metal products ...	44	43	-3	-1	9	3	Moderate-term O-J-T
Soldering and brazing machine operators and tenders	10	8	-17	-2	3	3	Moderate-term O-J-T
Welding machine setters, operators, and tenders	103	87	-16	-16	28	2	Moderate-term O-J-T
Metal and plastic processing machine setters, operators, and related workers	425	444	4	19	152		
Electrolytic plating machine operators and tenders, setters and set-up operators, metal and plastic	42	45	6	2	14	3	Moderate-term O-J-T
Foundry mold assembly and shakeout workers	10	8	-23	-2	4	3	Moderate-term O-J-T
Furnace operators and tenders	20	19	-8	-2	4	2	Moderate-term O-J-T
Heat treating machine operators and tenders, metal and plastic	20	17	-12	-2	5	3	Moderate-term O-J-T
Metal molding machine operators and tenders, setters and set-up operators	40	40	0	0	14	3	Moderate-term O- J-T
Plastic molding machine operators and tenders, setters and set-up operators	165	177	7	12	68	3	Moderate-term O-J-T
All other metal and plastic machine setters, operators, and related workers	127	137	8	10	44	3	Moderate-term O-J-T
Printing, binding, and related workers	384	387	1	3	108		
Bindery machine operators and set-up operators	72	77	7	5	18	2	Moderate-term O-J-T
Prepress printing workers, production	25	9	-64	-16	5		
Photoengraving and lithographic machine operators and tenders	5	3	-32	-2	1	2	Moderate-term O-J-T

Occupation	Employment		Employment change, 1994-2005		Total job openings due to growth and net replacements, 1994-2005	Earnings quartile	Most significant source of traning
	1994	Projected, 2005	Percent	Number			
Typesetting and composing machine operators and tenders	20	6	-71	-14	4	2	Moderate-term O-J-T
Printing press operators	218	223	2	5	62		Moderate-term O-J-T
Letterpress operators	14	4	-71	-10	3	2	Moderate-term O-J-T
Offset lithographic press operators	79	84	7	5	22	2	Moderate-term O-J-T
Printing press machine setters, operators and tenders	113	119	6	6	31	2	Moderate-term O-J-T
All other printing press setters and set-up operators	13	16	24	3	6	2	Moderate-term O-J-T
Screen printing machine setters and set-up operators	26	30	16	4	10	2	Moderate-term O-J-T
All other printing, binding, and related workers	43	48	10	5	13	2	Moderate-term O-J-T
Textile and related setters, operators, and related workers	1,018	829	-19	-188	222		
Extruding and forming machine operators and tenders, synthetic or glass fibers	22	28	28	6	11	4	Moderate-term O-J-T
Pressing machine operators and tenders, textile, garment, and related materials	77	76	-1	-1	19	4	Moderate-term O-J-T
Sewing machine operators, garment	531	391	-26	-140	106	4	Moderate-term O-J-T
Sewing machine operators, non-garment	129	117	-9	-12	26	4	Moderate-term O-J-T
Textile bleaching and dyeing machine operators and tenders	30	37	24	7	14	4	Moderate-term O-J-T
Textile draw-out and winding machine operators and tenders	190	143	-25	-47	38	4	Moderate-term O-J-T
Textile machine setters and set-up operators	39	36	-6	-2	8	4	Moderate-term O-J-T
Woodworking machine setters, operators, and other related workers	126	97	-23	-29	32		
Head sawyers and sawing machine operators and tenders, setters and set-up operators	62	47	-24	-15	16	4	Moderate-term O-J-T
Woodworking machine operators and tenders, setters and set-up operators	64	50	-22	-14	16	4	Moderate-term O-J-T
Other machine setters, set-up operators, operators, and tenders	1,779	1,799	1	20	554		
Boiler operators and tenders, low pressure	18	12	-32	-6	4	1	Moderate-term O-J-T
Cement and gluing machine operators and tenders	36	25	-30	-11	9	3	Moderate-term O-J-T
Chemical equipment controllers, operators and tenders	75	67	-11	-8	28	1	Moderate-term O-J-T
Cooking and roasting machine operators and tenders, food and tobacco	28	30	8	2	9	3	Moderate-term O-J-T
Crushing and mixing machine operators and tenders	137	136	-1	-1	36	3	Moderate-term O-J-T
Cutting and slicing machine setters, operators and tenders	92	103	12	11	29	3	Moderate-term O-J-T
Dairy processing equipment operators, including setters	14	14	-1	0	5	1	Moderate-term O-J-T
Electronic semiconductor processors	33	34	4	1	10	3	Moderate-term O-J-T
Extruding and forming machine setters, operators and tenders	102	95	-8	-8	27	3	Moderate-term O-J-T
Furnace, kiln, or kettle operators and tenders ...	28	24	-13	-4	5	2	Moderate-term O-J-T
Laundry and drycleaning machine operators and tenders, except pressing	175	198	13	23	68	4	Moderate-term O-J-T
Motion picture projectionists	8	4	-47	-4	2	3	Short-term O-J-T
Packaging and filling machine operators and tenders	329	359	9	30	119	4	Moderate-term O-J-T
Painting and coating machine operators	155	159	2	3	47		
Coating, painting, and spraying machine operators, tenders, setters, and set-up operators	111	110	-1	-1	31	3	Moderate-term O-J-T
Painters, transportation equipment	45	49	9	4	16	3	Moderate-term O-J-T
Paper goods machine setters and set-up operators	51	42	-16	-8	13	3	Moderate-term O-J-T
Photographic processing machine operators and tenders	43	49	15	6	17	3	Short-term O-J-T
Separating and still machine operators and tenders	20	19	-6	-1	8	1	Moderate-term O-J-T

Occupation	Employment		Employment change, 1994-2005		Total job openings due to growth and net replacements, 1994-2005	Earnings quartile	Most significant source of traning
	1994	Projected, 2005	Percent	Number			
Shoe sewing machine operators and tenders	14	5	-64	-9	2	4	Moderate-term O-J-T
Tire building machine operators	14	13	-6	-1	4	3	Moderate-term O-J-T
All other machine operators, tenders, setters, and set-up operators	407	409	1	2	111	3	Moderate-term O-J-T
Hand workers, including assemblers and fabricators	2,605	2,665	2	60	784		
Cannery workers	73	82	12	9	29	4	Short-term O-J-T
Coil winders, tapers, and finishers	21	15	-26	-5	5	3	Short-term O-J-T
Cutters and trimmers, hand	51	47	-8	-4	14	3	Short-term O-J-T
Electrical and electronic assemblers	212	182	-14	-30	52	3	Short-term O-J-T
Grinders and polishers, hand	74	70	-6	-4	21	3	Short-term O-J-T
Machine assemblers	51	55	8	4	17	3	Short-term O-J-T
Meat, poultry, and fish cutters and trimmers, hand	132	168	28	36	74	3	Short-term O-J-T
Painting, coating, and decorating workers, hand	33	36	10	3	13	3	Short-term O-J-T
Pressers, hand	16	15	-4	-1	5	3	Short-term O-J-T
Sewers, hand	19	17	-9	-2	2	4	Short-term O-J-T
Solderers and brazers	27	31	17	5	12	3	Short-term O-J-T
Welders and cutters	314	316	1	3	88	2	Postsecondary vocational training
All other assemblers, fabricators, and hand workers	1,583	1,630	3	46	453	3	Short-term O-J-T
Transportation and material moving machine and vehicle operators	4,959	5,459	10	500	1,434		
Motor vehicle operators	3,620	4,045	12	425	1,066		
Bus drivers	568	663	17	95	193		
Bus drivers, except school	165	193	17	29	57	3	Moderate-term O-J-T
Bus drivers, school	404	470	16	66	136	3	Short-term O-J-T
Taxi drivers and chauffeurs	129	157	22	28	43	3	Short-term O-J-T
Truck drivers	2,897	3,196	10	299	823		
Driver/sales workers	331	359	8	28	122	2	Short-term O-J-T
Truck drivers light and heavy	2,565	2,837	11	271	701	2	Short-term O-J-T
All other motor vehicle operators	26	29	11	3	8	2	Short-term O-J-T
Rail transportation workers	86	75	-12	-10	15		
Locomotive engineers	22	19	-14	-3	3	1	Work experience
Railroad brake, signal, and switch operators	19	13	-31	-6	3	1	Work experience
Railroad conductors and yardmasters	26	25	-6	-2	4	1	Work experience
Rail yard engineers, dinkey operators, and hostlers	6	4	-40	-2	1	1	Work experience
Subway and streetcar operators	12	15	23	3	5	1	Moderate-term O-J-T
Water transportation and related workers	48	48	0	0	10		
Able seamen, ordinary seamen, and marine oilers	20	20	-3	-1	4	1	Short-term O-J-T
Captains and pilots, ship	13	13	0	0	3	1	Work experience
Mates, ship, boat, and barge	7	8	6	0	2	1	Work experience
Ship engineers	8	8	3	0	2	1	Work experience
Material moving equipment operators	1,061	1,129	6	69	298		
Crane and tower operators	45	42	-6	-3	11	2	Moderate-term O-J-T
Excavation and loading machine operators	88	100	13	11	31	2	Moderate-term O-J-T
Grader, dozer, and scraper operators	108	113	5	6	27	2	Moderate-term O-J-T
Hoist and winch operators	9	9	-5	0	2	2	Moderate-term O-J-T
Industrial truck and tractor operators	464	493	6	29	132	2	Short-term O-J-T
Operating engineers	146	154	5	7	37	2	Moderate-term O-J-T
All other material moving equipment operators .	201	219	9	18	59	2	Moderate-term O-J-T
All other transportation and material moving equipment operators	145	161	11	16	44	2	Moderate-term O-J-T
Helpers, laborers, and material movers, hand	4,799	5,270	10	471	2,056		
Freight, stock, and material movers, hand	765	728	-5	-36	306	4	Short-term O-J-T
Hand packers and packagers	942	1,102	17	160	429	4	Short-term O-J-T
Helpers, construction trades	513	581	13	68	240	4	Short-term O-J-T
Machine feeders and offbearers	262	242	-8	-20	80	3	Short-term O-J-T
Parking lot attendants	64	76	20	13	25	2	Short-term O-J-T
Refuse collectors	111	115	4	4	31	3	Short-term O-J-T
Service station attendants	167	148	-12	-20	67	4	Short-term O-J-T
Vehicle washers and equipment cleaners	249	299	20	50	133	4	Short-term O-J-T
All other helpers, laborers, and material movers, hand	1,727	1,980	15	253	744	4	Short-term O-J-T

Good Jobs and the Education They Require

Fastest growing occupations	Occupations having the largest numerical increase in employment
First-professional degree	**First-professional degree**
Chiropractors	Lawyers
Lawyers	Physicians
Physicians	Clergy
Clergy	Chiropractors
Podiatrists	Dentists
Doctoral degree	**Doctoral degree**
Medical scientists	College and university faculty
Biological scientists	Biological scientists
College and university faculty	Medical scientists
Mathematicians and all other mathematical scientists	Mathematicians and all other mathematical scientists
Master's degree	**Master's degree**
Operations research analysts	Management analysts
Speech-language pathologists and audiologists	Counselors
Management analysts	Speech-language pathologists and audiologists
Counselors	Psychologists
Urban and regional planners	Operations research analysts
Work experience plus bachelor's degree	**Work experience plus bachelor's degree**
Engineering, mathematics, and natural science managers	General managers and top executives
Marketing, advertising, and public relations managers	Financial managers
Artists and commercial artists	Marketing, advertising, and public relations managers
Financial managers	Engineering, mathematics, and natural science managers
Education administrators	Education administrators
Bachelor's degree	**Bachelor's degree**
Systems analysts	Systems analysts
Computer engineers	Teachers, secondary school
Occupational therapists	Teachers, elementary school
Physical therapists	Teachers, special education
Special education teachers	Social workers
Associate degree	**Associate degree**
Paralegals	Registered nurses
Medical records technicians	Paralegals
Dental hygienists	Radiologic technologists and technicians
Respiratory therapists	Dental hygienists
Radiologic technologists and technicians	Medical records technicians

Postsecondary vocational training

- Secretaries, except legal and medical
- Licensed practical nurses
- Hairdressers, hairstylists, and cosmetologists
- Legal secretaries
- Medical secretaries
- Manicurists
- Surgical technologists
- Data processing equipment repairers
- Dancers and choreographers
- Emergency medical technicians

Work experience

- Marketing and sales worker supervisors
- Clerical supervisors and managers
- Food service and lodging managers
- Instructors, adult eduaction
- Teachers and instructors, vocational educational and training
- Nursery and greenhouse managers
- Lawn service managers
- Food service and lodging managers
- Clerical supervisors and managers
- Teachers and instructors, vocational and nonvocational training

Long-term training and experience (more than 12 months of on-the-job-training)

- Maintenance repairers, general utility
- Correction officers
- Automotive mechanics
- Cooks, restaurant
- Police patrol officers
- Electronic pagination systems workers
- Correction officers
- Securities and financial services sales workers
- Patternmakers and layout workers, fabric and apparel
- Producers, directors, actors, and entertainers

Moderate-length training and experience (1 to 12 months of combined on-the-job experience and informal training)

- Human services workers
- Medical assistants
- Instructors and coaches, sports and physical training
- Dental assistants
- Painters and paper hangers, construction and maintenance
- Physical and corrective therapy assistants and aides
- Occupational therapy assistants and aides
- Human services workers
- Medical assistants
- Detectives, except public

Short-term training and experience (up to 1 month of on-the-job experience)

- Cashiers
- Janitors and cleaners, including maids and housekeepers
- Salespersons, retail
- Waiters and waitresses
- Home health aides
- Personal and home care aides
- Home health aides
- Amusement and recreation attendants
- Guards
- Adjustment clerks

Source: United States Department of Labor, Bureau of Labor Statistics.

Computer Jobs

A job in computer technology requires continual updating of skills. If you let yourself get behind, you may find your job obsolete, as computer technology continues to grow at a phenomenal rate. Traditional mainframe-oriented technologies are dying as more and more companies look toward employees with networking and client/server skills.

As a result, the embattled U.S. computer industry in recent years has been hard hit by foreign competition and sliding prices. Even so, it holds the distinction of being among the few manufacturing industries in which the United States still enjoys strong trade surpluses.

One result of the profit squeeze is the teaming of the nation's two top computer suppliers: IBM and Apple. Formerly hot competitors, Big Blue and Apple have agreed to work together on technology to revive profits. In what can be viewed as a giant technological fortress, the joint IBM/Apple efforts may do much to hold the competitive line for America.

Much more than computer making has been reshaped by the industry's turmoil. A great deal of its retailing activity has moved away from conventional computer stores to consumer electronics chains, office products outlets, and super computer stores where the gear is sold at discounted prices.

Even computer users are not untouched by change. One trend to watch is "outsourcing." When a department is outsourced, employees are replaced with outside contractors, supposedly to save the company money. Observers say that data processing may become the next big wave of outsourced departments, similar to food and janitorial services.

What effect has all this change had on humans? Computers—a relatively young industry—already is old enough to see unemployment among its legions. This does not mean the demand for computer specialists has peaked. Most industry experts think demand

for experienced, *skilled* computer specialists will go on indefinitely.

What's more, computer-based occupations are still among the fastest growing in the job market. The problem is that so many people are hopping on a good thing that the rivalry for jobs, especially for beginning programmers, has become a deadly competition.

But when one door closes another opens. Some of the same sort of bright minds that two decades ago would have aspired to become computer programmers now work in PC networks, the fastest growing segment of the industry. As **computer network engineers**, they are at the forefront of the newest phase of computer system development. Increasingly the world's computers are being joined together into networks that make united PCs as powerful as the old mainframes and at much less cost. Network engineers connect everything together.

While formal education counts more than ever for the best jobs in computer occupations, employers regard experience almost as highly. In addition to a degree, seek an internship program to hone your skills.

What happens next? The fanciful future may become the practical present as computer technology gets smaller and smarter. In size we have the incredible shrinking machine: from desktops to laptops to palmtops and now, researchers say, we're on our way to pentops that understand handwriting. Voice-driven computers continue to be seriously flawed, but computer scientists say, "Give us five years."

Computer technology has invaded the industrialized world. It puts on an apron to turn kitchen appliances off and on. It tags along to school with students, giving them a humane electronic alternative to yesteryear's sadistic practice of cutting up live frogs in biology classes. It trains surgeons by inviting them into new electronically simulated environments called "virtual reality."

As you might suspect, the world of computers offers a colorful kaleidoscope of opportunities.

Network administrators oversee a crowd of PCs associated in networks. They may manage a large group of machines or a few, but increasingly they are in demand at companies that rely on computing power. **Computer programmers** include systems programmers and applications programmers. **Systems programmers** help design computer systems that mesh with the other parts of the organization. **Applications programmers** create software for specific purposes—accounting, inventory control, word-processing, for instance.

Programmers enjoy fairly bright occupational skies. But the occupation has hit a wall compared to the phenomenal growth of the past, as improved software and programming techniques simplify or eliminate some programming tasks.

Prospects are best for college graduates who know newer machine languages that apply to computer networking, database management, and artificial intelligence.

Database managers will find pivotal positions at many companies monitoring the creation and flow of facts and figures. Management information system (MIS) managers are finding jobs scarcer than before, but those who can broaden their qualifications from technical whiz to astute business executive can become members of top management as chief information officers.

Data security specialists—the "hackbusters" who keep computer data secrets safe—will continue to enjoy good jobs as companies try to avoid the annual loss of hundreds of millions of dollars in computer crime. Headline stories of hackers and viruses have created a $3 billion computer security industry. Opportunities are best for engineers, mathematicians, and systems programmers who work for top accounting firms, management consultants, and computer makers.

Systems analysts solve information problems, analyzing the way a company uses and stores information, then design methods to help the organization run more smoothly. No one expects a shortage of information problems in the years ahead.

Information brokers—electronic librarians for hire—use home computers to tap into big on-line information services and sell tailored research to clients, such as high-tech companies or real estate firms.

Other jobs in and around computers include selling and servicing them, and training people to use them.

Employers continue to have the upper hand in the entry-level computer job market, so the thing to do is gain experience through internships and part-time paid or volunteer jobs while you're a student. Consider, too, majoring in or studying a wider discipline, such as business, engineering, accounting, or a science. Whether you focus on computer technology or another field, having interdisciplinary skills will increase your marketability.

If you really want to do high-level work with computers, consider a master's or a doctorate in computer engineering or computer science.

Computer Graphics Designers

Designing print media such as newspapers and corporate newsletters, many professionals in this industry have backgrounds in fine arts and computer graphics software. Some glamour opportunities exist designing film titles and CD-ROMs, but there is tough competition. $20,000 to $45,000.

Computer Network Builders

Boasting a college degree in computer science, these specialists decide how computers should be connected and how data should flow among them. In this world of network architecture, those who can handle fire walls (computer security systems that keep intruders out) often have advanced technical degrees and earn higher salaries. $40,000 to $80,000.

GIS Specialists

Geographic information systems (GIS) is a hot neighborhood. This technology combines information in databases with computer-generated maps. GIS is a lure to people who can mouse-click their way through countless data points. You need a college degree, and perhaps an advanced degree, in geography, urban planning, or environmental studies. $20,000 to $65,000.

Multimedia Designers

This is an uphill climb in which you keep stopping to swat the competition, but if you're up for computer games and entertainment, multimedia designing can be irresistible. Game testing doesn't pay well, but it is a practical way to break into the industry. As with any glamour field, it helps to be either a genius or find friends in the industry. You'll need a college degree, supplemented by extension classes at a community college to get with the (software) program. $40,000 to $60,000.

Online Publishers

Hail writers, editors, and layout designers! Online publishing may be for you. Online publishers mix intensive graphics, audio, and sound for an exceptional multidimensional package. There are no formal entrance requirements, but nothing about this work is easy—including

getting in and getting paid in this highly competitive field. $20,000 to $40,000. Systems engineers can earn up to $75,000.

The Law

Is a law school graduate who passed a bar exam but who is working as an FBI agent a lawyer? What about one who works as a business executive? Counting lawyers depends on the criteria for inclusion. That's why you'll see different figures from various sources.

By the measure of the American Bar Foundation, the numbers are dramatic. "In 1971, the U.S. lawyer population was one third of a million; by 1980, it had grown to half a million; in early 1988, it had reached almost three quarters of a million; and, by the turn of the century, will probably exceed a million."

Other year 2000 predictions: The U.S. legal profession will be dominated by 20 to 50 mega firms—some employing 3,000 or more lawyers. Young lawyers will have a fiercely competitive time becoming partners and those who do will wait longer; some will never become a partner but instead settle for a mid-tier "career lawyer" position earning big six-figure salaries. Small law firms will continue to exist but they'll experience a constant struggle to stay gainfully operated. Women still will have to fight their way through a glass ceiling—too few become partners and judges, the pinnacles of a law career.

Look for hot practice specialties. For pure dramatic scope, our personal favorite is biotechnology law, focusing on rules to govern scientists' new and incredible power to remold human life. A quick example: If a human voice box were grafted to a chimpanzee and it could speak, would it be human? If the answer is no, the scientist who created the talking chimp could patent it. Enter the biotech lawyer.

Robotics law deals with damage robots cause. High-tech law protects ownership rights in breakthrough discoveries. Employment law represents employees in court challenges of personnel practices employers used to take for granted. Immigration law is thriving with the influx of new Americans. Bankruptcy and corporate reorganization look ripe for the times. International law is riding high as business globalizes.

Environmental law is viewed as a career bright spot. As baby boomers age, opportunities will multiply in estates, probate, pensions, Social Security, and health care. Space law is no longer light years away now that private industry is launching satellites into space. Communications and intellectual property law are moving smartly along. Golden oldies, such as real estate and personal injury law, are likely to keep successful lawyers in style.

Financial pressures are cutting deeply into the hide of most law firms. Some are taking on non-law business—services ranging from financial to environmental consulting—to pay the bills. Others are hiring more paralegals, who work cheaper than lawyers. Still others are hiring MBAs to tell them how to make strategic plans for the future—a practice traditionalist attorneys see as better for a bottom-line business than a learned profession.

Whether associate or partner, law firm managements want "rainmakers"—people who can bring in new business as well as service existing clients. As the practice of law becomes more cutthroat, it's no longer enough to be a good lawyer. Not only are you expected to bring in business but—horrors!—you may have to give the client a low price bid to keep it.

Many dignified law firm attorneys have erected a wall of resistance to sales activities and are looking for exits. Some decide they'll work in corporate legal departments. Others decide they'll go into nonlegal work in business and return to night school for an MBA, reasoning that the dual degree will add armor to their value in the corporate job market. Still others simply take down their shingle and retire.

Despite the pummeling law office profits are taking, some of the best and brightest young people in the 1990s will introduce themselves to the blindfolded lady with the sword and scales. Some analysts think that, with the exception of top graduates from top law schools, competition for jobs and clients will continue to be crushing throughout this decade. But the Department of Labor, for a variety of sound reasons, expects supply and demand to be in rough balance by 2000. Research and decide. The verdict is yours.

The number of **paralegals**—paraprofessionals who assist lawyers with structured, well-defined tasks—is growing like crazy. Some lawyers say the number of paralegals will double this decade. The hitch is that paralegals find their salaries topping out at about $25,000 or $30,000 annually and many, discouraged, leave the field.

Human Resource Management

If you've got superior leadership and management skills, human resource management (still called "personnel" by many companies) may be the career for you. The job of an **HR manager** is to make employees satisfied and productive. The manager might lobby for job sharing or flexible schedules, or recommend whether to restructure employee benefits, establish a workers' child-care center, offer parental leaves, or require applicants to be tested for drug abuse.

The field has shot up in status since the days when it mainly dealt with hiring and firing. With so many companies merging, buying other companies, closing plants, installing automation, and locating facilities in cheaper labor markets overseas, there's plenty of human resource work to do. Companies rely on HR experts as they try to develop leaner organizations and expand training programs to meet technological change, as well as make concerted efforts to operate without violating anti-discrimination laws and employee rights.

Two stars on the human resource scene are the **executives** who know enough about labor and employment law to keep their companies away from multimillion-dollar liability court cases, and **compensation specialists** who help companies control pay expenses, a gigantic slice of business costs. As minority and ethnic representation in the workplace grows, more corporations are hiring **cultural diversity managers**. Their function is to devise policies and programs to make all employees work in harmony.

A college degree is standard admission to the field, and the growing trend, particularly in large companies, is toward cross-functional expertise rather than specialization. Graduates are lined up to enter the HR field. Get a jump on the competition by making contacts in the industry. Try to line up an internship or enroll in a co-operative education program. Attend meetings of professional societies, such as the Employment Management Association or the American Society for Human Resource Management.

Be computer literate. And learn a foreign language, a skill that is in demand and of short supply among multinational companies.

Advancement in HR can land you a position as vice president of human resources with the potential of pulling in a six-figure income. Increasingly, however, the top positions are going to those with master's degrees.

The Fastest-Growing Occupations to 2005

Workers in more than half of the 20 fastest-growing occupations (e.g., those with the highest *rate* of growth) are involved in providing health or social services. Nursing and personal care facilities, for example, are projected to increase by 46 percent and add 751,000 jobs. The twenty fastest-growing occupations are listed below (the numbers given show the projected percentage of growth for each occupation):

- Personal and home care aides (119)
- Home health aides (102)
- Systems analysts (92)
- Computer engineers (90)
- Physical and corrective therapy aides (83)
- Electric pagination systems workers (83)
- Occupational therapy assistants and aides (82)
- Physical therapists (80)
- Residential counselors (76)
- Human services workers (75)

- Occupational therapists (72)
- Manicurists (69)
- Medical assistants (59)
- Paralegals (58)
- Medical records technicians (56)
- Teachers, special education (53)
- Amusement and recreation attendants (52)
- Correction officers (51)
- Operations research analysts (50)
- Guards (48)

Source: U.S. Department of Labor Bureau of Labor Statistics

You don't have to work inside a corporate human resources department—you may even make more money on the outside, as a **technical recruiter** or **executive search specialist**. Don't overlook a wide range of human resource jobs, including **employment agency counselor, outplacement consultant**, and **career counselor**.

Accounting and Auditing

Accounting or auditing could be the first rung on the corporate ladder for top graduates. Many senior corporation executives got started in accounting or auditing. Accounting requires accuracy, an aptitude for mathematics, computer proficiency, responsibility under limited supervision, high standards of integrity, and the ability to communicate effectively both orally and in writing. These qualities, combined with accounting finesse, could put you on the road to corporate success.

To be among the sought-after graduates, master accounting basics, from auditing to taxes, obtain work-related experience while in school, and become joined at the hip with a computer.

You need at least a bachelor's degree in accounting, and, for greater job market clout, a master's in the discipline or in business administration. After that, aim for certification: Pursue the CPA (certified public accountant) credential for accounting firm employment; the CMA (certified management accountant) for corporate jobs; the CIA (certified internal auditor) for auditing; the CISA (certified information systems auditor) for work with computer systems; and the CFE (certified fraud examiner) for uncovering financial crime such as embezzlement.

Approximately one million **accountants** and **auditors** mind the money in the American business world and they are likely to multiply as complexities grow in federal, state, and local tax laws. Major accounting firms keep the cash flowing by offering management consulting, software programming, and help to clients on everything from merger advice to computer shopping.

The Disassembling Line

Manufacturing is projected to lose 1.3 million jobs from 1994 to 2005. Much of the decline in this sector, which accounted for 16 percent of total employment in 1994, is related to the increasing efficiency of manufacturing production and restructuring, but some of the decline is due to production being shifted to other countries. The numbers given show the declines in thousands of jobs lost:

- ◆ Operators, fabricators, and laborers — -674,000
- ◆ Precision, production, craft, and repair occupations — -284,000
- ◆ All other manufacturing occupations — -355,000

Projected total occupational employment decline in manufacturing, 1994–2005: 1.3 million jobs

Source: U.S. Department of Labor Bureau of Labor Statistics

You could become a high-salaried corporate chief financial officer, but the biggest payoff may be as head of a major accounting firm where you could be looking at annual paychecks as long as a telephone number.

International accounting serving large global corporations is on everybody's list of promising practice areas. Ditto for turnaround and litigation accounting, where specialists clean up the financial excesses of the 1980s.

Accountants and auditors can also expand into software development. With their broad base in computer applications, some have specialized in correcting software problems or in developing new software to accommodate particular needs.

But accounting is no longer a "for sure" occupation. When the boom of the 1980s became the thrift of the 1990s, *a once unquestioned belief— that accounting is one of those transferrable skills that moves easily across occupational lines—became open to challenge.*

Public accounting firms too have embraced the concept of consolidation and are merger-minded. And they too want "rainmakers," partners who are able to herd business through the door.

Recent accounting firm mergers threw many senior accountants and partners into unemployment, particularly in firms serving troubled industries such as defense contracting and real estate development. The immediate assumption by the newly jobless was that they could go into corporations as financial executives because that used to be an easy move. Not so, it has turned out. Employers who discovered they had an abundance of accounting candidates from which to choose upped the requirements. They now want candidates with a specific number of years' experience in their industry working in corporate offices, not public accounting offices.

What is the career lesson to be learned from recent events? Obtain multiple certifications to cover as many bases as possible. Monitor industries and try to join hands with the strongest, either as a public or corporate accountant.

Always be alert to moving to a client company when audits show it enjoys vigor and good management.

The trend is for more education for tomorrow's accountants. After 2000, members of the American Institute of Certified Public Accountants will need 150 college credits instead of the current 120. Already 18 states have passed laws to match that requirement for graduates who want to sit for the CPA exam. The main idea is for a broader education, including liberal arts. Graduates will need classes in foreign language, cultural differences, and interpersonal and communications skills to survive in the global economy.

Banking

The advent of electronic banking has changed the nature of banking as we know it. As banks seek to cut costs in order to compete in today's technological wonderland, they look toward online services to cut back on spending. This allows people to do all of their banking through a machine.

Increasingly, banks seek to merge in an effort to compete with foreign financial muscle. By eliminating overlapping branches, merged banks can cut down on overhead even more by significantly reducing staff. As a result, while senior executives may have a relatively stable career, tellers and lower-level managers find their jobs given to machines.

Arguments are unceasing about the smoothest way to transition financial services into the 21st century. Agreement occurs only on one scenario: By the next century, banking, as your parents knew it, will be unrecognizable. Brutal global and domestic competition—and unprecedented new mergers, some with department stores and industrial companies—are radically reshaping a business nearly as old as civilization.

Golly, it makes one want to rush right out to a "secure" career in banking, doesn't it?

Banking certainly isn't a field for sissies. But it would be a mistake to assume that the banking industry is on the ropes. Most of the nation's banks are profitable and solvent.

Financial Planning

Financial planning is a growth industry populated with investment gurus—investment counselors, bank trust officers, attorneys, in-surance agents, accountants, and, the newest breed, financial planners.

Financial planners take stock of a client's money situation in order to develop a financial plan for the client. This plan may assist the client in meeting a specific financial goal; planning for retirement; reducing taxes; or devising a comprehensive financial plan focusing on taxes, real estate, investments, and insurance. The planner may also sell securities, insurance, real estate, or other financial products to facilitate the client's implementation of the financial plan. However, the possible commission earned from the sale of these products must not precede the client's needs. Above all, a planner must be ethical.

Where the Jobs Are (and Will Be)

Occupational growth will be very concentrated. These 20 occupations are projected to be the biggest gainers *in sheer number of jobs added*, accounting for more than 40 percent of total employment growth over the 1994–2005 period. Three of these occupations are also among the 20 fastest-growing occupations. The numbers given show the projected employment growth in thousands.

- Cashiers (562)
- Janitors and cleaners (559)
- Salespersons, retail (532)
- Waiters and waitresses (479)
- Registered nurses (473)
- General managers and top executives (466)
- Systems analysts (445)
- Home health aides (428)
- Guards (415)
- Nursing aides, orderlies, and attendants (387)
- Teachers, secondary school (386)

- Marketing and sales worker supervisors (380)
- Teacher aides and educational assistants (364)
- Receptionists and information clerks (318)
- Truck drivers, light and heavy (271)
- Secretaries, except legal and medical (267)
- Clerical supervisors and managers (261)
- Child care workers (248)
- Maintenance repairers, general utility (231)
- Teachers, elementary (220)

Source: U.S. Department of Labor Bureau of Labor Statistics

Financial planners work for banks and other financial institutions, financial planning service firms, and on their own.

Straight out of college, you'd be lucky to earn $20,000 as a trainee; once established, high five- and six- figure incomes are not unusual.

What's ahead for planners in this largely unregulated industry? Most likely more federal regulation to protect clients, and more education to deal with increasingly sophisticated financial products.

Planners approach the field from a variety of educational backgrounds in financial service, reflected by the string of initials after their names. A rundown: CFP (certified financial planner); ChFC (chartered financial consultant); CLU (chartered life underwriter); RIA (registered investment adviser); MSFS (master of science in financial services—a university degree, not a professional certification).

Although you can enter the field with a business administration major, an increasing number of specialized financial planning courses and degrees are being offered. Which avenue of entry is best for you depends on your professional goals. Research to get the right answer.

Other Business Jobs

Consultants are business doctors who increasingly diagnose the ills of nonprofit entities, like museums and charities, as well as industrial companies.

Purchasing agents in large industrial firms have better-than-average prospects of lucrative employment. **Mortgage brokers** find rewards taming monstrous loan applications, both locally and through nationwide computerized loan-search networks. **Corporate fitness directors**, who work to keep employees in good physical shape, will encounter more competition than job openings in corporate America.

Managed care managers, who work for companies to keep employee health costs down, earn high salaries to develop relationships with hospitals and physicians and negotiate discounts in exchange for sending employees to them for treatment. Taking aim at opportunities in the business and office sector could be right on target as a prize career choice.

■ ■ ■ ■

Communications and Media

From the gathering of breaking news to acting as the "watchdog" of the U.S. government, the communications network plays a vital role in keeping people informed on local, national, and international levels. A career in television or journalism can place you at the forefront of all the hot newsworthy events. Be prepared, though, for grueling assignments as you strive to meet deadlines in a hectic atmoshpere.

Television is one of the more popular forms of communication media, perhaps because of its immediacy—its quick, visible reporting of events as they happen. But professional communicators use many methods and avenues to inform, educate, persuade, or entertain. Ideas, information, and attitudes also move through journalism, photography, film, radio, audio, video, advertising, public relations, book publishing, magazines, and newspapers.

These categories shelter many of the economy's most interesting jobs—the kind that permit you to make money doing what you most like to do. Some put you in the spotlight—a **talk show hostess**, for example, or **news anchor**. Others bring status within a profession—

advertising creative director or major **advertising account executive**. Still others offer no public recognition, just well-paid obscurity in stimulating environments—**film librarian** or **radio traffic director**.

The next couple of decades will see stunning gains in communication capacity through computers and breakthrough electronic broadcast technology. This growth will create new jobs galore. The problem for you will be establishing a beachhead and beating off the competition. Got the message?

Journalism

Look for openings with small-town and suburban newspapers to get started, as competition for positions with the metropolitan newspapers and magazines can be daunting. Employers prefer you to have a degree in journalism, though they will often accept degrees in other majors.

Additional knowledge in a specific area, such as economics, political science, or photography will increase your marketability, as will fluency in a foreign language. Most employers require computer skills, and experience is a must; get involved with your school newspaper and investigate internship possibilities.

■ ■ ■ ■

Consumer and Home Economics

For many years a field that suggested women who worked in test kitchens or taught high school home arts, home and consumer economics has widened its focus. Here is a sampling of occupations in this cluster.

Interior Designers

The dual nature of interior design allows you to meld scientific knowledge with artistic creativity as you develop aesthetically pleasing, functional environments. Not to be confused with a decorator, an interior designer must have a certificate or diploma from a three-year professional school or a bachelor's degree with a major in interior design. Some states require licensing as well. While this profession is typically overcrowded, prospects look bright. With the growing numbers of dual-career couples, single-parent households, elderly people, and work-at-home arrangements, the demands on interior designers are changing and growing. Many designers struggle financially, but big names can warm their pockets with six-digit earnings.

Fashion Work

Fashion designers study in vocational schools that offer two-and three-year programs, or in college and university programs leading to a bachelor's degree. To become a household word, you probably will have to live in a garment center, such as New York or Los Angeles.

Fashion merchandisers work across the country, often starting out as trainees after graduation; a sure sense for what's going to sell is the most valuable talent. Most work in retailing, formerly a happy home for talented women, but a field that has turned into what many fashion merchandisers describe as a financially desperate industry buried under back-breaking debts. The huge debts were taken on to finance the mergers, takeovers, and leveraged buyouts that savaged retailing in recent years. Even so, young, smart, and energetic fashion merchandisers will find ways to exploit opportunities created by the retailing turbulence—especially in off-price stores.

While **fashion models** appear to live glamorous lives, stringent weight and height guidelines exclude many people right off and those who **do** meet the perfection standards find that modeling requires more than a great appearance; models must be able to "sell" merchandise while twirling under hot studio lights or floating down runways. A model's career typically ends before age 25 and only the top two percent of models ever see the really big bucks. The financial insecurity, shady promoters, and shallow values of the modeling industry make it a risky enterprise.

Child and Elder Care

Careers in child-care look bleak; American **child-care workers** earn substantially less than kindergarten or elementary school teachers. Aim for a position as **director of a child-care center** to earn a salary comparable to those earned by teachers.

At the other end of the age scale, careers in **elder care and gerontology** offer more opportunities than ever before. As the population ages, there is growing demand for people specializing in a field, (for example, law, social work, architecture, or business), with a focus on the needs of the elderly. If you are interested in improving the quality of life of older adults, look for educational programs in gerontology, aging studies, or human development.

A Starburst of Options

Future projections don't help much because graduates of home economics programs—and others in this cluster—follow pathways in many industries. Prospects are much dimmer for **home lighting consultants**, for instance, than for **dietitians**. There will be more jobs for **preschool teachers** than for **models. Independent retirement planners** have less security than **housing managers**.

The most that can be said is that concerns for the family and home continue to churn up attractive career positions for tens of thousands of people.

■ ■ ■ ■

Environment and Natural Resources

Environmental protection activities counteract the negative effects of technology and civilization—industrial failure, air and water toxicity, overcrowding, oil spills, asbestos, radon, the hole in the ozone layer, deforestation, and ocean pollution, just to name a few. As these environmental threats become more dire, the need for trained environmental protection specialists and activists will persist and possibly expand.

A positive sign for growth in these careers is the amount of attention corporations have been forced to give to environmental issues recently. In some companies more than half their profits are being used for environmental projects—new structures and equipment, upgrades on existing facilities, and site cleanup.

Many environmental protection specialists have advanced degrees in the life sciences (such as botany, zoology, microbiology, biochemistry, biophysics), and most work for government agencies.

Environmental and natural resources careers offer diverse opportunities. You may work on location or in a laboratory doing research and design, perhaps as an alternative fuels analyst. Jobs in environmental law, congressional action, conservation, environmental policy direction, natural resources management, and the like can accommodate almost anyone who seeks to combine a career objective with a love of the planet.

Many young adults see environment and natural resources careers as consisting of "freedom jobs"—and head for the Great Outdoors. It's easy to understand their yearning because the work can be enormously gratifying. As a generalization, the pay for professional-level positions is moderately good, often on a government pay schedule or comparable to it. As a certainty, the competition for such jobs as **park ranger** is grizzly.

Forestry

If you want to manage, develop, and protect forest lands, about one-third of the nation's land space, it's over the river and through the woods to a four-year collegiate school of forestry. Whether you work for private industry or government, the job market is always tight.

Hydrology

Water is almost sure to replace energy as the nation's next natural resource crisis. Nearly every part of the United States faces serious water troubles, either a shortage, pollution, or leaky pipes. Experts who have been warning there will be no creek to be up are being taken more seriously. Enter **hydrologists**, scientists who study the distribution, circulation, and physical properties of water. Other than government agencies, hydrologists work for utilities, mining companies, and industrial corporations. The water peril is real—people who can help solve it will be sought after.

Ocean Engineering

Oceanography is a field whose future always seems to look brighter than its present. Since the 1960s, people have been talking about great opportunities exploring earth's last frontier, but a bountiful job market has yet to spring from the sea. **Ocean engineers** explore and use the ocean, and although a mainstay of employment—oil exploration—has substantially dried up, the search for mineral deposits and ocean nutrients continues to attract pioneers to the field.

Recycling

Recycling will be a big growth industry in the 1990s. Governments are demanding it with landfills reaching capacity. **Recycling managers** will find opportunities in states and cities implementing use-it-again programs. Scientists and engineers who can handle hazardous-waste disposal are on the high-demand list.

■ ■ ■ ■

Fine Arts and Humanities

Fine arts celebrate aesthetic communication, functioning as media for profound expression of thoughts and feelings. Not all arts are high-brow. Many offer entertainment and a break from daily routine. In whatever realm, art contributes to the quality of life. Humanities encompass the social and moral values of a culture, enriching our existence as human beings.

Job families often included in this cluster are visual and performing arts, writing, religion, language, history, and museum management.

The statistical generalities for fine arts and humanities are somber: Many who cherish their hours in these pursuits cannot earn a living through their work. Fortunately, the job market has infinite exceptions and there will always be tremendous opportunities for people of superior talent or even genius who are in the right place at the right time.

Two tips: If you find yourself irresistibly drawn to an insecure occupation—**singer, free-lance photographer, sculptor, art critic**, and the like—thoroughly learn the ropes of *marketing* your talent. And prepare for a back-up occupation that pays the bills.

Acting

"Actors are like troubadors going through the country looking for castles. There's no job security," says actor James Earl Jones.

Jones well captured the insecurity of acting. Most **actors** and **actresses** are unemployed. More than 75 percent of those serious enough about the profession to join a union, Actors Equity, are out of work each year.

Formal training is the way to whiz in show biz: Study voice, stage movement, and acting in a college drama program, or in a conservatory.

Of the nation's three dozen or so acting conservatories, some are attached to universities, such as the Yale School of Drama, or the Professional Actor Training Program at the University of Washington. Others are separate entities, such as the Julliard School in New York City. A conservatory is studio-intensive compared to a regular college program that is liberal arts-oriented.

Although expansion in the movie and television industry is expected to result in tens of thousands of new jobs for actors, musicians, and other artists, the odds still are that the show will go on without you.

Filmmaking

Who are the people who make movies? Aside from **producers, directors, screenwriters**, and **film editors**, there are **casting directors, camera operators, unit managers**, and scores of other behind-the-screens specialists. Filmmaking reaches from feature movies, television shows, and video productions to documentaries, commercials, and industrial/educational films.

There are three basic ways of preparing for film life: college study, on-job training, and independent filmmaking. The college route is good because students get a chance to taste the kind of work they'll be doing, make important contacts, and shoot film for their portfolios. You can get into filmmaking without going through a college film program; the key is finding a friend who will open doors for you to be hired as a messenger, mailroom clerk, assistant, or other entry-level worker. Think about how you will make your entrance.

Museum Jobs

Competition for jobs in the nation's 5,500 or so museums is fierce and pay for all but directors of the best-known is on a scale nearly as antique as the items displayed. But the work can be soul-satisfying for those with advanced degrees in related disciplines—art history, anthropology, folklife studies, or zoology, for instance.

Large museums divide job categories into six specialties: **curator, educator, registrar, conservator, exhibit designer, and museum director**.

If you enter the field through a museum training graduate program, be sure the one you choose is affiliated with a museum, has a faculty experienced in museum work, and offers an internship experience of at least six months.

Music

As the sound and style of tomorrow's music moves beyond the range of entertainment into the fast tempo of electronics, career choices for music majors continue to grow. Among music lovers with relatively reliable careers are **music teachers, record company publicists, recording engineers, music arrangers**, and **disc jockeys**.

That's for opening bars in the scope of music opportunities; the industry contains at least 100 separate occupations, ranging from **symphony conductor and rock concert impresario** to **opera singer** and **music video performer**.

Within the music industry there's much argument about how electronic music will affect jobs. Machines may drum some live musicians offstage and out of the studio, but automation is creating a few new jobs for people who can combine music, computers, and sound technology.

Sound recording technology offers opportunities to use these elements in fields other than entertainment. Auto manufacturers, advertising agencies, and game makers all utilize high-tech audio and music recording to develop or sell their products.

The standard advice to music majors who need back-up help has been to get a teacher's certificate after obtaining a four-year degree in music. Now, however, many universities offer a degree in music with an emphasis in sound recording technology, allowing students greater choice in their field.

Since your chances of reaching the top in music are about the same as winning a state lottery, prepare to make your money in a related field. Unless you're a performing star or recording company executive, the music industry is not known for lush paychecks.

Visual Arts

Yes, you can earn a living in fine arts, but for most people, it continues to be a brave career choice.

Gifted **painters** and **sculptors** must find a support base—family, mate, patron, part-time job—until sales of their work enable them to be financially self-sufficient. Few artists ever reach financial independence. What it boils down to is talent—natural major talent honed by ambition, perseverance, endless hard work, and self-discipline.

Many artists pursue fine arts as a part-time career, or combine their artistic training with a related study: arts administration, stage design, museum work, or teaching. An art history PhD, for instance, might enjoy a luminous art-wrapped career as a combination **college professor, art author, museum researcher, curator**, or **gallery director**.

The field of graphic art, also called commercial art or design, offers steadier paychecks. **Editorial artists** illustrate magazines, album covers, posters, and other publications. **Illustrators** paint or draw pictures for books, magazines, advertisements, and film. **Fashion illustrators, cartoonists, animators**, and **medical illustrators** all find work in specialized markets. In an information age, jobs for graphic artists will increase faster than average.

Even artists can't escape computers: Computerized business graphics is coming of age. CAD (computer-aided design) technology is used in advertising, audiovisual presentations, business statistics, and corporate publications.

Regardless of computers, the big money in art will always depend on a touch of genius and savvy marketing, whether the work is museum quality—or the next Garfield.

■ ■ ■ ■

Health Care

Several years ago, the nation made a big swing to "managed care." Companies tried to get a tighter rein by contracting with hospitals and doctors for fixed fees—setting rules in advance to control costs. Employees were sent to health maintenance organizations (HMOs) and preferred provider organizations (PPOs). Managed care works to a degree, but it hasn't kept health costs from spiraling into the stratosphere.

Already health care researchers are turning to automation to cut the payroll. Computers monitor critical care patients so that a single nurse can watch over as many patients as two or more nurses could monitor a few years ago. Automated delivery systems send robot carts, rather than unskilled workers, to deliver food and supplies, and pick up trash and dirty dishes. Physicians use artificial intelligence computer banks to speed diagnoses and follow recommended treatment protocols.

The push to get patients out of the hospital quicker has caused home health care to become the fastest-growing sector within health services.

Staff in doctors' offices is multiplying, mainly to handle the escalating load of paperwork created by the cost-containment bureaucracy.

Medicine

If you apply to medical schools, you'll discover that it's harder than ever to get in, not because the requirements for admission have changed, but because the U.S. supposedly has a surplus of doctors. However, some specialists, such as reproductive endocrinologists, immunologists, and infectious disease specialists are in high demand.

The new technological trend in medicine is telemedicine. Patients no longer have to travel long distances to see a specialist; instead, they can visit a local office where they can communicate with a specialist by phone or video. The future may actually bring house "calls," where you see your doctor through videophone.

Many new physicians are avoiding solo practice and taking salaried jobs in group medical practices, clinics, and managed care groups because they can't afford the high costs of establishing a private practice while paying off killer student loans.

Even though employment of physicians is expected to grow faster than the average for all occupations throughout this century—due chiefly to population growth and aging—the growth is being constrained by the managed care system of hiring lots of physician assistants and nurse practitioners to hold the costs down.

Nursing

If job security is your primary goal, nursing, the nation's largest health profession, is a good bet. Of the more than two million U.S. nurses,

80 percent work. Nursing remains a career in which the threat of unemployment is rare. But he new economics are these: When nurses become more expensive, they become more vulnerable to layoffs. As one New York hospital official says, "Back when RNs were earning $18,000, they weren't likely to be laid off. But now, when many are making $35,000 to $50,000, those positions have to be personnel-budget sensitive."

The advent of managed care programs has resulted in briefer patient stays. This in turn results in staff cutbacks. "Unlike the past, where most graduates began their careers in hospitals, today's newly licensed RNs will look more to other fields in nursing, such a home care or community health," advises American Association of Colleges of Nursing (AACN) President Rachel Z. Booth, PhD, RN.

Bearing in mind that some options require advanced education or specific experience, here's a sampling of other alternatives to hospital jobs.

BY WORK SITE: private duty nurse, doctor's office nurse, school nurse, occupational nurse, military nurse.

BY SPECIALTY: psychiatric nurse, rehabilitation nurse, and other specialties that parallel those of medicine, such as **orthopedic, pediatric, cardiovascular**, and **oncology nurse**.

BY ADDITIONAL EDUCATION: nurse practitioner, nurse researcher, nurse attorney, hospital director of nursing, professor of nursing, health facility administrator.

BY RELATED OCCUPATION: hospital nurse recruiter, program specialist (for nursing organizations), **patient educator** (demonstrating new equipment), **sales representative** (for pharmaceutical or medical supply company).

BY ENTREPRENEURIAL VENTURE: nurse consultant (to insurance and drug companies), **business owner** of publishing, proprietary emergency services, medical temporary help, or home care services.

Currently there are two categories of practicing nurses. The first is **licensed practical nurse**, who studies for 12 to 14 months in vocational-technical training after high school.

The second category is **registered nurse**, who obtains education either through: 1) a four-year college program, receiving a bachelor of science in nursing (BSN) degree; 2) a two-year community college program, receiving an associate degree in nursing (ADN); or 3) a three-year hospital training program, receiving a hospital diploma.

In recent years, nursing education has shifted dramatically to academic institutions. RNs with two-year degrees or three-year diplomas are going back to college in record numbers for four-year degrees, and enrollments are also up for masters degree programs. Nurses are increasingly upgrading their skills to meet the more complex demands for today's patient care, as well as to increase their chances for advancement.

The nursing profession is attempting to obtain more autonomy and receive higher pay while doctors are resisting what they view as attempts to encroach on their preserve. The nurses are winning a few inches at a time and their power could indeed grow as insurers look for additional ways to shave the costs of health care.

There are growing opportunities for the delivery of primary and preventive care for **nurse practitioners (NPs)**, who on a national average are paid $43,000 to $50,000 yearly. The AACN says mounting studies show the quality of NP care is equal to, and at times better than, comparable care by physicians, and often at lower cost.

NPs are registered nurses whose education and experience goes beyond that of basic RN training. They are usually required to complete a masters degree. Most NPs work in clinical specialties such as pediatrics, family practice, ob-gyn/women's health, occupational health, and gerontology.

Of 48 states that allow NPs to prescribe medication, 11 allow them to do so independent of physician supervision or delegation. In 20 states, NPs can practice independently without a doctor's supervision or collaboration.

A large and growing market for NPs is in rural health care, as rural hospitals become endangered service providers.

Dentistry

Dentistry is regaining its smile. The profession will remain competitive but much less so than in recent years because not so many new dentists are coming through the pipeline.

The practice of dentistry is changing as a reflection of the dental care needs of the population. Kids have fewer cavities these days, but older patients need a lot of repair work, from bridges to denture implantation.

The big news is the trend toward specialization. **Orthodontists** straighten teeth. **Oral and maxillofacial surgeons** operate on the mouth and jaws. **Pediatric dentists** treat the lollipop crowd. **Periodontists** get to the root of gum disease.

Possibly the worst thing about being a dentist—frequently dealing with people in pain who don't want to be in a dental chair—is changing. Lasers are creeping into usage as a replacement for noisy, painful drills. Electric braces are being tried to straighten teeth in half the often uncomfortable time required by traditional dental corsets. Computer-assisted carving machines can make crowns and bridges in less than an hour, outdating the need for molds and metal castings. We've saved the best for last: By the end of the century we may have an anticavity vaccine.

Veterinary Science

Animals have never had a better chance of staying healthy and alive. As recently as a decade ago, euthanasia was routine for pets with such serious ailments as heart disease or cancer. Now there's a similar treatment available in veterinary treatment for almost every procedure in human health care. And more than ever, pet owners are willing to pay what it costs to save "a member of the family."

If doctors for humans specialize, why shouldn't doctors for animals? The neighborhood generalist who supplies everything from vaccination shots to major surgery will be around for a long time. But increasing numbers of vets are specializing by focusing on medical specialties or a single species.

Veterinarians are becoming surgeons, radiologists, anesthesiologists, dermatologists, ophthalmologists, dentists, cardiologists, and more.

They may choose to work on companion or farm animals, horses, aquatic creatures, wildlife, or still other groups.

Owners of small animal practices usually earn more than owners of food-animal or large-animal practices, but pay can reach six figures. Vets with a racehorse practice can look forward to riding high.

Other Health Practitioners

Chiropractors will encounter competition in establishing a practice as graduates continue to pour out of chiropractic colleges. There's much optimism about prospects for **podiatrists** because of increased interest in jogging, and older people have more foot problems. The outlook is encouraging for **optometrists**, too. Half of Americans have eye deficiencies and one-third of optometrists are pushing retirement age.

More Than 200 Allied Health Occupations

Many of the more than 200 occupations that assist, facilitate, and complement the work of physicians and other medical specialists emerged only within the last 30 years in response to the rapid advancements in health care technologies. Although the shortages in nursing care have been well publicized, those in the allied health areas have sometimes been ignored and have become even more acute. As a result, there are plenty of opportunities in allied health in most areas of the nation.

In health care there are no unimportant jobs. From the **perfusionists** and **dental hygienists** to the occupational therapists and **biological photographers**, all in some way save or improve lives.

Often the occupation, such as **physical therapist**, permits you to open a private practice and earn a high income.

Of the fastest-growing occupations in the 1990s, seven of 20 will be in the health care area: **physician assistant, home health aide, X-ray technologist, medical secretary, medical records specialist, physical therapist**, and **surgical technician**.

Allied health careers usually require less education than the profession of medicine, often from one to five years of postsecondary study and training. A few of the occupations can be learned on the job and a few require more than five years' training.

The Birth of the Age of Genes

Scientistis expect to complete the Human Genome Project, a genetic mapping of the human body, by 2005. It will help researchers understand the progression of many diseases and will enable the development of new drugs to combat those diseases.

Gene transfers will create enormous problems. "The more powerful the technology that allows us to intervene in living creatures, the more powerful the long-term disruption. We are changing the genetic blueprint," warns Jeremy Rifkin, a famous scientist who urges greater caution in genetic engineering. But even the aspect of solving problems created by genetic tinkering will offer fascinating careers in health.

Along with genetics, we are at the threshold of a time when we can refurbish the human body with robotic limbs and synthetic skin. Within your lifetime, scientists say a replacement component will be able to take the place of almost any portion of human anatomy, except, of course, the brain and central nervous system. Today we can replace joints and legs, tomorrow we may have contact lenses with zoom vision and artificial hearts that work as well as the originals.

If you want to be a maker of miracles for patients, obtain the best health-related education you can to ready you for the most exciting years of healing in history.

■ ■ ■ ■

Hospitality and Recreation

This is a fun group of jobs for which some forecasters expect great things in the years ahead. Hospitality means tourism in its broadest definition—travel, lodging, food. Recreation encompasses the activities that entertain tourists.

Jobs range from **airline travel club manager** to **bartender**, from **golf course superintendent** to **baseball umpire**. A leading reason why the hospitality and recreation industries may be headed for a prosperous period is that baby boomers are maturing, have more jingle in their jeans pockets, and see travel and leisure pursuits as a right, rather than a privilege.

as travel planners, comparison shoppers, and consumer advocates, helping clients to sort out the bewildering number of travel options. They'll establish larger firms and scout for more commercial accounts, even going so far as to locate personnel in large corporate offices.

Travel agents earn little and change jobs frequently. The real money is in business accounts, tours, and ownership of a large profitable agency.

Travel

The travel industry is predominantly owned, managed, and run by women. Women make up nearly 85 percent of full-time travel consultants, more than 80 percent of management positions in travel agencies, and 60 percent of travel agency owners.

For both women and men, the vast majority of those in the travel business have seen the inside of a college, and many have degrees.

Automation in ticket sales and travel planning may squeeze travel agency-related jobs in the years ahead. The travel industry is only as good as the economy; a downturn brings storm warnings, good times bring blue skies and lots of travelers.

The technical complexity of the equipment and the business leaves little room for beginners to sprout wings on the job—you need airline experience or formal training. You can take a four-year degree program in travel, but an intensive few months in a vo-tech travel program is the route most **travel agents** choose. For those who prefer learning at home, the American Society of Travel Agents and the Institute of Certified Travel Agents offer a travel correspondence course. You'll need computer skills and good selling skills. Travel experience is an asset.

When it becomes commonplace to buy tickets by telephone or computer, smart travel agents will survive by emphasizing counseling rather than order-taking. They'll function more

Lodging Industry

Competition in the lodging industry will be cutthroat until the turn of the century, or beyond, as hotel companies compete with global strategies, marketing warfare, and computer battles to win paying guests.

Find room in the inns one of two ways: formal education or work your way up the ranks. You can study for an associate, bachelor's, or master's degree in hotel administration. Some hotel corporations offer management training programs only to college graduates, while others will consider high school graduates.

Banquet sales is a good break-in area that, once you begin to earn commissions, can result in high earnings. A successful **banquet booker** might become an **assistant manager** and finally a **general manager**. Promotion opportunities are best in major chains, rather than in small companies, because you can transfer to other locations as positions open up. Ambitious people in the hospitality field should plan on relocating and on making a total commitment where hours are concerned. Hotel management is very demanding.

Pay ranges from barely adequate to above average. But don't forget that besides salary and other normal fringe benefits, many hotel executives have part or all of their room and board and other incidental living expenses paid for since they frequently live in the establishments for the convenience of their employers.

Food Service

Americans like to eat out and the steep rise in the number of two-income households allows them to pay for it. After putting in a hard day at work, people are too wiped out to hassle with kitchen chores.

The restaurant industry, like travel, is at the mercy of the economy.

Food service management offers a variety of attractive possibilities. Managerial jobs exist in restaurants, cafeterias, hotels, country clubs, fast-food places, airlines, steamships, catering companies, and corporate kitchens.

There's a full menu of ways to prepare. You can attend a two-year community college or vo-tech institute for an associate degree in food service management that qualifies you for the technical aspects of food management. A four-year program with a major in food service prepares you for a management position.

To accommodate the national feeding frenzy, America needs **chefs**, plain and gourmet. You can learn on the job, including in the armed forces, or through a three-year apprenticeship program.

A third option is to attend a school. It may be a culinary arts program in a vo-tech school or community college. Many hopefuls attend a *toque blanche* school, so named for the tall white hats worn by chefs. The toque blanche schools—such as the Culinary Institute of America at Hyde Park, N.Y., the California Culinary Academy in San Francisco, or the Washburne Trade School in Chicago—prepare you to handle 50 diners, each requiring a different combination of dishes served in sequence and concurrent with their table companions' varied choices. Other students enroll in *cordon bleu* schools that lead to careers in small-scale catering, teaching, writing about food, preparing food for photography, writing cookbooks, or cooking in a very small restaurant.

Earnings vary as much as the difference between Tex-Mex cooking and French cuisine. Entry salaries are modest, but superstar chefs who handle multimillion dollar budgets earn in the six-figure bracket.

If you can handle the long hours and stressful pace, you'll probably find yourself in a field with more jobs than chefs to fill them.

More Careers in Leisure Land

Club management differs from association management in its recreational focus and facilities management. **Managers** of the nation's private clubs—country, university, yacht, luncheon, and fraternal—earn handsome incomes when fringes are counted in.

Believe it: Love Boat jobs are hard to land. Cruise director positions are so scarce that some **cruise directors** break in as shipboard entertainers. When applying to cruise lines, it's important to apply for a specific job, not just to "do anything" on board. You can choose from such jobs as **shore excursion director, fitness director, children's activities coordinator**, and **purser**.

■ ■ ■ ■

Marketing and Distribution

The marketing function goes far beyond sales activities. It includes *everything* that must be done to move goods/services from producer to customer. Marketing encompasses the price at which the products are sold, the way they are promoted, the places where they are stored, and the manner in which they will be delivered.

Marketing is one of the most popular majors in college. It's a huge field, employing roughly 10 million people throughout the country in advertising agencies, consulting firms, manufacturers, product testing laboratories, retailers, and securities and financial services firms.

Competition for entry-level jobs? It can be compared to a couple of prize fighters jabbing at each other in title bouts. Maybe that's not so bad. Think of a tough job hunt as good training for your chosen work of stalking consumers with such new arsenals of persuaders as radio ads in supermarkets, interactive video kiosks, hologram displays, and "talking" posters in which people in the picture sing, whistle at, and beseech customers to buy.

Advertising

Prior to the 1990s, the advertising industry appeared to be growing nonstop, chock full of great jobs, big pay, and glamorous times. Then from 1990 to 1992, the champagne began to go-to-flat, and advertising is now growing at a rate of, only about 3 percent annually.

Most analysts think the glory days are over. Advertising's share of the marketing dollar has fallen from 43 percent vs. 37 percent for promotions a decade ago, to 30 percent for ads vs. 70 percent for promotions today.

What is the reason advertising may never make a full comeback? Experts say consumers are chilled out by the constant din of "buy this, buy that." The average adult is dive-bombed with 3,000 marketing messages a day—which makes it hard to remember any one pitch amid the media commotion.

The view is not unanimous. Other experts believe that advertising will bounce back vigorously once the economy picks up and companies recover from heavy debt loads of the 1980s'

mergers and buyouts. "The [tv] networks are still the Main Street of advertising," says Coca-Cola's chief of global marketing.

Jobs in advertising are now an employer's market. In the past, you could find a job straight out of high school and learn the trade through experience. Now a bachelor's degree in advertising, marketing, or journalism is necessary to land even an entry-level position. Add experience in some aspect of advertising to increase your desirability even more.

Advanced degrees are not necessary for the more creative, lower-level positions, but you should remain open to earning a master's degree for access to executive positions.

Two trends will influence your future prospects in an advertising career.

1. Tomorrow's advertising aces will fill themselves in on the whole marketing picture, including direct mail and such consumer promotions as coupons, sweepstakes, and discounts. Advertising agencies are beefing up profits by serving their clients' total marketing needs, not just providing print and broadcast ads.

2. Mega-agencies with worldwide offices are emerging to service giant multinational corporations. Some creative people, who prefer advertising's traditional free-wheeling atmosphere, find the new bureaucratic environments stifling. Talented specialists and strong managers may find the most attractive opportunities in smaller, independent agencies that offer highly personalized service.

Although creative geniuses are splendidly rewarded, the big money goes to account executives who handle a large national account and are in such control of it that they can take it along when they open their own advertising agencies.

Public Relations

A **public relations specialist** is no longer the person called in at the last minute to share the blame, but one who anticipates issues and shares those anticipations with top management.

In moving from apologist to futurist, public relations specialists need hard evidence to support insights, which means learning to use electronic databases. That, plus the necessity to maneuver through the maze of emerging electronic media, points to course work that promotes a high degree of computer and electronic communication literacy.

Because PR specialists are paid to generate favorable public opinion for employer organizations to many publics, success in the field requires much more than a generalized desire to work with people. Public relations requires considerable knowledge of communications and media, and writing ability is extremely helpful. Having the abilities to think clearly and devise strategies is essential for the top jobs. Nearly all PR professionals are college graduates.

In college, take your degree in communications, public relations, or journalism with a PR emphasis—or in liberal arts with a major in English and plenty of information science and computer courses.

Sales Promotion

A job in sales promotion certainly won't let you waste your creative imagination. Count on combining revolutionary sales ideas with great communication skills and a flair for relating with people to score in this profession. The trend toward targeted marketing is causing growth in sales promotion opportunities.

Activities in sales promotion include couponing, premiums, contests, sweepstakes, point-of-sale materials, sampling, demonstrations, trade and sports promotions, event sponsoring, videocassettes mailed to buyers to introduce new car models, collateral materials such as product flyers, and anything else that will inspire the consumer to purchase the product or service.

A sales promotion is inviting a high school football team to a fast-food hamburger place after a big game for a free feed. Spectators at the game are given coupons good for a free soda with the purchase of a hamburger. The spectators pour in to see the team. And, as an added public relations touch, the newspaper photographs the team chowing down.

Businesses are frenzied in their efforts to come up with new and more targeted ways to get their marketing messages across to consumers. Speaking of the proliferation of sponsored sporting events, one wag says that in years ahead, the only events left unsponsored will be press conferences, Supreme Court hearings, and funerals.

Market Research

Increasingly electronic, market research is a systematic and objective gathering of information to solve marketing problems. It's how producers of goods/services avoid groping in the business dark. Let's say a pet food maker wants to introduce a new health food for cats. Who will buy the greatest quantities of it? Will it sell best in health food or pet supply stores? Should it be packaged in red or blue paper? Market research personnel try to answer such questions, identifying opportunities and reducing risks. Computer skills are mandatory. Expect artificial intelligence expert systems to make inroads on demand for market research managers who design research projects.

Preparation for market research varies, from specializing in market research as part of a marketing degree to taking extra courses in math and statistics in liberal arts. Psychology or sociology courses are helpful when personal polling is involved. Fewer than several hundred people work in the new field of quantitative marketing science, a statistical and mathematical approach to marketing data. The path to this kind of numbers crunching is a master's degree in statistics, operations research, or an MBA program heavy on quantitative courses.

As a career opportunity, market research is a chastened field after a decade of growth. Clients have been disappointed with the game plans spewed out by expensive computer programs and—heavens to betsy!—a number are turning back to old-fashioned interviewing with people.

Sales

If you enjoy providing people with what they want, and you feel your earnings should directly reflect your ability and effort in your job, try commission-based sales. There's not much argument that sales is one of the most lucrative roads to the bank. And most sales jobs do not require a college education. What can you sell? Look in telephone yellow page directories—for starters! Many industrial products are listed only in obscure trade catalogs, print and electronic.

Jobs in technical sales, often in high-tech fields, are among the best paying and are the ones that most new sales-minded college graduates hope to land. Many products are for resale—goods for biosensors, components for satellites, membranes for mining, liquid crystals for computers, materials for seeing-eye robots, and a world of other industrial innovations or staples.

A handful of colleges offer industrial distribution as a major; the program may be located in schools of engineering, business, or education. Other people enter the technical sales field from management engineering, industrial technology, engineering technology, industrial engineering, or another engineering discipline related to the products being sold. The prevalent job title is **sales engineer**.

As a rule, earnings for industrial products salespeople are higher than for those in consumer product sales.

Why consider sales, particularly if you're not a white male? Most employers, even if they're racist or sexist, will pay for sales. Most will be glad to get any business they can even if it comes from a purple robot. Moreover, in sales, you don't have to face subjective or biased performance review systems. You either bring in the business or you don't. In this sense, sales is the last frontier of career fields.

Fund-Raising

Fund-raising, a form of direct marketing, helps make the world a better place. **Fund-raisers** for non-profit and charitable organizations use the same direct-mail and telemarketing techniques employed by *People* magazine and the May Company. Universities, museums, symphonies, animal rights organizations, research foundations, health facilities, and other groups all survive because of contributions.

Fund-raisers are becoming a more educated group—4 out of 10 have at least one master's degree. That's good. They'll need all the preparation they can get to market worthy causes in the 1990s. Large corporate contributions have topped out after a steady two-decade climb, leaving a gap that hopefully will be filled by medium-sized and small companies. Corporate chiefs are becoming more concerned with fierce business competition, and less with social concerns.

Fund-raising, an honorable profession, is occasionally sullied by crooks. Legitimate fund-raisers are adequately paid and the work can be enormously satisfying.

Selling to the New America

A wave of recent immigration is radically remaking the map of the American consumer marketplace. Marketing specialists have long known about seniors, yuppies, and female careerists. The new purchasing powerhouse is immigrants—most of them from Asia and Latin America.

A lightning-struck career field, marketing crackles with new challenge in new markets and new technologies. Concerning the latter, the savviest marketers will use technology, but not tie their whole professional life to it. The danger is in allowing the computer to crowd out people as crucial sources of information.

■ ■ ■ ■

Public Service

The unifying theme of this occupational cluster is services to people. Activities are not oriented toward making a profit; instead, they focus on providing the support systems that lubricate society's engine. Jobs are found in non-profit organizations and government agencies—national, regional, state, county, and municipal.

Teaching

If American education to prepare young people for life was a term paper, it would be lucky to be awarded a "C" grade. Critics have stood in line to revise the content, straighten out the grammar, and fix the typos since the early days of the Republic.

Educators, politicians, parents, and the public are once again demanding sweeping change. Studies of educational opinion say some renovations seem assured.

Why real change now and not before? Layered onto the genuine desire to better prepare youngsters for what the future holds, the chief reason some current proposals may succeed in altering the fabric of education is deep concern that America is slipping in the world order.

For the first time in history, U.S. global competitiveness is at stake. Almost any innovation seems worth trying, proponents of change insist, if it has a chance of improving the education of America's young. But talk is cheap and it remains to be seen how much real muscle business and industry put behind education on a long-term basis.

Future teachers face a paradox. On one side is contemporary frustration and burnout; on the other is teaching satisfaction and the thrill of being among the idealistic new legions who storm what critics call educational decay.

Unlike earlier generations of teachers, today's professionals are being asked to solve a host of urgent problems that the school system was never designed to combat. Teaching has become a high-stress job. Its landfills of paperwork may take 50–60 hours a week for pay that pales in comparison to other professionals with similar levels of education. Furthermore, its rewards are largely intangible.

Some teachers are lashed to the point of exhaustion trying to teach children for whom English is not their primary language or dealing with the disruptive personalities of children born addicted to crack. It has become commonplace for teachers to cope with students who have complex social problems: violence, AIDS, pregnancy, drugs, broken homes, child abuse, and poverty.

One manacle of frustration for teachers is trying to keep track of society's fickle goals; what they're told to accomplish on Monday may not be what they're told to accomplish on Tuesday. Moreover, studies show that a number of students attend school for reasons other than to learn and that they spend more time on games and television than on school studies. From this group, it's almost a taunt, "Teach me, if you can."

With virtually every city tapped out financially, teachers constantly are being asked to do more with less. It's hard to find job satisfaction when all you do is cut, cut, cut, say teaching veterans.

By contrast, not all teachers have problem classes day in and day out and for the less stressed educators, the rewards of self-fulfillment can be enormous. It's a joy to lead interested young minds to the wells of learning. As one engineer who changed careers to become a teacher says, "Making things is okay but I'd rather be involved in making lives."

One asset the profession could use more of is additional minority teachers. For decades, teaching was among the few professions that welcomed minority newcomers; now minority graduates are broadening their horizons and choosing other careers. The result is they remove themselves as everyday role models for minority students.

To paraphrase Aesop, teachers share the labors of the great, but they do not share the spoils. Some educators have as much education as physicians, but when it comes to remuneration, they're on different planets. Average salary for public high school teachers is in the $35,000 annual neighborhood.

Teachers at private elementary and secondary schools annually average $10,000 less than their counterparts in public schools. Teachers at both private and public schools can lose their jobs if a private school folds or if a public school district is ruptured by a tax deficit.

Counseling

Two-thirds of **counselors** are in educational services. In school settings, counselors are concerned with expanding the number of opportunities for students and with encouraging them to make good choices. A Maryland high school guidance counselor says, "Since I know you are in the 'process of becoming,' I work with your expectations because I want you to stretch to your potential."

The job market and pay for counselors in education roughly parallel those of teachers. But when budgets are tight, counselors may be laid off to retain a full staff of teachers or shifted to classroom teaching assignments. School counseling is a slow-growth field with the bulk of openings brought about by replacement needs.

Library Science

Librarians—finders and disseminators of information—are no longer stuck in the stacks, but have the chance to be part of the dramatic technological change sweeping through progressive libraries everywhere.

Of the nation's estimated 100,000 libraries, most are computerized in some substantial sense, which means librarians increasingly must know how to use a computer. But their professional judgment and knowledge will also be needed for years to come.

Austere government budgets are keeping the lid on hiring librarians for public and school libraries. Librarian ranks will grow slowly throughout the remainder of the century, with most job openings created by those who retire or leave the field.

A master's degree in library science (MLS) is necessary to obtain an entry-level professional position in most public, school, and special libraries. State requirements for school libraries vary widely, but most require that school librarians be certified as teachers; not all states require a degree in library science.

Public librarians work in a kaleidoscope of settings. **Children's librarians**, knowledge professionals for small fry, handle an encyclopedic range of duties, from conducting story hours to finding the right book for a child. **Acquisitions librarians** choose books, periodicals, films, and other library materials. **Reference librarians** directly provide people with access to the information they need and want.

Cybrarians, also called online librarians, are the librarians of cyberspace, who make it their business to know what kind of information is available on the Internet and where to find it. Cybrarians who design and maintain World Wide Web pages on the Internet are called **Webmasters**.

Media specialists, as librarians who work in school settings are often called, teach students how to use the school library or media center. They often work closely with classroom teachers in curriculum development. Sometimes they are saddled with the additional role of keeper of the study hall.

Academic librarians cooperate with faculty members at colleges and universities to ensure the library has reference materials for courses offered.

Special librarians work in information centers, or in libraries maintained by corporations and government agencies. When the focus is on a particular field, such as law or medicine, an advanced degree in the appropriate subject specialization (as well as an MLS) is highly desirable.

To find out more about the many worlds of library science—from children's outreach services, prisons, and urban administration offices to corporate information management, school media centers, and historical archives, check library career literature available at—you know where.

Social Work

Social workers provide the caulk that keeps many unfortunates from falling through society's cracks. In dealing with trouble spots in a community, social workers often counsel clients or refer them to helping agencies.

You can work in a government agency doing casework with a bachelor's degree in social work, but if you want professional clout and supervisory positions, obtain a master's degree in social work.

State and local governments have been the leading employers of social workers to date, so the market has relied primarily on funding. However, more and more corporations seek social workers to help employees who must deal with the stress of balancing work and family. Some corporations also expect social workers to help employees adjust to downsizing or layoffs and outplacement.

Prospects are favorable for social work graduates in the 1990s, particularly in Sun Belt states and rural areas. Geriatric care is a growing specialty—the elderly face complex problems in retirement, health care, finances, and housing. As a new wave of immigrants sweeps into the country, many will need social services to help make the transition to productive citizenship. Demand should expand for social workers in outpatient health facilities, including health maintenance organizations.

Social workers now provide the bulk of psychotherapy services in the United States, according to the National Association of Social Workers; social work services usually are less expensive than psychotherapy offered by psychologists and psychiatrists.

Social workers earn moderate incomes. Those who advance to executive positions in large organizations, corporations, or government agencies usually earn in the mid-five figures. An estimated 70,000 social workers in private therapeutic practice may earn upwards of $100,000 yearly.

■ ■ ■ ■

Transportation

Occupations in the transportation cluster involve moving humans, creatures, and objects from one place to another, by land or sea, by air, space, or pipeline.

The much touted "coming revolution" in transportation featuring people capsules, tube trains, sky lounges, and other futuristic vehicles is not quite ready to swing around the corner. Researchers *are* hard at work on hypersonic planes and computer-guided cars, but American transportation will look much the same at the beginning of the new century as it does today.

Autos and trucks will continue to clog the highways, creating gridlocks and commuter rage. Airplanes will dot the skies, stressing airports and traffic systems. Railroads will chug along with bulk cargo shipments and fewer and fewer passengers. Mass transit systems will have their wheels to the wall in the absence of massive federal government funding. Space transportation? Literally, it is up in the air as bureaucrats debate what to do next.

All these problems create employment opportunities. The transportation job market is rolling along toward employment of four and one-half million workers in 2000, but will not be uniformly merry in all types of transportation services. Here's a quick look.

Air Transportation

Skies are turbulent but clearing for the airline industry. Major airlines are becoming bigger and fewer in a rash of buyouts, mergers, and consolidations. Thousands of employees have lost jobs in this decade and it may get worse before it gets better. The market has been flooded with displaced employees who have inundated airlines with applications. On average, each major airline has 10,000 pilot applications on file.

Airline executives fear that the industry will be reregulated (it was deregulated in 1978) but industry observers say a more likely change will increase foreign ownership in American airlines.

Other predictions:

◆ The number of major airlines will be cut in half to five or six in the near future.

◆ The U.S. Air Force has halved ranks of military pilots from 25,000 to 13,000. The military pilot cutback means roughly 75 percent of new airline pilots will be civilian trained.

◆ Openings for **reservation agents** and **ticket agents** will continue to rise, but competition for this glamour industry with the travel benefits will not let up.

◆ FAPA, an Atlanta-based aviation career information service for flight personnel (call 770–997–8097 for cost of services) reports that the outlook continues positive until 2005. FAPA's hiring forecast for 1996–2005 calls for 53,000 new **pilots**, 115,000 **flight attendants**, and 73,000 **maintenance technicians/ mechanics**.

Despite an updraft in career prospects, competition is increasing and airlines expect more and more from their applicants. Not only do many airlines expect their pilots to have achieved a four-year college degree, but pilots may have to finance their training. This pay-for-training is not yet a widespread practice but it is growing. In most cases, you will first interview with an airline that then will make a conditional job offer. If you successfully complete a specified training program, paid for out of your pocket, you will be hired. If you don't pass the program, you may lose most or all of your invested money.

Air traffic controller is one of the highest paid occupations open to high school graduates who have at least three years' general work experience. These traffic cops of the skyways prevent mid-air collisions of aircraft. There aren't enough of them to handle increasingly crowded skies. Don't even think about this work unless you can do two things at once.

Trucking

Would you like someone to pay you for traveling all over the United States? Did you know it's possible to make six figures yearly as a truck-driver? If you have wanderlust and don't mind being away from home for weeks at a time, consider buying a tractor-trailer and leasing your rig and services to a nationwide moving company. You can earn over $100,000 annually.

Not quite three million truckdrivers are on the go over U.S. streets, roads, and highways. Behind the wheels are local truckdrivers, driver-sales workers, private mail drivers, long-distance drivers, and special drivers, such as the wheelers for dealers who haul massive triple-deckers laden with shiny new cars.

This occupation often carries the union label—lots of truckdrivers belong to the Teamsters or to unions associated with the industry in which they work. The union influence is seen in the high earnings of many truckers. There's not much upward mobility, though—truckdrivers rarely advance to terminal manager or trucking company executive. Some do buy their own trucks and equipment and become entrepreneurs.

Can truck-driving schools really help you get behind the wheel of a big rig? Yes, but be sure to talk with some of the school's graduates to see how satisfied they are with the school and its placement help (section 14 has more advice on dealing with a vo-tech school). Some proprietary truck-driving schools deliver the promised training but what they don't tell you is that many employers will not hire their graduates without experience. Be careful that you don't end up with a sizable debt for tuition and no job.

■ ■ ■ ■

Where Do You Go From Here?

Now that you've had an introductory look at what's in the career universe, let's return the spotlight to *you*. Begin with the following section.

Pay close attention. Discovering who you really are and letting that person shine through every day leads to true happiness.

■ ■ ■ ■

Everyone Can Help

No career exploration exists in isolation. None of us could find our way without the knowledge and kindness of others. This section shows who can help you as you seek career success, and how. It explains the role of career tests and test-givers, and it shares a simple but effective technique to maximize your chances of long-term success.

Weave a Tapestry of Contacts

Contacts have been a critical component of success since the dawn of civilization. They will be no less important in the 21st century.

"Who you know" has always, does now, and will forever make a huge difference in how high you rise, although contacts are no substitute for competence.

Making contacts is not dependent upon your family's socioeconomic status. Any number of special people may be willing to wave your banner once you reach out and hand it to them. Some of these special people are:

◆ Parents

◆ Teachers

◆ Relatives

◆ Friends

◆ Friends' parents

◆ Neighbors

◆ Interest clubs

◆ Clergy, church members

◆ Merchants

◆ Coworkers

◆ School leaders

◆ Scouting, youth leaders

◆ Coaches

◆ Team members

◆ Employers

◆ Doctors, dentists

◆ Real estate, insurance agents

◆ Bankers

◆ Friends of friends

◆ Fraternity brothers, sorority sisters

These special people and their contacts form your personal network.

Networking means seeking out acquaintances, advice-givers, potential mentors, and friends, and systematically building on these relationships.

Your first reaction may be that you're too shy to reach out. Fight shyness by recognizing that networking is a legitimate, proven technique in career development. Make just one contact. It will lead to another and another and another. Soon you'll have a network.

Many contacts will be introduced to you by a third person at parties, meetings, and other gatherings. Consider having cards printed with your name, address, and telephone number. When you are introduced to a businessperson, chat a few minutes, then offer your card and ask for your new contact's card in return:

"I enjoyed meeting you. I'd like to give you my card (pause)—and perhaps I could have yours? Thank you."

Exchanging cards with a businessperson helps you establish yourself as an equal. Your savvy makes a favorable impression on your new acquaintance, and you open the possibility of a future relationship.

Even when there's no third person to introduce you, it's okay to talk to strangers, assuming you exercise good judgment and avoid suspicious people.

Don't ignore the person in the seat next to you when you're traveling a long distance by bus, train, or air. Speaking to a stranger is acceptable behavior under these circumstances. Find out who the person is, what he or she does for a living, and all the relevant job facts you always wanted to know.

A young man in Michigan uses an advanced method to keep track of everyone he meets. He records names and details in a home computer database. His entire personal network is available on his computer screen.

John Sweeney discovered that computers are giving a whole new meaning to networking. Sweeney is a mechanical engineer who landed a job in San Jose by surfing on the Internet. The Online Career Center, which was started on the Internet in 1993, now serves more than 3,000 companies. There are a growing number of books available in bookstores and libraries on using the Internet in your job search. Joyce Lain Kennedy, the co-author of this book, has also written the book *Hook Up, Get Hired!*, which explains how to use the Internet more successfully. Another good choice is *The Guide to Internet Job Searching*, by Margaret Riley.

Creating a *personal contacts log* in a computer may not be practical for you, but you can build the same resource with index cards. When you meet an individual who might be of help to you in the future, add that person's name to your personal contacts log. There's a simple format to use; see below.

A tapestry is a beautiful fabric picture that looks more or less the same on both sides. During the career exploration portion of your life, most of the networking you initiate will flow one way: to your advantage. Generally speaking, adults enjoy lending a hand to young people. As you become established in a career, however, your networking must become dual-sided, like a tapestry. The following segment explains.

■ ■ ■ ■

Pumping Life Into Your Network

At the outset of a career search, your networking returns much more than you give. It's all take, take, take. But as you establish yourself on a campus or in a job, your network will not survive if you don't share the wealth.

In their book, *Working and Liking It*, career consultants Richard Germann and Diane Blumenson discuss the concept that benefits must flow two ways.

The authors note that a network of contacts is a human resource and information exchange system—one that allows you to tap into a vast reservoir of knowledge about practically everybody and everything.

Reciprocity in networking, they explain, is a concept to guide you securely throughout your career.

Networking provides the visibility you need to choose a career, land a job, and get ahead in your life.

■ ■ ■ ■

Personal Contacts Log

Name: _____   Phone No: _____

E-mail Address: _____   Fax No: _____

Address: _____

When & Where Last Seen: _____

_____

_____

Comments: _____

_____

_____

Referred by: _____

Need Help? This Beats Calling 911

When you begin to weave your tapestry of contacts, take a few minutes to analyze the types of help you need and from whom. Draw a line down the center of a sheet of paper. On the left side write the kind of help you need; on the right side jot down the people who are your prime candidates to offer each type of help. Glance at the example below.

How often should you ask for help? Don't be chintzy with your requests. As a leading business publisher said, "The smart ones ask when they don't know. And, sometimes, when they do."

Will a Career-Planning Course Help?

Besides high schools and colleges, a number of public and private organizations offer career-planning help in seminars, workshops, and formal courses.

How good are they? That's like asking how good is a mathematics course. The quality varies all over the lot.

To our tastes, some of the courses seem more like a sensitivity-training experience than an exercise in career planning. Other programs, laden with technical flowcharts and formulas, invite napping.

Help Resources

1. Emotional support

Family: Discuss my interests, values, aptitudes, and abilities; ask family for job ideas that match my traits.

Friends: Share with them some of my anxieties about beginning my career exploration and decision making. Find out how my friends feel about their career challenges.

2. Need help with interviewing skills

Family and school counselors: Practice interviews and ask them to critique, telling me what I do wrong. Use a video or cassette recorder and listen to myself.

3. Get to know more about careers that I am vaguely interested in

Family: Get the names of some of their friends and associates who are working in jobs of interest and arrange to spend the day at their workplaces learning more about what they really do.

Friends and their parents: Collect names from them to widen my network of contacts.

Neighbors: Do I know someone who is working in the jobs that interest me? Do they know someone who is?

Former employers: (You can usually count on them if you did a good job when on their payrolls.) Have I covered all bases with those for whom I worked, including my babysitting jobs?

Aim for a well-balanced course that seems to offer a blend of inspiration and introspection with occupational information and job-market reality.

Some high schools provide inadequate courses in careers; they are little more than four-week units paired with other courses. Others offer full-blown courses, often in night school programs.

You're more likely to find a comprehensive career-planning course in a community college or in the continuing education division of a four-year college or university. A call to the institution's admissions office should put you on the trail of available offerings.

If you are more troubled about your future than your friends seem to be, perhaps you should consider paying for a commercial life/work planning program. A number of private firms hold group sessions, but find out about the costs up front; most programs come in at over $1,500.

You can find private counselors and life/work planning consultants in telephone directories under "vocational guidance" or "careers and vocational counseling."

Ask, too, at such non-profit organizations as public library education and job information services, Y's, adult education centers, and community organizations.

You can acquire as much information from books as a counselor can impart, but some people can't learn that way. Others need hand holding. Still others gain needed confidence through counseling.

Do whatever works for you.

Tests also can help you. Let's look at them now.

■ ■ ■ ■

Here's the Story on Career Tests

Name your price! I'll pay anything you ask if you'll give my son a test to reveal what he should do with his life.
—Anxious father to school counselor

This type of call comes regularly from parents who would pay thousands of dollars for tests that lead their offspring to the good life with job satisfaction, high pay, a bright future, and work security.

Unfortunately, the magic-bullet test is a myth. It is a misperception. It is a figure of imagination. The reason is not complicated:

Career development is a process, not a test.
We repeat:
Career development is a process, not a test.

It's not surprising that vast numbers of people believe otherwise. Popular magazines print test after test to measure your assertiveness, your managerial ability, your marriage relationship, and your diet habits. And if that's not enough, pop questionnaires reveal your personality traits and your potential longevity on this planet. Still other clever exams will supposedly divulge your attractiveness to the opposite sex and evaluate whether you are ready for an adult relationship.

These tests usually include a scoring standard that lets you know whether you are okay, need help, or are a hopeless case. People love these harmless evaluations, which is fine unless you naively believe 100 percent in the results.

In school settings, counselors often use tests. There are too many students to spend hours and hours interviewing each one, drawing out interests, aptitudes, and personality traits. Tests are the practical substitute for lengthy interviewing. They provide counselors with foundation facts about what's right for you.

When administering tests, experienced counselors always explain that career development is a process in which tests are but one component. The problem is that even when a counselor spells it out, a listener may choose to hear a different story.

For example, one counselor did everything except shout through a bullhorn in emphasizing to a student that the career interest survey she was taking was exactly that—merely an indication of her general interests. Even so, the young woman later told her father she had taken a test at school that showed she should be a meat cutter.

How amazing, her father thought, that a test could be so specific. Intrigued, he called for enlightenment. When the father was accurately informed about the nature of the test, he learned that his daughter's interests indeed did appear to include the possibility of meat cutting, but the results also pointed toward 50 other possible occupations.

The young woman closed her ears to a simple truth:

Tests are a sample of behavior. They give valuable clues about oneself and about relevant career options. That's their maximum contribution to your future success.

How, you may ask, do some private testing organizations get away with advertising their instruments as miraculous bridges over rivers of indecision? The answer is that the value of the help is in the mind of the receiver.

Many career seekers who have paid as much as $2,500 for a test battery, with a little interpretive counseling thrown in, rave about how the experience set them on the pathway of a promising career.

Maybe it did. In reality, what probably occurred is that the tests erased some self-doubts and supplied the missing incentive to do additional research.

Another reason costly tests often work is that the "expensive-must-be-good" philosophy is in play. When you pay lots of dollars for a benefit, aren't you inclined to rate it above a similar benefit you could have obtained for a few dollars? We are. It's human nature.

Tests can open windows of understanding, but it is important to remember that career development is a process of which tests are but one part.

■ ■ ■ ■

The Career Tests You're Most Likely to Meet

Now that you have an idea of what tests can and can't do, here's a cram course on evaluations you are most likely to encounter:

Interests

These tests identify your preferences. They help you discover what you *want* to do. You are asked to rate various activities as to whether you "like," "dislike," or "feel indifferent" about them.

A profile of your answers is compared with profiles of people working in various occupations. If you like independent work, you'll receive a list of occupations that require independent performance, such as chemist or writer.

On the other hand, if you want to be near theater, shopping, sports events, and other resources in urban areas, your job possibility list will not include park ranger or agricultural equipment dealer.

There are no right or wrong answers, and interest surveys are not a measure of your intelligence. They are limited to suggesting what you want to do.

Conversely, if test results show a weakness in spatial relationships (how parts of an object relate to each other in three dimensions), your job possibility list will not include civil engineer or drafter.

Because aptitude tests are not intelligence tests, you are sometimes asked to demonstrate an aptitude by doing a work sample—you can't simply claim to have finger dexterity, you must demonstrate it.

Aptitude

These instruments do not measure whether you want to do the work, but whether you *can* do the work.

Aptitude tests predict "potential for doing." More precisely, these tests help you discover hidden talent. A hidden talent is an aptitude. An aptitude is a readiness to acquire a given skill, or to master a particular subject.

An aptitude is *not* an ability. An ability is a skill. When you have acquired an ability or a skill, it means you have developed a level of expertise in a given activity. You can do a thing well.

An aptitude or hidden talent is a promise; an ability or skill is its fulfillment.

You may have an aptitude for voice and music, but if you fail to develop it, you'll never make a skilled singer.

Again, a profile of your answers is compared with profiles of people working in various career fields. If you score high in mathematical aptitude, for instance, you'll receive a list of occupations in which that aptitude is important, such as telecommunications equipment designer and insurance actuary.

Personality

These tests look at whether you have the *right temperament* for the work. Questions ask how much you enjoy various activities (somewhat like interest tests), how you make decisions, how you think, how you view the world, and how you deal with other people.

Your personality type is compared with the personality profiles of people who work in various occupations, and once again you're given a list of occupations that could be a good match.

Assume that your dominant personality type is social. You like to work with people—informing, enlightening, training, and curing them. Your list of possibilities could include psychologist, professor, industrial trainer, and nurse.

It would not, however, include microwave oven repairer or space station transmitter engineer.

Types of Questions on Career Tests

To help you understand the differences in the types of career tests you may take, there are brief examples for each beginning on page 105.

Some Well-Known Career Tests

Test	Description	Publisher	Audience
JOB-O A (advanced)	A general career interest inventory designed to help students assess their work skills and career interests so that they can make valid career decisions. Twenty-seven job clusters cover 250 occupations, self-scored and self-administered.	CFKR Career Materials Suite 7 11860 Kemper Road Auburn, CA 95603	16–adult
COPS (Career Occupational Preference System)	An interest-inventory test developed to measure job activity preferences leading to 14 career clusters.	EDITS P.O. Box 7234 San Diego, CA 92167	14–adult (A variation—COPS–P—is for the college-bound adult.)
CAPS (Career Ability Placement)	A multi-dimensional test measuring aptitudes and abilities keyed to entry requirements for many jobs.	EDITS P.O. Box 7234 San Diego, CA 92167	14–adult
SDS R 1994 Edition (Self-Directed Search)	A survey of aptitudes and interests. Comes with an occupations-finder guide which lists jobs for each of six work styles: realistic, investigative, artistic, social, enterprising, conventional. Also includes the educational opportunities finder and leisure activities finder.	Psychological Assessment Resources P.O. Box 998 Odessa, FL 33556	14–adult
Strong-Campbell Interest Inventory	Compares interests with those of people successfully employed in a wide variety of occupations. Uses same work themes as SDS.	Consulting Psychologist Press 3803 E. Bayshore Road Palo Alto, CA 94303	14–adult
Myers-Briggs Type Indicator	Measures personality types and interests based on Jung's theory of 16 types. Booklet provides career implications.	Consulting Psychologist Press 3803 E. Bayshore Road Palo Alto, CA 94303	14–adult
Harrington-O'Shea Career Decision Making System	A comprehensive measure of career interests that combines abilities and values with extensive interpretive information.	AGS Inc. 4201 Woodland Road Circle Pines, MN 55014–1796	Level 1: 7th–10th grade Level 2: 10th grade-adult

Interest Surveys

Make an X under **L** for the activities you would like to do. Make an X under **D** for the things you would dislike doing or to which you would be indifferent.

	L	**D**
Realistic		
Fix electrical things.	____	____
Take a woodworking course.	____	____
Investigative		
Read scientific books, magazines.	____	____
Take a chemistry course.	____	____
Artistic		
Play in a musical group.	____	____
Take an art course.	____	____
Social		
Work as a volunteer.	____	____
Help others with their problems.	____	____

Enterprising
Participate in a political campaign.	____	____
Serve as an officer of any group.	____	____

Conventional
Update records or files.	____	____
Operate office machines.	____	____

(Reprinted from the *Self-Directed Search Assessment Booklet* by permission of the publisher, Psychological Assessment Resources, Inc.)

Aptitude Tests

Look over the following sample questions. These questions are just a sampling of four subtests typically found within aptitude tests.

1. MECHANICAL REASONING (MR)

This test is a measure of Mechanical Reasoning. Following are questions about mechanical facts and principals. Place a heavy black mark in the box corresponding to the best answer. Practice on the following examples.

Example 1:

Which person is carrying the heavier load?

❑ A
❑ B
❑ No difference

Example 2:

In which direction will the submarine move if the control fins are turned in the direction of the arrow?

❑ Dive
❑ Surface
❑ No difference

In Example 1, you should have darkened the space next to the letter **A**. **A** carries the heavier load since the bricks are closer to **A** than to **B**. In example 2 the correct answer is **surface**. The submarine will surface since the flow of water adds buoyancy by pushing up beneath the fins.

(Reprinted from the *Career Ability Placement Survey* by permission of the publisher, EDITS.)

2. SPATIAL RELATION (SR)

This is a test of Spatial Relations. Following are patterns which can be folded into figures. You are to choose which figure can be correctly made by folding the pattern and then darken the answer space above it. Only one of the four figures is correct for each pattern shown. Practice on these examples.

Example 1:

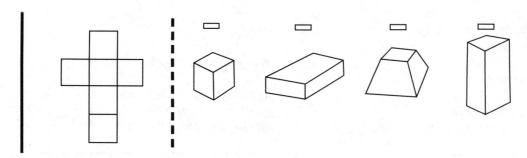

Example 2:

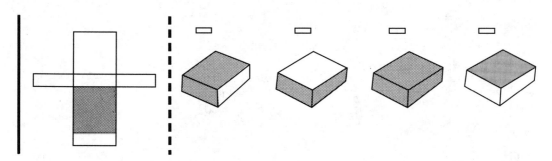

In Example 1, the first figure, the cube, is correct. You should have darkened the answer space above the first figure. In Example 2, all of the figures are correct in shape, but only one of them is shaded correctly. The last figure is correct.

Remember, the surfaces you are shown in the pattern must always be the outside of the folded figure.

(Reprinted from the *Career Ability Placement Survey* by permission of the publisher, EDITS.)

3.NUMERICAL ABILITY (NA)

This is a test of Numerical Ability. Below are two sample problems. To the right of each problem are five possible answers. Work each problem and then darken the space next to the correct answer. Only one answer is correct for each problem.

Example 1:
ADD

	⬜ 15
14	⬜ 16
+11	⬜ 25
	⬜ 26
	⬜ 27

Example 2:

MULTIPLY
	⬜ 34
11	⬜ 40
× 4	⬜ 43
	⬜ 46
	⬜ Not given

In Example 1, the correct answer is 25. You should have darkened the answer space to the left of 25.

In Example 2, the correct answer is 44. Since 44 is not among the given answers, you should have darkened the space next to Not given.

(Reprinted from the *Career Ability Placement Survey* by permission of the publisher, EDITS.)

Personality Surveys

Which answer comes closest to telling how you usually feel or act? Circle **A** or **B**.

Does following a schedule:
   A. appeal to you?
   B. cramp you?

Are you inclined to:
   A. value sentiment more than logic?
   B. value logic more than sentiment?

Which word in each pair appeals to you more?
   A. firm-minded   B. warmhearted
   A. hearty   B. quiet
   A. thinking   B. feeling
   A. speak   B. write

(Reprinted from the *Myers-Briggs Type Indicator*, Form F, with permission of the publisher.)

Interested in Taking Career Tests? Here's How

Most tests can be taken by making arrangements with high-school guidance departments, college counseling centers, public employment service offices, and private counseling firms. The tests may be free, cost a modest amount, or, in the case of private counseling firms, cost from $25 to several hundred dollars.

Most tests cannot be ordered individually. When you cannot find a place that offers the test you want, contact the test publisher for a referral.

■ ■ ■ ■

Doing It Your Way

Because you're going to be seeking out people for your contacts network, you'll be the recipient of many suggestions.

A downside to all of this advice may occur when the guidance of people who count (parents, teachers, friends, and so forth) is on a collision course with your idea of your own best future.

They may be right when they say you'll wind up as a mud-wrestler if you drop out of school, or that you won't get a job with a major in French unless you want to teach, interpret, or translate.

Pay attention when key people talk: There's a difference between having faith in your ability to make decisions and in being stubborn.

However, the final decision must be your own. You may think you're not an authority on anything, but you are—you are your own best authority on knowing what you want for yourself.

■ ■ ■ ■

CHAPTER
6

You and Only You: On the Road to Awareness

In this section the focus is on self-awareness. You learn how to use identity inventories to bring forth the real you. To create these identity inventories, you'll use a variety of activities designed to sharpen your perceptions.

You'll complete a separate identity inventory for each of these considerations:

- ◆ Your interests
- ◆ Your aptitudes and skills
- ◆ Your academic abilities
- ◆ Your personal values
- ◆ Your work values
- ◆ Your personality traits
- ◆ Your lifestyle preferences

At the end of the section, you'll put everything together in a brief summary, revealing your identity snapshot.

What Do You Like to Do Best?

Your interests are those things you like to do. Discover them. Here are three activities devoted to revealing your interests.

The Terrific Ten

Quickly write down 10 things you enjoy doing. Anything goes. Your likes can be related to leisure, work, hobbies, or whatever. Here's an example:

sports

reading

watching videos

working out

science

surfing the Internet

talking with friends

shopping

working

listening to music

Don't spend a lot of time constructing your list. Just write what pops into your head. Next to each item that you jot down, write the codes that apply. The codes are:

1. Place an **X** next to those things you have done within the last three weeks.

2. Place an **A** next to those things you like to do alone.

3. Place a **P** next to those things you prefer to do with other people.

4. Place a **$** next to those that cost $10 or more each time you do them.

5. Place an **O** next to those you would like to be a part of your occupation.

6. Place an **L** next to those you would like to be a part of your leisure.

7. Place a **C** next to those you would like your life's companion to have on his or her list.

8. Place an **R** next to those you think you'll be able to do after you retire.

Terrific Ten Summary

I like:	Code	Setting
_____	___	_____
_____	___	_____
_____	___	_____
_____	___	_____
_____	___	_____
_____	___	_____
_____	___	_____
_____	___	_____
_____	___	_____
_____	___	_____

Go back over your list and describe the setting where you could most likely do each of these things. This could include the mountains, a city, the suburbs, a coast, the country, a small town, and so forth.

The Terrific Ten activity doesn't have a scoring guide and it doesn't offer magic answers. What it does do is direct your thoughts to those activities you would do with a song in your heart, to how much they cost, and to whether you would like them to be a part of your job or a part of your leisure.

The Executive Summary

The process of reviewing your past to find leads to your future is called the *diary approach*.

A complete diary approach takes weeks and as many as 100 pages of writing. At some point in your life, you may need to experience the whole process.

For now, let's do a quick wrap-up, which we call an *executive summary*.

First, glance at the following list of words that describe activities and functions other people say they enjoy doing. After you have the general idea, reach into your own history and fill out the executive summary form that follows. We've filled in examples to get you started on the executive summary form.

Which words seem most like you—either what other people say or your own preferences?

Examples of Activities/Functions

accept challenge	change	data	evaluate
adapt/modify	classify	delegate	examine
administer	coach	demonstrate	exchange information
advise	collect	design	execute
analyze	communicate	develop	expedite
appraise	compare	direct	
approve	compile	discover	figure
assemble	compute	distribute	finance
assign duties	conceive ideas	do artwork	forecast
assist/help	conduct	do physical work	
audit	consolidate	do precision work	gather information
	construct	draft correspondence	give information
be free	consult	draw up standards	guide
brainstorm	contract		
budget	control	edit	handle detail
build	coordinate	efficiency	handle objects
build morale	correct	empathize	help people
build team	counsel	enjoy others	
	create	entertain	
calculate	critique	entrepreneur	identify needs
care for	cross cultural	establish priorities	implement
catalog	cut costs	estimate	improve *(continued)*

increase productivity
influence
inform
initiate
innovate
inspect
inspire
install
instruct
integrate
interpret
interview
invent
investigate

judge
justify

layout
lead
liaison
liberate
listen
lobby

make consensus
make decisions
make policy

manage
market
mentor
moderate
monitor
motivate

negotiate

observe
operate machines
optimize
organize
overhaul
own

people
perform
persuade
plan
policy
present
preside
procure
program
project
promote
protect

provide treatment
publicize
publish
purchase

raise funds
read/speak
   languages
realize ideas
recruit
repair
report
research
resolve conflict
review
risk

schedule
select
sell
service
set objectives
solve problems
speak
staff
strategy
supervise
support
survey

synthesize
systematize

teach
teamwork
tend
think
train
translate
travel
treat

unify
use tools

value
verbalize
volunteer

work independently
work outdoors
work well with others
   (teamwork)
work with children
write features/ads
write instructions
write proposals
write reports
write—

Executive Summary

Activities	Things I Like	Things I Dislike
School Subjects		
1. history	gather info.	review
2. _____	_____	_____
3. _____	_____	_____
Hobbies		
1. sports	accept challenge	train
2. _____	_____	_____
3. _____	_____	_____

Extra-Class Activities

1. yearbook _____   write _____   edit _____
2. _____   _____   _____
3. _____   _____   _____

Work Experience

1. movie usher _____   assist/help _____   monitor _____
2. _____   _____   _____
3. _____   _____   _____

Community Activities

1. environmental club _____   speak _____   fund-raising _____
2. _____   _____   _____
3. _____   _____   _____

(In identifying your likes and dislikes, you are not limited to the sample functions and activities just given. Write any aspect of an activity that turns you on or off.)

Although your interests are going to change as you mature, certain preferences are bedrock. If, for instance, you're a nature lover who enjoys nothing more than hiking the overland trails, its improbable that at age 35 you'll turn into someone who prefers the indoors, or into a professional athlete if you're a couch potato.

From the insights gathered in the Terrific Ten and executive summary activities, fill out the identity inventory (next page) of your interests.

What's the difference between aptitudes and skills?

An aptitude is a promise and a skill is that promise fulfilled.

An aptitude is the bud; the skill is the rose. You may have an aptitude or a talent for drawing, but until it's polished and perfected, you can't say you have a skill in art.

For brevity, we'll discuss only skills. We'll count on you to remember that while you may be on your way to acquiring certain skills, for some of them, you're not quite there yet.

What Can You Do Best?

In choosing a future that works for us, we need to know what we can do well—our aptitudes and our marketable skills.

Skills Up Close

All skills are not created equal. Some you can do like a champ, others moderately well, and still others only by hanging from your fingertips.

Identity Inventory:
MY INTERESTS

Interests I would like to pursue in my career:

1. _____

2. _____

3. _____

4. _____

5. _____

6. _____

7. _____

8. _____

9. _____

10. _____

SUMMARY: (Top three interests)

1. _____

2. _____

3. _____

---

1. *Formally-acquired skills* are those that come to you as a result of taking classes or reading books. Examples include learning HTML, practicing a martial art, or repairing a car.

2. *Informally-acquired skills* are the ones you learn by trying, failing, and trying again until you master them. You also gain these skills by watching another perform them, then giving it a go. Examples: riding a bike, in-line skating, or running a computer program.

3. *Natural skills* (talents) are those you were born with. They're in the genes. Examples: singing, a knack with children or animals, throwing a ball.

A skill formally acquired by one person may be informally acquired by another; it might be a natural skill for a third individual.

Except when it comes to credentials and professional licensure (such as acquiring a medical degree before attempting brain surgery), it's not all that important how you acquire skills.

What counts is that you can say "I can do that" and know how to evaluate how well you can do it.

As a warm-up, look over the extensive list of skills below. For more inspiration, look again at the examples of activities and functions people like to do that appeared earlier in this section. Other exercises follow.

A Sampling of Marketable Skills

abstract reasoning
accounting
acting
administrating
analyzing
animal grooming
arbitrating
assembling
athletics

baking
balancing checkbooks
bookkeeping
budgeting

carpentry
charting
checking
classifying
cleaning
clerical
collecting
color analysis
comparing
competing
compiling data
computer programming
conceptualizing
controlling
cooking
cooperating
coordinating
coping
copying
counting
creating
cutting hair

dancing
data entry
debating
defending
defining
delegating

developing rapport
diagnosing
diplomacy/tact
directing
driving

editing
electrical skills
enforcing
equipment operation
evaluating people/
   situations
expanding
experimenting

first-aid skills
following directions

gardening
getting along with
   others
good manners
guiding

handling detail
handling tools
healing/curing
home
human relations
hypothesizing

identifying
illustrating
imagining
implementing
improvising
influencing others
initiating
integrating
interior design/
   decorating
interpersonal
   relationships
interpreting

interviewing
inventing

judging

leading
listening

managing money
managing people
management
mathematics
mechanical repair
memorizing
modeling
motivating

navigating
negotiating

observing
organizing
overseeing

painting
photographing
planning
playing musical
   instrument
plumbing
precision working
preparing
presenting
problem solving
promoting
proofreading
public speaking
purchasing

questioning
quick learning

reading
recognizing

recombining ideas
recruiting
reevaluating
renovating houses
researching
responding

scheduling
selling
sewing
singing
sorting
speaking
speaking foreign
   language
speed with accuracy
spelling
summarizing
supervising
supporting others
systematizing

teaching
technical
   comprehension
tending
testing/screening
time management
training
transcribing
traveling
troubleshooting
tutoring
typing

verbalizing
visualizing in three
   dimensions

wallpapering
working in teams
writing

The Skills Employers Want

The American Society for Training and Development (ASTD) has conducted the largest study to date on this topic. According to this research, many employers indicate that the most important skills for any employee are academic skills—reading, writing, and computation. Employers are saying, "Give us people who can read, write, and do simple math, and we'll train them to do the jobs we have available." But, when we look more closely, we find that employers want good academic skills *and much more*. According to the ASTD publication, *Workplace Basics: The Skills Employers Want*, the "much more" refers to sixteen specific skills in the following seven skill groups:

Learning to learn
Knowing how to learn

Competence
Reading
Writing
Computation

Communication
Listening
Oral communication

Adaptability
Creative thinking
Problem-solving

Personal management
Self esteem
Goal setting and motivation
Personal and career development

Group effectiveness
Interpersonal skills
Negotiation
Teamwork

Influence
Organizational effectiveness
Leadership

A Test of Skills

In each of the following categories, check the statement that best describes your skills in this field.

Scientific

_____ 1. I can follow directions to measure things accurately either in volume or size, if directions are simple.

_____ 2. I can follow detailed instructions to do scientific experiments and have good ability to accomplish detailed observations of experiments and write down accurate accounts of these observations.

_____ 3. I understand scientific principles and have successfully performed scientific experiments. I am curious about scientific articles, and if asked, can explain detailed scientific ideas.

Mechanical

_____ 1. I can use a screwdriver and pliers to take apart or put together simple things.

_____ 2. I can make some repairs and understand the workings of mechanical objects and simple machines, plumbing and electrical devices. I have used power tools.

_____ 3. I usually figure out what is wrong with a machine, plumbing or electrical device, and am challenged to do so. I understand the principles of these devices and how they work. Friends come to me for a variety of mechanical difficulties.

Clerical

_____ 1. I can file and I know how to use a dictionary. If instructions are available, I can run a photocopy machine. I can use a computer for word processing.

_____ 2. I can type a business letter accurately and am well organized. I can figure out the details of an office quickly. I can follow directions. I occasionally find ways to streamline the procedures I am asked to accomplish.

_____ 3. I am a rapid and accurate typist and can take shorthand or use a dictating machine. Not only am I well organized, but I have the ability to supervise others. I can operate most office equipment. I can organize an efficient office. I can compose letters and write reports with a minimum of direction.

Computational

_____ 1. I can do basic math functions (adding, subtracting, dividing, and multiplication). I can make change and usually manage to balance my checkbook.

_____ 2. Numbers come fairly easy to me. I understand decimals and can compute percentages and interest. I know how to read graphs and tables.

_____ 3. I understand and can compute statistics. I can use advanced mathematics functions and prepare written and oral reports using mathematical equations and principles. I know how to prepare budgets. I understand the basic function of computers, golf and racing handicaps, and the stock market page.

Sales

_____ 1. I have difficulty trying to sell materials. If necessary, I allow people to look at merchandise, make a decision, and then I complete the sale.

_____ 2. I can comfortably point out assets of a given product for sales purposes. I am friendly and find talking to people easy.

_____ 3. I am very persuasive. It's easy for me to convince someone to endorse any idea or product. People enjoy my company and persuading someone to make a decision is a fascinating challenge.

Social Service

_____ 1. I dislike listening to other people's problems. I generally am at a loss about what to do if someone asks me for help with a personal problem.

_____ 2. I get along well with people. Many of my friends ask me to help them with their problems. At times I assist people in making decisions or in finding resources to help them.

_____ 3. Helping people discover solutions to their problems is easy and satisfying for me. I spend a lot of time helping people with their problems. I can refer people seeking help to appropriate agencies. If I am presented with a problem, I try to find a solution or a service that helps with the problem.

Verbal

_____ 1. I can talk with friends, but talking before large groups frightens me. I can write a letter to a friend, but writing a report is difficult. I do not read a great deal and often I do not understand what I read.

_____ 2. I can talk to small groups on a familiar subject. I can read and understand most materials if they are not extremely technical or difficult. I can write or present an oral report using a variety of sentence structures.

_____ 3. I am effective when speaking to large groups. My vocabulary is large and I use it well both in speaking and in writing. I can skillfully prepare extensive written materials and I am an excellent reader.

Art

_____ 1. I can dance simple steps, or play a musical instrument in an elementary way, or draw something if I can copy it, or originate a very simple design.

_____ 2. I can dance to most musical rhythms, or I have sung or played a musical instrument in a group or alone, or I have drawn or painted something that has been put on display.

_____ 3. I can easily pick up a new dance step or routine; I have danced either in a group or alone in a performance, or I have had extensive musical training either vocally or instrumentally.

Now that you've tested your skills in eight areas, let's get the results on paper. Fill in the following chart—and remember it well for future reference.

SKILLS

Career Field	I can do these well	I can do these OK	I can't do these well
Scientific			
Mechanical			
Clerical			
Computational			
Sales			
Social Service			
Verbal			
Art			

Although these pages focus on what you do well, here's a preview of how all the parts will fit together by the end of this section. Check over the eight categories again and, this time, decide how much you like each one. Fill in this chart, too.

INTERESTS

Career Field	Turns me off	Some interest	Really interesting
Scientific			
Mechanical			
Clerical			
Computational			
Sales			
Social Service			
Verbal			
Art			

You've already guessed that if you have both a high skill and interest in the same field, the merger is a sign that you may have hit on a happy choice.

Suppose your skills and interest coincide in the scientific, computational, and mechanical categories. This suggests that engineering is a lively option for you.

High ratings in mechanical, verbal, and art categories are a clue to look at architecture, printing, landscape architecture, and interior design.

Match-ups in clerical, sales, and verbal categories point to sales manager, travel agent, retail buyer, or personnel counselor.

One more illustration: If you ranked high in computational, clerical, and sales categories, don't overlook such options as store manager, computer programmer, computer sales representative, certified public accountant, or mathematics teacher.

Clearly, these informal self-help guides are like all tests—fallible. But they do help move you off point zero.

Behind Yesterday's Hills: New Skills

This activity is also based on the diary approach. On the theory that history is the best predictor of the future, we want you to take a backward look at your life for inklings of skills you'll use in the future.

Write at least two accomplishments for various life segments, starting at age seven. Seek help in the memory department from your family.

What is an accomplishment? It's anything you did that you think was wonderful. It's anything you have felt proud of doing and enjoyed. It's anything that was satisfying and meaningful.

Perhaps you were the spelling champ in the third grade or maybe you resisted enormous peer pressure to do drugs in the tenth grade.

It's possible you brought home an A in Spanish, even though you have a tinny ear for languages. Were you the features editor for your school paper? Did you earn the money to buy your own car? Even if the high spot of your life last year was to organize your class notes into neat files, that's an accomplishment.

Accomplishments need not be network news, just important to you personally.

Once you begin rolling down memory lane, you'll be surprised at how many accomplishments you have to your credit.

That's the easy part. The hard part is that for the activity to be of major value, you must analyze the skills used to make every accomplishment happen.

If you were a school newspaper features editor, you probably used these skills: planning page layouts, decision making, instructing writers, writing, editing, proofreading, researching, persuading people to be interviewed, and more.

Splitting accomplishments into skills is a challenging task. It's not the sort of thing you do every day, so it may take awhile to get into the swing of it. Don't be discouraged if you're stymied.

When you're stuck, just take your time and review the examples of activities and functions again, and the list of marketable skills listed earlier in this section. Inspiration will strike.

Here's a format for your convenience, but you'll probably want to expand it on sheets of blank paper.

Yesterday's Hills and New Skills Format		
Life Segments	Accomplishments	Skills
5–9 years old		
10–12 years old		
13–15 years old		
16–18 years old		
19–21 years old		
22–25 years old		

Skills From Data, People, and Things

Another way to part the curtain of uncertainty surrounding your future is to look for skills you can market by using the data, people, and things concept.

♦ *Data* are information, ideas, statistics, and facts.

♦ *People*—all ages, both genders, every ethnic and racial group, and social class.

♦ *Things* means tools, machines, equipment, and materials.

All jobs involve all three categories of data, people, and things, but most jobs emphasize one over the other. The researcher works with data; the nurse with people; and the engineer with things.

When you get within striking distance of making a career choice, you'll want to keep these broad divisions in mind, but in this section we use the concept as a treasure chest from which to pull skills you may have.

DATA ARE:

words ♦ symbols ♦ knowledge ♦ facts ♦ information ♦ numbers ♦ ideas ♦ charts ♦ graphs ♦ designs ♦ blueprints ♦ statistics ♦ opinions ♦ theories ♦ techniques ♦ budgets ♦ evaluation measures ♦ tests ♦ drawings ♦ flowcharts ♦ surveys ♦ costs ♦ work assignments ♦ objectives ♦ goals ♦ policies ♦ procedures ♦ recommendations ♦ memoranda ♦ curriculum ♦ monitor systems ♦ stock-figures ♦ handbooks ♦ guidelines ♦ literature ♦ historical documents ♦ catalogs ♦ reports ♦ regulations ♦ briefs ♦ future plans

What skills can you use in working with data? In the list below, circle those that most appeal to you. Underline those you have used.

examining ♦ comparing ♦ calculating ♦ computing ♦ gathering ♦ compiling ♦ classifying ♦ filing ♦ analyzing ♦ collating ♦ observing ♦ investigating ♦ composing ♦ reporting ♦ presenting ♦ organizing ♦ writing ♦ reading ♦ copying ♦ creating ♦ transcribing ♦ coordinating ♦ combining ♦ synthesizing ♦ interpreting

PEOPLE MIGHT BE:

children ◆ young adults ◆ elderly ◆ Asian American ◆ Latino ◆ African American ◆ Caucasian ◆ gifted ◆ college students ◆ professional ◆ tradespeople ◆ economically disadvantaged ◆ powerful ◆ influential ◆ physically or mentally challenged ◆ extroverted ◆ introverted ◆ middle-aged ◆ ill ◆ ex-offenders ◆ abused ◆ religious ◆ foreigners ◆ political ◆ chemically dependent ◆ wealthy ◆ middle-class ◆ rigid ◆ flexible ◆ conformist ◆ free-spirited ◆ high achieving ◆ ambitious

What skills can you use in working with people? Circle those that most appeal to you. Underline those you have used.

attending to ◆ serving ◆ taking instruction from ◆ supervising ◆ communicating ◆ instructing ◆ caring for ◆ persuading ◆ managing ◆ training ◆ teaching ◆ entertaining ◆ motivating ◆ coaching ◆ consulting ◆ coordinating ◆ treating ◆ leading ◆ facilitating ◆ criticizing ◆ counseling ◆ advising ◆ negotiating ◆ confronting ◆ informing ◆ empathizing ◆ problem-solving ◆ supporting

THINGS INCLUDE:

electrical sockets ◆ lamps ◆ photocopy machines ◆ computers ◆ stoves ◆ brooms ◆ vacuum sweepers ◆ ovens ◆ pots ◆ paper ◆ chain saws ◆ pliers ◆ screwdrivers ◆ lawn mowers ◆ power tools ◆ heavy equipment ◆ fork-lift trucks ◆ cars ◆ bicycles ◆ motor bikes ◆ telephones ◆ gauges ◆ controls ◆ hair dryers ◆ laser equipment ◆ microwave ovens ◆ furnaces ◆ air conditioners ◆ nuclear reactors ◆ gasoline motors ◆ electric motors ◆ transformers ◆ gas turbines ◆ cleaning equipment ◆ cameras ◆ showers ◆ spinning wheels ◆ building supplies ◆ dental equipment ◆ airplanes

What skills can you use in working with things? Circle those that most appeal to you. Underline those you have used.

moving ◆ pushing ◆ carrying ◆ feeding ◆ loading ◆ running ◆ emptying ◆ stacking ◆ flying ◆ starting ◆ delivering ◆ adjusting ◆ monitoring ◆ manipulating ◆ cutting ◆ guiding ◆ assembling ◆ operating ◆ controlling ◆ regulating ◆ setting ◆ overseeing ◆ adapting ◆ designing ◆ demonstrating ◆ repairing ◆ keyboarding ◆ painting ◆ calibrating ◆ selling

Summarize the skills you prefer to use in each category on the following form:

Skills Summary	Data	People	Things
Skills I prefer to use in working with:			

Now that you've pulled together market-able skills, you have—or can easily develop— information for the identity inventory of your aptitudes and skills.

Identity Inventory:
MY APTITUDES & SKILLS

What I may be able to do in the future with training and experience—or can do now—that will help my career.

1. _____
2. _____
3. _____
4. _____
5. _____
6. _____
7. _____
8. _____
9. _____
10. _____
11. _____
12. _____
13. _____
14. _____
15. _____

16. _____
17. _____
18. _____
19. _____
20. _____
21. _____
22. _____
23. _____
24. _____

SUMMARY: (Five job skills that I have right now.)

1. _____
2. _____
3. _____
4. _____
5. _____

Skill Secrets From School Records

Your educational track record is set in black and white. By bringing your grades to the fore now, you'll clearly see how they reflect both skills and interests.

And you'll have to face up to the possibility that your academic talents aren't up to your aspirations. When you're panting to be a veterinarian but are going down the tubes in chemistry, you'll have to bring your grades up or choose another career.

If reports of your grades seem to have been eaten by the family dog, obtain a transcript from your guidance counselor or registrar.

Working with the transcript, fill in the identity inventory of your academic abilities.

Identity Inventory:
MY ACADEMIC ABILITIES

My most important educational experience:

_____

_____

Job-related courses I liked and did well in: | Knowledge & skills gained in this course:

General courses I liked and did well in: | Knowledge & skills gained in this course:

What Are Your Personal Values?

No matter how many frills are added, the concept of personal values is simply a matter of what is and what isn't important to you.

These two no-nonsense activities will help to sort out your personal priorities, always an important consideration in a career choice.

What Counts Most

Rank the following considerations. Place the number **1** before the item most important to you, the number **2** before the item that is next in importance, and so on.

_____ Satisfying and successful career

_____ Job security

_____ Good family relationships

_____ A world without discrimination

_____ International fame

_____ Pleasure

_____ Strong religious faith

_____ Lovely home in a beautiful setting

_____ Self-knowledge

_____ Ability or position to influence world affairs

_____ Satisfying love relationship

_____ The right to do what I want

_____ Excitement

_____ Ability to stimulate and/or influence the minds of others

_____ Enough money to live comfortably

_____ Sense of accomplishment

_____ A world in which humans and nature are in balance

_____ Love and understanding of friends

Feel free to talk over your ranking with family and friends. Consider what you would accept as a substitute—a trade-off—for each value; suppose job security is a high-ranking value but you would consider unusual opportunity as a substitute. These are lively discussion topics and new doors of understanding may open. There are no right or wrong answers. After doing this exercise, summarize what's important to you on the values identity inventory.

How Do You Really Feel About Work?

Now that you have a better idea of where you stand on personal values, shift gears and determine how you feel about work values.

Which of the following statements most accurately reflect your feelings about work?

Nothing is really work unless you would rather be doing something else. (SIR JAMES BARRIE)

By working faithfully eight hours a day, you may eventually get to be a boss and work 12 hours a day. (ROBERT FROST)

If you first don't succeed, try, try again. Then quit. There's no use being a damn fool about it. (W. C. FIELDS)

Identity Inventory:
MY PERSONAL LIFE VALUES

Value (Order of importance)

1. _____

2. _____

3. _____

4. _____

5. _____

Trade-off (What I would accept as a substitute)

1. _____

2. _____

3. _____

4. _____

5. _____

SUMMARY: (Top two values, which are "must haves")

1. _____

2. _____

As motivational expert Denis Waitley has said, "Attitude is a choice you make." Note your attitudes about work on the following evaluation form. It may be interesting to ask family members and friends to try this activity, too, and compare your response with theirs.

WORK VALUES EVALUATION

I would prefer (Select A or B)

_____ A. Work for organization
_____ B. Self-employment

_____ A. Structured environment: well defined duties and responsibilities
_____ B. Unstructured work: room for creativity and initiative

_____ A. Short hours: maximum eight hours per day
_____ B. Long hours and weekend work usual

_____ A. Similar duties every day
_____ B. Variety of duties every day

_____ A. Fast pace, high pressure
_____ B. Slow pace, low pressure

_____ A. Work indoors in pleasant environment
_____ B. Work outdoors in all weather and conditions

_____ A. Work for large business
_____ B. Work for small business

_____ A. High prestige and status
_____ B. Low prestige and status

_____ A. Work opportunities after 65
_____ B. Early retirement

_____ A. Few opportunities for advancement and professional development
_____ B. Many opportunities for advancement and professional development

_____ A. Work alone
_____ B. Work with other people

_____ A. Close supervision
_____ B. No supervision

_____ A. High level of responsibility: make key decisions
_____ B. Low level of responsibility: no critical decisions

_____ A. Guaranteed regular hours
_____ B. Possible overtime

_____ A. Challenges and risks in work
_____ B. Work offers security

_____ A. Visible end products: specific achievable goals
_____ B. Can't see results of work, long-range goals

_____ A. Work in specific geographical area
_____ B. Willing to relocate anywhere

_____ A. Live close to work
_____ B. Live half hour or more from work

_____ A. Little or no travel
_____ B. Frequent travel

_____ A. Little work with machines
_____ B. Close work with machines

Now that you know you want a job in which you're not required to work more than two hours a day, that will pay $200,000 a year, and that guarantees lifetime security, what more is there to say? Say it anyway and say it on your identity inventory for work values.

Identity Inventory:
MY WORK VALUES

Values (Order of importance)

1. _____
2. _____
3. _____
4. _____
5. _____
6. _____
7. _____

Trade-off (What I would accept as a substitute)

1. _____
2. _____
3. _____
4. _____
5. _____
6. _____
7. _____

SUMMARY: (Top three values, which are "must haves")

1. _____
2. _____
3. _____   3. _____

Your Personality: Which Type Are You?

What do Madonna, Ricki Lake, Bruce Willis, Damon Wayans, Janet Jackson, and Joan Chen have in common? None of them is an ISTP or an ISTJ. (You'll understand once you study the charts on the following pages.)

The alphabet soup refers to scores in a widely used personality measure, the Myers-Briggs Type Indicator (MBTI). It is based on Swiss psychiatrist Carl Jung's theory that there are 16 basic personality types. Jung's theory was embellished by two women before it became a popular test.

In the early 1940s, Katharine Briggs and her daughter, Isabel Briggs Myers, questioned people whose personality types they already had identified.

They asked about general attitudes toward the world, how information was processed, and how decisions were made. From that research the mother-daughter team designed the MBTI.

SENSING TYPES

INTROVERTS

1. ISTJ (INTROVERT, SENSING, THINKING, JUDGING)
Serious, quiet, earn success by concentration and thoroughness. Practical, orderly, matter-of-fact, logical, realistic, and dependable. See to it that everything is well organized. Take responsibility. Make up their own minds as to what should be accomplished and work toward it steadily, regardless of protests or distractions.

2. ISFJ (INTROVERT, SENSING, FEELING, JUDGING)
Quiet, friendly, responsible, and conscientious. Work devotedly to meet their obligations and serve their friends and school. Thorough, painstaking, accurate. May need time to master technical subjects, as their interests are usually not technical. Patient with detail and routine. Loyal, considerate, concerned with how other people feel.

5. ISTP (INTROVERT, SENSING, THINKING, PERCEPTIVE)
Cool onlookers—quiet, reserved, observing, and analyzing life with detached curiosity and unexpected flashes of original humor. Usually interested in impersonal principles, cause and effect, how and why mechanical things work. Exert themselves no more than they think necessary, because any waste of energy would be inefficient.

6. ISFP (INTROVERT, SENSING, FEELING, PERCEPTIVE)
Retiring, quietly friendly, sensitive, kind, modest about their abilities. Shun disagreements, do not force their opinions or values on others. Usually do not care to lead but are often loyal followers. Often relaxed about getting things done, because they enjoy the present moment and do not want to spoil it by undue haste or exertion.

EXTROVERTS

9. ESTP (EXTROVERT, SENSING, THINKING, PERCEPTIVE)
Matter-of-fact, do not worry or hurry, enjoy whatever comes along. Tend to like mechanical things and sports, with friends on the side. May be a bit blunt or insensitive. Can do math or science when they see the need. Dislike long explanations. Are best with real things that can be worked, handled, taken apart, or put together.

10. ESFP (EXTROVERT, SENSING, FEELING, PERCEPTIVE)
Outgoing, easygoing, accepting, friendly, fond of a good time. Like sports and making things. Know what's going on and join in eagerly. Find remembering facts easier than mastering theories. Are best in situations that need sound common sense and practical ability with people as well as with things.

13. ESTJ (EXTROVERT, SENSING, THINKING, JUDGING)
Practical, realistic, matter-of-fact with a natural head for business or mechanics. Not interested in subjects they see no use for, but can apply themselves when necessary. Like to organize and run activities. May make good administrators, especially if they remember to consider others' feelings and points of view.

14. ESFJ (EXTROVERT, SENSING, FEELING, JUDGING)
Warm-hearted, talkative, popular, conscientious, born cooperators, active committee members. Always doing some thing nice for someone. Work best with encouragement and praise. Little interest in abstract thinking or technical subjects. Main interest is in things that directly and visibly affect people's lives.

INTUITIVE TYPES

3. INFJ (INTROVERT, INTUITIVE, FEELING, JUDGING) Succeed by perseverance, originality, and desire to do whatever is needed or wanted. Put their best efforts into their work. Quietly forceful, conscientious, concerned for others. Respected for their firm principles. Likely to be honored and followed for their clear convictions as to how best to serve the common good.	4. INTJ (INTROVERT, INTUITIVE, THINKING, JUDGING) Usually have original minds and great drive when they choose to use them. In fields that appeal to them, they have a fine power to organize a job and carry it through with or without help. Skeptical, critical, independent, determined, often stubborn. Must learn to yield less important points in order to win the most important.
7. INFP (INTROVERT, INTUITIVE, FEELING, PERCEPTIVE) Full of enthusiasms and loyalties, but seldom talk of these until they know you well. Care about learning ideas, language, and independent projects of their own. Tend to undertake too much, then somehow get it done. Friendly, but often too absorbed in what they are doing to be sociable. Little concerned with possessions or physical surroundings.	8. INTP (INTROVERT, INTUITIVE, THINKING, PERCEPTIVE) Quiet, reserved, brilliant in exams, especially in theoretical or scientific subjects. Logical to the point of hair-splitting. Usually interested mainly in ideas, with little liking for parties or small talk. Need to have sharply defined interests. Tend to choose careers where some strong interest can be used and useful.
11. ENFP (EXTROVERT, INTUITIVE, FEELING, PERCEPTIVE) Warmly enthusiastic, high-spirited, ingenious, imaginative. Able to do almost anything that interests them. Quick with a solution for any difficulty and ready to help anyone with a problem. Often rely on their ability to improvise instead of preparing in advance. Can usually find compelling reasons for whatever they want.	12. ENTP (EXTROVERT, INTUITIVE, THINKING, PERCEPTIVE) Quick, ingenious, good at many things. Stimulating company, alert and out-spoken. May argue for fun on either side of a question. Resourceful in solving new and challenging problems, but may neglect routine assignments. Often turn to one new interest after another. Skillful in finding logical reasons for what they want.
15. ENFJ (EXTROVERT, INTUITIVE, FEELING, JUDGING) Responsive and responsible. Generally feel real concern for what others think or want, and try to handle things with due regard for other people's feelings. Can present a proposal or lead a group discussion with ease and tact. Sociable, popular, active in school affairs, but time enough on their studies to do good work.	16. ENTJ (EXTROVERT, INTUITIVE, THINKING, JUDGING) Hearty, frank, able in studies, leaders in activities. Usually good in anything that requires reasoning and intelligent talk, such as public speaking. Are usually well-informed and keep adding to their fund of knowledge. May sometimes be more positive and confident than experience in an area warrants.

INTROVERTS

EXTROVERTS

The test takes about 45 minutes to an hour to complete. It is designed to identify your preferences in four dimensions:

1. **Extroversion or introversion (E or I)**

2. **Sensing or intuition (S or N)**

3. **Thinking or feeling (T or F)**

4. **Judging or perception (J or P)**

Once you identify your type, you are given possible career options.

If you want to take the Myers-Briggs Type Indicator, published by the Consulting Psychologist Press, ask at a school counseling center or private counseling service.

Before looking for advance clues as to which type you are, remember that all people usually possess, in varying degrees, each of the described characteristics. The Myers-Briggs scores suggest those the test taker prefers. Moreover, while results identify occupations in which people with similar qualities have done well, others with differing scores may be suited for the same occupations.

Your Working Style

Have you found your personality type? If so, reflect on these typical working styles associated with each characteristic.

Extroverts

like variety and action

tend to be faster than average

dislike complicated procedures

are often good at greeting people

are often impatient with long, slow jobs

often don't mind interruptions

often act quickly, sometimes without thinking

like to have people around

communicate freely

Introverts

like quiet for concentration

tend to be careful with details

dislike sweeping statements

don't like interruptions

work contentedly alone

may have problems communicating

Sensing Types

dislike new problems

like established way of doing things

enjoy using skills already learned more than learning new ones

work along steadily with realistic idea of how long it will take

reach a conclusion step by step

are patient with routine details

are impatient with complicated details

are seldom inspired and rarely trust inspiration

seldom make errors of fact

Intuitive Types

like solving new problems

dislike doing the same things over and over again

enjoy learning a new skill and using it

put two and two together quickly

are impatient with routine details

follow their inspirations—good or bad

often get their facts a bit wrong

Thinking Types

are relatively unemotional and uninterested in people's feelings

may hurt people's feelings without knowing it

like analysis and putting things into logical order

can get along without harmony

tend to decide impersonally, sometimes ignoring people's wishes

need to be treated fairly

are able to reprimand people or fire them when necessary

tend to relate well only to other thinking types

may seem hardhearted

Feeling Types

tend to be very aware of other people's feelings

like harmony; efficiency may be badly disturbed by office feuds

often let decisions be influenced by their own or other people's likes and dislikes

need occasional praise

dislike telling people unpleasant things

relate well to most people

tend to be sympathetic

Judging Types

are best when they can plan their work and follow the plan

like to get things settled and wrapped up

may decide things too quickly

may dislike to interrupt the project they are working on for one more urgent

may not notice new things that need to be done

want only the essentials needed to get on with a job

tend to be satisfied once they reach a judgment on a thing, situation, or person

Perceptive Types

tend to be good at adapting to changing situations

don't mind leaving things open for alterations

may have trouble making decisions

may start too many projects and have difficulty finishing them

may postpone unpleasant jobs

want to know all about a new job

tend to be curious and welcome new light on a thing, situation, or person

Occupations and Types

Some of the career choices that seem to be associated with each personality type follow.

Caution: Do not consider only these examples. Each activity and example in this section is selected to help you expand your options—not to limit them.

Later on we'll discuss the best time and the best way to narrow your choices.

1. ISTJ (introvert, sensing, thinking, judging)

6 percent of the general population

Words/Phrases Describing This Type
decisiveness in practical affairs
super dependable
their word is their bond
quiet and serious
very persevering
conserve resources of employer
dedicated
thorough
good at details
don't take chances
orderly
traditionalist

Examples of Suitable Careers
accountant
auditor
bank examiner
business executive
computer programmer
financial planner
legal secretary
library supervisor
mechanical engineer
mortician
tax examiner
traffic analyst

2. ISFJ (introvert, sensing, feeling, judging)

6 percent of the general population

Words/Phrases Describing This Type
desire to be of service
minister to individual needs
seek continuity in relationships
value traditions
believe work is good and play must be earned
efficient
procedures of the company are law

irritated when others don't follow rules
dependable
thorough
steady
loyal

Examples of Suitable Careers
accountant
animal caretaker
counselor
dietician
librarian
nurse
pharmacist
physical therapist
physician
secretary
social worker
teacher

3. INFJ (introvert, intuitive, feeling, judging)

1 percent of the general population

Words/Phrases Describing This Type
want to help
can deal with complex issues
achievers
take work seriously
enjoy academic activity
perfectionists
exert quiet influence
reserved
easily hurt
find conflict disagreeable
imaginative
artistic

Examples of Suitable Careers
air traffic controller
chemist
clergyperson
composer
counselor
dentist
mathematician
nurse

pilot
poet
psychologist
writer

4. INTJ (introvert, intuitive, thinking, judging)
1 percent of the general population

Words/Phrases Describing This Type
self-confident
introspective
realistic
not impressed by authority
conform to rules if they make sense
open to new ideas
good at generalizing and summarizing
stimulated by challenges
creative
unemotional
independent
future-oriented

Examples of Suitable Careers
auditor
bank examiner
chemist
engineer
executive
geologist
lawyer
librarian
mathematics teacher
scientific researcher
systems analyst
tax examiner

5. ISTP (introvert, sensing, thinking, perceptive)
6 percent of the general population

Words/Phrases Describing This Type
detached
action-oriented
like factual, practical matters
work long hours on activities of interest
unpredictable

impulsive
restless
tolerate solitude
enjoy hands-on activities
prefer to gain expertise through experience
troubleshooter
negotiator

Examples of Suitable Careers
antique dealer
appliance repairer
art historian
automobile mechanic
cabinetmaker
economist
electrical engineer
jeweler
pilot
statistician
surgeon
tool designer

6. ISFP (introvert, sensing, feeling, perceptive)
6 percent of the general population

Words/Phrases Describing This Type
free spirit
experience intensity of feeling
sensuous
practical
enjoy nature
not interested in fitting in
communicate through action, not words
independent
live for the moment
seek excitement
have wanderlust
adaptable

Examples of Suitable Careers
animal keeper
artist
biologist
chef
counselor
environmentalist

forester
musician
oceanographer
sailor
truckdriver
wildlife worker

7. INFP (introvert, intuitive, feeling, perceptive)

1 percent of the general population

Words/Phrases Describing This Type
capacity for caring
shy
reserved
idealistic
sense of honor
deep commitment
welcome new ideas
work well alone
dislike interruptions
impatient with routine
scholarly
creative

Examples of Suitable Careers
character actor
clergyperson
counselor
dietitian
historian
interior decorator
journalist
music teacher
novelist
public relations writer
reference librarian
translator

8. INTP (introvert, intuitive, thinking, perceptive)

1 percent of the general population

Words/Phrases Describing This Type
precise in thought and language
architect of ideas and systems
principled

desire to understand the universe
curious
intellectual
analytical
logical
taskmaster
prize intelligence in others
work quietly without interruption
tend to be arrogant

Examples of Suitable Careers
actuary
architect
artist
credit analyst
economist
financial planner
lawyer
logician
mathematician
philosopher
professor
systems analyst

9. ESTP (extrovert, sensing, thinking, perceptive)

13 percent of the general population

Words/Phrases Describing This Type
resourceful
people of action
friendly
do things with a flourish
social
unpredictable
witty and clever
fun to be with
pragmatic
don't care to justify actions
initiator
sophisticated

Examples of Suitable Careers
advertising executive
announcer
coach
consultant

diplomat
disc jockey
entrepreneur
landscape architect
marketing specialist
sales representative
secretary
travel agent

10. ESFP (extrovert, sensing, feeling, perceptive)
13 percent of the general population

Words/Phrases Describing This Type
radiate warmth and optimism
smooth
witty and clever
charming
fun to be with
avoid being alone
sophisticated
enjoy good things in life
unpredictable
generous
impulsive

Examples of Suitable Careers
actor
advertising executive
chef
clergyperson
fashion designer
marketing specialist
model
nurse
photographer
physician
secretary
teacher

11. ENFP (extrovert, intuitive, feeling, perceptive)
5 percent of the general population

Words/Phrases Describing This Type
see life as an exciting drama
spontaneous

believe intense emotional experiences are vital
keen observers
very alert
easily bored
enjoy creating ideas or projects
not interested in follow through
enthusiastic
independent
optimistic
creative

Examples of Suitable Careers
actor
advertising specialist
counselor
defense attorney
drama teacher
editorial writer
foreign service officer
newspaper reporter
playwright
politician
psychologist
salesperson

12. ENTP (extrovert, intuitive, thinking, perceptive)
5 percent of the general population

Words/Phrases Describing This Type
enthusiastic
analytical
look for better ways to do things
confident
will not believe "It can't be done"
good conversationalist
enjoy debate
adaptable
innovative
improvise
life of the party
avoid unpleasant situations

Examples of Suitable Careers
actor
architect

fashion designer
job analyst
journalist
landscape architect
lawyer
marketing specialist
photographer
physician
political scientist
teacher

13. ESTJ (extrovert, sensing, thinking, judging)

13 percent of the general population

Words/Phrases Describing This Type
pillars of strength
responsible
like to see things done correctly
analytical
realistic
punctual
follow routines
well organized
dependable
consistent
preserve the establishment
tend to accumulate responsibilities

Examples of Suitable Careers
bank executive
building contractor
church administrator
claims adjuster
curator
economist
judge
lawyer
loan officer
military officer
office manager
urban planner

14. ESFJ (extrovert, sensing, feeling, judging)

13 percent of the general population

Words/Phrases Describing This Type
sociable
dislike conflict
traditions are important
conscientious
orderly
hurt by indifference
nostalgic
idealistic
conscious of appearances
value opinion of others
loyal
sympathetic

Examples of Suitable Careers
athletic director
clergyperson
cosmetologist
counselor
nurse supervisor
military officer
occupational therapist
physician
professor
salesperson
secretary
veterinarian

15. ENFJ (extrovert, intuitive, feeling, judging)

5 percent of the general population

Words/Phrases Describing This Type
leader
socially adept
try to please
feel responsible for feelings of others
tend to idealize relationships
involved
supportive
commitment to people
comfortable in unstructured situations
tolerant
trustworthy
articulate effectively

Examples of Suitable Careers
actor
arbitrator
clergyperson
counselor
family therapist
graphic designer
lawyer
newscaster
public relations specialist
salesperson
teacher
urban planner

16. ENTJ (extrovert, intuitive, thinking, judging)

5 percent of the general population

Words/Phrases Describing This Type
leader
urge to structure
task-oriented
tolerant
efficient
tend to take over
look to long-range goals
tend to be visionaries
devoted to their job
decisive
impersonal
organize people into smooth running groups

Examples of Suitable Careers
auditor
buyer
city manager
fund-raiser
funeral director
hospital administrator
hotel manager
military officer
office administrator
school principal
store manager
teacher

You'll notice that some occupations are suggested for several personality types. One reason is that some occupations are divided into specialties. A trial lawyer, for instance, probably would be an extrovert, whereas a patent lawyer might be an introvert. A public relations writer may be an introvert, while a public relations account executive who deals with media is likely to be an extrovert.

Another reason is that people who fall into categories that differ only on one trait (letter) will share similar characteristics and thus certain careers may be common to them.

These examples are for general information only. For more details on the MBTI, see a career counselor.

Lifestyle: Figuring Out What You Want

Maybe you still aren't 100 percent sure whether you want to share the sky with eagles or the ground with prairie chickens, but by now you do have an insider's knowledge of yourself. (See "To The Reader" p. xx.)

Use this enlightenment to anticipate your preferred lifestyle. When people gripe about their jobs being dismal or their lives uninspiring, look for a lifestyle that is incompatible with their values.

What is lifestyle, exactly? The answer is profound, yet simple: It's how you live your entire life.

NOTE: The data on percentages, type descriptions, and sample career options are drawn from the tapes and writings of Isabel Briggs-Myers, as well as independent research conducted by one of the authors, Dr. Darryl Laramore.

Identity Inventory:
MY PERSONALITY TRAITS

Evaluations by myself and others suggest that I have the following characteristics:

1. _____
2. _____
3. _____
4. _____
5. _____
6. _____
7. _____
8. _____
9. _____
10. _____
11. _____
12. _____

SUMMARY: My five most dominant traits are:

1. _____
2. _____
3. _____
4. _____
5. _____

Lifestyle includes where you reside geographically—North, South, East, or West. It includes whether you live in a small town, large city, farm, military base, or convent. It includes whether you live in a rental apartment, condominium, detached family dwelling, houseboat, or estate with guarded gates.

No matter where you live, area and residence color your life. Your days living near the ocean or in the mountains will be quite different from your days in the desert or the flat Midwest.

Lifestyle also includes leisure-time pursuits. If fishing every other day is your idea of heaven and you live in New York City, the odds are you will not be completely satisfied with your lifestyle.

Your lifestyle includes the kind of car you drive, the amount of traveling you do, and the kinds of vacations you take. It includes the types of friends you have.

What decides lifestyle? In most major ways, your decisions set the stage. Contributing factors are your education, marital status, and family responsibilities.

Beyond that, the chief determiner of how your lifestyle shapes up is your career, and, increasingly, in an age of two-income families, the career of your spouse.

Unless you live off an inheritance, your career determines whether you can pay for the lifestyle you want and whether you have enough time from your job to enjoy it.

Your Own Crystal Ball

There's no time like the present to pick up a tablet of paper, find a quiet corner, and jot down your visions of what a lifestyle should be. Be sure to include your values and try to project yourself into the future. These headings can serve as a guide:

Residence. Where do I want to live? (Describe in detail the geographical location, the kind of apartment or house, and your surroundings.)

Work Values. What kinds of things do I want to do on the job? (Include a description of the physical location of your workplace and the kinds of people you want to work with. Example: I want to work where I can be outside a great deal and work mostly by myself.)

Friends. What kinds of people do I want to be associating with socially?

Family Life. What do I want my family to be like? This includes marriage, children, and so forth.

Recreation and Cultural. Which cultural resources do I want to be available? Libraries?

Theater? Museums? (Don't just jot things down; describe in detail where you want to go and how often.)

Hobbies. Which hobbies do I want to participate in?

Education. How much education do I want?

Finances. How much money do I want to make?

Scenarios

As the saying goes: "Just when you've got it together, somebody moves it."

So it is with lifestyles. Unforeseen changes may dramatically alter your wish list.

Here are a number of stories about the lifestyles several people wished for, and what happened in real life. For each case history, ask yourself how you would cope in the situation.

What would pull you through—education, skills, reserves of personal strength?

This activity could makes for great after-dinner discussion at the family dining table.

Debbie

Debbie wants to live in a small town, where she will be close to nature and away from the pressures of a big city. She wants to work outdoors most of the time. She would like to raise animals. She wants to ride and show horses as a hobby. She wants to get married and have four children, she thinks. She would like her husband to share her interest in animals.

Debbie also likes camping and would like her family to share her interests. She enjoys the company of a few friends, but does not care for large gatherings or parties. She wants to be active behind the scenes in some community activities. Debbie wants secure careers for herself and her husband, but her needs are simple and most of her leisure pursuits are simple.

She figures that extra income can be made by breeding horses. Because Debbie wants to spend time with her children when they are young, she would like a career that could be interrupted or continued on a part-time basis.

Real life: Debbie went to a dude ranch on vacation, met Joe, and married him. Joe, an investment banker, was offered a Wall Street position too good to turn down. The newlyweds moved to New York City. Two years after their marriage, Joe decided he did not want children.

How would you cope with this unforeseen change?

Peter

Peter wants a job that will utilize his creative ability and isn't routine. He would like some travel in his job. The idea of working from 9 to 5 sounds awful to Peter. He would prefer to have a job where he can perform a task at a time of his choosing. He wouldn't mind having several projects to work on at the same time.

The atmosphere of Peter's work environment must be modern and neat. He also wants a nice house. Peter wants his wife to work, too. He hopes both he and his wife will have professional careers so their circle of friends will be stimulating. He believes that a suburb would best suit his needs.

Real life: Peter became an insurance broker. He married a librarian who worked for two years before she became pregnant and quit her job. She told Peter she felt she should stay home with their child for several years at least. Peter has to choose between scrimping and lowering their lifestyle, or accepting a higher-paying but rigid job.

How would you cope with this unforeseen change?

Cheryl

Cheryl loves the ocean and water sports. She loves to boat, water ski, and surf. She hates cold weather. She wants to own a boat and a house with a view of the ocean.

All these things are expensive, so she knows that she will need a career that pays well but will allow enough time for her to enjoy leisure pursuits. She wouldn't mind working in the city if she can enjoy a home on the beach. She would also like access to tennis courts. She would eventually like a family, but has no desire to marry soon. She likes structure, so she wants a job where she knows what to expect.

Real life: Cheryl graduated from high school but decided against further education or training. She was in a hurry to get to the sun and fun. Cheryl moved to Maui, Hawaii, from her native Ohio, knowing no one in her new state.

Cheryl was lucky and quickly found evening work as a waitress at a resort hotel, a job that left her days free for the beach.

After three years, Cheryl became weary of her life. She decided she'd had it with living on an island without good friends. She was tired of her job, and of the people she met on the beach—they didn't seem to think the same way about things as she did.

Cheryl was debating whether she should return to Ohio where she knew people and where the values of the community were those she had grown up with when she was fired from her job.

How would you cope with this unforeseen change?

John

John never missed a police show on TV. From the time he was 12, he talked about going into police work when he grew up.

John's father, a doctor, wanted him to become a doctor, too, or at least a lawyer. He believed John would outgrow his early passion.

To please his father, John enrolled in a college and began to prepare for a life as a professional and the good-life rewards it would bring. But John never stopped saying he wanted to be a detective.

Real life: John hated book work and dropped out of college after one miserable year. During the ensuing shouting match with his father, John kept trying to explain that he just wasn't a student.

He preferred action, being out and around all day—not being behind a desk or around a bunch of sick people.

John never married and his dream came true. He became a fine police officer and was on his way to becoming a detective when he was shot in the line of duty. Afterwards, John was destined to spend the remainder of his life in a wheelchair.

The police chief personally offered John a desk job in personnel. John was grateful. Then it hit him: John would never be promoted in the personnel department until he returned to college and obtained his sheepskin. What an ironic twist of fate, John thought, being forced back to the very schooling he'd escaped a decade earlier.

How would you cope with this unforeseen change?

■ ■ ■ ■

Fairy Tales and Reality

You've been a good sport, sticking with us through both your wish list and the harsh doses of reality that sometimes happen in real life. For that kindness, we have a special treat for you.

Here's a fantasy capsule of Snow White's lifestyle. We admit we carried her life a bit further than the Brothers Grimm intended.

The Lifestyle of Snow White

Age	Residence	Major Activities	People Close to Snow White
15	luxurious castle	being tutored playing with dukes and duchesses	father governess
20	small cottage	feeding dwarfs cleaning cottage buying apples from queens dressed as witches	Happy Sleepy Grumpy Sneezy Dopey Doc Bashful
30	castle	raising young princess redecorating castle giving parties	husband princess
60	small cottage on castle grounds	watching TV playing bingo babysitting young princes and princesses	daughter grandkids

Don't give up yet. There's only one more identity inventory to complete—it's on lifestyle preferences.

Identity Inventory:
MY LIFESTYLE PREFERENCES

First choice

If I could design my life, I would prefer:

Urban, rural area _____

Part of country _____

Have extra leisure time _____
(yes, no)

Working indoors, outdoors _____

Working days, evenings, nights _____

Working weekends, off week days _____
(yes, no)

Not working weekends _____
(yes, no)

To run my own business _____
(yes, no)

To leave my work at the office _____
(yes, no)

To carry my work in my head _____
(yes, no)

Other preferences: _____

_____

_____

_____

_____

_____

_____

_____

_____

Trade-off

What I would accept as a substitute, at least temporarily:

_____

_____

_____

_____

_____

_____

_____

_____

_____

_____

_____

_____

_____

_____

_____

_____

_____

_____

IDENTITY SNAPSHOT
—A Summary of Myself—

Interests:

_____

_____

_____

Aptitudes/Skills:

_____

_____

_____

Academic Abilities:

_____

_____

_____

Personal Values:

_____

_____

_____

Work Values:

_____

_____

_____

Personality Traits:

_____

_____

_____

Lifestyle Preferences:

_____

_____

_____

(Note: Do not include physical characteristics, including disabilities, on your identity snapshot. These considerations are discussed in Chapter 7 of the *Career Book*.)

The Wrap-Up

Casey Stengel was one of baseball's greatest and most colorful characters. He was also a good judge of baseball talent.

Out on the coaching line one day he pointed to a player and asked, "See that fella over there?"

His companion nodded and prompted, "What about him?" "He's 20 years old. In 10 years he's got a chance to be a star. Now that other fella over there, he's 20 years old. In 10 years he's got a chance to be 30."

Having persevered through all seven of your identity inventories, we're betting that in a decade you'll be more than merely 10 years older. You'll be, as Casey might have said, ahead of the game.

The work you have done in creating your profile will help you move toward what you want in life. Knowing yourself raises red flags to the sort of work you certainly don't want, and opens vistas to the kinds of work that, upon further exploration, you may want with a passion.

One of the biggest wastes of young lives occurs because so many new workers flounder. They aimlessly drift from one thing to another with no sense of direction or purpose. Some of those who wobble back and forth through the job market have failed to develop self-awareness—they don't know what they want. They are trying to find the right careers but they don't even know themselves.

If it is true—as many analysts predict—that by 2000 the average college graduate will make as many as 10 job changes and five *career* changes—you can see the mark of wisdom in developing self-awareness.

Nobody ever sets out to be a person who never seems to find the right job. One who keeps starting one job, quitting, and starting another. By taking the time to explore yourself, you can make better choices.

Now with a clearer idea of your desires, abilities, potential skills, personal values, work values, personality, and priorities, the next step is to summarize the data on the form provided for your *identity snapshot*. Choose only the most relevant, most important items.

In case you're still not convinced that filling out a bunch of charts beats just thinking about your self-identity, humor us and try it. Thinking, writing, and boiling down helps organize and fix the information in your mind. Trust us.

■ ■ ■ ■

Your Career Awareness

When you want your dreams to come true, wake up! Waking up is what awareness means. This section and the one that follows tell you how to develop awareness as a skill and use it to make intelligent choices about your career path.

Without the freedom to choose your own career, your personal dignity as a unique individual is denied. Because stereotypes, biases, and other misperceptions limit your chances to be a successful career-climber, it's important to understand how you may acquire slanted viewpoints. This section recommends methods of pushing aside self-limiting images.

We let you in on many ways to acquire career information you need, and conclude with a list of 700 job ideas.

Awareness: A Life Force

Awareness means you take note of the change when your best friend's braces are removed, when the trees begin to bud, when your family pet grays and grows old.

You recognize these things because you sense, feel, observe, and understand what's going on. You stay awake, tune in, are in touch with the world.

For your career growth, awareness means you perceive job-related facts and impressions and realize what they mean. You actively gather and store information you can use later. Let's use aviation as an example.

Boarding an airplane is routine today, so much so that you probably give little thought to the wonder of jet travel. But during a visit to the Smithsonian Institution's National Air and Space Museum in Washington, D.C., you quickly become very aware of how far people have soared in only a few years.

You see the *Spirit of St. Louis*, the silvery monoplane in which Charles Lindbergh spanned the Atlantic in a single gulp of determined flying. Nearby, *Friendship 7* stands, the dark plexiglass spacecraft piloted by John Glenn, the first American in orbit.

A brief 35 years separates the heroic feats of these men. Imagine: Propeller blades became rocket launchers in one-third of a century! Your awareness can be electrifying as you realize that scheduled commuter flights between planets may begin within your lifetime and as you consider how such progress may affect your personal career plans. In this case, your awareness can lead to an expansion of career options in a variety of ways. To name a few imaginative choices, maybe you can become:

◆ A space flight instructor

◆ A shuttle reservation agent

◆ An importer of outer space goods

Awareness is a skill you can sharpen every day if you're alert to what's happening around you. Lack of awareness can mean missed opportunities.

By any measure, awareness is a powerful force in life.

■ ■ ■ ■

You Are Unique

Gee, Son, people will really wonder about you if you become a ballet dancer.

Now that you've lost a hand, you'll need to change from the automobile design curriculum, won't you?

My little girl doesn't need to know about careers. She's a beauty and when she grows up, she'll marry a fine man who will be attracted to her accomplishments and she will lead a country-club life.

You're quite short. Most managers are taller than average. Why don't you consider accounting?

Our career center has a pamphlet on opportunities for Jewish youth in retailing but no publication about auto mechanics.

City kids aren't likely to be happy as forest rangers. Blacks aren't either.

The drop-out rate for Hispanics in high school is so high that we try to get them into a trades program.

Statements of this nature are more than ludicrous—they are sexist and racist, discriminatory and objectionable. Believe in yourself (and all others) as a unique human being who will have the liberty to live up to your personal capacity. Such stereotyping steals your freedom of choice and contaminates the way we see one another.

■ ■ ■ ■

It's Okay to Be Different

Delightful comedian Marty Ingels tells a wise fable. Here's the gist of it.

Conk a scientist on the head and, with his memory gone, stick him in the middle of a jungle. He sees thousands of monkeys swinging through the trees. He knows he isn't one of them, but he doesn't know he's superior.

Looking around he thinks he must be second-rate because he can't jump and swing like the monkeys. Even if he had a few swinging lessons, in his heart he knows he'd still be a lousy monkey.

But if he knew what he was, a scientist, he would get to the high ground, build a fence, and own all the monkeys.

Being different, Ingels explains, doesn't mean you have to be inferior. You can be a scientist in a world of monkeys.

■ ■ ■ ■

The Days of the Greek Gods Are Fading

We said this in the introduction but it's worth repeating: This is a new age for Americans with disabilities, giving those with special challenges their best shot ever at employment.

The 1990 *Americans with Disabilities Act* kicked in with full force in 1992 in areas ranging from public accommodations and transportation to telecommunications and jobs.

The ADA builds on an earlier battery of laws benefiting people with disabilities in the job market. Until these laws were in place, you didn't stand much chance of being employed at many American corporations unless you were some stereotypical Greek god.

Now secretaries who are blind type dictation using a braille dictionary; company supervisors learn basic sign language to communicate with deaf technicians; and people with cerebral palsy operate computers.

If you have a characteristic that has traditionally limited career choices, don't assume you need a list of good jobs for persons with disabilities. That's an outdated notion.

You choose a career the same way persons who do not have disabilities do. Only you have to be resourceful enough to figure out a way the occupation can be adapted to your special needs. It will not be possible in every instance, but in many cases, you will have other strong skills that may compensate for your limitation.

Having a disability does *not* prevent you from perfecting other job skills that can crown your career with success. You can show ingenuity in solving problems, demonstrate careful planning, show perseverance, and other positive attributes.

Your challenge will be to get managers and supervisors to think of a disability as only a single characteristic and not as something that is all-embracing. You want them to focus on abilities plural, not disability singular. This is how it is explained by Rami Rabby, a New York City-based management consultant and senior author of *Take Charge: A Strategic Guide for Blind Job Seekers* (National Braille Press).

Rabby says that "Once you think of my blindness as only one part of the body that happens not to work as well as it might on the same level as any other kind of limitation that anybody has, then you're beginning to look at it in the kind of perspective that I think the industry should."

To illustrate, Rabby once presented a training program on disability and employment at a major bank that does a lot of overseas business. After Rabby explained that emotional perceptions are to blame for blocking the entrance of disabled people into mainstream society, a vice president said, "All this stuff in the seminar is interesting, but in the final analysis, I feel sorry for you because you're blind."

In his response, Rabby countered her emotionalism with logic: "I understand that you do and that is the problem. There is no reason that you should feel any more sorry for me because I'm blind than I should feel sorry for you (in dealing with job-related international banking) because you don't happen to know Hebrew, French, and Spanish, as I do. Because in the practical situation of employment, the two are absolutely identical."

A manager, after all, plans, organizes, coordinates, and controls. Which is the more restrictive in a supervisory job—a lack of vision or a lack of organizing ability? Is it easier for a person to learn dictation skills or interpersonal skills? Is it reasonable to assume that one cannot think because one cannot see?

As Rabby explains, disabled applicants must try to make interviewers grasp the whole package they offer, not zero in on a single feature. Blindness, for instance, must *not* be perceived as the central aspect of a candidate. If the interviewer starts out asking "How are you going to do this job?," give a factual, brief answer, but immediately move the conversation to your technical qualifications and your experience or education.

The principle is the same as for any job seeker: Deal briefly with shortcomings and refocus on your strengths.

While American industry has a long way to go before debunking the Greek-god hiring standard once and for all, progress is being made.

It's ironic that it existed in the first place. In ancient legends, Hephaestus—the Greek god of crafts—used his strong arms over the fires of his smithy to create world-class works. Hephaestus was lame.

■ ■ ■ ■

Getting on With Success—No Matter What

Arthur Godfrey was a famous radio and television personality. Author Robert Metz tells the story about Godfrey's frustrating efforts to be a patriot. During World War II Godfrey tried to join the Navy. He was turned down time after time.

Finally Godfrey asked for help from President Franklin D. Roosevelt, who called the Navy and asked why Godfrey was being rejected. An officer told President Roosevelt that the Navy couldn't give Godfrey a commission because of leg injuries he suffered in an automobile accident.

When Godfrey told the story many years later, he said F.D.R. asked, "Can he walk?" "Yes, he can walk," the Navy officer replied.

"Then give him the commission," F.D.R. roared. "I can't walk and I'm the Commander in Chief!"

This anecdote illustrates preconceptions that often hinder persons with disabilities in the job market.

Bruce McNeil is another who dispels the myth that a person with disabilities cannot participate as a valuable member of the workforce.

Bruce McNeil, reported to be mentally impaired (his IQ has been measured at 79), is admired in the coastal town of Gloucester, Mass. McNeil was 30 when he founded a tiny housecleaning service. He employs a dozen people on and off, all of them formerly homeless or alcohol abusers. A likeable, persuasive person, McNeil hopes to expand his business into a laundry service.

McNeil and millions of other people with disabilities want careers, no matter what.

In spite of barriers to openness and accessibility in the job market, they want the same things most of us want out of life—including using our abilities to the fullest, participating in the workplace, and being judged on how well we do with what we have.

The *Americans With Disabilities Act of* 1990 makes this goal easier to reach for everyone— from cleaning service owners to the Commander in Chief.

■ ■ ■ ■

Freedom Starts in Your Mind

The next activity reveals how you feel about stereotypes.

Close your eyes and see a pilot. Envision the pilot in full uniform walking out to the plane. Now the pilot is sitting behind the controls of the plane.

Do you see a woman? Probably not; based on the reactions of thousands of students who did this exercise, you most likely see a man.

All of us suffer from occupational stereotypes that not only are sex related, but personality and image related as well.

Imagine that you are a Hollywood casting director. After each of the following occupations, jot down your impression of how you would cast each role. Consider appearance, personality, age, gender, racial, or ethnic group.

accountant: _____

_____

_____

heavy equipment operator: _____

_____

_____

nurse: _____

_____

_____

sporting goods store manager: _____

_____

_____

civil engineer: _____

_____

_____

surgeon: _____

_____

_____

flight attendant: _____

_____

_____

secretary: _____

_____

_____

professional athlete: _____

_____

_____

When you can't see yourself in a role you've described, you probably won't consider the occupation for yourself. In your mind, it's not "you."

If you can't match yourself with the image you hold of a career field, your mind is closed about a particular occupation and you are prematurely limiting your choices. Open your mind.

■ ■ ■ ■

The Stork Doesn't Bring Stereotypes

As you surmised from the previous activity, you are probably not without your own stereotypical notions. Where do they come from? We are not born with them. Several possible culprits are:

◆ Newspapers, magazines, books

◆ Television, radio

◆ Not knowing many people in the field of your stereotype

◆ Your parents and friends

Sometimes wrong perceptions of an occupation become so widespread that it's humorous. In *Powermom* by Hester Mundis, the author gives her hilarious version of a "career guide."

Of airline pilots, she says it's a good choice because you travel extensively on the job, but bad because you never get to watch the movie. A stereotype.

As a retail buyer, you buy beautiful clothes with other people's money, but you can't afford the same clothing for yourself. Another stereotype.

Photographers, Mundis explains, can make money attending gala social functions just by taking pictures, but the downside is your friends expect you to take pictures for free. Still another stereotype.

When you're surrounded by stereotypes, what's the answer? Take direct fact-finding action. Make an appointment to spend a day with someone in the career field in question. Watch, observe. Compare the factual information you acquire with your previous perception.

If we were to shadow Hester Mundis's examples, we'd find that pilots often are stranded in faraway places and must return to home base as passengers, in which case they can watch any movie shown.

Buyers may be given big discounts on beautiful clothing for their own wardrobes.

Photographers need only insist to friends that photography is their living and they do it only on a professional basis.

Hester Mundis was joking, of course, but you can see how stereotypes, like rumors, get into the culture.

By now you know that the stork doesn't bring stereotypes; misinformation does. The only cure is to get the facts.

■ ■ ■ ■

The Myths about Women and Work

◆ Women should not take jobs away from men by entering the workforce.

◆ Women are not physically or mentally equipped to perform many work tasks.

◆ Women choose work as an extra thing to do, not because they want to pursue their own career goals.

◆ Women don't have to be concerned about work because they almost always end up getting married.

◆ Women only go to college to find their future husbands.

◆ Women are intellectually inferior to men in certain academic studies, such as math, science, and politics.

◆ Women do not belong in selected occupations, such as President of the United States, the Armed Services, and religious roles as ordained clergy.

◆ Women are incapable of owning and operating their own businesses because they lack financial savvy.

Two decades ago women across America thought they were well on the way to putting these myths in history's attic, says Patricia L. Duffy, senior author of *Hire Learning*. Nevertheless, some of today's students may not have come to grips with equality, achievement, and rewards, this career education authority says. Duffy urges vigilance in continuing to show new generations of young people how myths that put women in the career shadows not only lack substance, but can be self-limiting.

■ ■ ■ ■

Women: The Sky's The Limit

Eileen Nester is the editor of *Career Woman* magazine. She was surprised recently to receive a letter from a woman who noted the emphasis the magazine placed on women in traditional male careers.

"Over the past two decades," Nester says, "women in growing numbers have found success as accountants, lawyers, engineers, and doctors—all fields that once were considered to be the sole domain of men. So how many women have to enter a profession before it stops being classified as 'male'? As far as I'm concerned, the sky's the limit for women in today's workforce," Nester says.

Women Are Working Everywhere

Millions of women across America are proving that they are excellent stockbrokers and business owners, wildlife managers and project engineers, psychologists and public accountants, physics professors and newspaper editors—and more.

Already the nation has more than 100,000 female physicians. The American Medical Women's Association anticipates that women may comprise a third or more of the nation's physicians by the year 2010.

Women are beginning to break through in business, too. Kathy Prasnicki is founder and CEO of the gasoline distributor Sun Coast Resources. Prasnicki, 33, is from East Texas and has built a booming $200-million-a-year company. Prasnicki says she never planned to be a success. She grew up in a working-class family and worked part time in high school as an accounting clerk at Jasper Oil Company. She liked working and so skipped college. She became a sales representative for Jasper and was able to strike out on her own nine years ago. Prasnicki works 60 to 70 hour weeks and her only vacation was taking seven days off for the birth of her daughter, Kaely, in 1994. She then built a nursery at Sun Coast for her daughter and the children of her 51 employees.

Even the tough turf of law enforcement is beginning to see change. Louise O'Leary has become the first Black woman ever to be named Secretary of Transportation of the United States. Janet Reno is the Attorney General, the country's highest law enforcement position. The Clinton Administration has appointed more women into top posts than any other administration.

Even female stereotypes like "all women sew" can be turned into money-making ventures. Francine Huff, founder of Wyoming Woolens, turned her flair for sewing and designing into an outerwear manufacturing company. The company started from home with one sewing machine and now has 100 employees. Sales topped 3.2 million dollars in 1994. Huff overcame numerous setbacks, including business and personal bankruptcy, before starting Wyoming Woolens. Determined, Huff worked as a waitress, saving enough money to buy a sewing machine, and started over. "The Japanese are just discovering the outdoor market," says Huff, 44, "and we want to be in on it."

Barriers to Women's Advancement

An exhaustive study of a generation of American men and women concludes that women's educational achievement is superior to men's, but that the labor market rewards them much less than it does men.

The National Longitudinal Study of the High School Class of 1972 describes the educational and labor market experiences of that class until its members were 32 years old.

"It is the richest archive ever assembled on a generation of Americans," according to a spokesperson for the U.S. Department of Education which conducted the study.

Among the study's findings:

♦ *Men are almost always paid more than women, even when the women are better qualified educationally. Women also have a higher rate of unemployment.*

♦ *One notable exception is in math majors. Women who have at least eight college math credits earn on average 16.5 percent more than men with the same math background. For women, more math means more money, particularly in business careers.*

♦ *It's a myth that women don't care about monetary reward; they value it more than men do.*

Another new study by the American Association of University Women shows that girls emerge from adolescence with a poor self-image, relatively low expectations from life, and much less confidence in themselves than boys do. At age nine, a majority of the girls were confident, assertive, and felt positive about

themselves. But by the time they reach high school, fewer than a third feel that way.

The search for the case of the disappearing adolescent self-esteem continues—most authorities agree it's more than hormones. There are heavy hints of cultural contributions from institutions ranging from schools to media. Feature stories still portray successful women as the exception, suggesting that they are vastly different from other women. They must have some mysterious qualities not likely to be found in "normal" women.

Writing in the *Fort Worth Star-Telegram*, Katie Sherrod describes a recent ceremony honoring achieving women in Texas. Only one or two of the women fell into the self-destructive trap of saying they don't deserve the honor, Sherrod reports. Most expressed quiet pride in their accomplishment and thanked others for their help. Sherrod continues:

"These women knew they were not standing up there alone, that they were standing on the shoulders of women who had gone before them, opening doors through which they passed. These women did not see themselves as particularly exceptional. They had worked hard and overcome barriers, but women have been doing that for centuries. The message for our daughters was a clear and welcome one: I *did this, and you can, too.* It's a message we must send more often. Then maybe one day, our girls will believe it."

More High-Performance Women

Women still make only 72 cents on a man's dollar. Overall, women now hold 38 percent of all managerial positions in America (only 3 percent of the top jobs at the largest 500 companies), but these female supervisors are paid only 64 percent as much as their male counterparts, says U.S. *News & World Report.*

The figures don't tell the entire story—the sky really can be the limit for high performance women.

From *Savvy* magazine's annual *Savvy* 60 survey ranking America's leading women business owners, we spot Susie Tompkins, who heads Esprit De Corp., a San Francisco apparel maker with 4,000 employees. Jenny Craig is president of Jenny Craig International, a Del Mar, California weight-loss company with 5,500 employees. Lana Jane Lewis-Brent is CEO (chief executive officer) of Sunshine-Jr. Stores Inc., a Panama City, Florida convenience store chain with 1,900 employees.

In *Working Woman* magazine's 12th annual survey, we find that Marion Sandler, CEO of Golden West Financial, earns more than $600,000 a year. Elizabeth Lederer, an assistant district attorney in New York, is compensated at $74,500. Robin Burns, CEO of Estee Lauder Inc. cosmetics, is paid a reported $1.3 million.

And then there's Kristin Baker. A 1990 graduate of West Point, Baker was the institution's first female Cadet Captain. The job, awarded on the basis of academic, athletic, and leadership ability, is the school's most challenging assignment. The Cadet Captain oversees all aspects of life for 4,400 cadets. This includes marching, parading, and managing a support staff of 40 upperclassmen—all while carrying a regular course load.

At first, some cadets griped about taking orders from a female. Old-line West Point graduates wrote to her saying a female shouldn't have the job. It was a tense time. Baker had to do "twice as well as anyone else," observed a classmate. Ultimately, her performance won over most of the critics.

We'd guess that Kristin Baker strongly believes that women should have the opportunity of being all that they are capable of becoming. At graduation, Baker dismissed the class for the last time and then, with the other 895 cheering graduating cadets, tossed her hat—skyward.

We admit we loaded the deck by showcasing high flyers. Remember, though, these achieving women are not so different from you. They are good role models, certainly, but they are not so exceptional that you cannot achieve—as they achieved.

Some women decide, for part or most of their working years, to put their energy into child-rearing. Indeed, in one recent study, eight of ten working women said they would choose a career path with flexible hours and more family time but slower career advancement than inflexible hours and faster advancement.

Other women will have few options. As an Atlanta mother who supported her five children through a series of clerical jobs says, "Career? No. I was just trying to feed my kids."

If you want to think about this with the help of a wonderful book loaded with interesting, thought-provoking exercises, read *Choices: A Teen Woman's Journal for Self-Awareness and Personal Planning* by Mindy Bingham, Judy Edmondson, and Sandy Stryker (order from Academic Innovations, Suite 267, 3463 State St., Santa Barbara, CA 93105; 800–967–8016).

■ ■ ■ ■

Words Are Tools of The Brain

Use language that helps smash stereotypes. It's in your best interests to say letter carrier, not mailman; repairer, not repairman; advertising lay-out planner, not advertising lay-out man.

A foreman is a supervisor and a new car salesman is a new car sales associate. A poetess is a poet.

Why should you strive to use sex-neutral language?

Sexist communication assigns either females or males into roles solely on the basis of sex. Nonsexist communication does not pre-label. It does not assert that male is the norm (repairman) and that female is something less than the norm.

An old saying suggests, "Tell me a people's language and I'll tell you the values of that people."

In addition to the fact that sexist communication indicates that one is behind the times and has a patriarchal view of the job market, we urge you to think in sex-neutral job titles because doing so keeps your mind open to opportunities. Watch your thoughts, warns writer Frank Outlaw. Thoughts become words, then actions, then habits, then character—then destiny.

Sexist job titles do not encourage you to think about being all you can be.

■ ■ ■ ■

Minorities Come of Age

The 1990s have been the decade of the minorities: Large numbers of newcomers into the workplace have been women and minorities. The shrinking youth demographics are largely responsible for the rush to attract African-Americans, Asian-Americans, Latinos, and native Americans to the professions and corporate America. If you're one of these groups, seize this window of opportunity. You're in the right place at the right time.

■ ■ ■ ■

African Americans, Claim Your Career

Herman Miller Inc. is the second largest office furniture company in the nation. Located in Zeeland, Mich., it is a Fortune 400 company with annual sales of $865 million.

Michele Hunt was the first African American to hold the position of vice president at Herman Miller. A member of the executive committee (top management team reporting to the CEO, or chief executive officer), Hunt is vice president of quality and people development.

She has a big job with responsibility for quality and communications initiatives, human resources, education and development, information services, and safety/security.

Her career began in the public sector (Michigan Department of Corrections) when Hunt was the first woman to direct treatment in a male prison and supervise men on probation. The executive has had considerable experience in advising young people how to achieve their goals. She says:

"Focus on your dreams, not on your disabilities. Being a minority, being disabled, being shy, being poor, or being burdened with any other so-called barrier should be looked upon as a stepping-stone, not as a block.

"Those of us who the world identifies as being in a group of minorities or people with disabilities have been taught to blame. When we blame we become powerless. The only road to success is to take *total* responsibility for our successes and failures. It does not mean we do not understand the realities of racism, sexism, and other "isms," but it does mean that once we understand the situation, we can choose how to deal with it. That's where our focus can serve us well.

"It's kind of like traveling on a road, with your baggage and dreams—wanting desperately to get to your destination—when a tree falls on the road. Racism, sexism, and other "isms" are *only* trees that have fallen on your road. You have the power to move them out of your way," Michele Hunt says.

More good advice comes from African American men who excel in their careers.

Richard D. Parsons was the first African American to become CEO of a major United States bank. The chairman of The Dime Savings Bank of New York offers advice to students:

"Luck is the residue of design. Those people who are working hard and doing the best they can tend to position themselves to catch the lucky breaks. Those who are doing the minimum to get by won't be so 'lucky.' In the long run, hard work and diligence pay off."

Two other insightful African-American executives offer tips on trashing old stereotypes and succeeding in corporate America.

♦ Wisconsin Power & Light CEO Erroll B. Davis:

"You cannot be perceived as antisocial or difficult to deal with. That means you may have to exhibit a higher tolerance for ignorance than your non-minority colleagues."

♦ Floyd Dickens, president of Cincinnati's 21st Century Management Services:

"Multiracial networking is strongly urged. Minorities tend to shy away from interaction and offer the excuse of 'I'm uncomfortable with whites all day—why should I be uncomfortable with them after work?' Look at after-work activity as being an extension of the workday."

Away from the civilian job market, Desert Storm won the military new stature as an institution of opportunity for African Americans. Throughout the chain of command, the gulf war spotlighted models of African American achievement, from former Joint Chiefs Chairman Colin Powell, to deputy Desert Storm commander Gen. Calvin Waller, to three members of the Patriot missile crew decorated for shooting down Scuds over Saudi Arabia.

As reported in *Newsweek* magazine, Sgt. Charles Lewis Davis, a Los Angeles Army recruiter says "The military is so far advanced from the civilian population, it's pathetic."

This doesn't mean the military playing field is level—the general feeling is that African Americans have to be not just as good but better to get a promotion in the military. But it does mean the battle for respect has been helped by the stunning performance of the desert warriors, 20 percent of whom were African Americans—this for a group comprising just 12 percent of the U.S. population.

Stereotyping and prejudice is taking a long time to die off. As Michele Hunt warns, letting it get to you lowers your self-esteem and keeps you from achieving the rewards you want. Find mentors, get good grades, and do a superior job. If you want to choose a minority-friendly location, head for New England, Washington, DC, or the West Coast—that's where a University of Michigan study shows African Americans fare best economically.

■ ■ ■ ■

The Aspirations of Latino Students

Sometimes it's in our best interests to ignore statistics. For example, some statistics claim that the Latino population in the United States is burgeoning, but the proportion of Latino youths who finish high school is not keeping pace with gains by African Americans and other minority groups.

Educators who do these studies are concerned that without immediate intervention to provide education and training, not only those in school now, but Latinos who already have left school will miss out on the good jobs.

But an advocate for fairness in the educational image of Latinos sees a downside to the concern: a negative stereotype that communicates the wrong message to young Latinos.

"Latinos don't finish school. Many don't attend college, and those who do, don't finish. We are told this every day by 'experts' who conduct surveys and studies," says Raoul Lowery Contreras.

A syndicated newspaper columnist, Contreras explains that the stereotype is debatable, basically because it mixes in millions of uneducated people from Mexico and Central America who often do not speak English.

As a single example, native-born Americans of Mexican descent attend and finish school in percentages comparable to anyone, Contreras says. Sometimes they're at the top of the charts.

Los Angeles teacher Jaime Escalante (portrayed in the film *Stand and Deliver*) taught calculus to Mexican-American students from a barrio high school. All passed the national Advanced Placement Test given for college credit.

Their achievement was questioned by test administrators who, remembering the stereotype, figured they must have cheated and made the Latino students take the test over. They did and all once again passed.

"Escalante doubled and tripled his output of college-level achievers and proved that Mexican-American students, regardless of economic status, can compete with anyone in the country, anyone," Contreras observes.

The columnist urges young Latinos to forget about falling behind because the stereotype says they're expected to. *Mexican-Americans can succeed at calculus, at college, at anything they choose, as long as they're willing to study and work hard.*

So much for stereotypes.

■ ■ ■ ■

The Best Life— How to Find It

You may have a general idea of the kind of life you would like to have. You may already have some information about several career areas.

That's not enough.

It is only the beginning.

To be rewarded with a blockbuster career, you must become a comparison shopper, looking at all possibilities within your awareness range.

You may not have thought about it in quite this way, but the lifestyle you want can be fulfilled by more than one career pattern. Perhaps two dozen occupations have your name on them. If you like people and faraway places, for instance, you might like to be a travel agent or a tour guide or an airline reservation agent or a corporate travel department manager or a trade association convention manager—or maybe you'll see a recruiting poster and join the Navy.

The point is that you have to scout far and wide before you can answer such key questions as these:

What are the jobs?

Where are they?

What do I have to do to get them?

A logical way to begin is to write down all the career fields that look good. Before you settle down to serious selecting—before narrowing your sights to a handful of outstanding prospects—you first must be aware of all the wonderful things in the world from which you can choose.

There's so much, in fact, that the array of opportunities can be dumbfounding. Not only is the sheer volume of ways to earn a living nearly overwhelming, but they cram a constantly changing careerscape.

The classic way to deal with a mass of unwieldy information is to break it into several small stacks.

In career development, groups of related occupations are often called *career clusters* or *job families*. Career clusters are formed in several different ways.

♦ Some occupations share a cluster because they are part of the same industry—both physicians and respiratory therapists are in the health cluster.

♦ Other occupations are kindred because they require a certain kind of training, such as apprenticeship (plumbers and electricians).

♦ Still other occupations are clustered because they involve similar activities, such as working with people. Sales engineers and technical manufacturer's representatives work with customers in similar ways.

♦ The common bond for some groups of occupations is a shared interest, such as in the environment or in music.

♦ A particular skill is the glue that holds together other groups of occupations. Mechanical ability is an example.

♦ A clustering system, known as *worker traits*, combines both interests and skills. Artists and sculptors illustrate this concept.

As you can imagine, a job can be slotted into several career clusters, depending on how it is viewed. For example, clerical occupations are found in all clusters.

There are two main reasons why it's important to understand how the cluster concept works.

1. If you discover an occupation you like, you may spot one you like even more by exploring the cluster. A young man interested in the work of a marine geophysicist should scan the entire environment-and-natural-resources cluster. Other options in marine science, such as hydrologist or marine meteorologist, might be more attractive to a specific individual.

2. If you have an avid desire to enter a particular field but fail to qualify for some reason, you may come upon a satisfying related opportunity by exploring alternatives within a cluster. A young woman whose eyesight does not meet vision requirements to become a pilot might choose to become a marketing specialist for an airline rather than exclude aviation as a career area.

Career clusters are a tool to help you shop for the best work niche in life.

Clusters related to industries and broad functions are found at the end of this section.

■ ■ ■ ■

Make a Future File

Career information is more usable if you organize it in a file. Because it deals with your future, let's call it a *future file*.

You can use notebooks—say, one notebook per career field. If you don't want to use notebooks, use file folders. Keep copies of articles and notes on interviews you conduct. If you have a computer, you can create an electronic future file.

The way you keep your file is far less important than the care with which you do research, take notes, and organize your findings.

Organizing is in itself a technique that will enhance your career awareness.

Samples of forms you can use to summarize the information in your future file appear next. The forms show you how to organize information you gather. Examples of how the forms might be filled out follow.

EXPLORATION INTERVIEW REPORT

Name: _____

Title: _____

Organization: _____

Address: _____

Date of interview: _____

Key information obtained: _____

_____

_____

_____

_____

_____

(Don't forget to add this name to your contacts log described in section 5.)

EXPLORATION INTERVIEW REPORT

Name: Chris Littlejohn

Title: Employee Benefits Administrator

Orgnization: Sun Up Clothing Company

Address: 1234 Horizon Parkway, Poway CA 92888

Date of interview: July 6

Key information obtained: Littlejohn is very happy in his work. Says most benefits people like the field. He says that if I am not mathematically talented but prefer English, I might want to consider becoming a communications specialist in benefits, because after the plan is designed and implemented, employees must be made aware of programs.

Career Field/Occupation

EXPLORATION SUMMARY
After exploring this option, am I interested in it as a potential career choice?

Yes ❑   Maybe ❑   No ❑

Likes   **Dislikes**

Nature of Work

_____   _____

_____   _____

Working Conditions

_____   _____

_____   _____

Employment

_____   _____

_____   _____

Training

_____   _____

_____   _____

Other Qualifications

_____   _____

Advancement

_____   _____

Earnings

_____   _____

Job Outlook

_____   _____

Related Jobs

_____   _____

_____   _____

Sources of More Information

_____   _____

_____   _____

Career Field/Occupation

EMPLOYEE BENEFITS MANAGER
(also called employee benefits
administrator)

EXPLORATION SUMMARY

After exploring this option, am I interested
in it as a potential career choice?

Yes ❑   Maybe ❑   No ❑

Likes   **Dislikes**

Nature of Work

Handling employee fringe benefits   Probably need more math and

such as insurance & retirement   finance courses.

funds. Satisfaction from helping

people by protecting them from

injury, sickness, old age.

Working Conditions

Pleasant office environment.   Would like to get out of office more

                                           often.

Employment

Jobs are available in most kinds of   Jobs are in cities. I'm not sure but I

industries and companies; jobs are   might like to live in a more rural

located throughout the United States   area.

so I could probably live wherever I

want.

Training

At least a college education.

Other Qualifications

Need analytical ability, good judgment, organizational skills, personality to deal with people.

Must understand accounting, economics, finance; too technical for my liking.

Advancement

Can become top compensation & benefits executive.

Is a position that rarely leads to top corporate management.

Earnings

Often between $25,000 and $40,000 + bonus of 10% to 20%. Pays well.

Job Outlook

Expanding field.

Related Jobs

Personnel jobs, insurance work, investment and financial services, banking.

Sources of More Information

1. International Foundation of Employee Benefit Plans Box 69 Brookfield, Wisc. 53005

2. Employee Benefit News, a trade journal.

What's Your Twenty-First Century Career Quotient?

A flood of new occupations came with the 20th century. More are on the way.

Many are new titles—such as computer graphics technician—that may become commonplace in the 21st century.

Among thousands of job titles, there are men and women working as bonsai culturists and cosmetologists, wedding brokers and well drillers, humor awareness therapy consultants, speech writers and bodyguards, ultrasonic hand solderers, video game arcade managers, banjo musicians, and thousands more.

Of this multitude of occupations, how many job titles can you name? Time yourself for two minutes; list as many occupations as possible.

1. _____	2. _____
3. _____	4. _____
5. _____	6. _____
7. _____	8. _____
9. _____	10. _____
11. _____	12. _____
13. _____	14. _____
15. _____	16. _____
17. _____	18. _____
19. _____	20. _____
21. _____	22. _____
23. _____	24. _____
25. _____	26. _____
27. _____	28. _____
29. _____	30. _____
31. _____	32. _____
33. _____	34. _____
35. _____	36. _____
37. _____	38. _____
39. _____	40. _____

How many titles did you jot down? If you listed 25, you have average awareness of the world of work. And you want to be more than average, right?

■ ■ ■ ■

You Won't Know Unless You Ask

Chances are, you need to beef up your career knowledge.

The technique: Ask questions in a structured interview.

Select people who work in your favorite jobs or jobs you want to know more about. Use a tape recorder, if possible. Locate interviewees through teachers, friends, relatives, neighbors, bankers, physicians, merchants, and graduates of your school. You also can call employers and professional associations to locate other people who work in jobs you like. Some school counselors maintain a list of resource people.

Don't be frightened because you fear interviewing is an imposition. Most people really like to talk about their jobs, and it's flattering to be asked for advice. Tell prospective interviewees that you are a student doing a career study. Although the career study is not homework assigned by a teacher, nevertheless it is a career study and you are making a truthful statement.

You might want to ease into interviewing by practicing first on family members. Here's a list of questions to ask.

1. What type of formal training have you had?

2. What fields have you worked in over the years?

3. What other training or experiences have you had that were helpful to you?

4. What other occupations did you consider before deciding on this one?

5. Can you describe briefly an average day's activities?

6. What do you like best about your present position?

7. What do you dislike most about your present position?

8. What are the main problems or frustrations you encounter in your work?

9. What activities other than your job are you involved with that are a source of satisfaction to you?

10. What kinds of training or experiences would be helpful to the person entering your field now?

11. What advice do you have for someone considering your field today?

12. Are there related fields I should explore?

13. Do you think that your past mistakes help you to make better decisions?

14. What interests do you have? Did they help you decide what job you wanted?

15. What school subjects do you use in your work and how? What subjects do you recommend someone taking in school that would help in your job?

16. How has your particular job changed over the past 10 or 20 years? What do you think the job will be like in another 10 years?

17. Are your personal hobbies very different from your job or are they similar?

18. How does this job support your way of living in terms of income, knowledge, working hours, and leisure time?

19. Why is this job important to you?

20. Do you know of any common characteristics a person should possess to be successful in your field of work?

You also can use this technique to interview someone who lives far away. Send a thoughtful letter that includes the questions you want answered, a blank audio cassette tape, and return postage. It works!

■ ■ ■ ■

Before You Ask, Prepare

Time is a non-renewable resource. Treat it with respect, especially when it belongs to someone else.

An ounce of preparation is worth a pound of dumb questions you could have learned answers to by reading. Spend an hour in the library's business reference section checking on an individual, organization, or career field.

Even if you're not a whiz at library research, librarians usually enjoy lending a hand to sincere knowledge-seekers. You may be surprised at how much advance information you can uncover. Write out your questions before an interview.

Your show of respect for the interviewee's time will keep the door open for other young people coming behind you. In addition, making a good impression on someone who could become a valuable professional contact in a field that you may someday want to enter is like having money in the bank.

■ ■ ■ ■

Alternatively, you can say, "I am researching my future career"; "I am gathering information to use in making my career decisions"; "I have read a great deal about this career field but I need the kind of personal interpretation that only someone in your position can supply to a young person."

Ask your prospective interviewee for 15 minutes and keep the meeting within that limit, unless you clearly are invited to stay longer.

As a term, "informational interview" is shopworn, but the technique itself remains vital and effective. Use it correctly—the same way a reporter collects facts and impressions for an article.

An Update on Informational Interviewing

Informational interviewing means asking someone for data you genuinely need. It is not a synonym for job interviewing; you are not asking to be hired.

During the last 15 years, many job seekers thought informational interviewing, along with networking, was the "secret of the job search." Although millions of individuals probably found the technique invaluable in their career decision-making process, others abused it.

Too many job hunters used informational interviewing like a trick or gimmick. As a result, business people today tend to be skeptical if you ask for such an interview.

Advice: Never mention the term "informational interview." Instead, clearly announce yourself as a student. Say that you're still in the dark about what to do with your post-graduation life.

Keep it simple and state, as earlier suggested, "I am doing a career study."

How to Get Career Research Interviews

Telephoning

Step 1

Find out the name of the individual you wish to interview. Simply ask the receptionist at the company's office for the name of the person holding the position.

I wish to write a letter to the marketing manager. Can you spell the manager's name, please? It's Mary Lee Ferrari, you say?

That's F-e-r-r-a-r-i. Thank you very much.

(Slight pause). Oh yes, while I have you on the phone, what is Ms. Ferrari's secretary's name, please? Ms. Fields—F-i-e-l-d-s? Got it. Thanks again.

Step 2

The following week, call back and introduce yourself to the marketing manager's secretary. It helps to keep a smile on your face even when talking on the phone.

Good afternoon, Ms. Fields. My name is Rolf Preisendorfer.

Step 3

Explain your reason for calling. Keep it simple but persuasive.

I am a student researching my future career. I am not looking for a job. It would mean a lot to me if I could speak for a few minutes to someone who is successful in marketing, a field that interests me very much. Do you think you could help me out by arranging a short 15-minute appointment with Ms. Ferrari sometime within the next two weeks? I could come early in the morning or late in the afternoon. It won't take long and I'll have my questions ready in advance. Could you set up an appointment?

Step 4

Chances are the secretary won't give you an answer on the spot. He or she will want to check with the boss, and probably ask you to call back. But if the answer sounds like a rejection, don't give up. Try for a future time.

Oh, Ms. Ferrari will be out of the city for the next two weeks? In that case, I'll check back with you in a month, Ms. Fields. Thank you for talking with me. Obviously you understand what it's like to need advice.

Step 5

If you are turned down flat, ask the secretary to suggest another marketing manager who would be willing to speak with you. Try to make the secretary an ally. If you are granted an interview, be sure to write a thank-you note to the secretary, as well as to the manager.

Writing

Arranging a career research interview by mail is basically the same as arranging one by telephone. You must obtain the name (and its correct spelling) of the person you wish to reach. Your letter must state the purpose of the appointment you seek, and it must close by saying you will follow up by telephoning to find out when an appointment would be convenient. Keep your letter to one page.

Career research interviewing gives your career direction. Two other gains are possible. You can acquire poise to use in future job interviews and you may meet an individual who one day will be in a position to support your upward climb.

Impress the interviewer by mentioning in your letter one or two books you have read on the career being discussed. Say the books raised several issues about which you would value the interviewer's opinion.

■ ■ ■ ■

Newspapers Are Goldmines

Your daily newspaper is another source of career information.

Look for two types of advertisements: classified help-wanted ads, which are concise requests for applicants, and larger recruitment display ads, which are more complete requests for applicants.

The classified ads are grouped together in one section. The display ads may be grouped in one section, or they may be spread throughout the paper, particularly in the business, sports, and features sections.

As you look through, clip the ads that immediately catch your eyes. Put these standouts in your future file. Wait several weeks, then call or write to request an interview with the employer, saying that you are a young person researching your future career. The reason to wait several weeks is that until the job is filled, the employer will be busy interviewing applicants.

News articles and features often give information that relates to jobs. For instance, look for announcements of new business managers, store openings, and coming events such as fairs and concerts.

Here's the program: Each day for one week, choose a newspaper article that contains some career information. Read the article carefully to see how many of the blanks on the following form you can fill in using only information from the article.

Rarely will you fill in every blank from a single article, but the exercise will snap up your career awareness.

You'll never read the newspaper the same way again. You'll be alert to picking up career information—not only from newspapers, but also from magazines and other print materials.

Career Awareness Capsule (from news articles)

Job title: _____

Personal qualities needed: _____

Skills needed: _____

Education needed: _____

Salary range: _____

Disadvantages of job: _____

Advantages of job: _____

Career outlook (are jobs available; does the future look bright or dim?):

_____

_____

Job duties: _____

Lifestyle: _____

Free Help From the Yellow Pages

Step 1

Whenever you have a spare three minutes, sit down with the thickest telephone yellow pages directory you can find. The only other tools you need are a felt-tip pen or a pencil, a tablet of paper, and your identity inventories from Chapter 6. Go through the directory, A to Z, circling each classification that appeals to you.

Ask yourself only one question: "Does this subject interest me?" If the answer is "no," move on. If the answer is "yes" or "not sure," write the heading on your tablet.

Trust your immediate reactions; don't linger over the heading, weighing one factor against another. Be quick about it.

By the time you finish scanning the telephone directory, you may have listed hundreds of headings.

Step 2

Reduce the number of headings on your list to the 30 you like best.

Step 3

For each of the 30 headings, ask yourself: "What in my education, training, or experience validates my interest in this particular field?"

There are exceptions, but if you are genuinely interested in a subject, you probably have read about it, studied it, worked or played at it.

Step 4

By now you have trimmed your list of interesting headings to 15 or so. The next question to ask yourself is: "In view of my requirements, such as lifestyle desires, travel, and earnings potential, which fields should I consider?"

If you can't answer this question for certain of your choices, or perhaps most of them, do more research. Turn to Chapter 8, "Your Career, Your Research."

Step 5

By now your list should be a manageable size, and you will treat the yellow pages directory headings like career headings. Rank the headings, putting the most appealing at the top.

Ten Interesting Career Fields/ Occupations

1. _____

2. _____

3. _____

4. _____

5. _____

6. _____

7. _____

8. _____

9. _____

10. _____

Step 6

Turn back to the yellow pages directory and find a list of companies that have the kinds of jobs you chose. After doing enough research to ensure that you respect your interviewee's time, set up appointments with people at the firms where you can get more information. Start with your first choice.

The object of the yellow pages directory exploration is to broaden your horizons: You will discover entire career fields you may otherwise have overlooked.

■ ■ ■ ■

Extend Your Vision

Choosing a career makes you a chooser. Like writers and artists, choosers do best with what they know.

You can know a lot about careers with a minimum of effort. You've already gained sophistication in using newspapers and yellow pages directories to boost your career awareness.

Now take a look at other possibilities.

Libraries

In addition to general-interest media, some of America's libraries have career centers filled with guidance publications and occupational literature. Many public libraries now also offer online job-searching resources, which are growing exponentially. These centers can open exciting new vistas to you. Read all about it in Chapter 8 and treat yourself to a library visit soon.

Television

Television shows that depict careers rarely are accurate, but at least they often contain some information.

As you watch TV programs, be aware of more than the plot. Think about the characters' job responsibilities and personal qualities. What about the skills needed for employment and the training necessary?

Are there clues to the quality of family life made possible by the job and the availability of leisure time?

If you have sufficient interest, the next step is to find real life people in the job and begin a series of interviews.

Cultural and Sports Events

Use museums, art galleries, theatrical productions, and ball parks for more than cultural enrichment and recreation. Try to talk to the people who make the events happen. Ask what they do, how they like their jobs, and how they live their lives.

If you're an opera buff, for example, ask the stage-door guard if you may speak with the stage manager. Explain that you are a student exploring your future career and that you would like to check on the various jobs involved with producing an opera. Depending on your manner and appearance, the stage manager may allow you backstage. If not, you lose nothing by trying.

If you have the opportunity, talk with people working in the jobs of stagehand, hairdresser, make-up artist, musician, singer, lighting technician, sound technician, and photographer.

At the ball park, interview an usher. Why? You may realize that somebody manages the usher corps for the ball park; somebody manages the usher corps managers for many establishments; and somebody must own the company that hires the ushers and their managers.

Movies and More

When you watch a film, notice the credits of who did what. Try to think of the variety of occupations that were required to make the motion picture.

Use the same thought process when you dine out. Make a game of naming all the people who provide you with a restaurant meal. Examples: agriculture specialist, fertilizer manufacturer, farm equipment sales representative, farmer, truckdriver, cook, server, and cashier.

Who makes a zoo function? In a fire station, who responds to an emergency? Who built the zoo enclosures or fire station?

Extend the same who-does-it reasoning to products. Who works to make possible the tapes and discs you buy? Cosmetics? Jewelry? School supplies? Books? Furniture? Cars? Think about it.

Person-in-the-Street Interviews

Anyone who imparts information has the potential to increase your awareness.

(Use common sense, of course. Stay away from suspicious-looking people. Never put yourself in a position where your safety may be in jeopardy.)

A dialogue with a letter carrier may reveal that permanent postal employees enjoy super job security—they cannot be laid off.

Speaking with a young physician might bring forth the competitive dimension: Increasing numbers of doctors make it more difficult for newcomers to launch careers.

No matter that you have no desire to enter a given field. Let's suppose that retailing doesn't ring your register. By talking with retail clerks, you may zero in on a previously unrecognized

factor, such as the satisfaction of owning your own shop, or the physical demands of standing all day. You'll perhaps remember such factors when considering other careers.

With a bit of practice you'll soon see careers everywhere you look.

■ ■ ■ ■

700 Job Ideas

This career awareness section is painted with a broad brush. In a general way, we discuss how to acquire career information and apply it to yourself.

(The finer points of career research are revealed in Chapter 8.)

If your career awareness is still dim, stoke your creative fires by reviewing the following 700 job ideas, 50 for each of 14 occupational clusters. Remember, an occupation can be slotted into more than one career cluster. A copywriter, for instance, could be placed in *Communication and Media* or in *Marketing and Distribution*.

A number of the job titles will seem puzzling or unclear. That's because many of them reflect new ways to earn a living in an information age.

Here's our recommendation when you come across an interesting but unfamiliar title: View your uncertainty as an opportunity to practice research skills. Make it a point of pride to find out what the job entails.

One immediate reward for uncovering what lies behind a mystery job title is a feeling of accomplishment. (*Translation*: Don't write to us for an explanation of a particular job title—in effect, asking us to do your homework for you; that's not what this book is about.)

Clusters: Job Ideas at a Glance

Agriculture (including Agribusiness)

agricultural attache (foreign service)

agricultural broker

agricultural cooperative manager

agricultural economist

agricultural engineer

agricultural journalist

agricultural produce commission agent

agricultural research chemist

agricultural sales representative

agriculture instructor

agronomist

arborist

beekeeper

botanist

commodity broker

county extension agent

crop insurance specialist

dairy technologist

entomologist

farm appraiser

farm broadcaster

farm machine operator

farm manager

farm products advertising manager

farm realtor

feed research aide

floral designer

florist

food technologist

4-H Club staff member

fruitgrower

grain buyer

grain farmer

greenhouse superintendent

horticulturalist

hydroponics horticulturalist

irrigation engineer

landscape architect

landscape contractor

meat inspector

milk processing plant manager

ornamental horticulturalist

plant geneticist

plant nursery owner

plant propagator

rancher

silviculturist

soil scientist

veterinarian

vineyard manager

Business and Office

accountant

actuary

administrative assistant

applications programmer

collection company representative

company treasurer

computer liaison specialist

computer operator

computer security specialist

computer tape librarian

corporate attorney

corporate fitness director

credit officer

database manager

data communications programmer

data processing auditor

data processing customer support specialist

data processing training specialist

documentation specialist

electronic mail supervisor

employment interviewer

financial analyst

foreign exchange trader

human factors engineer

human resources director

immigration attorney

information scientist

information systems consultant

insurance sales agent

internal auditor

investment counselor

job retraining specialist

legal secretary

loan officer

management consultant

management information systems manager

messenger service owner

operations officer

paralegal

personnel recruiter

real estate appraiser

secretary

software attorney

statistician

systems analyst

systems programmer

technical services manager

telephone answering service supervisor

title examiner

word processing specialist

Communication and Media

art director

book editor

cable television station manager

camera operator

columnist

commentator

commercials producer

computer conference network director

copywriter

critic

educational television consortium coordinator

electronic communications technician

electronic news editor

foreign language teacher

humorist

interpreter

journalism professor

media director

microwave engineer

newspaper editor

newspaper syndicate executive

newswriter

photographic laboratory technician

photojournalist

phototypesetter

printing company supervisor

proofreader

radar systems engineer

radio station manager

recording engineer

satellite-instruction educational facilitator

screenwriter

sign painting company owner

singing messenger service owner

space payload preparation specialist

special events director

technical writer

telecommunications equipment designer

telecommunications installation engineer

telecommunications manager

teleconferencing design engineer

teletext editor

television announcer

television news anchorperson

television news editor

television reporter

translator

transmitter operator

video manager

video-taping service owner

Construction

architect

architectural drafter

boatbuilder

bricklayer

building contractor

building inspector

building materials purchasing agent

building trades instructor

building trades union leader

cabinetmaker

carpenter

cement mason

civil engineer

combination welder

construction apprentice program administrator

construction association executive director

construction engineering professor

construction estimator

construction expediter

construction manager

construction painter

construction project manager

custom home builder

demolition specialist

electrician

equipment subcontractor

excavator

facilities planner

furnace installer

general contractor

glazier

heating/air-conditioning contractor

heavy equipment operator

insulation installer

land developer

lather

marine architect

pipefitter

plasterer

plumber

roofing contractor

sandblaster

sheet-metal worker

solar heating installer

stonemason

structural steel worker

subdivision marketing manager

surveyor

television cable installer

tilesetter

Consumer and Home Economics

adult education instructor

advertising agency stylist

better business bureau manager

business home economist

cafeteria food operations manager

cake decorator

child-care service owner

child development specialist

children's institution director

community fund-raising coordinator

consultant dietitian

consumer information specialist

consumer protection government agent

cooking instructor

credit counselor

customer service representative

educational toy maker

fashion coordinator

fashion designer

fashion model

federal food inspector

food chemist

food editor

food photography stylist

food service supervisor

food technologist

furniture refinisher

gerontologist

home economics instructor

home furnishings editor

home lighting consultant

homemaker rehabilitation specialist

housing manager

interior decorator

interior designer

nutritionist

pattern designer

picture framer

preschool teacher

product information manager

public information director

research dietitian

residence director

retirement planner

television consumer advocate

test kitchen researcher

upholstery company owner

wine maker

women's magazine beauty editor

Environment and Natural Resources (including Marine Science)

air pollution control specialist

aquaculturist

astronomer

biogas conversion tester

chemical engineer

chemical oceanographer

conservation officer

conservation organization executive director

energy utilization manager

environmental analyst

environmental epidemiologist

environmental physicist

exterminator

fisher

forester

forestry technician

geodesist

geothermal geologist

groundwater protection specialist

hydroelectric systems engineer

hydrologist

ichthyologist

industrial hygienist

land reclamation specialist

marine animal trainer

marine biologist

metallurgical engineer

meteorologist

microbiologist

mine manager

minerals economist

noise pollution engineer

ocean engineer

oil company executive

petroleum engineer

photovoltaic energy researcher

pollution control engineer

recycling director

refinery manager

resource recovery engineer

safety engineer

seismologist

solar energy engineer

timber buyer

toxicologist

volcanologist

wastewater treatment plant supervisor

water pollution control inspector

wind energy systems engineer

wood technologist

Fine Arts and Humanities

actor

animator

anthropologist

archaeologist

archivist

art appraiser

art dealer

art director

art teacher

art therapist

calligrapher

cartoonist

choral director

choreographer

cinematographer

comedian

costumer

creative writing teacher

dancer

film director

film editor

genealogist

historian

illustrator

industrial designer

industrial filmmaker

jewelry designer

lighting designer

make-up artist

mathematician

motion picture producer

muralist

museum curator

music composer

music conductor

musical instrument maker

musician

philologist

philosophy professor

photographer

playwright

religious education director

scene designer

sculptor

singer

sociologist

special effects technician

stage director

stage manager

textile designer

Health

anesthesiologist

animal health technician

audiometrist

biochemist

biological photographer

biomedical engineer

cardiologist

cardiovascular perfusionist

child abuse therapist

chiropractor

computerized tomography (CT) technician

dental hygienist

dentist

dialysis technician

electroencephalographic (EEG) technician

emergency medical technician

genetic biologist

geriatric specialist

health physicist

hospital administrator

licensed practical nurse

medical assistant

medical illustrator

medical laboratory technician

medical records administrator

medical social worker

mobile medical clinic director

nuclear magnetic resonance (NMR) technician

nuclear medicine technologist

nurse-midwife

nurse practitioner

occupational therapist

oncologist

ophthalmologist

optometrist

oral surgeon

orthoptist

osteopathic physician

pediatrician

pharmacist

physical therapist

podiatrist

positron emission tomography (PET) technician

psychiatrist

psychologist

radiologic technologist

recreational therapist

registered nurse

respiratory therapist

sonographer

Hospitality and Recreation

airline travel club manager

athletic director

athletic trainer

banquet manager

bartender

botanical gardens public relations director

camp director

caterer

catering sales manager

clown

convention manager

corporate travel manager

country club manager

cruise director

dude ranch operator

executive chef

food and beverage director

golf course superintendent

health spa manager

hotel controller

hotel/motel manager

industrial recreation program director

jockey

laserist (light show)

lifeguard

nursing home activities director

physical fitness instructor

professional athlete

pro sports scout

puppeteer

pyrotechnician

recreation director

recreation establishment manager

reservation agent

resident manager

resort vice president, sales and marketing

restaurant manager

show animal trainer

sports coach

sports equipment supplier

stunt performer

theme park manager

tour guide

travel agency owner

travel school president

travel wholesale tour packager

umpire

video dating service director

yacht rental agent

youth program director

Manufacture and Repair

aeronautical drafter

air-conditioning mechanic

anodizer

biomedical equipment repairer

bookbinder

business machine servicer

CAD/CAM (computer aided design/manufacture)

camera repairer

ceramic engineer

chemical engineer

computer games manufacturer

computer graphics simulation technician

computer service technician

cost control manager

cost estimator

digital design engineer

director of product engineering

electrical engineer

electronics engineer

farm equipment mechanic

fiber optics researcher

food and drug inspector

home-based skate board builder

industrial engineer

instrument repairer

knowledge engineer (artificial intelligence)

laser technician

magnetics manufacturing technician

manufacturing engineer

manufacturer's service representative

materials manager

mechanical drafter

mechanical engineer

model maker

numerical-control operator

package engineer

petroleum engineer

planning and scheduling manager

plant engineer

quality control supervisor

refrigeration mechanic

robotic line supervisor

roboticist

systems engineer

tool-and-die maker

tool designer

vice president, manufacturing

vice president, research and development

watch repairer

welding engineer

Marketing and Distribution

advertising manager

air freight manager

antiques dealer

auctioneer

branch store coordinator

clothing manufacturer's representative

college recruiter

commodities broker

computer memory products representative

computer software distributor

contract administrator

direct mail entrepreneur

expediter

fashion merchandiser

fitness equipment retailer

import-export agent

inventory control supervisor

laser equipment sales engineer

mail-order wholesaler

marketing consultant

marketing information systems manager

marketing research analyst

material handler

media buyer

medical imaging equipment distributor

memorial consultant

merchandise displayer

microcomputer sales engineer

microwave component sales manager

mobile radio/paging device sales engineer

multi-level marketer

new product development manager

package designer

package research specialist

physical distribution manager

product demonstrator

public relations representative

real estate sales agent

retail buyer

retail store manager

robotics sales engineer

sales manager

securities sales agent

semiconductor sales

strategic marketing engineer representative

telecommunications equipment sales representative

telephone long-distance carrier sales representative

television time sales representative

vice president, marketing

warehouse manager

Personal Services

alteration tailor

astrologer

attendant to physically disabled

barber

beauty salon chain owner

biofeedback technician

blade-sharpening service owner

bodyguard

career adviser

carpet cleaning contractor

chauffeur

color consultant

companion

cosmetics representative

cosmetologist

cosmetology instructor

custom tailor

day-care director

delegate guide

domestic cook

dressmaker

electrologist

embalmer

escort for the blind

family and marriage counselor

funeral director

graphologist

hair stylist

home attendant

housekeeping service owner

house-sitting service owner

hypnotherapist

laundry plant supervisor

limousine service operator

manicurist

massage therapist

party planner

personal pilot

personal shopper

pet animal trainer

pet-grooming shop owner

reducing salon manager

shoe-repair shop manager

shoe-shine stand owner

social secretary

tattoo artist

tax preparer

taxi driver

wedding consultant

window-cleaning service owner

Public Service

administrative officer

bailiff

blood bank donor recruiter

border guard

CIA intelligence specialist

city manager

college alumni director

coroner

correction officer

cultural affairs officer

customs inspector

deputy attorney general

detective

economic development coordinator

education lobbyist

equal opportunity representative

faculty adviser (college or university)

federal aid coordinator

financial aid planner

fire protection engineer

foreign service officer

foreign student adviser

harbor pilot

Internal Revenue Service agent

judge

labor standards director

law enforcement community relations specialist

license inspector

mail carrier

military recruiter

police officer

port authority manager

postmaster

psychiatric social worker

public defender

public works commissioner

public works inspector

reference librarian

school guidance counselor

school principal

secondary school teacher

sheriff

special education director

state governor

substance abuse counselor

urban planner

U.S. senator

volunteer services coordinator

welfare director

young adult librarian

Transportation

aircraft company president

aircraft mechanic

Air Force officer

air traffic assistant

air traffic controller

airline pilot

airport ground equipment supervisor

airport manager

ambulance service contractor

automobile design engineer

automobile electronics repairer

automobile manufacture chief executive officer

barge captain

bicycle mechanic

bus driver

bus line operations manager

command module pilot

contract carrier operations manager

corporate airplane pilot

cruise ship captain

diesel mechanic

electronic flight control engineer

express-delivery service contractor

flight attendant

flight school director

flight test engineer

helicopter pilot

hot-air balloon operator

hydrofoil boat pilot

hypertechnology engineer (aerospace research)

independent trucking contractor

launch station operations manager

local truckdriver

locomotive engineer

long-distance truckdriver

motor home rental agent

motor vehicle dispatcher

motorboat mechanic

motorcycle mechanic

passenger service representative

passenger train dispatcher

rapid transit manager

satellite launch preparation specialist

service station manager

space mission specialist

taxi garage manager

terminal operations manager

traffic engineer

traffic safety administrator

wind tunnel model designer

Career Awareness: Make It Work for You

Careers are like colors: If you haven't seen a rainbow, you might think your choices are limited to black and white.

For more shades of discovery, turn to the next section. In it, we tell you how to find out anything you want to know about any occupation.

■ ■ ■

CHAPTER 8

Your Career, Your Research

Information is power. Without factual information about careers and the job market, you are without power, flying in a sandstorm.

While most people require career market research to see where they might find a home for their goals, others will be stimulated in their career search by the "shopper effect"—wanting something they find while browsing in the marketplace.

This section deals with the quality of the market research you need and how to get it.

What Career Information Really Means

Having increased your career awareness (read Chapter 7 if you haven't done so) and compiled future files of possible careers, you're ready for graduate work in the finer points of career market research.

First, let's be clear about the importance of such career characteristics as:

◆ What's involved in the work

◆ The places of work

◆ The size of the occupation

◆ The training to enter the field

◆ Career paths

◆ Personal qualifications

◆ Earnings

◆ Working conditions

◆ Future prospects

What's Involved in the Work

The need to know what a job is all about may well seem obvious. After all, you know whether a particular occupation requires you to shuffle electronics in a bank, sit at a computer work station in an engineering office, or seat people in a restaurant. But if a specific career is a serious contender for your affections, it's time to go beyond the basic outline and get to the nuts and bolts.

Here's a consumer checklist of questions.

1. Exactly what tasks might I do on the job?

2. What would a typical day or month be like?

3. What is the product or service?

4. Would I chiefly work with data, people, or things?

5. Would I travel? Where and how often?

6. Would I sit all day? Stand? Get outside the office?

7. How closely would I be supervised?

8. How would my tasks relate to coworkers?

9. What distasteful things would I have to do?

10. Is there any danger to my health or physical safety?

The Places of Work

While schools and campuses tend to be alike in appearance, work sites are as different as night and day.

You might be working on the 95th floor of a 100-story office building, or deep in the earth in a mine shaft. You might be working at a construction site, a factory, a restaurant, a store, or in a ship, a plane, even a space station.

The place where you work also is dictated by your employer—private industry, government agency or nonprofit organization.

Do beautiful surroundings count with you? The most glamorous offices are those connected with executive headquarters of large corporations, banks, utilities, and well-endowed foundations. At the opposite end of the luxury scale are the offices of small, struggling companies, charities, and low-level government offices.

Another aspect is where the work is located— in cities or rural areas. For career mobility, learn whether the occupation is available only in a few places or is found in most states.

The greater the number of places where you can find employment, the greater your control over your career and lifestyle.

Here are questions to consider.

1. Do I have ample opportunity to relocate to any number of states if I choose?

2. Are the jobs available in the geographic areas I prefer?

3. If the job is available only in government agencies, am I cut out to be a civil servant?

4. If the job is available only in large corporations, am I able to function in a bureaucracy?

5. If the job is available only in marginally profitable businesses, can I tolerate the instability?

6. Are the companies where I might work respected as good corporate citizens and fair employers?

The Size of an Occupation

The size of an occupation is a clue to how many job openings it will have year after year.

Because a small career field has a rocketing rate of growth, don't assume there'll be tons of job openings. On the other hand, because a huge, sleepy career field has modest growth, don't assume job openings will be scarce.

For example: Assume an occupation of 5,000 people and a growth rate of 35 percent annually. That's 1,750 job openings each year.

Now assume an occupation of 500,000 people and a growth rate of 10 percent annually. That's 50,000 job openings a year.

The ideal combination is a fairly large occupation that is showing rapid growth.

Among the questions to answer are:

1. How large is the occupation?

2. Does it have a fast, average, or slow rate of growth?

3. How many job openings are expected each year?

4. Is there a high personnel turnover because the work is poorly paid or dull or unattractive in some other way?

The Training to Enter the Field

If you're in school now, be certain not to overlook the high school and college courses useful or necessary to prepare for the career you have in mind.

You can get ready for jobs in many ways, including enrollment in college programs, vo-tech schools, home study courses, government training programs, military services training, apprenticeships, and more.

The amount of training you have usually determines the kinds of jobs available to you. In many cases, it is also a major factor in how fast you're promoted to higher-level positions.

For some occupations you'll need to be certified or get a license. Doctors, nurses, school teachers, barbers, cosmetologists, electricians and plumbers are examples of those who must be licensed to practice or do business. If you are considering an occupation that requires state licensing, be certain that you check the requirements for it in the state in which you plan to work. After you invest heavily in an education, you don't want surprises.

Here are appropriate training questions:

1. How much education or training is required to qualify in the job market and to meet legal certification or licensing requirements?

2. How long does it take?

3. What does it include?

4. How much does it cost?

5. Where can I get a list of accredited schools?

6. What kind of high school or college program is required? What subjects should or must be chosen?

7. Is there more than one way to prepare? If so, what are the alternatives?

8. Is it possible that instead of formal training, I could learn on the job?

6. Would I need additional education?

7. Would I need another type of work experience?

8. What are the related occupations to which I could move?

9. Is this a field that might permit me to start my own business?

10. Should I expect "employability" security?

Personal Qualifications

Look for information in your career research that will help you determine whether the occupation fits in with your unique personal characteristics. For a particular job, you may need to use specific skills and talents.

For example, an occupation could require that you motivate others, work under close supervision, work in a highly competitive atmosphere, enjoy solving problems, work as part of a team, or use creative talents.

There's only one question for this category: Is this occupation compatible with me as revealed in my identity inventory for personality traits (Chapter 6)?

Career Paths

Try these career path questions:

1. What proportion of workers are promoted?

2. What are the upward steps?

3. How long would it normally take to receive my first promotion? My second?

4. How high could I rise in the field?

5. How long would it take to reach the top?

Earnings

When you are researching a career in depth, you'll probably come across the average earnings for an occupation. Sometimes, instead of average earnings, the figures are expressed as median earnings, which means that half of the people in the career earn more and half earn less.

Although income figures give you an inkling of the relative ranking of jobs by earnings, don't bronze the figures. At best, they are statistical compilations. Look at earnings figures as hints of what you might be paid.

Your paycheck will depend on many things: your experience and ability, the industry you work in, and the section of the country where you live.

Differing pay scales among companies, unionization, seniority, and quality of performance are other factors that explain why often there is a vast spread in the earnings of people in the same occupation.

Another factor in the size of your paycheck is your ability to negotiate a salary equivalent to your value; some people are persuasive and fairly rewarded, while others never bother to learn negotiating skills and are underpaid.

When you're looking at what an occupation typically pays, don't overlook the dollar value of employee benefits. These include such items as health insurance, paid vacation, retirement funds, social security, and sick leave.

In round numbers, employment "bennies" (benefits) are worth nearly 38 percent of your salary; the national annual average is $11,500 per person, according to the Bureau of National Affairs Inc.

Some jobs offer special "perks" (perquisites) that can save you a bundle. Flight attendants may receive reduced airline fares, sales supervisors may receive cars, and hotel employees may receive uniforms.

If self-employment is your tycoonish aim, forget about average earnings. There are too many variables. If you can scratch out a living after six months in your own business, count your blessings. You may be a millionaire before age 30 or you may be in Chapter 13 (bankruptcy) by 25.

Young entrepreneurs tend to ignore benefits, too. As one young electronics company head whose business is run out of his garage says:

"Health insurance? That's the last thing on my mind. The meter doesn't tick when you're sick."

Questions to help evaluate pay scales include these.

1. What is the base annual salary for the job at the entry-, mid-, and top-level?

2. Are bonuses given for superior performance?

3. Does a sales job pay salary plus commission or only commission? (High-performance salespeople often prefer commission only because they can earn astronomical incomes. It's safer for beginners to ask for salary plus commission.)

4. Does the job pay overtime? (Overtime is a feature of clerical and craft jobs.)

5. Does the occupation typically offer an expense account?

6. What employee benefits are usual with this occupation?

7. How much money could I reasonably expect to earn in this occupation after five years? Is this my idea of "good money"?

8. Are raises based on merit, or on rigid pay scales determined largely by seniority? Is this the way I want to work?

9. Have others in this field gone on to open their own businesses and have they prospered?

10. Does this occupation leave time for me to moonlight and earn a second income, if I choose? Does the occupation pay so little that I probably would have to have a second job to accumulate any savings?

Working Conditions

By checking out working conditions, you make sure that when an occupation calls to you, it's with a smile. How well you like the way things are on the job is a big part of career satisfaction.

Considerations discussed in this category are somewhat related to those in the category of "places to work." Here's an analogy to something familiar. "Places to work" are like houses or apartments for living. "Working conditions" are everything that affects the way you live in a building.

There are several aspects of working conditions to consider:

Overtime work. When overtime is required, you must give up some of your free time and be flexible in your personal life. Could you cancel a vacation at the last minute if necessary to finish a crash project and meet a deadline? The trade-off for overtime is more money and/or promotion.

Shift work. People who work nights—such as nurses or auto repossessors—have their days free for shopping, hunting, fishing, gardening, or education. They can also spend their days looking for a better job. A downside is that an individual's biological clock may rebel at night-owl hours.

Environment. Work settings vary from clean air-conditioned offices to dirty, greasy, or poorly ventilated establishments that bear remarkable resemblance to municipal landfills.

Variable settings are a fact even within the same occupation. Take sludge professionals, as an example. Sludge is the slushy, revolting mass left over after water and sewage treatments. While you may be an up-and-coming environmental engineer working in a cushy office punching a pristine computer keyboard most of the time, every now and then you might have to take field trips to collect sludge for testing and review. The samples may drop on your carpet and stain it forever.

One more illustration: When you work in a bureaucracy, space is usually at a premium. So plan on being a cubicle creature surrounded by a few inches of space and portable partitions that never offer total privacy.

Outdoor work. Breathing in fresh air is terrific except on smog-alert days and when it snows, rains, hails, sleets, blows, or overheats.

Hazards. Some jobs are downright dangerous. You could fall, burn, or cut yourself in a kitchen, tumble from a roof during construction, inhale a cancerous substance in manufacturing or chemical plants or suffer heaven knows what as a stunt performer in a film. Some people like leaping from airplanes to fight forest fires, but others prefer seeing it on television. Which type are you?

Physical demands. If you really like working out, you can find a job that requires standing, stooping, crawling, or heavy lifting. Be sure you have the physical strength and stamina required before seeking one of these jobs. Also think ahead 10 or 20 years. Does a physically demanding job offer less strenuous options for older workers?

These questions can help you realize what working conditions are really like in a given career field.

1. What do people in the job say they like most about their work? The least?

2. Are the hours regular or irregular? Long or short? Does the work involve a part-time or flextime schedule? Would you work evenings, weekends or holidays?

3. How much vacation is usual for the industry?

4. Is the work steady or seasonal?

5. Would the job become harder as you get older?

6. Is the work hazardous?

7. Is the occupation one that would eventually depress you or lift your spirits?

Future Prospects

How's the job market? That is the question of questions.

If surgeons are in oversupply, would you really want to spend 13 or more years training with the real possibility that you'll be under-employed?

Do you want to spend six months in mani-curing school when every manicurist in your area has had difficulty keeping busy three days a week?

Is it realistic to invest your time and money in becoming a PhD archaeologist when the job market is nearly nonexistent?

Is it smart to spend years and years getting ready to be a professor of English literature if jobs are few and far between?

These are the kinds of reasons why you must get facts straight about the job market for any career field you are considering. Wishful guess-ing doesn't count.

When you check on job prospects, here are a few tips to keep in mind.

◆ Because there's a shortage in an occupation one year doesn't mean it will continue for-ever. Demand may be cyclical. To illustrate, in some years, engineers are in short supply. The word gets around and soon students are pouring into engineering schools. When the economy takes a dip, the market is stuffed full of engineers. During the energy crunch of the 1970s, petroleum engineers were the hottest things on two legs. Demand dropped in the late 1980s, then zoomed up again in the early 1990s.

◆ Think of your own life cycles in relationship to job outlook. Age discrimination is illegal but nevertheless alive and well in America.

Again focusing on engineers, the ones who stick to the technical side and do not switch to management roles can expect job troubles (if they're ever unemployed) once they're past their 50th birthdays, and sometimes sooner.

Professional athletes are yet another and even more dramatic example of short-career people. If age will impact on your job future, what could you do as a second career? Think about it now.

◆ Revolutionary technology is a fact of the Information Age you can't ignore. In a time of robotics, fiber optics, artificial intelligence, laser marvels, space and ocean exploration— whirlwind scientific and technological change—another question you must deal with is whether choosing a particular occu-pation would paint you into a corner. Ask yourself: "Will I develop skills in this career that I can transfer elsewhere if my job be-comes obsolete?"

◆ When you hear that demand is going through the roof in certain fields—such as immigra-tion law or computer programming—realize that the demand is for *experienced* people. Neophytes have an uphill battle. Getting that first job can be a killer! Anticipate how you are going to overcome the no-experience barrier. The answer usually is to make friends in the field while you are a student, and to obtain experience as a student intern.

◆ Remember that because you learn that a job is in great demand, there's no guarantee that it's in demand where you live. College towns often are teaming with jobless graduates who never moved away, but who could find em-ployment if they would relocate to another community. Competition is almost always greater in warm places than cold, except skiing country.

◆ Any occupation that depends on government action is subject to immediate change. When the government mandated mainstream education for the disabled, demand for special education teachers shot up. The opposite is true too. When the the government cancels a big defense project—such as a warplane—many thousands of defense workers lose their jobs.

◆ Swings in the economy have a dramatic effect on your future prospects. Because an industry's kitty of jobs is closely related to demand for its output, enterprises providing necessity goods or services usually offer more job security than those dealing with luxury goods. Here's an overview of recession winners and losers.

Capital goods are items bought by companies to manufacture products, such as tools for assembly lines. Consumer goods are finished products used by people like you and us; an example is running shoes. Traditionally, makers of capital goods are more vulnerable to downturns than are those that supply consumer goods. A changing world economy, however, may modify this pattern. Thanks to rising export demand, machine tools, heavy equipment, and other capital goods may hold up fairly well in the 1990s. The once-Communist countries of Eastern Europe have large consumer demands that at the present time can only be satisfied by imports.

Durable goods are things that last for a number of years, such as refrigerators and automobiles. Nondurable goods are often used within a year, such as margarine or facial tissues. In tough times, jobs are less secure in durable goods industries, because people tend to put off purchases of big-ticket items.

Even in hard times, some industries buck the trend and do well. Those with a silver-lining track record in past recessions include enterprises that help customers make do with what they have.

The next decade looks good for travel agents, private detectives, and subway operators. But don't even think about becoming a butcher, watchmaker, or ship fitter, says the federal Bureau of Labor Statistics (BLS).

The bureau is fallible since, as we have mentioned, many things can happen to upset the employment apple cart. However, Uncle Sam's predictions are based on good information.

Predictably, practically every unskilled or semiskilled job linked to manufacturing is a loser. Ronald Kutscher, associate commissioner of the Bureau of Labor Statistics, says that manufacturing output will grow, but productivity is rising more rapidly than demand, which undermines employment.

Jobs that are most vulnerable to imports will likely be a drag on the market, as well.

The number of child-care workers is expected to increase by 60 percent by the year 2005, as more mothers with young children go back to work. The number of legal child-care workers in private households, however, is expected to decline, as servants become a less affordable luxury. Jobs for private cooks and maids are also in jeopardy, as the demand shifts to restaurant cooks, bakers, manicurists, bellhops, and laundry and dry-cleaning workers.

The number of farmers will continue to decline while the number of nursery-farm workers will increase.

The entertainment industry is booming, opening jobs for producers, directors, actors, and amusement park attendants.

The BLS projects a 72 percent increase in the ranks of occupational therapists and an 80 percent increase in the number of physical therapists. There will also be increased demand for medical secretaries, registered nurses, and psychologists—in short, anyone who can reduce the workload of high-priced physicians, where there will only be a 22 percent rise in demand.

In a similar vein, the BLS predicts that there will be 58 percent more paralegals in the year 2005, but only 28 percent more lawyers.

Hundreds of thousands of jobs will disappear in telecommunications and office work, as microprocessors and radio transmitters replace humans. Jobs for bank tellers are on the decrease as automated teller machines are being used for more and more routine transactions. At some financial institutions, a fee is charged for speaking with a human teller.

Many new jobs will be created in computer design and repair, software innovation, and computerized page layout for magazines and newspapers.

All of these predictions point up the need to do extensive, ongoing research, since the market can change in a moment.

In searching for a citadel strong enough to keep the wolves away from your door, your choice of employer is important—how well is the organization managed and how strong is its position in an industry?

Even job function affects the stability of your employment—how vital is your work to the company's survival?

Size counts too. The larger the department the weaker your security because there's more fat to trim than in a small department.

Where you live is another factor in job security. Among area hot spots that will add the *most jobs* from now to 2010 (based on forecasts by NPA Data Services, a Washington, D.C. research firm) are these. In California: Los Angeles, Anaheim/Santa Ana, San Diego, Riverside/San Bernardino. Also Washington, Atlanta, Houston, Dallas, Phoenix, Boston, Chicago, Seattle, Tampa/St. Petersburg, Minneapolis/St. Paul, Philadelphia, and Denver.

Among areas with the *fastest rate* of job growth are these. In Florida: Naples, Ft. Myers/Cape Coral, Ft. Pierce/Stuart, W. Palm Beach, Ocala, Orlando, Bradenton, Ft. Lauderdale. In California: Anaheim/Santa Ana and Santa Rosa/Petaluma. In Nevada: Las Vegas and Reno. Also: Santa Fe, N.M., Bryan/College Station, Texas, Ft. Collins/Loveland, Colo., Phoenix, Ariz.

Recession job jitters can clobber workers with the fewest skills; young women and men who offer little more than willing hands may find no takers.

"Last-in, first-out" (LIFO) is a common condition in recessions. It means there is security in seniority and that the most recently hired workers are the first to go when there are reductions in staff. Being "lifo'd" has been particularly hurtful to women and minorities.

Because any young person is subject to being lifo'd, it's wise to devise a back-up plan to use while the skies clear. Here are several plans others have employed.

Rita J., a laid-off trade show manager with office skills, worked for a temporary help agency until she turned up a job in her field.

Harold B., a furloughed pilot, expanded his part-time real estate sales business into a full-time venture while waiting to be recalled to work.

Irene P., a civil service employee who was fired when her agency's budget was cut, found a temporary appointment in another agency while waiting for a permanent job in the merit system.

At this point in your life, you probably haven't idea one about an appropriate back-up plan—you're having lots of trouble coming up with a primary plan! Even so, we confidently suggest that your circuits will not become overloaded if you spend a little time here and there thinking about the perfect back-up plan for you.

To recap, here are questions that should be on your mind as you evaluate a potential career.

1. Do I have a reasonable chance to find a job in this field?

2. Will I be able to work as long as my health is good? if not, what could I do in advance to prepare for a second career?

3. Have I done enough research to know that technology isn't likely to cut my career short if I choose this field?

4. Does this field offer adequate opportunites to develop transferable skills?

5. Am I willing to live where the best jobs in this field are located? Where is that?

6. Does this occupation depend on government action for its ups and downs?

7. Is this occupation strongly affected by swings in the economy?

8. If I should be lifo'd, do I have an alternate plan? What is it?

■ ■ ■ ■

Always go after the secondary sources first; use original sources to validate or disprove what you think you've learned. You get the most from interviews when you know the right questions to ask.

We'll look at secondary sources of career information before examining techniques of field interviewing, bearing these two considerations in mind.

The Keys to Gathering Career Market Research

Now that you know *what* you're supposed to find out, the question is, *how*?

Chances are, you've met more than one dead end trying to track down intelligence on careers that may be right for you. That's not surprising. A lot of this information is tedious or tough to get. Read with us and you'll become a master sleuth in no time.

To paraphrase the great 19th-century British Prime Minister Benjamin Disraeli:

The most successful person in life usually is the person who has the best information.

As you move from career awareness (Chapter 7) to digging for in-depth, specific information for a few favored careers, think about original sources and secondary sources of research data.

Original sources include people doing the work in the fields you like and their employers.

Secondary sources are printed materials, electronic texts and everything else pertinent to the fields.

The Material Must Be Objective

Pamphlets, books, films, and other career information can be biased or incorrect. Company recruiters want their organizations to attract the cream of job candidates so you'll never see recruitment literature that says a company is anything other than wonderful.

All educational institutions—from private vocational schools to well-known universities—need students. They need business. The job opportunities flowing from a given course of study may be overstated; beware of the phrase "unlimited opportunities." There are no such things—all opportunities are finite.

As a generalization, labor unions and professional societies tend to think there are too many people in their fields, while educational institutions tend to think there are too few. Viewpoints frequently benefit those who hold them, which is another way of warning you to watch out for vested interests.

Finally, determine the age of the career material. Anything older than three years is questionable. Anything older than five years is suspect. The working world is moving *that fast*!

Answers to the following questions will help you assess secondary information:

1. Is the material objective?

2. Does the material describe the important abilities and personality traits needed?

3. Does it mention the drawbacks as well as the good points?

4. Does it present realisitic salary data—not just the higher ranges?

5. Does it suggest that you will become rich and famous if you choose this career?

6. Is the material older than three years? five years?

Create Your Own Super Future Files

You learned in Chapter 7 to create future files in building career awareness. Now it's time to use the same concept and create super future files, in which you save every scrap of information on the field you're researching. You will be uncovering data too important to misplace.

As we mentioned earlier, the very experience of researching, filing and retrieving information can help you come to a well-reasoned career decision.

■ ■ ■ ■

The Career Hunter's Guide to the Library

For career seekers, a library is more exciting than a candy store is for 10-year-olds.

Well-equipped public and school libraries have almost everything you need to get started in your research. If they don't have an item you want, they can borrow it from another library through the interlibrary loan system.

We're talking beyond books. Libraries collect and lend films, videos, records, artwork, and pamphlets, and the librarians can help you use on-site computerized guidance systems.

While libraries have always been sources for career information, many are establishing special career centers. Many libraries that haven't established education and job centers because they are strapped for funds have reorganized the materials they own into career sections.

Try Library "Cousins"— School Career Centers

Career centers have sprung up over the past quarter century in high schools and colleges. They offer resources similar to those described in contemporary libraries. The centers may be extensions of the school libraries or separate entities.

In both libraries and career centers, ask the librarian or career technician for help before starting an exhaustive search. These specialists will be very familiar with materials and can show you how to do some serious digging for information.

■ ■ ■ ■

Here Are the Meatiest Resources

While no rundown on career materials can be complete in a single section, here are the categories and resources we consider to be basic or unusually valuable.

High-Tech Job Research, Even for Low-Tech Work

Computers, online research and job search, and the Internet have become household words in the past few years. The term "get wired" has come to mean becoming computer literate and hooking up to the Internet, the network of computer networks.

At first, a familiar phrase was "Get wired, get hired!" Now the phrase making the rounds of professional offices is "Get wired or get fired!"

Even if you do not have a computer of your own, many schools and libraries offer free access to computers wired to the Internet. Assistants may be available to help you learn how to go online and "surf" around the Net.

The electronic universe has made it easier than ever before to collect the details of career information you need to make good career decisions.

Here is a small sampling of several outstanding Internet World Wide Web career sites that are free to the public. The strange-looking letters in the parentheses are the electronic addresses. An Internet savvy person can help you find these resources on the computer. Once you see how easy it is, you'll be an online convert.

America's Job Bank (www.ajb.dni.us)

This is the site of a cooperative effort by the U.S. Department of Labor and 1,800 state employment service offices. It lists hundreds of thousands of job openings each day. Jobs in the private sector and government jobs are included. When the site is finished, a million job openings will flow through every day.

JobWeb (www.jobweb.org)

Sponsored by the National Association of Colleges and Employers, this is *the* resource for new college graduates, and increasingly for job-seeking alumni. This is a high quality, A-to-Z resource that includes job openings, resume postings, job hunting advice, career field comments, and the Catapult, a huge "link page." A link page allows you to mouse-click from one Web site to another without starting from scratch. You see a place you'd like to go, click on it, and presto—you're there!

E-Span (www.espan.com)

This is the pioneer and award-winning online job advertising service. The graphic design is super attractive. E-Span offers a wide variety of career information including salary surveys. Don't miss it.

Online Career Center (www.occ.org)

This pioneer service is one of the best of the comprehensive career search sites. New material appears daily at this one-step resource. You'll want to put this one at the top of your "hot" list for regular visits.

Good Works
(www.tripod.com/work/ goodworks)

More than 1,000 national organizations are profiled here by their type of nonprofit service, including internship opportunities. The resources listed here are described as "The pay is modest, the work is important, the satisfaction is incredible!"

Employment Resources for People with Disabilities
(www.disserv.stu.umn.edu/ TC/Grants/COL/listing/ disemp)

A no-frills site, artistically speaking, but filled with good information for people with disabilities who are conducting a job search.

Business Job Finder
(www.cob.ohio-state.edu/ dept/fin/osujobs.htm)

Operated by Ohio State University, this superior Web site gives direct information about specific business career opportunities, such as finance, accounting, and management consulting.

Monster Board
(www.monster.com)

Many college career seekers say this is their favorite career information and job search site, probably because of its impressive graphics and young, current language.

Career Mosaic
(www.careermosaic.com)

This is huge site with a wide range of career information and links to other resources. You can search by keywords such as "state," "industry," and so forth.

Student Center
(www.studentcenter.com)

Visit this adventurous Web site and check out such offerings as "Fortune-tellin'/Career-pickin' " and a virtual interview feature.

Career Choices
(www.jobweb.org/catapult/ choice.htm)

This Web site gives information about how various majors have led to specific careers. Try the "What can I do with a major in?" and "Major confusion" links. This is very good for career planning.

Resources for Minorities on the Internet (www.vjf.com/ pub/docs/jobsearch.html)

A listing of Internet sites filled with career information for minorities such as African–Americans, Native Americans, Latinos, and Asian–Americans.

JobSmart (jobsmart.org)

An all-around career site, but the first to offer links to some 70 salary studies in various career fields. If money is an important consideration in your career selection, don't miss this site.

General Graduate School Information (minerva.acc.virginia.edu/ ~career/grdsch.html)

Maintained by the University of Virginia, this site is of interest to anyone applying to graduate school.

GRE Online (www.gre.org)

This is the site to look at for test dates, questions about, and other data concerning the Graduate Record Examinations.

Law School Admissions Council (www.lsac.org/ list.htm)

Here's a good site if you're thinking about law school; it includes links to all law schools with Web sites.

Pre-Law Handbook (www.urich.edu/~polisci/ prelaw.htm)

This is a plain but main site to get good advice if you're thinking about law school.

Yahoo's List of Universities (www.yahoo.com/ Education/Universities)

If the colleges and universities you're considering have a presence on the World Wide Web, you'll be able to zip to it from this Web site. You can also click for a "United States Only" list.

AAMC Website (www.aamc.org)

Pre-med on your mind? This comprehensive site by the Association of American Medical Colleges tells you plenty of what you should know.

For lots of information on high-tech research, see Margaret Riley's book, *The Guide to Internet Job Searching* (VGM Career Horizons), and *Hook Up, Get Hired* (John Wiley and Sons) by one of the authors of this book, Joyce Lain Kennedy.

Government References

The *Occupational Outlook Handbook* is issued every two years by the U.S. Department of Labor's Bureau of Labor Statistics. It is the ancestor of all collections of occupational information. Although other publishers may rehash and repackage the book, only the federal government has the money and the resources to gather the original data and evaluate it. A minimum of 35 economist-writers and their editors work on the reference.

The OOH is a superb accomplishment that should be supported and expanded. A downside is that two years often pass between gathering information and printing the book.

The presentation is cautious and bland, never bluntly warning readers to avoid a given occupation that seems headed for oblivion. But

OOH is a topnotch starting place and you should never begin a career search without looking through it.

With each government budget cut, the *Occupational Outlook Handbook* becomes thinner and describes in detail fewer occupations. Included for each occupation is information on what the job is like, working conditions, personal qualifications, training and educational requirements, chances for advancement, job prospects to 2005, earnings, related occupations, and where to find additional information.

The U.S. *Industrial Outlook* is published by the U.S. Department of Commerce. It appears each January with forecasts for specific industries. The reference is an easy way to check that you're not planning to enter a declining industry.

In addition, don't overlook free career briefs provided by states. California, for instance, has hundreds of free guides in its series.

Specialized Career Books

Thousands of books are available that deal with specific career topics, such as *Careers for Bookworms & Other Literary Types*, by Majorie Eberts & Margaret Gisler (VGM Career Horizons/NTC Publishing Group); 101 *Careers: A Guide to The Fastest-Growing Opportunities*, by Michael Harkavy (John Wiley & Sons); *Careers in Advertising*, by S. William Pattis (VGM Career Horizons/NTC Publishing Group); *Career Choices for the 90's: For Students of Mathematics*, by Career Associates (Walker Publishing Co., Inc.); *Great Careers: The Fourth of July Guide to Careers, Internships, and Volunteer Opportunities in the Nonprofit Sector*, edited by Devon C. Smith (Garrett Park Press); and *Opportunities in Performing Arts Careers*, by Bonnie Bjorguine Bekken (VGM Career Horizons/NTC Publishing Group).

A librarian can help you discover career books that relate to your interest by checking in a major reference titled *Subject Guide to Books in Print* (R.R. Bowker Co.).

Sometimes you will want to buy and keep a particular book. If you cannot find the book in a store near you, you may want to order it directly from the publisher. While you can order titles through traditional bookstores, many discount bookstores will not take special orders. Publishers' addresses are listed in several references available in libraries and bookstores.

You can write to the publisher, asking the prepaid price, including postage and handling charges, or, if you are in a hurry and know the book's price, take a chance and add $3.00 to your order to cover shipping costs.

A growing number of publishers maintain toll-free telephone numbers. You can call the number to learn the exact mail-order price of the book. To determine whether a publisher has a toll-free number, call 800-555-1212. (In some areas, you must dial "1" before dialing the information number.) If there is no toll-free number and you want the book as soon as possible, you might want to spend a few dollars on a long-distance call.

Career Briefs

Career briefs are short articles on specific occupations or industries. The following companies are representative of publishers of career briefs.

Careers Inc. (P.O. Box 135, Largo, FL 34649) publishes for high school students briefs, summaries, and job guides describing hundreds of careers. For both students and adults, a new book, *Occu-Facts*, is written in a useful outline format providing a quick reference to almost 600 careers.

Chronicle Guidance Publications, Inc. (P.O. Box 1190, Moravia, NY 13118) publishes a set of some 600 briefs covering 3,500 occupations. The briefs are written in a straightforward language and always include a helpful list of additional aids. This is a valuable resource.

Vocational Biographies (P.O. Box 31, Sauk Center, MN 56378) presents briefs enlivened by stories of real people. Hundreds of occupations are available, including unusual ones hard to find, such as music video producer. Occupational titles are available individually, in book form, and in cluster collections. An idea garden.

Magazines

Specialized career magazines are basic for research. Additionally, the motivated researcher will find that reading general interest and specialized magazines focused on other topics also can save countless hours of frustration and many false starts down rewardless roads.

Some periodicals, such as *Working Woman*, *Black Collegian*, and *Careers & The Disabled*, aim toward specific groups.

In *High Technology*, you might be inspired to explore computer science after reading about the twilight zone of the microchip age—the world of artificial reality where environments only seem to exist.

Business Week is a basic tool for keeping up with trends that directly affect career choices.

American Demographics also reports on early warning signals that influence career trends.

To move from outsider to insider in an industry, the trade press functions as a perfect conveyor belt.

This category of magazines comprises trade journals and professional magazines, like these:

Construction Week

Datamation

Nurse Practitioner

Human Resource Management

Journal of Marketing

Supermarket News

Telecommunications

Chances are that your library or career center subscribes to very few trade magazines; you'll probably have to ante up for the publications you want, but the returns are enormous. You'll know the hot new trends in an industry, see ads for special training opportunities, and learn the jargon so that you can speak like a native when you interview for a job. By regularly reading the recruitment ads, you can anticipate the job market and determine what you must do to become a prime candidate.

A simple way to identify the right trade journals is merely to ask people in the field what they read. A librarian can help you find the appropriate publications by checking under the subject index in *Ulrich's International Periodicals Directory* (R.R. Bowker Co.).

Indexes

Other notable references useful in ferreting out magazine articles of particular interest include:

Readers' Guide to Periodical Literature

Magazine Index

Business Periodicals Index

Subject indexes help you find articles in specific fields, such as finance or science. Examples are:

Art Index

Education Index

Agricultural & Biological Index

The Social Science Index

Directories

One of the richest mines of information is *The Encyclopedia of Associations* (Gale Research, Inc.). Here you'll find 22,000 organizations whose sole reason for existing is to promote their special interests. There are associations for virtually every subject you can imagine. A specialized reference, also from Gale Research, Inc., is the *Professional Careers Sourcebook: An Information Guide for Career Planning*. Featuring a phenomenal resource list for each of more than 100 occupations requiring education or training beyond high school, the big compiling task has been done for you. The directory is updated yearly.

After finding the associations that fit your interest, it's often possible to obtain free or inexpensive career materials from them. If your library or career center hasn't acquired the booklets and pamphlets published by organizations of interest to you, write a letter along these lines:

Dear Association Executive:

Please send me a copy of the free career literature that your organization publishes. In addition, please include a bibliography of the career materials you offer that are available for a charge.

Sincerely,

Your name,
address

After receiving the initial material, you may have questions, or you may want to get in touch with the association's members in your area. To follow up, you can address your letter to the association's education director, public relations director, or membership director.

Other Directories

At least 5,000 directories identify numerous topics, ranging from convention meeting dates to employers of engineers to newspapers.

The easiest source to find which of these information motherlodes you need is called *Directories in Print* (Gale Research, Inc.).

Here are a few examples of available resources:

◆ *The Directory of Conventions* (Successful Meetings/Databank). Every day of the year a convention or conference is held somewhere in the nation. If you want to become a sports doctor, a venture capitalist, or a psychologist, wouldn't it be great to attend a meeting of the American Academy of Sports Physicians, the National Association of Small Business Investment Companies, or the American Psychological Association?

Job interviewing often takes place at these meetings and even if you're still a student, you may meet a manager this year who will hire you another year. Always ask about special student rates because these meetings can be costly to attend.

◆ *Chronicle Career Index* (Chronicle Guidance Publications Inc.) is a rich reference listing of career guidance materials.

Directories that are useful in job hunts include these:

◆ *Hoover's Handbook: Profiles of Over 500 Major Corporations*, edited by Gary Hoover and Alta Campbell (Publisher's Group West). Launched in 1990, this modestly priced reference contains one-page profiles of over 500 major corporations: their history, management, products, and performance. Plans call for updating each fall.

◆ *Standard & Poor's Register of Corporations, Directors and Executives* (Standard & Poor), three volumes. The first volume lists the names of companies and describes what they do. The second volume lists the names of company executives and directors. The third volume is an index telling you the name of each company and where to find information about it in the other two volumes.

◆ *The Career Guide: Dun's Employment Opportunities Directory* (Dun's Marketing Services) contains the addresses, contact people, hiring practices, career-development programs, benefits and company overviews of thousands of U.S. companies with more than 1,000 employees.

◆ *Thomas Register of American Manufacturers* (Thomas). This book tells you who makes what across the country, including manufacturers' names and addresses. For most states there also is a state directory of manufacturers published by Manufacturers' News Inc.

◆ Various local directories of businesses are published by both state and city chambers of commerce.

Finding What Jobs Will Be in Demand in Your State

When you want to know about demand for various occupations in your state, call your state's occupational information coordinating committee (OICC). Generally, your state's OICC is located in the state capital; you can find out by calling the National OICC in Washington, D.C. at (202) 653-5665. NOICC is an independent federal agency located at 2100 M St. N.W., Ste. 156, Washington, D.C. 20037.

The committees give educated guesses that include the top growth jobs and the jobs with the most openings. Because they are speculative, they are not guaranteed to be right on target. Even so, it's useful to know what experts think who have studied your state's economy.

Some states publish their own occupational outlooks and will send a free copy upon request.

Your high school guidance office or college career services office is likely to have an OICC copy of your state's job outlook.

Beyond the Library: Original Research to the Rescue

After unearthing career information from media and recording it in your super future files, you're ready to move to primary sources and interview people and their bosses at work in the field you're considering.

Refresh your memory by turning back to the career awareness discussion (Chapter 7) and rereading the techniques for obtaining interviews and conducting them.

In case you've forgotten the difference between career awareness and the original research you're about to do, it's a matter of volume and details.

In career awareness interviews, you scan the world of work and become aware of many career options. You are cruising, doing brief interviews with many people. You are screening out options that seem to clash with your preferences.

Now, after weeding out all but the most attractive options, you get down to brass tacks. Now you are considering just a few fields, maybe only one. You are getting ready to set goals and make decisions.

For each finalist field on which you are gathering information, you'll want to dig, dig, dig. You need not only chapter and verse, but paragraph and period. And the way you are going to get it is to validate your extensive media research with person-to-person interviews in depth.

The moment has arrived—go out and interview! This is no time to suffer an attack of shyness. As we said earlier, try not to get yourself in a tizzy about the possibility of being turned down.

If it happens, simply try someone else. Being refused an interview is of no consequence. Most people will give you an appointment. They understand that your career search is not a trivial matter.

■ ■ ■ ■

Youth Work Clubs Are Valuable Resources

On an imaginary spectrum of career exploration, you find at one end the activity of data gathering; at the other, working in student jobs. Somewhere in the middle is a group of top-notch organizations that let you sample occupations in various ways.

Collectively, these groups are called *youth work clubs.*

Their purpose is to help you meet and learn from people who already are in the career fields you are thinking of entering. Most of the groups aim at high school students. If an organization seems right for you, find out how you can join—or start—a chapter.

Community-Based Clubs

Aspira of America provides educational assistance to the Hispanic community in high schools and colleges through Aspira Leadership Club. (*Aspira* is the Spanish word for "aspire.") The clubs offer career information programs, and, in some instances, internships. (Aspira Association, Inc.,

1444 I Street NW, Ste. 800, Washington, DC 20005)

Boys and Girls Clubs of America emphasize youth development and offer a self-directed job search program. (Boys & Girls Clubs of America, 1230 West Peachtree Street NW, Atlanta, GA 30309)

Business Professionals of America is for high school and postsecondary students preparing for careers in the business world. The organization, through its chapters across the country, sparks business skill development, leadership, and ambition. (Business Professionals of America, 5455 Cleveland Avenue, Columbus, OH 43231)

Exploring is the coed, high school division of the Boy Scouts of America. The program, the largest of its kind in the nation, is established in a series of "posts"—places where you can find out what the work world is really like. Each post has different divisions, such as law and criminal justice, computer science, commercial art, and business management. (Boy Scouts of America, 1325 W. Walnut Hill Lane, Irving, TX 75015-2079)

From Dreams to Reality, is the career exploration program of the Girl Scouts of the U.S.A. The activity encourages girls to explore a wide variety of careers, strengthen decision-making skills, and evaluate experiences as they relate to personal life and career choices. (Girl Scouts of the U.S.A., 420 Fifth Ave., New York, NY 10018)

Girls Incorporated (formerly Girls Clubs of America) offers to members, up to 18 years old, career awareness programs with an emphasis on non-traditional careers for women, such as science, math, and technology. (Girls Incorporated, 30 E. 33rd St., New York, NY 10016)

Horizon, the Camp Fire career program, encourages members to pursue volunteer work as a way to explore work interests and skills. Participants assess their talents and values relative to work, obtain basic employment information, and focus on career preparation requirements, plus they provide valuable services. (Camp Fire Boys and Girls, 4601 Madison Avenue, Kansas City, MO 64112)

JETS is the popular name for the *Junior Engineering Technical Society*, an organization with student chapters for those considering engineering or applied science as a career. Students explore technology through project work and activities. JETS is funded by engineering societies, engineering schools, and corporations. (Junior Engineering Technical Society, 1420 King Street, St. 405, Alexandria, VA 22314)

Junior Achievement Inc. provides young people with practical economic education programs and experiences in the competitive private enterprise system. The international organization forms a partnership with businesses and schools. (Junior Achievement Inc., One Education Way, Colorado Springs, CO 80906)

The *National 4-H Council* programs offer training in automotive skills, business management, economics, career planning and management, and other fields. (National 4-H Council, 7100 Connecticut Ave., Chevy Chase, MD 20815)

recognize abilities acquired through agricultural education. (FFA National Center, 5632 Mt. Vernon Memorial Highway, Alexandria, VA 22309)

Future Homemakers of America is an organization for students in home economics and consumer homemaking courses. One program stresses career preparation with recognition that workers also fill roles as family and community leaders. (Future Homemakers of America, Inc., 1910 Association Drive, Reston, VA 20191-1584)

Vocational Industrial Clubs of America is the group for trade, industrial, technical, and health occupations students in high school and post-secondary institutions. Members join clubs in their own occupational area; their activities are a part of the curriculum. A Skills Olympics is held each year to recognize outstanding achievements (National VICA, 14001 James Monroe Highway, Leesburg, VA 22075)

Vocational Education Clubs

DECA students take marketing, merchandising, and management courses, along with related student jobs, in high school or college. (DECA Association of Marketing Students, 1908 Association Drive, Reston, VA 20191)

Future Business Leaders of America—Phi Beta Lambda is an organization for students preparing for careers in business. FBLA is for high school students, while PBL is for postsecondary students. Membership offers students a variety of networking and leadership development opportunities/programs to give them the edge in the competitive career marketplace. (Future Business Leaders of America—Phi Beta Lambda, Inc., 1912 Association Drive, Reston, VA 20191)

FFA is a national organization preparing students for careers in agriculture—its science, technology, and business. Awards and activities

How Youth Clubs Help

Because youth club activities allow you to test the waters of your career interest, sometimes you discover that a decision you made was wrong.

One would-be lawyer—after talking to judges and attorneys lined up through his Boy Scouts Explorer post—found that he wasn't cut out for the law and switched to an Explorer journalism division. Out of school now, he is writing broadcast commercials and loving every word of it.

"Without Exploring," he says, "I would have wasted thousands of my parents' dollars and years of my time in school before finding out that what I really like to do is write."

After completing this section, you are well equipped for career sleuthing. Not bad for one who, until picking up this book, didn't know clusters from career mobility.

■ ■ ■ ■

CHAPTER
9

Your Goals

Setting and reaching goals helps you focus on the best place for you to be in life. Without goals, it's easy to become distracted in your journey toward success. Knowing the difference between striving for goals and drifting along often separates winners from near misses.

This section supplies a variety of thought-provoking activities to help you understand the nature of goals, objectives, reality testing, and how to handle disappointment when things don't work out.

Goals Along Life's Winding Road

What! No star, and you are going out to sea? Marching, and you have no music? Traveling, and you have no map?

This astonishment at impetuosity is taken from the French.

For young men and women puzzling over their careers, the American version could be: *What! No goals and you are trying to pick a career?* Without goals, you can't predict where you're going.

From the beginning of time, successful people have realized that if you don't know where you're going, you won't wind up any place you recognize. Yes, you might stumble into good fortune, maybe you'll win a state lottery. But you can't count on luck or serendipity pulling you through.

Zig Ziglar, a major-league motivational speaker, agrees. In his book *See You at the Top*, Ziglar notes that, while it is safer not to set goals and risk being embarrassed in front of friends, it would also be safer for a ship to stay in port or a plane to stay on the ground. But the ship would collect barnacles and become a bucket of bolts in the harbor, and the plane would rust and fall apart on the ground.

A worthwhile but realistic goal is one that makes you reach and stretch, and one that you have at least a 50–50 chance of achieving. Is there really any point of wanting to be a top athlete when you lack coordination, or aiming to become the President of the United States when you prefer reading a book to meeting people?

It is not, however, unrealistic to have riches as a goal, or visualizing how you will put those little green dollars to work. And it's reasonable to set a high and noble goal, such as deciding you want to play a recognizable role in conquering cancer. Once you fully decide to commit yourself to unlocking your potential, to being all you can be, you begin to grow. Sometimes the whole becomes larger than the parts, an effect seen in people who believe they have a calling and are able to do seemingly miraculous things.

Goals express your belief in yourself. Gather together your star, music, and map.

■ ■ ■ ■

Take Your Best Shot

Author Katherine Nash also believes in aiming as high as your potential. In her book, *Getting the Best of Yourself*, she says:

The goal, the objective—the dream!—they are all attainable. The first step is to TAKE the first steps—raise one foot off dead center.

You're not compelled to achieve your aspiration by one soaring flight, not even by giant steps, only one foot at a time. After the first footstep, the second is easier, the third is surer, the fourth is faster. Suddenly the miracle happens. Your mind is off the footsteps and only on the dream.

Only you're not dreaming the dream anymore—you're living it. Winning. Getting the best of yourself.

Valuable Goals

The work you've already done will give you a head start on this discovery. Turn back to Chapter 6 and review your identity inventory for values.

Write the five most important values on the left side of the following chart. In the right column, write a goal that reflects each value. There are two examples to start you off.

(Reprinted by permission of Grosset & Dunlap/Putnam.)

VALUES CHECKLIST

Value	Goal
Having personal freedom on the job.	Owning my own business.
Helping others.	Finding an attractive career in
	which I can be of service to others.
1.	1.
2.	2.
3.	3.
4.	4.
5.	5.

In Memory Of—

A great way to find out what you want from life is to write your own obituary. Limit your accomplishments and personal factors to 150 words. Style it on the order of newspaper obituaries. In anticipating your own mortality, you'll zero in on goals that are really meaningful to you.

_____

_____

_____

_____

_____

_____

_____

P. S. You were 98 when you passed away peacefully in your sleep.

Goals and Objectives: The Difference

Although you may hear the words used interchangeably, goals are *not* objectives.

Businesses set goals and identify the steps necessary to reach the goals. Objectives are the steps. An objective can be measured, so you'll know when you've accomplished it.

Goals are broad and involve long-range periods. Objectives are concrete, specific accomplishments necessary to achieve goals, and they usually involve a shorter time period.

Many successful people use the basic goals-objectives method to climb to success. Let's look at an example of using goals and objectives to get what you want.

Pete's Goals

Pete is a junior and Sara is a very attractive sophomore. All the young men want to date Sara. Pete would like to date her himself. He has one problem. He doesn't have a fancy car. He can use the family station wagon—but who wants to pick up a date (one you want to impress) with a station wagon that has rips in the seat covers and dog hair everywhere?

Pete would really like to buy a car, but to do so, he figures he needs $2,800. He found out he can get the perfect car for that price. The guy who will sell it to him will let him have it for $400 down and he can pay the balance by the month.

Pete has $500 in a savings account. He's been saving it for college. At present, he doesn't have a job and his parents don't want him to use his college savings for a car.

Pete has a real flair for landscaping and, by borrowing his dad's lawn mower, leaf blower, and weed eater, he opened "Pete's Lawn Ser-

vice." He placed neighborhood ads suggesting clients could save money by contracting for the season. Evidently, his advertisement was impressive, because within a week he had eight clients.

Pete talked his parents into a plan whereby he would borrow the money from his savings account, buy the car, and then pay back the money to the savings account and also make monthly payments on the car from his lawn service earnings.

Sure enough, Pete got a date with Sara and she was impressed with his car. Interestingly enough, Sara was less impressive. He's decided that she is rather shallow. But Pete's wildly enthusiastic about his business, which he says is "blooming."

Pete thinks that horticulture is a possible career option and plans to research colleges that offer it as a major. He's also decided to talk to some people working in the field.

You can see that Pete had a goal and how he was motivated to reach it. Pete achieved his goal by having specific objectives. Write Pete's goal and the objectives to reach it. Also point out what new goals and objectives Pete has set for himself.

Pete's goal:

_____

_____

Pete's objectives leading to his goal:

_____

_____

_____

Pete's new goal:

_____

_____

Possible objectives leading to this goal:

_____

_____

_____

Get Specific

The more specific you are in stating a goal and the objectives for reaching it, the better your chance for success. Goals such as "I want to be happy" are too vague.

Break your goals into small, more immediate steps—ones that you can measure. What are some specific things that would make you happy? Looking better? Having more friends?

Then objectives might be: 1. Be able to run 3 miles by July 1, and 2. make a point to talk with five people this week whom you think you would like to know better.

Winners Reach Their Goals

Setting goals is no guarantee that you'll reach them. To continue the self-improvement example, here's another goal and the well-planned objectives that would lead to its achievement:

Goal: To lose 20 pounds by June 1 so I won't feel self-conscious in my bathing suit.

Objective: Visit my doctor by March 1; get a diet recommendation that is both safe and effective.

Objective: Tell my family of my plan and give them a list of the kind of food I will need and ask for their support. I want to start no later than March 15.

Objective: Stick to my diet and tell all of my friends the day I begin so they will support my effort and not encourage me to cheat on the diet.

Objective: Weigh myself every three days and keep a record of my weight loss.

Your Turn at the Goal Post

Practice is the best way to become an expert goal setter and objective chooser. Try this:

For each time period listed below, write one goal. Be sure to consider whether the goal is realistic and whether the objectives leading to the goal are measurable. (If you are 4 feet tall, a goal to be a basketball star is unrealistic.)

Bear in mind that you should have a 50–50 chance of reaching your goal and that it should be challenging.

Today's goal:

_____

_____

Objectives to reach it: _____

_____

_____

_____

This week's goal:

_____

_____

Objectives to reach it: _____

_____

_____

_____

This year's goal:

_____

_____

Objectives to reach it: _____

_____

_____

_____

The goal to reach by the time I am 30:

_____

_____

Objectives to reach it: _____

_____

_____

_____

■ ■ ■ ■

Choose Your Goals Wisely

When you consider goal ideas, you'll probably want to consider two types of goals: short- and long-range goals. Short-range goals are those to be achieved in the immediate future, the next day, or the next couple of weeks.

Long-range goals are those you plan to reach in the future, within the next few months, or in more than a year.

The biggest difference between winners who reach their goals and those who don't is in goal selection. Goal-reachers aim neither impossibly high nor uninspiringly low. They think carefully about the kinds of goals they set and calculate the risks involved in reaching them.

■ ■ ■ ■

What Others Say About Goals

You need to start with hopes and dreams. More of them may be attainable than you think if you set your goals creatively.
—*Career Development Pioneer* BERNARD HALDANE

In a way, you have something to look forward to only if you lose. After we won the Super Bowl, I looked over at Charlie Waters and whispered, "But who do we play next?" When you win the Super Bowl—I hesitate to say it—you're depressed.
—*Former Dallas Cowboy* CLIFF HARRIS

You have to make a decision, "I am going to be such and such," even if that is not, in the end, the great answer. You have to set your sight on a goal to get anywhere.
—*Advertising Guru* MARY WELLS LAWRENCE

There's a word that you should always keep in mind if you aren't sure which way to turn. That word is "goal"—the end result you want in return for your work. . . . With [goals] you'll always know the right direction in times of trouble.
—*Author* ROBERT M. HOCHHEISER

I push in just one direction, not in every direction.
—*Nobel Prize Winner* RITA LEVI-MONTALCINI

Ready! Fire! Aim!
—ANONYMOUS

You've got to think about "big things" while you're doing small things, so that all the small things go in the right direction.
—*Futurist and Writer* ALVIN TOFFLER

To tend, unfallingly, unflinchingly, towards a goal, is the secret of success.
—*Russian Ballerina* ANNA PAVLOVA

Do not aim lower than your potential. Few people have ever attained a higher level than the one to which they aspired.
—*Former U.S. Cabinet Officer* PATRICIA HARRIS

There is no achievement without goals. Perhaps through some magical piece of luck or coincidence you will manage a great coup someday, but coincidence is not something you'll want to put your money on. It's safe to say that without knowing where you want to go, and without making some specific plans about how to get there, you will either move backward or drift sideways.
—*Planning Consultant and Author* ROBERT J. MCKAIN

The shadow of your goalpost is better than no shade at all.
—ANONYMOUS

If you shoot for the stars and hit the moon it's okay. But you've got to shoot for something. A lot of people don't even shoot.
—*Business Expert and Writer* ROBERT TOWNSEND

Parties who want milk should not seat themselves on a stool in the middle of a field in hope that the cow will back up to them.
—*Writer* ELBERT HUBBARD

A life that hasn't a definite plan is likely to become driftwood.
—*Business Titan* DAVID SARNOFF

Reality Testing: Facing Facts About Your Goals

Do you recognize anyone in this cast of dreamers?

◆ Marsha, a lead dancer in the sophomore follies, who, not recognizing the big difference between school shows and tapping her heart out on Broadway, has a goal of becoming a musical comedy superstar.

◆ Rolf, a determined premed student whose C grades in organic chemistry, biology, and math make him an unlikely candidate for an American medical school, refuses to admit that, academically speaking, he is overmatched by many other premed students.

◆ Tim, a young man whose drawings everyone admires, insists that he will become an architect although his technical aptitude is slight. He knows that automation is drastically reducing the job market for architects but feels he will be an exception, succeeding where many others will fail.

◆ Joe, a foreign student whose family sacrificed to send him to the United States to become an engineer, stubbornly insists on pursuing this goal although counselors have told him there is ample evidence that people with comparable academic records have consistently failed or done poorly when admitted to an engineering program. Joe fears failure could result in disgrace for his entire family.

■ ■ ■ ■

Make Your Own Reality Test

It's easy to look at others and see why they are headed for disappointment. But are you as objective about your own goals? Will they survive reality testing? Try this checklist and see:

	Yes	No	Not Sure (Need more facts)

1. Do I *have the intellectual capacity to achieve my goal*?
   (To verify, ask your counselor to profile a successful student in your goal area. This should include SAT or ACT scores, preparatory courses, and grades and other academic measures. After reviewing the profile, ask yourself, "In the light of this information, what is it in my academic background that could lead me to succeed at this career goal?")

2. Do I *have the necessary physical characteristics to reach my goal*?
   (Speed won't compensate for height in pro basketball if you're under 6 feet; motivation won't make up for lack of talent in entertainment; determination won't make it magically possible for a blind person to become an air traffic controller. Decide which physical characteristics are required for your goal. If there are shortcomings, maybe you can find ways to compensate. And maybe not.)

3. Do I *have the financial backing to reach my goal*?
   (Think ahead. Brainstorm for ways to find the money you'll need.)

4. Do I *have the energy to achieve my goal*?
   (Are you in good health? Will your stamina get you through a career of stress-filled days, if that's the kind of goal you select? For example, high stress jobs include practical nurse, public relations specialist, and city manager, among many others.)

5. Do I *have the commitment to reach my goal*?
   (Are you willing to postpone things you want now to achieve your long-range goals? A college junior, for instance, may be impatient living on nickels and dimes and tempted to drop out of school and take a job that seems, at the time, to pay a fortune. Another example: Can you wait to marry until you and your spouse can have your own place?)

6. Do I *really, deep down, want this goal*?
   (Sometimes we choose goals merely to please others and we don't enjoy the journey to the destination, a sure formula for dissatisfaction. This is the person who can't stand the sight of blood but signs up for medical school to please a parent.)

How to Handle Disappointment

Even though you've planned your goals well and reality-tested them, there's no assurance that everything will work out.

Losing a job you really want is an example of a missed goal. You're disappointed and that's understandable.

Disappointment is a fact of life and a recent study at the Institute for Social Research at the University of Michigan shows that only one-third of Americans feel pretty sure their life will work out the way they want it.

When things don't work out as you expect, here are several ways to deal with your disappointment.

◆ Admit disappointment to yourself rather than pretending it doesn't hurt; this acknowledgment helps get grieving out of the way.

◆ Have a sense of perspective on the loss, realizing that there are alternative ways to satisfy your yearnings. Your challenge is to find them. There are countless examples of disappointments that turn out to be blessings in disguise—you probably can think of several in your own life.

◆ Analyze what went wrong and determine whether any action on your part (better planning, more attention to details, less indulgence in mere wishful thinking) could have changed the outcome. If so, learn by your mistakes and look at your disappointment as a learning experience—as an opportunity for growth.

For your bulletin board: As Thomas Edison said, "When down in the mouth, remember Jonah. He came out all right."

■ ■ ■ ■

Realizing Your Potential

When you find that you need straight answers for life's winding road, review your goals and objectives, making sure that they are clearly defined and you have at least a 50–50 chance of achieving them.

■ ■ ■ ■

CHAPTER
10

Your Decisions

As a decision maker, you take responsibility for your own success or failure. While it may be a frightening challenge, the rewards can be fantastic. Controlling your own destiny puts sunshine and music into reaching for your goals.

This section explains why taking control of your life and making your own decisions is the most rewarding road to follow. There are activities to help you rate your decision-making ability. We offer a seven-step formula for decision making and explain the importance of making flexible, responsible decisions.

Decisions and Dirty Sweet Potatoes

People who don't learn to make good and timely decisions may, figuratively speaking, eat a lot of dirty sweet potatoes. Here's what we mean.

In the 1950s, a colony of monkeys on Japan's island of Koshima were studied by scientists. The monkeys were fed sweet potatoes dropped in the sand. The monkeys liked the taste of the raw sweet potatoes but hated the taste of the dirt.

Imo, a young female, decided to solve the problem. We can't know what decision-making steps Imo worked through but whatever she did, she came to the correct conclusion: Imo washed the potatoes in a nearby stream. Imo then taught the positive results of her decision to her mother and to playmates, who also taught their mothers how to solve the problem of gritty tasting sweet potatoes.

Between 1952 and 1958, all the young monkeys and parents who imitated their children learned this social improvement. Other adults—who did not make a decision to solve the problem—continued to eat the unclean tubers.

Unless you're fond of dirty sweet potatoes, remember that the ultimate responsibility for making decisions that affect your life is yours.

■ ■ ■ ■

Where Do You Stand on Decisions?

Decisions, decisions. In your younger days, many of them were made for you. Now it's time to seize the freedom you've always wanted by drawing your own conclusions.

You cleverly realize that many of the choices you make today will define your life tomorrow. Knowing that, you'll be careful about choosing, won't you?

A favorite friend of ours wasn't. At 34, the young man is starting over, a veteran of five wasted years on ski slopes, a victim of embezzlement of his company, and a subsequent filer of bankruptcy. As this honors graduate of the school of hard knocks said:

I wish I had taken my choices more seriously. When I knew it was time to make my own decisions, I did. But I went off half-cocked. I had the power to make decisions, but not the practice to make the right ones.

When people tried to warn me to watch out for this or that, or not to make a rash decision, I thought to myself, "I'm no dummy, I can think for myself."

What I hadn't anticipated when I made so many foolish decisions is that there are a lot of people in the world who spend a lot of time figuring out how to get the best of you. I know that now. I found out the hard way.

Facing adulthood is an appropriate time to take stock of your personal style of handling weighty decisions.

Are you one who clutches, panics, agonizes endlessly, and secretly hopes someone else will take the torturous decision off your hands? Or do you rush into the first thing that pops into your head on the theory that God takes care of fools, drunks, and you?

Either approach hurts your chances to succeed in life. One of the reasons people do things they later regret bitterly is that they have not learned how to make good decisions. You were not born knowing how to choose well. You learn by trial and error.

Here's an illustration. If your mother always chooses the clothes you wear, you have had few opportunities to look like a horror show and suffer endless teasing from friends. If you select your own clothing, you have learned through criticism to be careful about the way you dress— you have learned lessons in being responsible for your own actions.

It's not a happy thought, but most people learn to make good decisions by making mistakes. It's what happens later that counts.

Losers view failure as an excuse to quit, while winners view failure as the chance to learn not to do something the same way again.

Some of us learn faster than others who go through life never understanding why the things they do often end badly.

Here are two activities to help you see a true picture of yourself in relation to the way you make decisions.

Are You Satisfied With Your Past?

How do you feel about the decisions you have made? List four decisions you made that turned out well:

Decision	Age When Made	What Happened?
Example: **Said "no" to drug pusher.**	14	Boosted self-esteem and respect from friends. Drugs never messed up life.
1.		
2.		
3.		

(continued)

Decision	Age When Made	What Happened?
4. _____	_____	_____
_____	_____	_____
_____	_____	_____
_____	_____	_____

List four of your decisions that you now regret:

Decision	Age When Made	What Happened?
Example: Dropped out of school.	16	Couldn't get a decent job; talked parents into letting me go back to school at 18. Lost two years.
1. _____	_____	_____
_____	_____	_____
_____	_____	_____
2. _____	_____	_____
_____	_____	_____
_____	_____	_____
3. _____	_____	_____
_____	_____	_____
_____	_____	_____
4. _____	_____	_____
_____	_____	_____
_____	_____	_____

Who Makes Your Decisions?

You may not realize how much control of your life you hand over to others. The next activity helps you see to what extent your friends exert their will over your decisions.

Decision-Making Checkup

Type of Decision	Amount of Control Friends Exert		
	None	Some	A Lot
1. What classes or major I take			
2. What books I read			
3. What I will do after graduation			
4. Whether and where I will go to college, graduate school			
5. Whom I will date			
6. Who my friends are			
7. What grades I get			
8. How I treat others my age			
9. What songs I like			
10. What I would like to be			
11. Whether I smoke, drink, do drugs			
12. Whether I get a part-time job			
13. How I treat my teachers, professors, parents			
14. What clothes I buy			
15. What politicians I support			
16. What my hobbies are			
17. Whether I cheat on tests			
18. Whether I get married after graduation			
19. Whether I go to class			
20. Whether I finish school			

The Art of Choosing

Decision making can be sliced up into orderly stages. Our formula uses seven steps.

Once you get them down pat and practice a bit, the steps tend to merge into a continuous process.

Our seven-step formula simplifies all decisions, whether you're deciding something important, such as your choice of career, or something minor, such as which entree you will order for dinner.

Here's how it works.

1. Define the Problem

The precise nature of a problem is not always self-evident. Sometimes you need family and friends to help blow away the fog.

For example, suppose you're feeling unsure, restless, and frustrated without knowing exactly why. After listening to you for awhile, others—who can be more objective about you than you yourself are—may pick up clues and offer a suggestion: "It sounds as though you need to change your major."

You're astonished! It's true! The revelation hits like thunder. Now that you mull it over, your classes have seemed incredibly boring and you aren't quite sure to what end your education is leading. Once you know the problem, you can decide what to do about it.

2. Identify Options

At first, you may think of few or no options. Seek advice. In addition to home-based consultants (family and friends), pull in information from other sources, too.

If you're eyeing another major that seems promising, ask people who are already enrolled in that major what they think about it both as a discipline, and as the basis for a future career or foundation for graduate study.

3. Anticipate Probable Outcomes

As you will recall from our earlier discussion of expert predictions, you know that everybody's crystal ball is cracked from time to time. Nevertheless, you should make an educated guess about how each option might turn out.

Let's say you switch your major from English to engineering. While your immediate job prospects will be immensely better as a new technical graduate than as a graduate in liberal arts, some of your credits may not count toward graduation. This means you'll have to go to school longer. Are you prepared to extend your studies?

Some people hate to make decisons because they fear they'll make errors. The way to put this fear in perspective is to make a good guess about the outcomes of each option. "What is the worst thing that could happen?" "What is the best thing that could happen?"

4. Make a Values Impact Statement

People make choices because they value one thing more than another.

Looking back at the discussions on values in previous sections, you'll recall that your values include how you feel about yourself; how you feel about others; your moral, ethical, and religious beliefs; your emotional needs and your motivations. When making a decision you must weigh all these values.

When you act in conflict with your values, you usually pay not only the piper, but also the percussion section and maybe the whole orchestra.

Often you can eliminate a number of your options because you can't live with the consequences. Engineering is a good idea—for others. You just don't want to go to school long enough to get an engineering degree.

If it's an important decision, it's not a bad idea to write a brief statement about how your values relate to each option.

5. Review Your Goals

Analyze whether a decision you're about to make fits with the goals you've set.

Suppose you hanker to become a world-wide travel tour operator (ah, Rome, Venice, Paris . . . dream on). This is another reason to reject engineering as a major. It's out of synch with your goal.

Before finalizing a decision, ask yourself two key questions: 1. Does this decision support my aspirations? 2. Is it realistic or am I kidding myself about my chances to pull it off?

6. Make a Decision

Ready, aim, decide. If you're still shaky and can't bring yourself to decide something, chances are you can break the mental logjam by acquiring more information.

Without adequate information, it's easy to make damaging decisions; with enough relevant facts about the subject in question, you stack the cards in your favor.

Decide! Write it out: After reflecting on this problem, my decision is: _____.

7. Write an Action Plan

Once you make a decision, writing a plan to implement it will help cut the ropes of lethargy and send your decision ballooning upward. It need not be an elaborate plan; one paragraph will do.

Let's say you finally decide to drop English, consider fields that would include working as a world-wide tour operator, and switch to a recreation major. Your plan might read like this:

Decide to discuss new direction with current advisor. Request new advisor in recreation department to plan new courses for next term. Launch career research immediately to determine all career options within recreation field. Use Internet to gather additional information.

Apply the Technique

Now let's see what you've learned about those rascal decisions hanging over your head. Think of two problems that are causing you to lose sleep and work your way through the seven-step process:

1. Define the problem.

2. Identify options.

3. Anticipate probable outcomes.

4. Make a values impact statement.

5. Review your goals.

6. Make a decision.

7. Write an action plan.

Use the forms on pages, 220 and 221.

■ ■ ■ ■

An Age for Decisions

"How can I make decisions now that will affect me for life?" you ask. "Aren't I too young? What if I change my mind?"

Good questions. But remember, you choose the kinds of people you want for friends. You select subjects to study. You determine whether joining clubs or teams is right for you. You choose the college you wish to attend. You elect whether or not to find part-time work. These and other decisions reinforce your decision-making skills. No decision is irrevocable if you consciously try to make decisions that allow flexibility in the future.

Here are a few examples of flexible decisions.

1. Taking math through 12th grade calculus is a flexible decision. It permits you to choose either a technical or non-technical major in college. Should you ultimately choose a non-technical major, you've lost nothing and gained a head start on understanding an increasingly complex world.

2. Enrolling in a communications program rather than in a traditional journalism curriculum is a flexible decision. Journalism prepares you to work in media; communications includes such courses as speech, sales, public relations, and advertising. The 360-degree approach gives you basic skills to move back and forth among media, public relations, and advertising, should the winds of the job market so require.

3. A flexible decision for a music major would be to add to a skills repertoire by using electives to study such subjects as business and psychology. If you can't support yourself as a performer, you could become a music therapist, concert promoter, recording manager, or other specialist in the music careers cluster.

Now we give you a few examples of inflexible decisions.

1. Unless you want to design the software that runs computers, a computer science major is an inflexible choice. It does not prepare you for many different opportunities. You would have many more options by majoring in accounting, finance, marketing, or another foundation discipline. You would take only enough computer science courses to have a sophisticated understanding of how to use computers as tools.

2. A major in driver-and-safety education is too narrowly focused. During tight budget times in some states, driver education is one of the first things school systems do away with. The same concept applies to other narrowly defined majors, such as African American studies. If you want to go into education, think of something with a wide scope, such as a major in a specific academic subject (social studies, for instance), followed by a master's degree in secondary school curriculum and instruction.

3. Another decision that could limit your options is to begin your career in a non-profit organization, rather than a profit-making private business. Business employers tend to look at people who work in non-profit organizations and government agencies as slow-moving and unable to make a commitment to the bottom line in business—making money. As a rule, you can move from a profit-making business to a non-profit organization much more easily than you can make the opposite move.

What's the best way to prepare so that you can more easily go with the flow of jobs? The answer is clear: Acquire solid foundation knowledge that lets you add on new knowledge as needed. Try not to specialize too soon.

If you acquire a broad background in language, math, and science, you can move ahead making decisions with confidence.

■ ■ ■ ■

A Dozen Suggestions for Choosing a Career

When you're still in a quandary about which road to take, check your tentative decisions against this timeless list of good advice from Dr. Robert Hoppock, the father of modern career information evaluation. Here's what Dr. Hoppock recommends:

◆ Choose an occupation because you like the work, not solely because of the rewards in money or prestige.

◆ Choose an occupation that will use the abilities you possess.

◆ Choose an occupation in which there is likely to be an active demand for workers when you are ready to go to work.

◆ Do not choose an occupation just because a friend or someone else you admire chose it.

◆ Avoid occupations that require abilities you do not possess or cannot acquire.

◆ Do not confuse interest and ability.

◆ Before making a final choice of occupation, find out what are *all* the things you might have to do in it. Find out which of these will take most of your time.

◆ Do not expect to find a job in which you will never have to do anything you dislike.

◆ Do not stay permanently in a job in which you dislike most of the things you have to do.

◆ Beware of biased information from recruiters and other sources.

◆ Take all the advice that is offered, then act on your own judgment.

◆ Remember Robert Louis Stevenson's counsel, "To know what you prefer, instead of humbly saying 'Amen' to what the world tells you you ought to prefer, is to have kept your soul alive."

■ ■ ■ ■

Problem One

Step 1. _____

_____

_____

_____

Step 2. _____

_____

_____

_____

Step 3. _____

_____

_____

_____

Step 4. _____

_____

_____

_____

Step 5. _____

_____

_____

_____

Step 6. _____

_____

_____

Step 7. _____

_____

_____

_____

Problem Two

Step 1. _____

_____

_____

_____

Step 2. _____

_____

_____

_____

Step 3. _____

_____

_____

_____

Step 4. _____

_____

_____

_____

Step 5. _____

_____

_____

_____

Step 6. _____

_____

_____

_____

Step 7. _____

_____

_____

_____

CHAPTER
11

Student Jobs Are Good For You

Work activities—both paid and volunteer—are vital to your healthy career development.

This section challenges the notion that student jobs threaten academic achievement, or that they rob you of "only-young-once" good times.

It examines the array of benefits generated by part-time employment, summer jobs, and internships.

In addition, it explains how to construct a beginning Resume, how to find student jobs, and how to star in an employment interview even though it's your first time out.

The section concludes with tips on making the most of the student jobs you land. It tells how to start off on a good note, how to polish selected skills, and why it's a good idea to keep a log of your achievements.

(In Chapter 16, which is geared to helping you succeed on your first full-time job, we give you accelerated information. For now, though, be sure you master the basics of making good on a job.)

Need a Job?
Get Experience.
Need Experience?
Get a Job.

The no-experience dilemma is a vicious cycle: If you have no experience, you can't get a job, and if you can't get a job, then how can you get experience?

We hear frequently about the problem from your point of view:

I am a recent college graduate who is very interested in a career in the computer field. But employers want experience. How do you get experience when you have been going to school most of your life? It's all so unfair.

I graduated from high school and applied for a job as a cashier at a drug store. I thought I was all set, but the manager said that the only thing he could offer me was a part-time job. The reason he gave was that I had no experience. He said that if I had had part-time experience while I was in school, I could have been given the full-time job. Isn't that ridiculous?

Unfair or ridiculous? Maybe. But have you heard the joke that asks where an 800-pound gorilla sleeps? The answer is, "Wherever it likes."

That's the way it is with employers. Because they control the jobs you want, they hire whomever they like, and the people they usually like best have experience.

The reasoning isn't too hard to understand. Experience is proof you can do the work. When you have no experience, how can you document your claim that although you can't do the job immediately, you soon can?

The market is minimal for those who think they are very interested in work they know little about or simply want to learn at the employer's expense.

Few employers are anxious to risk hundreds or thousands of dollars training a beginner who, after finding out what the work is really like, may bow out.

Moreover, it's a matter of psychology. Employers are far more interested in their own profit pictures than in people who are out merely to improve themselves.

The voice of experience says, "I have made the effort to gain the skills that will benefit your organization."

Breaking the no-experience barrier is just one of the reasons why obtaining paid or unpaid student jobs is so important to your career climb.

■ ■ ■ ■

Student Jobs:
What Else Is In
Them for You?

In sports, exhibition games help players shape up before the real season begins. So it is with student jobs. The practice you get by working during summers and after school provides opportunities to learn some moves to repeat and some moves to avoid when you enter the full-time job market.

Try to find jobs that relate to a career you think you would like to pursue. When you observe others who work in the field, you gain clues to the satisfactions and frustrations of the work, as well as to the kinds of people who choose it. You make contacts who may one day advance your career.

Moreover, you will learn that the work world expects you to have not only technical competence in handling a particular job, but also a general understanding of how to behave in business and an ability to work smoothly with others. The result may be that you decide to switch some remaining school courses to more precisely focus on your specific career goals.

When a job in your chosen field isn't available, it's still well worth your time to juggle fast-food orders or take tickets in a movie theater. You may be pleasantly surprised at all the good things that can happen to you.

◆ You gain independence. As you do your job well, you acquire a sense of responsibility and begin to feel more self-reliant. The independence of having a job and earning some of your own money is a great feeling.

◆ You gain a new dimension in personality and become a more interesting person. Your self-confidence gets a boost. You'll do things that open new horizons, giving you new subjects to talk about to friends.

◆ You gain new friends. Shared experience on the job is a good basis for getting to know someone.

◆ You gain experience with supervisor relationships, in learning how to cooperate with co-workers, and in polishing skills for serving clients and customers. These are skills you can take anywhere.

Whether you work for someone else, are self-employed, or do a volunteer stint, student jobs are a conveyor belt to your future. They can carry you from the sandlot league to the ranks of promising young starters.

■ ■ ■ ■

After-School Jobs: The Naysayers

Much debate has taken place during the past few years about whether working has a negative effect on a student's education, family life, and behavior.

The criticisms can be divided into six main groups: overextension, inappropriate rewards, negative outcomes, wasted youth, family status, and child-labor exploitation. What follows is a closer look at each criticism and a response.

Overextension

Criticism: Exhausted students doze in class, skip homework, and fail to keep their grades up.

Response: Certainly students can overextend and that's why students and family should jointly consider how much work is too much.

The majority of high school and college students hold part-time or summer jobs. During the school year, most students who work are on the job 10 to 20 hours a week. A job requiring more hours should be questioned.

The number of hours worked should be evaluated on an individual basis. For some students, five hours a week are too many, while others, highly organized and competent, can handle 20 hours with ease.

Another factor is the time of day you work. Working three hours in the afternoon from 2:30 until 5:30 is less taxing than working on school nights from 8:00 to 11:00.

Still another consideration is time off for school studies. Arrange in advance with an employer your right to take leave from work the day before mid-term and final exams.

One more tip: Until you are settled into your first year at college or your first year in a new school, don't take a job at all unless it's a matter of financial survival. Spend your time learning the campus ropes.

As for academic problems, no study proves that working per se causes grades to drop on a group basis. What may happen to cause such assertions by some teachers is that students who are less academically able or are not interested in school simply prefer to work longer hours.

A countercharge by other teachers and counselors holds that students who work up to 10 hours a week tend to be better students because they learn to budget their time more efficiently and, consequently, may apply this skill to their study time.

Keep in mind, too, that a major study of the effects jobs have on students made for the National Center for Education Statistics (NCES) shows that those who worked and those who didn't both averaged less than an hour of homework a day. Many students have nothing to do but watch TV if they don't work. In some locales, without jobs, students just join neighborhood gangs.

Criticism: Busy students cut back on extracurricular activities, sapping enjoyment of school and thus moving school away from the center of their world.

Response: The NCES research indicates that working does not seem to drastically affect extra-curricular student activities.

Criticism: Exhausted and busy students spend less time with family, do fewer chores around the house, and sleep when home, causing a change in family relationships and structure.

Response: Exhausted students probably do sack out at home. If so, a time analysis study would indicate whether the problem really is the job or something else, like too much social life.

Inappropriate Rewards

Criticism: Student earnings are wasted on material concerns, such as trendy clothing, cars, and rock concert tickets.

Response: Some students are saving their pay for college expenses or are helping their families. But the bulk of spending does go toward things students want to buy.

Isn't the freedom to spend your earnings the way you wish one of the rewards of working?

What's more, blowing money on 10 cases of purple bubble gum while a student may help you to learn how to minimize frivolous expenditures as an adult.

Criticism: What students learn in low-level jobs is not skill- and training-oriented.

Response: Every experience teaches something, even grass-cutting.

Jobs that offer considerable interaction with others, such as fast-food service, retail and telephone sales, help you learn how to communicate and how to persuade.

In particular, a major survey among fast-food workers conducted by the National Institute for Work & Learning shows that thousands of young people feel they have gleaned valuable skills and work habits, such as how to take direction; how to work in a disciplined setting; how to cooperate with others; and understanding why it's necessary to come to work on time. Another plus: They learned how to operate electronic equipment.

Any job will teach you something, even if it's only that a particular field doesn't agree with you.

Negative Outcomes

Criticism: Students' jobs tend to place them in adolescent ghettos with little opportunity to learn from adults. In this ghetto, they find the workplace to be a school for petty crime as they give away goods to friends, take things from employers, call in sick when they aren't, and work while drunk or are strung out on drugs.

Response: Young people usually prefer to be with others in their age range whether they are working or playing. Petty crime is a societal issue, not an employment issue.

Criticism: Rather than create healthy attitudes for work, the low-level jobs breed cynicism as students begin to believe that hard work gets you nowhere.

Response: Thoughtful employers, teachers, and parents help students understand that a long journey begins one step at a time, that all of us must "pay our dues," that all honest work has value, and that you get out of a work/learning experience what you put into it. The drone jobs will communicate another fact to students: The best jobs are achieved by people who learn to work *smart* as well as hard.

Wasted Youth

Criticism: Because students have the remainder of their lives to work, holding a job robs them of a precious time period.

Response: A student who maintains a proper balance between an after-school job and classroom studies gains a head start on students who do not work.

A California study suggests that a job imparts consumer sense in money management, and an increased sense of responsibility. Both young men and women reported that their jobs encouraged their willingness to stick to a task and take pleasure in getting it done.

No one argues for all work—no play. On the contrary, in the NCES research, the study direc-

tor writes that "high school students seem to have an abundance of time at their disposal—so much that even a fairly strong commitment to work does not seriously impinge on their other activities."

The youth-robbing argument lacks substance.

Family Status

Criticism: Some parents resist allowing their children to hold after-school jobs because they fear it will appear they need the money. They think Junior's working reflects unfavorably on their image as providers.

Response: It is selfish to place status ahead of a young person's career welfare.

Exploitation

Criticism: More young workers than ever are getting ripped off as businesses violate child-labor laws.

Response: This is true—but it's not a crystal clear issue. Child-labor laws date back to the late 19th century, when eight-year-olds were losing their fingers in factories. Young workers still get hurt once in a great while—a 13-year-old lost his leg working in a car wash and a 17-year-old died in a car crash while making a pizza delivery, for instance.

Child-labor law is a puzzling web of regulation and bureaucracy, regulated by governments at all levels. In California, a five-year-old can work as an actor but a 13-year-old cannot flip hamburgers. A 17-year-old high school graduate is an adult, but a drop-out, even one supporting a family, is not.

Obviously, a parent's input should be sought when children work. It's a good idea to talk over the job with counselors and teachers too. It would be a crime to turn back a clock that victimized young workers for years.

What Students Say about Working

Students themselves explain that they work for different reasons. They use the money for entertainment, to buy a car or clothes, and for a college eduaction. They also state that working gives them a broader outlook and helps to build character.

"Working gives you the experience you need to survive out in the world," says 16-year-old Nancy Root of Santa Rosa High, who works as a junior dance instructor at Nordquist Ballroom Dancing Studio. "Also, having a job teaches you how to manage money."

Zach Barrett, a senior at Santa Rosa High who works at Round Table Pizza, says that working teaches responsibility, too. "With a job," Barrett says, "You learn about not being late, and about being there when you're scheduled. You learn to work hard."

Barrett also points out that having a job alleviates some of the tensions at home. "I think it offers freedom, because you don't have to ask your mom for 20 dollars here and there."

As to how they get their jobs, it varies from student to student. Maria Bianchini, a senior at Santa Rosa High, got her job at Windsor Waterworks after seeing the position advertised in the local paper. John Bollinger, a senior at Montgomery High, says he landed his job at Bennett Valley Pizza by being persistent. "I had a friend who worked there," Bollinger says, "and I went in and asked him for an application. Then I went back and bothered the manager for a couple of weeks and finally ended up getting the job."

Zach Barrett got his job at Round Table Pizza through networking. "My ninth grade English teacher's husband is the manager of the store," Barrett says. "I knew her, so I asked if I could get an application and interview, and he gave me the job."

The Wildlife Museum in Petaluma, California, is managed and staffed by teens and has the distinction of being the first high-school facility of its kind in the country. Students built most of the exhibits themselves. "I've done a lot of work throughout the whole museum," says Rina Borodkin, a senior at Petaluma High who has been on the museum staff for three years.

Shawn Thorsson, another Petaluma High School senior on the staff, says that when she applied for the museum class, there were three types of jobs offered: maintenance, clerical, and tour guide. "I applied for clerical, but I ended up doing whatever was needed. In my junior year, I ran the maintenance crew. A lot of what I've been doing this year is conducing tours and teaching underclassmen how to run tours."

Many of the students in these nature classes are interested in affiliated careers. For example, Borodkin plans to major in animal science and wildland resources at the University of California at Davis.

■ ■ ■ ■

"Gee, All I Ever Did Was Baby-Sit"

To explain how any job can teach you something or look good on your resume, let's take babysitting, the most pedestrian of all youth jobs.

(These interview excerpts are reprinted with permission, Sheri Graves/The Press Democrat, Santa Rosa, CA.)

Here's how to show baby-sitting as solid work experience on your resume.

Work Experience

1992–94   Extensive experience in child-sitting for numerous customers.
Demonstrated:

- *Supervisory ability.* Often responsible for welfare of two or more children. A customer described me as "competent in handling disagreements, good in human relations." (Mrs. John Apple, address on request.)

- *Sense of responsibility.* No child ever injured while in my care.

- *Good work attitudes.* Never late for job. Another customer said, "You show a mature attitude." (Mrs. Robert White, address on request.)

The essential idea is to translate aspects of any student job into characteristics all employers want.

Even if an employer doesn't take your interpretation of your accomplishments as seriously as you would like—and some won't—the employer will be impressed that you rate your abilities high enough to make such a strong presentation.

It certainly beats a blase "Gee, all I ever did was baby-sit."

■ ■ ■ ■

Here's a Short List of Student Jobs

For an idea of the kinds of paid jobs students often obtain, glance over this sampling:

- *Banks and insurance offices*
  clerical worker
  janitorial worker
  mail department messenger
  word-processing operator

- *Restaurant and fast-food shops*
  counter worker
  dining room attendant
  janitorial worker
  kitchen helper
  waiter and waitress

- *Retail stores (department, drug, food, and hardware)*
  cashier
  counter attendant
  delivery helper
  janitorial worker
  messenger
  packer and wrapper
  sales worker
  stock clerk

- *Community recreation centers*
  cashier
  clerical worker
  concession stand worker
  crafts instructor
  groundskeeper
  recreation leader

- *Resorts and camps*
  beach attendant
  camp counselor
  clerical worker
  crafts instructor
  dining room attendant
  lifeguard
  sales worker
  trip leader

- *Construction companies*
  carpenter's helper
  clerk

handyperson
laborer
painter's helper

◆ *Campus jobs*
cashier
clerk-typist
data-processing assistant
dormitory assistant
food worker
research assistant
science lab assistant
tutor
word-processing operator

◆ *Manufacturing companies*
assembler (assembles parts for products)
clerk
handyperson
janitorial worker
laborer
shipping room and stockroom helper

◆ *Miscellaneous*
amusement park worker
auto agency rental clerk
car washer
gas station attendant
landscape maintenance worker
library clerk
newspaper delivery worker
private postal-service delivery worker
receptionist
security guard
taxi driver
toll collector

Extensive lists of student jobs appear in a variety of books, such as *Summer Jobs* and the *Summer Employment Directory of the United States*, both published by Peterson's.

■ ■ ■ ■

Internships Are Calls to Audition

You can test your interest in a field—and its interest in you—without making a long-term commitment. How? By obtaining an internship.

Internships are work experiences that offer definite objectives for learning. They are usually short-term work arrangements and may be part- or full-time, paid or unpaid. An internship arrangement with an employer can last up to a year, but most are for three to six months.

Your school counselor may help you locate such work, and you'll find additional internship resources listed in Chapter 12.

■ ■ ■ ■

What the Laws Say About Your Working

Let's banish a myth: "You must be 16 to get a job."

In fact, in many states, you can be as young as 14 and work in some jobs outside of school hours and during school vacations.

There are two kinds of laws that apply to minors in the job market—those made by the federal government (Fair Labor Standards Act) and those made by the state in which you live. When both the federal and state laws apply, the tougher law must be observed.

What the federal law basically says is that persons who are 14 years old and older can work in certain non-farm jobs that are not dangerous. A few examples of dangerous work: If you're under 18, you can't drive a school bus, operate power-driven meat-slicing equipment, or operate power-driven machinery used in processing waste paper. Under the federal law, the child labor provisions do not apply to anyone aged 18 and over.

Federal law does not require work permits.

The vast majority of states, however, do require employers to obtain employment certification (work permits) for employees under 18.

Even 12-year-olds can work in some cases: delivering newspapers, baby-sitting, doing chores. They can work on farms, too, as long as the employment is not detrimental to their health or education.

To find out about particulars of the federal law, you can call a compliance officer at a local office of the Wage and Hour Division, listed in phone directories under U.S. Government, Department of Labor, Employment Standards Administration.

Particulars about your state's laws regarding the employment of minors can be obtained from your counselor, librarian, or state department of labor.

■ ■ ■ ■

Try Volunteering

Most career fields offer related volunteer jobs you can use to acquire experience, make contacts, and build up your resume.

A teaching hopeful might try being a volunteer in a recreation program. A would-be veterinarian might clean cages in animal shelters to learn the necessary skill of handling animals. A future forester could volunteer at a botanical garden.

A psychology major at a large state university says she tutors a boy in his home because she gets only theory in class and wants to validate her interest in counseling psychology.

Since volunteering is a 50–50 deal—you're getting but you're also giving—carefully evaluate the organization in which you may invest your time from the viewpoint of what it can do for you in return. What follows are checkpoints you can use to be sure you're receiving maximum career exploration as well as the safisfaction of helping others.

- Does the organization's training consist merely of an explanation of the group's goals, or does it actually train you for specific jobs? What skills will you develop?

- Will you be in a visible position where you'll meet other people, or isolated in a back office?

- Will your volunteer hours be recorded, along with your job description, so you can refer to them on your Resume?

- If you find you've made a mistake in choosing an organization, quit. Analyze your reasons for leaving so you'll avoid poor choices the next time.

When you can't obtain a referral to volunteer jobs at high school or college, try a volunteer center (also called voluntary action center). Hundreds of volunteer centers across the nation screen and refer applicants to agencies that need volunteers.

Look in a telephone directory under "Volunteer Center of (name of city)." If you can't locate a center and need a referral, or if you want more general tips on volunteer jobs, write to: The Volunteer National Center, Suite 500, 1111 N. 19th St., Arlington, VA 22209.

More than one in every 10 Americans your age does some volunteer work for church, school, and other organizations.

■ ■ ■ ■

Job Search News: First Edition

Just as champion tennis players and skiers begin mastering their techniques at a young age, you are wise to learn the basics of an effective job search early in life.

First, look at job hunting in the right perspective. It's a skill you acquire. In a way, it's like learning to drive a car. You learn what is expected of you, think about it, and practice.

Your presentations will become more sophisticated as you progress in a career, but basic strategy and tactics will not change. Job search verities really are eternal.

Next we're going to show you how to put down on paper a convincing argument about why an employer should hire you. If you don't, who will?

· · · ·

A Practical Guide to a First-Rate Resume

You must convince employers that you will become an asset, not a liability.

To do this, frame your presentation in such a way that employers will answer *yes* to each of these three main questions:

1. Can this applicant do the job?

2. Does this applicant have a positive work attitude?

3. Does this applicant get along well with others?

In your case, since you are short on experience, what employers are really looking for are signs of promise, of potential, of the ability (if not experience) to do the job.

Beyond that, employers want employees who are dependable, enthusiastic, and hard working. They want your presentation to clearly communicate that your personality will fit in well with coworkers.

Rarely do employers want to hire only breathing bodies. They want specific people to do specific jobs.

Your challenge is to convince employers that you have the specific qualifications to do the specific jobs.

One of the tools you need to do this is called a resume (REH-zoo-may).

Why You Need a Resume

A resume essentially is a piece of paper. (Sometimes it's stored in a computer, but more about that later.) It serves as a calling card, a self-advertisement. It tells the employer that you have the ability—based on your skills—to do the job you seek. It tells the employer you have positive work attitudes. It tells the employer you have positive personality traits.

Strictly speaking, a resume is a series of written statements that highlight your previous education, paid and unpaid work experiences, and other pertinent background.

Most resumes are washouts. They do not interest anyone. That's because they are filled with trivia, or because they are a bare-bones, boring history of an applicant's background.

A famous salesperson talked about "selling the sizzle, not the steak." He meant that people are not interested in buying a slab of meat. What they are interested in is buying the good taste of the meat, the nourishment of the meat, and the satisfaction derived from eating it.

That's why the resumes that employers actually read dwell on accomplishments. They accent abilities. They describe qualifications.

They zero in on skills. All of these factors combine to focus on meeting employers' specific needs.

You list your education and work experience merely to prove that what you say about your accomplishments, abilities, qualifications, and skills is true.

It may surprise you to know that on the average employers spend a mere 30 seconds scanning each resume. If this seems insensitive, particularly after you slaved over every word, what would you do if you had a stack of 300 or 400 resumes on your desk in answer to a single recruitment ad?

You must train yourself to write the kind of resume that—at a glance—tells an employer why it is to his or her advantage to invest time in talking with wonderful you.

Employers aren't focused on what they can do for you. They are focused on what you can do for them.

So when in doubt about what to put in or what to leave out of your resume, apply this two-question test:

1. *Does this information add anything to my objective of being hired for this job?* If not, leave it out.

2. *Does this information say (or suggest) what I can do for the employer?* Again, if not, leave it out.

As you prepare work sheets and later the finished document, never lose sight of the *concept* of what your resume should say.

In every statement, your resume will in some way tell employers you have the ability to do the job, possess positive work attitudes, and can get along with others.

Overall, your resume will convince employers that they can benefit by interviewing you.

Start With Work Sheets

Begin drafting a resume by putting together a personal evaluation of your qualifications.

Use four work sheets, one each for *education, paid work, unpaid work,* and *outside interests.*

On each work sheet, make a conscious effort to list accomplishments, abilities, and skills—not just the dry facts of your life to date.

You've already compiled a large percentage of the information you need on your identity inventories in Chapter 6.

Look back and transfer the appropriate data from your identity inventories for academic abilities, aptitudes and skills, work values, interests, and personality traits.

Step 1:
Educational Work Sheet

(Use your identity inventory for academic abilities here.)

Focus on the school or training program that did the most to prepare you for the job you seek, as you fill out a work sheet like the one that follows.

Stress the most important educational institution. If you are a high school graduate, don't mention your elementary school years. If you are a vocational school or college graduate, skip details of your high school experiences.

Write down all the separate courses you took. Put a check mark beside those that are useful in jobs. Zero in on the courses related to the job you have in mind—give as many details about each as you can concerning what you learned, skills you acquired and your accomplishments.

Tip: As you write down the details about your knowledge, skills, and accomplishments, make a strong effort to come up with concrete examples that can be <u>measured</u> in some way.

Simply claiming that you are a hard worker (or have another particular strength) is not enough. You need proof to back up your claims.

Here's an example: If someone says, "I am a good dancer," you may think the person is just bragging. But if someone *shows* you how well he or she can dance, you believe the person. The claim now has *credibility*.

In looking for a job, you rarely have the chance to show what you can do, except when you must demonstrate skills like operating a word processor.

That's why you need concrete examples of your strengths that can be measured in some way. The examples give credibility to your claims of being a strong applicant.

How can you give concrete examples that can be measured? In four basic ways. You can use:

1. *Numbers*—"Waited on about 100 customers on a typical day." "Missed only one day of work last year."

2. *Percentages*—"Waited on more customers than 90 percent of my co-workers." "Missed fewer days of work than 95 percent of my co-workers."

3. *Amounts*—"Saved my employer $50 a month by suggesting a way to cut photocopy costs." "Increased sales on paper route by $200 per month."

4. *Supreme statements*—"My employer said I was the hardest-working counter clerk she had ever hired." "Was the only student ever twice elected secretary of the Young Tycoons Club at Dover College."

Using concrete examples in your Resume highlights your qualifications in a way that does not seem like bragging,

Before filling in your educational work sheet, glance at the sample for Carrie on page 236. Carrie graduated from high school and now hopes to become a secretary in a recording company.

Educational Work Sheet

Name of school/training program: _____

Address & telephone: _____

Year(s) graduated or attended; credential received, if any: _____

Class rank: _____

Teachers who will give references: _____

_____

_____

Summary of courses: check (✓) those related to the job you have in mind.

_____

_____

_____

Details on these job-related courses: _____

Course: _____

What I learned: _____

_____

_____

Skills acquired: _____

_____

Accomplishments: _____

_____

Course: _____

_____

What I learned: _____

_____

_____

Skills acquired: _____

_____

Accomplishments: _____

_____

Course: _____

_____

What I learned: _____

_____

_____

Skills acquired: _____

_____

Accomplishments: _____

_____

Carrie's Educational Work Sheet

Name of school/training program: Richard Montgomery High School

Address & telephone: 2700 Monroe St., Caldonia, Utah 78904; 725/555-9999

Year(s) graduated or attended; credential received, if any: 1996, diploma

Class rank: Upper one-third in business subjects

Teachers who will give references: Robert Red, English teacher; Roberta Hope,

business teacher; Claire Voyant, coach; Ted Tiger, home room teacher

Summary of courses: check (✓) those related to the job you have in mind.

English I, II, III, IV ✓ Typing I, II ✓ Word processing I, II ✓

Accounting I, II ✓ Office procedures I, II ✓ History I, II, III

Physical education   Art I

Details on these job-related courses:

Course: Typing and word processing

What I learned: Keyboard touch typing, accuracy, speed, letter styles,

tabulation, special functions of word processing

Skills acquired: Can type accurately 70 words per minute, can use contemporary

office equipment

Accomplishments: Received certificate of accomplishment for typing proficiency;

two certificates were awarded among three typing classes

Course: Office procedures

What I learned: Learned variety of office machines: dictating equipment,

photocopiers

Skills acquired: Techniques of answering telephones, filing and office systems,

equipment operation

Accomplishments: Was selected by teacher to aid fellow students on word processor

Step 2: Paid-Work Work Sheet

(Use your identity inventories for aptitudes and skills, work values, and personality traits here.)

Fill out a work sheet like the one shown for each paid job you have held—from newspaper carrier to store manager. Baby-sitting jobs can be grouped on a single work sheet.

Once again, look for accomplishments, abilities, and skills. Back these up with concrete examples.

Study the summary for Dan on page 238 before beginning your work sheet. Dan is a college graduate who hopes to find employment as a department store management trainee.

Paid-Work Work Sheet

Employer's name, address, phone: _____

_____

Supervisor's name: _____

Dates employed: _____

Starting, ending pay: _____

Nature of job: _____

List of duties: _____

_____

_____

_____

_____

Skills learned: _____

_____

_____

_____

Accomplishments; give concrete examples of each: _____

_____

_____

_____

_____

Dan's Paid-Work Work Sheet

Employer's name, address, phone: **Exmoor Flagship Service Station,**

3881 Market St., New Madrid, R.I. 78888; 314/555-5647

Supervisor's name: **Wes Pumps**

Dates employed: **Sept., 1995 to present**

Starting, ending pay: **$4.25 per hour/$5.50 per hour**

Nature of job: **Service station attendant**

List of duties: **Pump gas, collect cash payments, fill out credit card sales slips,**

wipe windows, check engine oil & water, jockey cars

Skills learned: **Handle customers, handle cash, keep records of sales**

transactions, responsibly handle valuable property, give favorable image

of employer

Accomplishments; give concrete examples of each:

Superior worker—supervisor kept me on when two other part-time workers

were laid off due to shortened station hours; supervisor said I was fast

learner, hard worker

(Note: In real life, Dan's work sheet would also describe an earlier job as a sales supervisor at Woolwow Corp. For brevity, the details are omitted here, but are shown on Dan's Resume.)

Step 3:
Unpaid-Work Work Sheet

(Use your identity inventories for aptitudes and skills, work values, and personality traits here.)

Fill out a work sheet, like the following one, for each unpaid job you've ever had. The exam-ple given for Chitra may inspire you. Chitra at-tended college for two years. She hopes to land a job as a meeting manager, one who arranges conferences and seminars for companies and organizations.

Unpaid-Work Work Sheet

Volunteer job: _____

Location: _____

_____

Supervisor's name, telephone: _____

Duties: _____

_____

Skills learned: _____

_____

Accomplishments; give concrete examples of each:

_____

_____

_____

Chitra's Unpaid-Work Work Sheet

Volunteer job: **Activities coordinator assistant**

Location: **Peaceful Nursing Home, 18 Grove Lane, Delight, N.M. 35776**

Supervisor's name, telephone: **Sally Bird, 989/555-5309 or 741/555-3429 (She travels between two facilities)**

Duties: **Advance work in planning field trips for nursing home residents; assisted residents on trips**

Skills learned: **Researching, planning, problem-solving, negotiating, preparing reports, managing groups of people**

Accomplishments; give concrete examples of each:

Showed resourcefulness and creative ability by thinking up need for this work, approaching activities coordinator, persuading her to give me a try; she says I am the most helpful volunteer she has ever worked with

Step 4:
Outside Interests Work Sheet

(Use your identity inventory for interests here.)

Make a work sheet—similar to your other summaries—of all extra-curricular activities, hobbies, and personal pursuits.

List everything you've done for the past few years. Analyze the information to see which interests helped you develop skills and accomplishments related to the job you want. Put a check mark beside job-related outside interests, and then develop your work sheet like the example.

Dan's outside interests are wide ranging, as his work sheet illustrates.

Outside Interests Work Sheet

A. Interest: _____

   Skills learned: _____

   Accomplishment: _____

   _____

B. Interest: _____

   Skills learned: _____

   Accomplishment: _____

   _____

C. Interest: _____

   Skills learned: _____

   Accomplishment: _____

   _____

D. Interest: _____

   Skills learned: _____

   Accomplishment: _____

   _____

E. Interest: _____

   Skills learned: _____

   Accomplishment: _____

   _____

Dan's Outside Interests Work Sheet

A. Interest: **Writing**

Skills learned: **Organization of thoughts, self-expression**

Accomplishment: **Won city-wide essay contest on merchandising with 150 entrants/Block St. Merchants Assn.**

B. Interest: **Reading**

Skills learned: **Awareness of trends**

Accomplishment: **Read regularly several consumer magazines**

C. Interest: **Travel**

Skills learned: **Awareness of various consumer tastes**

Accomplishment: **Am widely traveled in U.S.**

Step 5: Job Target Research

Decide which jobs you want to apply for. Do advance research on each.

For student jobs, find out what the company does—what goods it makes or sells, what services it provides.

If the company has a personnel or human resources department, ask the receptionist if a job description is available for the job you want. You can pick it up in person or telephone and ask that it be mailed to you. Study the job description carefully. List the qualifications (skills, abilities, accomplishments, education) you have that match the job's requirements.

For example, if you know the job requires the ability to read well and to be reliable, identify your reading skills and the times you have shown reliability.

Add this proof to your finished resume. You are giving the employer what the employer wants.

If you can't get a job description, invent one. Ask yourself: If I were hiring a person for this job, what qualificatons would I want? Admittedly, this is not an easy task. Family and friends who are in the job market can offer suggestions. You can get more tips by reading related newspaper help-wanted ads, which often go into detail about job requirements.

Whether real or imagined, working from a job description as you write a resume will help you to "get inside the employer's head," and, therefore, present yourself as an applicant well matched to the job in question.

The notes you make on the job—and how you match its requirements—are your *job target sheets*.

Job target sheets can be made in any style you like; an example of a blank job target sheet form, followed by a filled-out job target sheet for Carrie, illustrates the technique.

You'll refer to your job target sheets along with your work sheets and identity inventories when you put together your finished resumes.

Resumes? Did we say resumes? That's right. You may write a dozen or more versions after you learn to tailor a resume to a specific job.

Some students do an all-purpose resume and let it go at that. But then, they're not practicing to be expert job seekers.

You can, of course, construct a general resume and use a cover letter to customize your application to each employer. More about cover letters in Chapter 15.

Job Target Sheet

Company: _____

Contact: _____

Address: _____

Telephone: _____

Job Description/Key Elements: _____

_____

_____

_____

Carrie's Job Target Sheet

Company: Gary Witt Publishing Co.

Contact: Patricia Witt, Vice President

Address: 2889 Sunburst Blvd., Northbrook, Ill. 76767

Telephone: 555-7777

Job Description/Key Elements: Secretary, Editorial Dept; strong skills in typing, word processing; knowledge of office procedures and systems; will provide clerical support for three editors; good interpersonal skills required

Writing the Winning Resume

You've done most of the work, and now it's time to whip your information together.

Your resume needs to be more than mere words. It needs to be a powerful, potent sales message. In today's competitive job world, your resume will show that as a young person you have great potential. It will show that you are punctual, a hard worker, willing to learn, and dependable.

Remember: In every statement, your resume will tell employers that you *can* do the job, that you *will* do the job, and that you *will get along* with others while doing it.

Appearance Creates an Instant Image

The appearance of your resume is usually the first impression you make on an employer. How a resume looks says as much about you as its content.

Here are tips on how to look alert:

◆ *Length*. At your age, hold your resume to one page, two pages at the most.

◆ *White Space*. Leave lots of space for margins. Leave some space between paragraphs. Use capital letters to call attention to key points. Short lines are easier to read than long lines.

◆ *Paper*. Use standard-size (8½" × 11"), quality paper. Stick to white or an eggshell color.

◆ *Printing*. A copy of your resume that is individually printed on a laser printer is a wonderful way of telling an employer you really care about a job. It shows you went to a lot of trouble because you respect the employer, and you respect the job offer that may be made. It is a subtle compliment.

But typing 50 or more original copies can wear your fingers to the nub. And there's plenty of room to make typing errors.

The best solution is to use a computer's word processing program. Often computers are available free in schools and offices. Most major cities have desktop publishing shops with equipment you can pay to use on their premises.

A computer can automatically type the same resume over and over. A computer-generated resume is easy to change. Moreover, each copy is an original. All the operator does is feed in paper and push several buttons. A resume should be beautifully produced, so if you can't operate a computer's keyboard, find someone who can.

If possible, have your resume printed on a laser printer. This makes it look super. But if you don't have access to a laser printer, be sure your printer turns out a crisp, sharp image (no faded ribbons).

When a typewriter is what you have to work with, type a clean original copy and have clean photocopies made.

◆ *Spelling*. Spelling and typing errors ruin the best of resumes. Employers tend to think if you are careless on your resume, you will be careless on the job.

Most word processing programs now offer automatic spelling checks, which is an enormous help. But dictionaries are not extinct, so use them.

Do not scribble data in handwriting to correct or update your resume. Start over. Look fresh!

Use Action Words

Use as many action verbs as possible in your resume. Use words like: *managed, coordinated, sold, improved, planned*.

Drop introductory phrases such as "I was in charge of . . ." Just say "Supervised . . ." This way, you save valuable space for your additional accomplishments.

The more "I's" you can make disappear from your resume, the better.

Use Words That Measure

As we said earlier, when describing accomplishments, give concrete examples that can be measured in some way. Use numbers, percentages, amounts, and supreme statements.

Use Job Objectives

Because employers' eyes streak across resumes like comets in the sky, tell them right away what kind of a job or career field you want.

Begin your resume with a job objective—"Wish to work as hotel front-desk clerk" or "Seeking to be assistant at amusement park."

You may hear that stating a job objective limits employment prospects because there may be job openings of which you are unaware. You can minimize the risk by keeping a job objective fairly broad.

Stating your job objective becomes more important later, as you apply for jobs of greater responsibility. Employers are apt to see students as a blank canvas, but after you gain experience, they'll expect to see the color and form that make a recognizable picture of who you are and what you can do for them.

An alternative to using a job-objective statement to begin your resume is to start with a benefits capsule. Here you state what you are offering, such as "Offering typing skills and the willingness to work hard and the ability to learn fast." See resume examples of job-objective statements later in this section.

Choose the Best Format for You

Just as certain colors and clothing styles flatter one person but not another, resume styles can boost or lower your chances for an interview.

Aim for a format—the form used to give information—that is most flattering to you. It will be one that shouts your strengths and keeps quiet about your faults.

Some people say it is dishonest not to mention your faults in a resume. Does this make sense to you? Have you ever read a recruitment ad like this?

Worker wanted for a company that almost went out of business last year. The boss is a nag. The customers are worse. Co-workers are known for giving beginners a hard time. But the money's good.

Probably not. That's because no one would apply.

During an employment interview, there is ample time to raise any problem you feel you must reveal as an honest person.

Study format choices carefully. You can choose from one of three types—*chronological, functional,* or *hybrid* formats.

Chronological Format

Chronological, of course, means related to the order of time. In this style, you begin with your most recent experiences and work backwards.

The chronological format is best for people who have a steady school and work record showing constant growth.

The chronological format is the easiest to write, but it is not always advantageous. It is a poor choice for those who have employment gaps or other problems in their work backgrounds.

Young people rarely have a lot of work experience; listing only one or two jobs is somewhat like putting only one or two pieces of furniture in a big, empty room.

It is possible to highlight your accomplishments—other than work experiences—in a chronological format, but it is hard to do without making your resume look cluttered.

Functional Format

A function is an activity for which one is specially fitted. The functional format groups your qualifications by function—selling, purchasing, organizing, managing, or repairing, for example.

In a functional format, it is not important when or where you gained your qualifications. Dates, employers, and schools, are not given.

Perhaps the most valuable advantage for the young applicant is that the functional style makes the most of scant work experience.

A functional format highlights what you can do rather than merely reporting what you have done.

Moreover, it allows you to disregard experiences that do not relate to the kind of work you want. Suppose the job you want requires good spelling skills. You can emphasize the experiences that show your spelling skills and ignore the non-related job where you learned to read sun dials.

Another advantage to the functional format is that it allows you to lead the reader's attention away from a spotty work history or a poor school record.

As useful as it can be, the functional format has two major disadvantages:

1. It can be very confusing.

2. It may make an employer suspicious of your past because it is not straightforward.

Hybrid Format

A hybrid style combines the best features of the chronological and functional formats. For young people, it can be an ideal choice.

You can put together a hybrid resume in one of three ways:

1. A functional summary can be placed on top of a chronological resume (two pages).

2. A functional resume is followed by a short chronological page that gives dates, employers, and schools, as well as a summary of each experience (two pages).

3. A page contains functional groupings and is followed by chronological details (one page).

Checklist for Excellence

At this point, stop reading and begin writing your resume. We know it's hard to do, but keep writing.

When you finish, see if you can answer *yes* to all these questions:

1. Overall, does my resume show how an employer would benefit by interviewing me?

2. Does it stress my accomplishments and skills—instead of being a dry list of things I studied and tasks I performed?

3. Is it inviting to read, with a good layout, enough white space, good typing, and an emphasis on key points?

4. Is my writing style action-oriented and clear?

5. Is my resume free of facts unrelated to the job?

6. Does it contain only positive information?

7. Are all my claims believable—backed up by concrete, measurable examples?

8. Is my resume a powerful and potent sales message?

If you cannot answer *yes* to all these questions, go back to the drawing board and try again.

Keep at it until you succeed. Resume-writing is a skill you will most probably use again and again. And you already know more about it than most people learn in a lifetime.

What About References?

Arrange for personal references by asking people for permission to use their names. Don't list the names and addresses of your references on your resume, but have them ready on a separate sheet of paper.

Use your references only when an employer asks for them. If you overuse your references, they may become weary of saying how outstanding you are and mumble that you're okay.

With a little effort, you can make it easy for your references to sell you to employers. After an interview, on the left side of a sheet of paper, jot down a brief description of what the job requires in skills and personal characteristics. On the right side, note your matching qualifications. Call this paper a "reference summary" and give each of your references a copy of it. Use different words on each reference summary so when an employer calls to check up on you, all your references don't sound like an answering machine saying exactly the same thing.

Examples of Resumes

We know that individuals who write inadequate resumes as students tend to write inadequate resumes as 40-year-olds. They go through life failing to grasp the central idea of resumes.

The following resumes incorporate this central theme. Each begins with a job objective, telling the reader the type of job being sought. (A cover letter accompanying an all-purpose resume could do the same thing.)

The examples continue with Chitra, Carrie, and Dan. Unless otherwise noted, the informa-

The central resume idea is to create a document saying you and the job are a good match. A good match means that you know the job's requirements; that you can do the work; that you will do the work; and that you will behave pleasantly while doing it.

tion about each person has not been previously mentioned.

Notice in Chitra's resume how she gives measurable proof of how she can do the job of coordinating a convention. This job requires handling a zillion details in a hectic environment. Chitra says immediately that she is experienced, competent, and calm. Then she gives examples to back up her claims.

Why did Chitra begin by noting her unpaid work experience rather than her education?

Because Carrie is short on experience, she uses her education as a function. Notice how she takes the positive approach: Carrie's overall class rank was in the bottom one-half. But Carrie stresses her rank in business courses, which is higher and more impressive.

Why does Carrie make a big thing out of being able to work well with others?

Dan's resume is a single page that leads with functional groupings and is followed by chronological details. Notice how he shifts experience in an unrelated field (gas station) to make it seem perfect for retail stores.

Now that you've finished your own resume, you've noticed that some of the data you compiled for your work sheets fell on the cutting room floor.

The information isn't wasted. After being dredged up from your memory, it is on standby status in your mind, ready to use during job interviews.

Resume ready, our next concern is how to hunt for a job.

■ ■ ■ ■

Chronological Resume

CHITRA SAXENA

932 Sandy Lane   Phone: (989) 555-8021, 6–9 p.m.
Delight, New Mexico 35776   Day messages: (989) 555-7878

Seek position as meeting coordinator . . . to use planning and organizing abilities. Management experience in large and small events. Proven skill in handling many complex details, smoothly and calmly.

EXPERIENCE:

<u>Member</u>, Special Events Committee, University of New Mexico, Albuquerque; 1994–1996. As part of the six-person team, was responsible for $100,000 annual budget, and for bringing 27 major performances and 10 speakers to campus. Both years ended with a profit of $25,000 annually.

From Outside Interests Work Sheet.

♦ Became completely familiar with special event contract negotiations, handling large sums of money, securing facilities, dealing with people.

♦ Learned to work efficiently under pressure and to handle setbacks in even-tempered, creative manner, according to faculty advisor, Dr. Roger Gomez.

<u>Activities Coordinator Assistant</u>, Peaceful Nursing Home, 18 Grove Lane, Delight, N.M. 34776; 1993–1996. Initiated and planned full program of field trips for 25 nursing home residents and accompanied them on trips.

From Unpaid-Work Work Sheet.

♦ Researched possibilities, negotiated costs, solved transportation problems, managed group of elderly people.

♦ Showed resourcefulness in seeing need for program. Evaluation study by supervisor Sally Bird showed 100% of participants felt trips were "outstanding."

♦ My supervisor said I am "The most helpful volunteer she ever worked with."

EDUCATION:

Attended University of New Mexico, 1994–1996. Major study: social psychology. Particularly enjoyed research-related courses.

From Educational Work Sheet.

PERSONAL:

Enjoy people, have good social skills . . . get satisfaction in creating order from chaos.

Functional Resume

CARRIE RICHARDS

27 Girard Ave.   725/555-1245   Caldonia, Utah 98905

Offering excellent skills in typing, word processing, knowledge of office machines and systems. Seek to apply these as secretary. Available July 1, 1996.

strong business skills	Accurately type at 70 words per minute. Can use computer. Familiar with databases, Microsoft Word, ClarisWorks, Windows '95, PageMaker, and the Internet. Understand filing and general office systems, as well as correct procedures for telephones.	From Educational work Sheet.
computer	Took a part-time job assisting small companies to utilize effective computer use, arranged by computer teacher. Clients were always satisfied with work and in many cases have been offered permanent positions.	From Paid-Work Work Sheet.
proofreading	Copy editor of high school newspaper, two years; often praised for careful work in spotting errors.	
planning & coordinating	Assisted my father in setting up a new branch office of his company: helped arrange the office, organize the files, negotiate with telephone company for phone system. Trained staff in use of computers.	From Outside Interests Work Sheet.
education: business diploma	High school diploma with four years of English and a concentration in business applications of computers.	

Accomplishments:

♦ Received one of only two proficiency certificates awarded among three computer classes

♦ Selected to aid fellow students on computers.

♦ Overall rank in computer subjects: top twenty percent.

From Educational Work Sheet.

work well with others	Directed volunteers to do mailings for a political campaign. We were able to mail 10,000 letters in one week's time, with volunteers enjoying the project and feeling useful.	From Unpaid-Work Work Sheet.
	The campaign manager, Will Raindrop, complimented me before the entire staff, saying that I am "an easy person to get along with."	From Identity Inventory for Personality.

Hybrid Resume

DAN MAHLUM
1221 Center Street   315/555-0213 (work)
Pawtucket, R.I. 78888   315/555-0069 (home)

Seek manager-trainee position in retail field.
Qualifications include college degree, and ability to handle
merchandise and sales transactions responsibly; longtime interest
in merchandising.

Education: Bachelor of Arts—English. Emphasis of electives has
              been on business and marketing.

Sales: At gas service station, handle cash and credit sales for
              an average of 200 customers daily. Supervisor kept me   From Paid-Work
              on when two others were laid off due to shortened   Work Sheet.
              business hours, saying I am a "fast learner and hard
              worker." Missed only one-half day of work, never late.

Merchandising: Won a city-wide essay contest on merchandising with   From Outside
                150 entrants. Sponsored by Block Street Merchants   Interests Work
                Assn.   Sheets.

Supervising: At variety store, trained 10 new part-time clerks;
              devised one-week course to orient trainees. Worked in   From Paid-work
              all areas restocking merchandise, making sales,   Work Sheet.
              counting receipts.

Awareness: Regularly read several consumer magazines. Have
              traveled throughout the U.S. with my family and
              understand regional differences in consumer taste.

                            ******

Experience: Service Station Attendant, Exmoor Flagship Service
              Station, 3881 Market St., New Madrid, R.I. 78888;   From Paid-Work
              314/876-5647; Supervisor, Wes Pumps. Sept.'94 to   Work sheet.
              present.

              Sales supervisor, Woolwow's, 49 Hand Court,
              Pawtucket, R.I. 78889; 314/942-5656; Supervisor,
              Michelle Bryanowski. Sept. '93-Sept. '94 (part-time).

College: Apple University, Carson, PA: B.A. 1992. Earned   From Identity
              approximately 50% of tuition while student.   Inventory for Work
                                                                        Values and
                                                                        Education work
                                                                        Sheet.

When You Need a Crash Course in Finding Student Jobs

No matter how wonderful your resume, you won't receive a job offer until you've been through a job interview. Resumes help you get interviews, but during the interview you sell yourself as a good match for a job. Sometimes you won't even present a resume until the interview.

The trick is to line up interviews. Here are ways to do it.

Schools

Your campus career planning and placement center is an obvious place to start looking for a part-time or summer job. In some high schools, a counselor or career center specialist maintains a clearinghouse of student jobs. In both colleges and high schools, notices of student opportunities find their way to bulletin boards.

Don't overlook professors in your major field, and teachers who coordinate vocational education work-study programs. Since these educators stay in touch year-round with employers, they may know of opportunities

Networking

Use contacts to obtain referrals to other people who can direct you to opportunities. Include parents, relatives, neighbors, classmates, past employers, and school and community youth placement agencies, as well as teachers and counselors. Add to your personal contacts log for future reference all new acquaintances.

Direct Application

About one-fourth of all employees find their jobs by going directly to employers and asking to be hired.

Newspaper Ads

Check local weekly papers, as well as the metropolitan daily papers, for job leads. In addition to recruitment ads, learn to read business news stories with an eye toward developing job opportunities. Is a new store opening? If so, you could get in on the ground floor.

Employment Services

Community centers, civic organizations, religious groups, city governments, school districts, and others often sponsor student job programs.

Y's and similar organizations frequently post help-wanted notices on bulletin boards, as do some shopping centers.

The chamber of commerce may have a list of firms that hire summer workers. A quick reference to these services may be found by checking with campus career planning and placement centers and school counselors.

A call to the mayor's office, or a visit to a large library, may turn up a list of potential job opportunities.

Some civic-minded private employment agencies post free-of-charge summer student jobs. Don't forget to check with the local public employment service office, in some states called the Job Service, which we discuss in detail in Chapter 15.

■ ■ ■ ■

Timetable for Summer Job Hunting

October to November

1. Identify potential employers: companies, agencies, programs.

2. Research the 20 employers you'd most like to work for; write job target sheets.

3. Write (or redo) your resume to match your qualifications to the requirements of the top 20 job prospects.

November to January

1. Each year a booklet is published that catalogs federal summer jobs. Most jobs are for college students, but some are available to high school students. The booklet, known as Announcement 414, is titled "Summer Jobs in the Federal Government for [year]." Copies are available in Federal Job Information Centers. You can write for a free copy to: Washington Area Service Center, OPM, 1900 E St. N.W., Washington, DC 20415. Send your request for the announcement no later than December 1 so you'll get it when it comes off the press in late December each year. Don't delay. Some application deadlines are as early as January and there's crushing competition for the jobs.

   In addition to federal jobs, ask your counselor or librarian to steer you to lists of city and state government summer jobs.

2. Over holidays, contact people who can hire or refer you to a job. See as many in person as you can. To others, send letters of application and resumes. Submit applications for special programs.

January to March

1. Meet deadlines for any governmental job applications.

2. Continue to apply for jobs.

March to May

Contact all companies and agencies that have not replied. Expand your contacts to as many more prospects as you can identify.

June

Push the panic button. Try for any type of summer job. Once again, drop a note to your top 20 prospects saying that you are still available if circumstances should change.

■ ■ ■ ■

Use the Phone to Line Up Job Interviews

Try these three top techniques for landing interviews by phone.

1. The number-one method is to arrange to be referred by an official source. This might be a counselor, career center employee, or employment service specialist. It could be a teacher or professor. The official source probably has knowledge, or at least an inkling, that the target (person you are calling) is in a hiring mode.

   "My name is Roy Pfautch. Charlie Pitman at the Baron University Career Center thought that I might be exactly the person to consider hiring for a summer job. With your agreement, I'd like to stop by next Tuesday at 2 o'clock. Would that be convenient or would after 4 be better?"

   Keep it simple. All you want to achieve in this call is to gain an interview appointment. Do not give the target an opening to interview you on the phone. If pressed, say "I really want to talk to you about that face to face. When would be the best time?"

2. The second method is to be referred by an unofficial source—friend, relative, just about anyone.

"My name is Claire Burns. Dr. Scott, I'm a student at Freemont Community College where I'm studying medical assisting. Our friend Allison Cook asked me to call you. She thinks we ought to meet because one day you may need a reliable part-time assistant and I'd like to be at the top of the list. Knowing how busy you are, I'm asking you to set the time at your convenience. When would be the best day?"

You are saying quickly who you are, who knows you, and what you want. You are implying that someone known to the target asked you to call and that the target will gain a benefit by meeting with you.

3. The third in a trio of effective techniques is the telemarketing call. Never call the personnel department and only say, "Do you have any openings?" It is too easy to say "No, sorry." Instead, try this (to a personnel department employment interviewer, whose name you got from the telephone receptionist):

"Hello, my name is Agatha Wisti. I'd like to stop by your office tomorrow to talk about working part time for your company. Would tomorrow morning around 11 be a good time for your schedule or would after lunch be more convenient?"

Although many of you will take this fairly simple approach, there's still a better way.

Do advance research on the name of the person who has the power to hire you. Usually this is the individual who will supervise you. In a small firm of 25 employees or less, ask for the name of the company manager. In a larger firm, ask for the name of the person to whom you would report.

Practice what you are going to say before you call. If you are given a "no help wanted" answer, don't fizzle out like a punctured balloon—keep talking, keep asking for an interview. If you seem to be talking to a stone wall, ask if you can call back in a few days. Your persistence will make a good impression.

Get yourself in an upbeat mood before making your calls. Sound as though you are an enthusiastic person who has a high energy level. Your telephone personality is the only basis upon which the employer can judge you at this point.

Here's the kind of technique to use. The example is adapted from the book *Who's Hiring Who*, by Richard Lathrop (Ten Speed Press).

"Mrs. Botticelli, I'm sure I can do a great job in your department when a part-time job opens up. May I come in to see you?"

Botticelli resists: "But we don't have an opening."

"What I'd like to do is show you that I'm the best applicant to hire the next time you do. May I come to see you?"

If Botticelli asks you about your experience, don't crumple because you don't have any. Instead, turn to related strengths.

"In school I showed that I worked hard, fast, and with care. People have always liked the jobs I've done for them."

If Botticelli says that's all very nice but that they need better experience than that, keep your mouth running.

"I learn fast and you can count on the fact that I'll work hard for you. I'd sure appreciate the chance to prove it to you. Can I come in to see you?"

Botticelli may say you've earned an interview and set the date, or she may continue to say no. If so, ask if you can call back in several weeks, and ask if she can suggest someone else who can use your abilities.

After you thank her, immediately call any person to whom she referred you and say, "Mrs. Botticelli suggested I call you . . ."

You have lost nothing. If you did not gain an appointment with Mrs. Botticelli, you may have promoted yourself upstairs to the second best way of using a telephone to arrange for a job interview.

■ ■ ■ ■

Looking Like You Belong

Whether or not you will be offered a job often depends on what happens during the first few minutes of contact in an interview.

The reason may be what psychologists call the *halo effect*—if you excel in one area, it is assumed you excel in others.

Dress and grooming play major roles in creating your halo effect.

Although we'll discuss image in greater detail later, the thing to remember is to look as though you belong in the setting to which you aspire.

As a student, your school clothing may be perfect, but, if there's doubt in your mind, ask a counselor, or reconnoiter the workplace in advance of your interview and see what everybody else is wearing.

■ ■ ■ ■

How to Make the Interviewer Select You

It's showtime! You have Resume in hand and you've arranged a job interview. It's time to show your stuff.

Although it may do little to calm your nerves, remember that you will be offered the job or rejected because of the impression you make on the interviewer.

Arrive for interviews about five minutes early—never be late. Nobody cares if you got caught in traffic.

Be friendly and well-mannered. Avoid the urge to chew gum or smoke. Stand still until you're invited to sit. Give the interviewer a good handshake and remember that a smile improves your looks.

Sit straight, leaning a little forward in your chair. Avoid crossing your legs and keep both feet on the floor. When nervous, people often move their feet when their legs are crossed. Also sometimes even experienced interviewees will use too much motion with their hands. It's a good idea to have your hands sitting in your lap, relaxed and touching one another so that you are aware of their location.

The biggest favor you can do yourself is to anticipate questions and then rehearse good answers.

Some typical questions for student jobs include these brain-breakers:

◆ Tell me about yourself. (Tip: Keep your answer brief. Cover your education, skills, abilities, and work attitudes.)

◆ What school courses do you like best? Least? Why?

◆ In which subjects do you do best? Worst? Why?

◆ In what activities have you participated?

◆ Do you drive? Own your car?

- What are your skills?

- What are your career plans?

- What hours could you work?

- Why do you want to do this kind of work?

- Why do you want to work for this company?

- Why should we hire you? (Tip: You learn fast, you work hard, and you are reliable.)

- Have you ever failed a course in school? (Tip: If the answer is affirmative, admit it and quickly change the subject to a course in which you did well.)

It would be unusual if you were not nervous during your interview performance. As a student, your nervousness will be overlooked as long as your teeth don't chatter and you don't fidget in your chair. The cure for nervousness is to interview often. Practice makes poised.

Watch for clues that the interview is drawing to a close. The interviewer may stand up, or thank you for coming in.

You, in turn, express your thanks to the interviewer. Ask about the next step:

"This job sounds very challenging and I would be grateful for the chance to show you I can do it. When do you think I might hear from you?"

Another tack you can take at this point eliminates the anxiety of waiting long, fingernail-biting days for the phone to ring with a job offer. Say that you may be hard to reach in the next few days and ask if it would be okay if you check back with the employer on a given date.

Going home and writing a thank-you note to the interviewer for the time and and consideration given you is one more way to make a favorable impression. For advanced interviewing suggestions, turn to Chapter 15.

■ ■ ■ ■

When You're Not Offered the Job

Columnist Tony Perry, writing in the *Los Angeles Times*, says young workers are becoming less satisfactory by the hour. Perry speaks for many adults when he describes youthful disinterest.

You see it everywhere: the deli sandwich-maker who wipes her nose and continues assembling your ham on rye. The ice cream scooper who can't keep her hands out of her hair.

The clerks who are determined not to make eye contact with customers. And always the discussion among them of hours and working conditions: Did you start at 10 a.m.? Are you working tonight? Can I take my break now?

Okay, so this is another whopping stereotype. Nevertheless, you may face someone who shares Perry's opinion just when the opening is exactly the job you want. Here's what to do after you wait a week for an answer:

Wait no more. Pick up the telephone and politely ask the interviewer if a decision has been made, or if there is additional information you can supply. Restate your interest in the job.

Your refreshing interest may tilt the odds in your favor. Assuming the interviewer doesn't faint dead away.

■ ■ ■ ■

Hired! Start Your Job on the Right Foot

Once you land a job, there's a simple way to get off to a good start with your boss. On your first day at work ask for guidance on what is expected of you and the kinds of achievements most valued.

Say something like this: "I'm going to try hard to be the best person on your team. To be sure I've got my signals straight, will you tell me which duties are most important to you? I want to do things your way but I need to double-check that I know what you prefer."

■ ■ ■ ■

How to Avoid Flops, Flubs, Failures, and Fiascoes

The reasons businesses give for not hiring young applicants can double as a guide to success on your student job. On the left are 10 reasons and on the right, the corollaries for good performance.

Negative Factor

1. Poor personal appearance.

2. Overbearing know-it-all.

3. Inability to express self clearly, poor diction and grammar.

4. Lack of interest, enthusiasm.

5. Interested only in paycheck.

6. Unwilling to start at bottom, expects too much too soon.

7. Makes excuses, is evasive.

8. Lack of tact.

9. Lack of courtesy.

10. Lazy.

Corollary

1. Dress appropriately; be neat and clean. Use deodorant.

2. Figuratively speaking, don't rearrange the furniture until you're the boss.

3. As a Chinese fortune cookie says: "Engage brain, then start mouth."

4. Focus on the job, get involved, show interest. Being lost in space is better left to starships.

5. Do a fair day's work, remembering that if you goof off, you'll be fired and someone else will get your job.

6. Sweep as fast as you can.

7. When you mess up, don't invent excuses that shift the blame. Accept the responsibility by apologizing and if you have an acceptable reason for a mistake, blurt it out.

8. It's okay to be a bit blunt, but never say that your boss is "actually quite perceptive and not entirely stupid."

9. Show your politeness in every way every day. Never elbow the boss aside when racing for the door.

10. Walk briskly, respond to directions quickly, ask for assignments when you have time on your hands.

More Basics for Beginners

Attitude is the magic word for success in a student job. Employers say it makes all the difference. Attitude covers a lot of ground, including criticism.

When your supervisor criticizes you, accept it gracefully because it's not likely you'll do a near-perfect job in the beginning.

Your work habits will be under scrutiny as well. Don't let the company phone grow out of your head by making frequent or lengthy personal calls. Keep personal chats with co-workers to a minimum. A radio is an appliance that belongs in your home. Disappearing acts from your work station may result in your permanent departure.

Most employers go through the roof when you are absent without giving advance notice and getting approval. If you're part of a team, your absence can cause major problems. Whenever you will be late, call as soon as you know you'll be among the missing and explain why.

Be sure to honor the time limits of lunch hours and breaks, and stay until quitting time.

Light-fingeredness is very risky business. Walking out with anything that is not yours is stealing and employers are getting tougher on employee theft.

Refuse no assignment within reason or you'll remind the boss of the message inside a greeting card: "I'd wish you a happy birthday, but it's not in my job description."

■ ■ ■ ■

What Employers Think About You

A survey of employers reported by VICA (Vocational Industrial Clubs of America) asked three questions. Here are the results.

1. *What do you consider to be the major problem of new employees?*
   - ◆ Dependability, responsibility.
   - ◆ Lack of motivation, initiative.
   - ◆ Attendance, punctuality.
   - ◆ Selfish attitudes (wants pay without work).

2. *What is your major reason for terminating an employee?*
   - ◆ Poor attendance.
   - ◆ Poor job performance.
   - ◆ Poor punctuality.
     [Other studies show that interpersonal factors—inability to get along with others and politics—is the number-one reason why people are fired.]

3. *What is important for advancement?*
   - ◆ Self-motivation, initiative, extra effort.
   - ◆ Willingness to accept responsibility.
   - ◆ Dependability, reliability.
   - ◆ Interest, enthusiasm.

■ ■ ■ ■

Keep a Log of Accomplishments

Buy an inexpensive little notebook and as soon as you've mastered your job, begin writing down any accomplishment or contribution you make to the employer's success.

Every few months, summarize your achievements. Remember the measurement technique.

As you'll recall, there are four basic ways to measure. You can use:

1. *Numbers.* "Saved 200 carry-out food cartons from being dumped by mistake."

2. *Percentages.* "By carefully following maintenance procedures, cut service calls on photocopy machine by 50 percent over previous three-month period."

3. *Amounts.* "In needlepoint store, sold $100 more per week than in previous quarter."

4. *Supreme statements.* "Regional supervisor said this movie theater concession stand is the cleanest of any in his group."

As simple as it sounds, keeping a measurable record of your accomplishments can make a big difference at raise time—and on future Resumes. Moreover, it's a valuable habit to develop for later in your career.

■ ■ ■ ■

Capitalists Prosper (Sometimes) in Own Business

Adventuresome students may decide to get off to a fast start in the business world by starting their own mini-businesses.

Some ideas are simple: furniture refinishing, swimming pool cleaning, lawn mowing. Others involve organization: coordinating local garage sales for a percentage of the profits.

Still others—principally created by hard-charging college students—are a megasuccess. A Stanford University student customized tax and accounting software for companies, grossing $300,000 in sales his senior year.

Not all student businesses amount to much. Most don't. In fact some young business owners have a first-hand opportunity to learn about losing money.

Still, some notable successes remind us of this remark by author John Andrew Holmes:

Never tell a young person that anything cannot be done. God may have been waiting for centuries for somebody ignorant enough of the impossible to do that very thing.

■ ■ ■ ■

CHAPTER
12

After High School, What?

What will you do after high school? That's the question of the year—preferably of the year in which you are a high school junior. Matters can get hectic if you wait until your senior year to make plans.

Often the question of the year is approached through a series of *should* I questions.

◆ Should I go right to work immediately?
◆ Should I wait a year before continuing school?
◆ Should I attend a vocational school to learn a trade?
◆ Should I go to a small college or a big university?
◆ Should I choose a technical or liberal arts major?
◆ Should I join the military?

This chapter is the first of three that respond to questions about your direction after high school. It addresses the college-bound student, offering a roadmap of considerations that bear on your future career. Students who are not bound for college can turn to Chapter 14.

Among the topics we discuss are education in a changing world; the case for college in a techno-tomorrow; the dwindling importance of admission tests in the majority of colleges; coaching and test-taking for competitive colleges; paying for college; rating the colleges; black colleges; cooperative education programs; college internships; federal service academies; and taking the first two years at a community college.

The section concludes with an explanation of what accreditation really means, a checklist for selecting your college, and a college planning calendar.

Education in a Changing World

Hundreds of thousands of jobs in steel mills, textile plants, shoe factories, and other traditional smokestack workplaces are slipping into history. Caught in the void of bygone industries are a group of unfortunate people, officially called *displaced workers*, whose jobs are gone forever and who often lack the flexibility and skills to effectively seek employment alternatives.

What does the plight of displaced older citizens have to do with you? You're part of a brave new high-tech world, right? Yes and no.

Your generation will be trained to direct computers, lasers, robots, and other wonders, but there's also a strong possibility that you'll come up against increasingly sophisticated, gee-whiz machines that can outperform humans in the operation of lesser machines.

Even now there are computers that program other computers and robots that boss robots.

Super automation may create a new generation of displaced workers. That's a distressing thought, but you can take strong, positive steps to protect yourself against becoming a future casualty of a "brotherhood of machines."

The secret to doing well in a rapidly changing society is to acquire the skill of learning.

Learning is a renewable resource. In the years ahead, you may be required to draw upon that resource again and again. If technology should close one door, it may open another. By consciously developing a flexible attitude and by never hesitating to add to your educational power base, you position yourself among those who can cross over new thresholds.

Whether you join the military, go to a vo-tech school, or obtain an advanced university degree, it is important to master fundamental skills upon which future learning can be built.

What are fundamental skills? There are many definitions, but they certainly include written and oral expression, mathematics, analytical thinking, and creative responsiveness to problems.

No matter what basic mix you accept, the point is: From a strong foundation, you can branch out in many directions—as required by changing circumstances.

Learn to think.
Learn to learn.

■ ■ ■ ■

Making Plans for College

Each year, nearly one and a half million students move directly from secondary school to colleges and universities across the nation. Thousands more hit America's campuses after a stint in the military or in the civilian workplace.

While in the 9th grade you can begin to get your thoughts together about your education after high school. Continue thinking in the 10th grade.

If you plan to attend a selective college, you should know that the 11th grade is the make-or-break year. Take the most demanding course load you can handle and still maintain a good grade point average (GPA). The 11th grade is the last *full* year in which your grades are reviewed by most admission committees. Sophomore and freshman grades are less important, but don't let your senior year grades slide—if they nosedive, you could be unadmitted or admitted on probation.

For more tips, see *How To Prepare for College*, by Marjorie Eberts and Margaret Gisler (VGM Career Horizons).

■ ■ ■ ■

Why We Favor College for Many Students

A U.S. Labor Department study says college programs lasting four years or longer provide qualifying training to more workers than all the other postsecondary school categories combined.

Even so, remember that not everyone shows championship form in the most traveled waters and you may find your best prospects are not found on college campuses but elsewhere. We'll discuss that later. But for now—college, here we come!

■ ■ ■ ■

The Case for College in a Techno-Tomorrow

As you envision a lifetime when computers sometimes outthink humans, customers shop by video terminal, and robots do windows, you're probably thinking "college."

If so, you are among the majority of high school graduates who see college on the horizon. When this decade began, six of 10 high school graduates enrolled in college—the highest proportion ever.

But that's not surprising. Americans in recent decades have been climbing on the educational bandwagon as never before. Today about two of 10 American adults are four-year college graduates, a percentage roughly double what it was a mere 20 years ago.

It's obvious the word has gotten out: In a highly technical age, a college degree offers a competitive edge.

As a college graduate, you are likely to earn more money than do non-graduates, suffer less unemployment, and hold superior positions. Lifetime earnings of a man with a college degree are 50 percent more than those of a man with only a high school diploma.

According to the 1995 *Salary Survey* published by the National Association of Colleges and Employers, the job market for 1995 graduates is improving.

Other findings included the following:

♦ 45 percent of all job offers went to technical grads

♦ 70 percent of the non-technical graduates received job offers from the service sector

♦ 21 percent of all offers to non-technical grads came from accounting firms

Starting salary offers to most types of engineering graduates increased significantly, with industrial engineers seeing the biggest increase (to $35, 244). However, chemical engineers had the highest average starting salaries ($39,863).

Computer science graduates had average starting salaries of $32,607, with the largest percentage of job offers coming from computer software/data processing employers.

Average offers for management information systems graduates rose to $30,654 and average salaries for accounting graduates went down to $27,873.

The following table shows average salary offers in a number of curriculum areas.

Business	Total Offers	Average Offer
Economics & Finance	273	$26,597
Hotel/Restaurant	28	$21,762
Marketing	379	$24,726
Real Estate	5	$24,100
Communications		
Advertising	22	$22,031
Communications	82	$23,457
Telecommunication	21	$19,278
Education		
Elementary	152	$22,164
Special Education	27	$23,427
Home Economics		
Textiles	7	$18,643
Home Economics	18	$19,883
Humanities & Social Sciences		
Foreign Languages	14	$21,821
Political Science	47	$23,812
Psychology	78	$20,487
Visual and Performing Arts	42	$23,004
Agriculture & Natural Resources		
Agribusiness	19	$26,201
Natural Resources	7	$23,100
Health Sciences		
Allied Health	25	$33,810
Nursing	45	$31,798
Pharmacy	40	$43,234
Sciences		
Actuarial	6	$34,333
Architectural & Environmental Design	5	$23,210
Biological Sciences	41	$22,471
Chemistry	31	$29,945
Environmental	7	$23,098
Mathematics	29	$26,587
Polymer	3	$30,080

College graduates have the edge in job security too. A 20-year study of unemployment rates reveals that high school graduates have suffered increasingly more joblessness compared with college graduates. Today a high school graduate is twice as likely to be out of a job as a college graduate.

Why has the collegiate crowd fared so well? When employers have a choice, they almost always select the applicant with the highest academic credential. For beginning jobs, at least, credentials have become the basis for pay and position.

Is it true that it doesn't matter what you major in, that nobody sticks with a college major once work has begun? That's a debatable issue. But various studies do report that most college graduates obtain their first jobs in fields related to their majors, that several years after graduation most male graduates have relatively high status occupations, and that roughly 90 percent of college graduates are satisfied with their chosen occupations.

Other research says college is valuable for the contacts you make—old-school ties. Some employers regard the college you attended as one of the most important considerations in first-job hiring decisions.

Finally, in looking at college for the effect it will have on your career, some of the most attractive occupations, such as engineers and teachers, are closed to those who lack a college degree.

Jobs, though, aren't the only reason to study yourself into the ground and perhaps go in debt for an education.

The following comments are by a former U.S. Secretary of Education, William J. Bennett. To understand what else college can do for you as a person, read this.

College *should* be a road to your ambitions. But every student should take the time to tread the ground outside his or her major, and to spend some time in the company of the great travelers who have come before.

Why? Put simply, because they can help you lead a better and perhaps happier life. If we give time to studying how men and women of the past have dealt with life's enduring problems, then we will be better prepared when those same problems come our way. We may be a little less surprised to find treachery at work in the world about us, a little less startled by unselfish devotion, a little readier to believe in the capacity of the human mind.

And what does that do for a future career? As Hamlet said, "readiness is all." In the end, the problems we face during the course of a career are the same kind that we face in the general course of life. If you want to be a corporate executive, how can you learn about not missing the right opportunities? One way is to read *Hamlet*. Do you want to learn about the dangers of overweening ambition? Read *Macbeth*. Want to know the pitfalls of playing around on the job? Read *Antony and Cleopatra*. The importance of fulfilling the responsibilities entrusted to leadership? Read *King Lear*.

Even in the modern world, it is still that peculiar mix of literature, science, history, math, philosophy, and language that can help mature minds come to grips with the age-old issues, the problems that transverse every plane of life. Students who bring to college the willingness to seek out those issues, to enliven the spirit and broaden the mind, will be more likely to profit in any endeavor.

■ ■ ■ ■

More Good Reasons for Going to College

As you approach the milestone of high school graduation, you may need help in clarifying your thoughts about college. Here are more reasons to invest in a college education.

Knowledge and Intellectual Development

No overwhelming research *proves* that intellectual development and training to think are nourished by the college experience, but it is logical to assume few students know less about a subject at the end of a course than they knew at the beginning.

Even so, couldn't you do just as well by reading books on your own? Perhaps, but educators say most people will find the college experience far more enriching. Going to class, reciting, asking questions of the professor, being stimulated by other students, reviewing for exams, gathering your thoughts and knowledge to prepare a term paper—all these factors reinforce learning in ways that independent reading can't.

Social Development

College attendance is associated with growing up socially.

Researchers say that college students often become more liberal in their attitudes, more politically and socially sophisticated, and more competent in working with others than do non-students.

Researchers assert that college graduates are more at ease with and exhibit less prejudice toward persons who are different from themselves.

Personal Growth

Individual self-esteem seems to bloom in college students. A theory is that higher education provides a range of resources from which you can build a sound psychological base. You learn, for example, where to find the information you need, which helps you remain open to new ideas.

College—A Good Investment for Many

College attendance is associated with career enhancement, intellectual attainment, and social and personal growth. Compared with those who have not gone to college, college graduates know more, hold better jobs, and earn more money.

improve reading and study skills, b) to prepare for graduate or professional school, c) to make more money, and d) because parents wanted students to attend college.

Whatever your reason for going to college is, don't you think it's worth investing just a few years towards a better life?

■ ■ ■ ■

Reasons College Students Give for Going to College

The cooperative Institutional Research Program on Education has published data from a student survey beginning in 1971 and every year thereafter on this topic. In their 1995 publication the following highlights were published:

◆ College frosh give three main reasons for attending college: economic, liberal education, and parental influence. This pattern has persisted over more than two decades.

◆ College students from lower family income backgrounds give greater weight to economic influences.

◆ Students in public colleges and universities give greater weight to economic influences.

◆ Students in private institutions give greater weight to liberal education.

◆ Students from the lowest and highest family income backgrounds gave the greatest weight to liberal education, while middle family income backgrounds gave the least weight to liberal education.

◆ Between 1971 and 1994, the greatest growth in motivation for attending college was a) to

College and Students With Disabilities

In 1949 the University of Illinois at Urbana-Champaign was the only institution equipped to accommodate physically disabled veterans returning from World War II. Today, in many ways, the picture is much brighter. Most schools across the country have taken steps to make their campuses accessible not only to students with physical disabilities, but to individuals who have sensory or learning disabilities.

Moreover, most students with disabilities are admitted to America's colleges on much the same basis as nondisabled applicants with comparable qualifications, according to a College Board study.

Not all disabilities are treated equally in admission decisions, however. Admissions were lower than expected for students with learning disabilities, visual impairments, and physical disabilities, but applicants with hearing impairments were admitted more often than their grades and test scores would suggest.

There are a number of good books available for students with disabilities. These include *College and Career Success for Students with Learning Disabilities*, by Roslyn Dolber, and *Career Success* for *People with Physical Disabilities*, by Sharon F. Kissane, Ph.D. Both books are published by VGM Career Horizons, and are available in bookstores and libraries. Two other useful publications are *How to Choose a College: Guide for the Student with a Disability*, and *Financial Aid and Disabled Students*. Both of these publications are available free from the HEATH Resource Center, Suite 800, One Dupont Circle, Washington, DC 20036; toll-free telephone: (800)544–3284; District of Columbia residents call (202)939–9320.

■ ■ ■ ■

Is College for You? Questions and Answers

Q. *My grades in high school were terrible. What college would have me?*

A. No matter how dismal your high school grades, you can find a college that will accept you. Open admissions (the policy of accepting all high school graduates to an institution's limit of capacity) is more prevalent now than it was a decade ago. You will, of course, have to take remedial courses in college to make up for what you didn't learn in high school.

Q. *I hated high school. Isn't college more of the same?*

A. An odd thing happens to many students who thought high school was the pits. Once they get on campus, they find they like it! In high school, teachers and school authorities were breathing down your neck. Even as a senior, you had to follow many of the same rules you faced as a freshman.

In college, the rigid atmosphere is gone. You'll have freedom you've never known before. No one is breathing down your neck or even looking over your shoulder. If you need help, however, *you* have to go after it.

Q. *Nobody in my family ever went to college. I am afraid that other students will look down on me because I have not had their advantages and we do not have a lot of money. My high school wasn't the best. I sometimes think about going to college, but then I think that I should stick with the kind of life I know.*

A. These fears remind us of fleet-footed huskies pulling sleds in Alaska: The scenery only changes for the lead dog.

Move ahead. In any family, one individual has to pioneer. Can you think of any reason why it shouldn't be you? Sure, there's a possibility that in your first days at college, you'll feel uncomfortable and even a bit inferior. You're not alone. As you make friends on campus, you will discover that others feel uneasy too. Gaining confidence, you'll begin to think college is a pretty good idea after all.

Here are a couple of common-sense suggestions to help.

If your educational preparation wasn't all it could have been, look into ways to obtain tutorial or special catch-up help. Many colleges offer classes or workshops to strengthen students' academic skills.

As for money, become expert on how the student financial-aid system operates. Do not rely solely on awards from the financial aid specialist at your college.

Q. *I am interested in trying college but to be honest, I never stick with any one hobby or activity for very long. What can I do to stay in school once I start?*

A. Campus involvement is the tie that binds. Get involved.

Q. *If I decide late in my senior year that I really do want to go to college, can I still go?*

A. The majority of colleges have openings as late as a *month* before the start of a semester. Once you make up your mind, race to your high school counselor's office.

Many community colleges will accept you as late as the day of registration.

Q. Will *a college degree guarantee me a good job*?

A. No. You cannot be certain you'll get a good job just because you're a college graduate. If you have decided on a major, you can compare the job placement results for similar majors at different schools. Ask career service centers at various colleges for the figures. If 85 percent of plastics engineers from one college found jobs, but only 45 percent were hired from another school, find out what accounts for the difference.

■ ■ ■ ■

The Tests to Take

Test taking for college admission is one of life's necessary evils. Because you usually can't avoid testing if you're campus bound, learn good test-taking practices from a book, a course, or your counselor.

Now, here are the most commonly given tests.

Preliminary Scholastic Aptitude Test/National Merit Scholarship Qualifying Test (PSAT/NMSQT)

This test, administered by the College Board, is divided into two segments: verbal and mathematical. Scores on each part range from 20 to 80. Designed for juniors, it is also given to interested sophomores as a practice test.

Scores become a National Merit Selection Index. National Merit Scholarship semifinalists are determined by the Selection Index. Generally, to be ranked as a semifinalist, a student must have an index of 200 or more (this varies from year to year). At a level just below the semifinalists are the commended students who usually have an index of 185 or more.

The test must be taken in the junior year to qualify for National Merit consideration.

The PSAT/NMSQT is changing to a shorter, preliminary version of the new SAT-I (described below), including more critical reading in the verbal section and the inclusion of student-produced responses (rather than multiple choice) in the math portion.

Scholastic Aptitude Test (SAT)

This test currently includes three sections: verbal, mathematical, and a test of standard written English. Scores on the verbal and math sections range from 200 to 800 per section (a total of 1600 points for both), with the average score in the 900 neighborhood.

Many students take the test in the spring of their junior year; all college hopefuls should plan to take the SAT before January of their senior year. Students planning to apply for early admission decision programs should complete all required testing by the end of their junior year. College-bound students usually score at least 800 (out of 1600) total points.

Producers of the SAT (The College Board, a nonprofit membership organization of 2,600 schools and colleges that sponsor the test, and the Educational Testing Service, which administers it), are introducing radical revisions which were largely in place by 1994.

The SAT has been divided into two parts: SAT-I and SAT-II.

SAT-I are tests of reasoning skills that cut across both school and college curriculum areas (comparable to the current SAT-Verbal and SAT-Math tests).

The biggest change is in the math portion; about 15 of the 60 math questions will require computation and short answers rather than multiple choices to pick from. Students can use calculators. The message is that problem-solving ability is important.

The verbal section of the SAT-I will test more vocabulary in longer critical reading passages and drop some of the isolated word exercises, such as the antonyms.

The achievement tests of specific subject areas (foreign languages, history, literature, for instance) which are not required by as many colleges as math and verbal reasoning tests, will be regrouped as SAT-II. New tests will include language exams in Japanese and Chinese, a non-Western history test and an English-as-a-second language exam. And for brave souls, a new writing test in SAT-II will include an essay.

All who take the SAT will take SAT-I. Individual colleges and universities will indicate which tests in SAT-II they require.

At this writing, the mechanics of scoring and expected average tests scores for SAT-I and II had not been established.

American College Test (ACT)

The nation's other major college-admission test is the ACT Assessment, which has been completely revised for the 1990s. The new ACT includes tests in English, mathematics, reading, and science reasoning. The Assessment score scale ranges from 1 to 36, with the average score running between 20 and 21. College-bound students usually score a minimum of 15 points.

Although ACT traditionally has been used by colleges in midwestern, southeastern, and mountain/plains states, today most colleges accept either ACT or SAT scores.

Studies reveal that average ACT scores are related to types of high school course work. In a recent year, the average ACT composite score for students who took a college preparatory high school program (four years of English and three years each of math, social studies, and natural sciences) was 22, three points higher than the average score, 19, for students who did not complete such a program.

P-ACT + (Preliminary American College Test Plus) is a practice test with added components for career planning. You can take it when you are a sophomore.

Achievement Tests (ACH)

These College Board tests are administered in 15 subjects: American history and social studies, biology, chemistry, English composition, European history and world cultures, French, German, Hebrew, Latin, literature, mathematics-level I, mathematics-level II, physics, Russian, and Spanish. Scores range from 200 to 800. Not all colleges require achievement tests, and many colleges say they do not use the results for admissions purposes.

These achievement tests are gradually being reorganized as SAT-II tests.

Advanced Placement Tests (AP)

These College Board tests are for high school students who are taking college-level course work in certain subjects. The tests are graded 1 through 5. Many colleges award credits, usually three to five, to students who earn high scores. Students decide whether to submit these test results to the colleges.

Test of English as a Foreign Language (TOEFL)

Students—mostly from other countries—whose first language is not English take this test. The results will help the college evaluate their verbal ability.

■ ■ ■ ■

Critics Give Some Tests Failing Grades

Standardized college admissions tests are under fire.

Critics question whether the exams can accurately predict academic performance. They say the tests do not measure aptitude (your potential) but simply achievement (what you already know).

Detractors insist the existing tests measure only minimum levels of skills, factual recall, and theoretical knowledge. They say tests ignore such qualities as judgment, ambition, drive, and values. Tests do not show how well individuals would apply their knowledge in meeting daily challenges.

Moreover, some critics say the exams are biased against women, minorities, and the poor.

Even recent revisions by test-makers have failed to silence antagonists. Some call the leading testing organization an "unregulated monopoly," and would rather see their products scrapped than made over.

FairTest, a Massachusetts advocacy organization, has let loose a firestorm of criticism toward the standardized testing industry, insisting that as it now exists, their exams do not make fair, accurate, or relevant assessments of students or their teachers.

Defenders of standardized testing argue convincingly that tests are like messengers in the Middle Ages who brought reports of the plague from neighboring towns and were put to death for being the bearers of bad news.

Ohio State English professor John Sena insists that we don't like what the SAT tells us about our society and we take out our frustrations and anger on it. "Attacking the SAT may provide us with a measure of comfort, but it is a comfort based on the illusion that the problem is the exam, and not the discrimination, poverty, and neglect that it mirrors."

The test-or-not-to-test controversy isn't likely to be resolved during this century. Draw your own conclusions about admissions testing and fairness, but, from a practical point of view, let's consider the exams as they apply to you.

■ ■ ■ ■

A Contemporary Perspective on Tests and Admissions

The pool of 18-year-olds is shrinking. Except for the top schools—the ones that are harder to get into than Fort Knox—colleges and universities are marketing hard to keep their doors open.

Higher education has moved from a seller's market of a generation ago to a buyer's market today. With one-quarter fewer teen-aged students to draw from, colleges are looking for ways to invite you in, not screen you out.

What this means is that you can put off having a nervous breakdown because your SAT or ACT scores leave much to be desired. You can get into some college somewhere.

But there are still times when your SAT and ACT scores matter a lot.

■ ■ ■ ■

When the SAT and ACT Loom Large

Earning very high scores on the SAT or ACT is not of earth-shaking consequence for entrance into most institutions of higher education, except in three instances:

1. When you are trying to get into one of the most selective colleges.

2. When you want to attend a state university (or federal service academy) that limits enrollments by requiring minimum SAT or ACT scores.

3. When you are competing for a scholarship that partly depends on your SAT or ACT scores (merit scholarship, state scholarship programs, Proposition 42 athletic scholarships).

If you are interested in applying to one of the most highly selective schools, listen to Marge Loennig, the college admission counselor at the well-known private Holton-Arms School in Bethesda, Md.

For the most highly selective 10 to 15 colleges, students need a SAT total of 1350 plus or an ACT total of 32 or better; three Achievement tests at the least in the high 600s; an unweighted 3.8 (out of 4.0) grade-point average in rigorous academic subjects (physical education, business law, and journalism are not academic subjects); and a rank in the top 5 percent of a public high school class. Colleges like students who have held major leadership positions, competed on athletic teams, made a major volunteer commitment, worked outside of school, and who show independence and initiative.

While you will want to check college guide books for more details on relationships between test scores and specific institutions, Loennig gives a concise overview:

Students need a minimum SAT score of 1000 or an ACT score of 25 to be competitive at most flagship state universities, although the recent flood of applicants is causing some public institutions to ask for SAT scores of 1100 or higher or ACT scores of 26 or higher.

Generally speaking, almost any college that can afford the luxury of turning away applicants probably will use test scores as a key screening device.

There's one more thing to know about admission tests. College officials use tests for more than admission decisions; they use them to help place students once they have been admitted. If, for instance, your math scores are on the low side, you may be required to take certain basic math courses.

Allow plenty of time if you decide to prepare for your admission tests, remembering the Chinese proverb: Dig a well before you are thirsty.

■ ■ ■ ■

Can Coaching Boost Your Scores?

Does coaching for the SAT and ACT work? A decade ago, several groups—ranging from the federal government to Ralph Nader to Harvard professors—studying the coaching issue affirmed the value of test preparation. They said it works.

In fact, top commercial training groups claim they can boost SAT scores by an average of 100 to 150 points out of a maximum of 1,600. (We believe improvement of ACT scores is comparable.) Not everyone agrees.

Test proponents continue to insist that the SAT is the least coachable of tests. The College Board concludes that so far no one has demonstrated that coaching is sufficiently effective for all students to recommend spending significant amounts of time or money on it.

"Students can accomplish at least as much in school or on their own," according to a College Board statement. "Well-verified research shows that not all coaching works (certainly not for all students) and that, on the average, the effects are relatively modest. Some students who participate in coaching activities do not improve their scores. Others who do nothing but take the SAT a second time enjoy score gains comparable to the unverified claims of commercial coaching companies," says the College Board.

Coaching advocates reply that nothing works all the time for everyone. In any case, coaching classes are multiplying like garage sales in a recession and students are rushing to sign up. Stanley H. Kaplan, the man who practically invented the coaching business, says, "The more who go for coaching, the more who want it."

At the very least, coaching makes you familiar with the testing process. If you're a person who panics at the mention of the word "test," a dress rehearsal will give you the confidence to score up to your potential.

The cost of test-prep courses—$50 to $700—probably makes you wonder if you can't turn coaching into a do-it-yourself project. Yes, of course, you can. The drawback is that while you may learn as much on your own about test *content*, you may overlook important *strategies* known by test-wise instructors.

As one young woman has said, "It would be better to prepare on your own than not at all, but I feel the course gave me a little edge over what I could produce myself. I found questions on my exam that were very similar to what I had been given in the course. You make up so much time when that happens and then you do better overall."

But if you do want to study on your own, find how-to guides at bookstores, libraries, and counseling offices.

High-Tech Studying

High-school students can now study for the Scholastic Aptitude Test on their computers. "Inside the SAT" is a Windows and Macintosh-compatible program that helps students to prepare for the test using friendly, comic-book-like graphics and confidence-building comments. Results can then be analyzed for test-taking strengths and weaknesses. A CD-ROM version was released in September 1995.

The Impact of Test Scores

Although test-prep may be in your future, remember that getting a high test score—after intense preparation—will not necessarily provide the winning ticket in the Great American Selective College Sweepstakes. High test scores alone are unlikely to force admission to a school that wants a total package other than what you offer.

If you want coaching, get it well before the first SAT is taken in the spring of your junior year. Test-prep programs vary in length from five to a dozen weeks.

Because *all* SAT scores are sent to colleges, a single high score is more likely to put a smile on an admission officer's face than a series of varying scores. The officer has to wonder which score reflects more accurately your academic capacity—"Will the real test score please stand up?"

However, if you have a particular college in mind and you haven't scored in that school's range, it can be worthwhile to retake the tests.

With ACT, the student can specify which score is to be sent to colleges.

The authors believe that coaching classes indeed can boost scores. But unfortunately, in a few cases, they may boost them too much for students who lack the motivation to compete in a fast-track environment. These students may be better served at a less competitive campus. As Publius Syrus, a phrasemaker of antiquity, said:

You cannot put the same shoe on every foot.

■ ■ ■ ■

What Colleges Look For

Selective institutions—also called competitive institutions—can afford to be choosy. They enjoy swarms of applicants, many more than they can absorb.

The number of selective colleges in the United States is disputed. We agree with most education authorities who use the figure of 50 to 60 institutions. Others maintain that 117 institutions are in the most selective category—those that accept less than half of their applicants. Still other authorities generously find 300 colleges to count as competitive because entering students have done better than average on both national tests and in their high schools.

Studies show that while two college admission committees rarely paint on the same canvas, most picture the following criteria as the major factors influencing their decisions.

The two big numbers are *grade point average* (GPA) and *class rank*. Next comes *admission* test *scores*. If you've got lousy grades, you usually can save the day with great test scores; if your test scores are weak but your GPA is impressive, you still can look like a desirable student. In a selective college, academic factors range from between 50 percent and 75 percent of the overall evaluation.

Your school's *academic challenge* receives consideration. Top grades from a secondary school known for the rigor of its studies command more respect than top grades from a school thought to be mediocre. This is why prep school students often have an advantage over public school students in seeking entry to competitive colleges.

Course selection counts too. Students who have labored through tough courses are more impressive to admission people than students who have taken soft loads.

Advanced placement and *honors courses* add a few gold stars to your application.

After GPA, class rank and admission test scores, admission evaluators are interested in your *extracurricular activities*—and in this case, less may be more.

Rather than hopping all over the activities map, concentrate on doing a few things extremely well. The qualities you want to show are persistence, that you can follow through on a project with significant results, and that your activities have focus. Leadership positions in school organizations are ideal for this.

Next on the entry scale comes *recommendations* from teachers, counselors, and alumni.

While glowing references do make a favorable impression, run-of-the-mill references may not count for much because recommendations no longer are confidential. Fearing a lawsuit, reference givers are reluctant to say anything bad about you and the admission people know this.

What about personal interviews? Don't they count in the admission process? Surveys say not. In a recent study by the Educational Testing Service, colleges report they place little credence on personal interviews in admission decisions. Use your meetings with admission officers to gather information about institutions.

Beyond basic criteria, some students enjoy what can be called an "ace in the hole." When all else is equal, they may have an edge. Who fits in this elite group? Minority students, athletes, musicians, and others with notable talents.

Sons and daughters of alumni get special consideration, too. A U.S. Department of Education study shows that alumni children get a big break on admission to Harvard. Only 16.9 percent of all those who apply to Harvard get in, but alumni children were admitted at a 35.7 rate.

Yale, Dartmouth, Stanford, and other prestigious schools say they, too, have legacy preference policies, giving a "tip" to offspring of alumni. The rationale is that alumni give money and legacy admissions keep it coming.

But some alums are more equal than others. Privately, admission officers say children of big givers have an even bigger advantage than children of the average alum.

Most colleges claim to be "need-blind" in their admission policy, which means they don't consider whether or not a student needs financial aid in deciding who gets in. But, in these tight financial times when institutions of higher education need every dollar they can scrape up, when a college's financial aid purse is empty, it's empty. If openings remain, the institution may be forced to consider students who can pay but whose academic qualifications lack desirable luster. This means that if a college you want turns you down in the spring, it's worth a second telephone call in the fall to be sure the freshman class indeed is filled.

When the time comes to set facts to paper, keep a couple of common-sense points in mind.

Fill out your applications neatly. Hard-to-read forms are annoying. Set aside enough time to write or type a legible, clean, neat, grammatical, properly spelled, and altogether well-done application.

The same rule applies to essays, if you are asked to write one. If you have a choice, choose a personal topic, perhaps an event that affected your life, rather than an abstract subject such as world peace. When college representatives ask you to submit an essay, count on its being read.

Sometimes it will pay to include documentation along with your application. If you are a musician, it may be wise to send a tape of your music. If you are an artist, enclose a couple of slides of your best work. Be very selective in sending supplemental materials.

When you do everything right to get into a competitive school but find yourself on the outside looking in, remember this comment in *Newsweek* magazine about legacy preference: *No surprise, just a reminder that the myth of the campus as pure meritocracy is just that—fantasy.*

Even though for most colleges it is a buyer's market, a great sorting takes place among nearly one and a half million students who leave high school each year across the country. If you want to be sorted into the category of your choice, do what you must do to ensure your best presentation.

For more tips, read about admission dynamics in *Peterson's Guide to College Admissions*. Inexpensive brochures, such as A *Guide to the College Admission Process*, and college maps are available from the National Association of College Admission Counselors, Suite 430, 1800 Diagonal Road, Alexandria, VA 22314.

■ ■ ■ ■

10 Popular Essay Topics

From The College Board we learn the most frequent topics on which student applicants are asked to write an essay.

1. A personal statement describing you as an individual.

2. A significant interest/experience that holds special meaning.

3. How have you grown and developed?

4. Why have you selected this college?

5. Why have you chosen a given career field?

6. Describe an important issue of personal, local or national concern.

7. Name and say why you'd like to interview a prominent person (living, dead, or fictional).

8. Name a person who significantly influenced you and explain the influence.

9. Write a speech for delivery before some group; or write an article, letter, or editorial for publication.

10. Write about a book that has special significance for you.

■ ■ ■ ■

Early Acceptance: Getting the Jump on Admission

Many top colleges admit a large portion of their incoming freshmen before Christmas of their senior year.

Applying early may improve your chances of getting into a top school, despite many college officials' denials. You may gain what one candid admission dean describes as a "small but significant" edge. Two more advantages: You can skip weeks of filling out an avalanche of paperwork, and, because you know where you're going, you can feel less pressured during your senior year.

But there's a downside to early admission. You may change your mind during your senior year about where you want to enroll. Also, you may be disappointed in the student financial aid offer that doesn't come through until the spring. By then, if you have a binding agreement, it's too late to change colleges for the year.

Some early admission plans are nonbinding, and allow students until May 1 to change their minds. When reading college catalogs, pay attention to the terminology. Programs described as "early decision" usually require a binding student commitment. Programs described as "early action" or "early notification" usually do not.

"Rolling admission" is the most permissive early admission plan; it lets students apply as early as their senior September, hear back within three weeks and change plans any time during the senior year.

Popular guidebooks like *Peterson's Four-Year Colleges* note early-decision plans under the "Freshman Admissions" section. Another book, *Peterson's National College Databank: The College Book of Lists*, includes names of colleges and universities that offer early filing deadlines, usually from October 15 to November 15.

Is early acceptance a good idea? This is one of those issues you can argue either way. Critics say rather than commit early, students should spend extra time visiting campuses and comparing academic programs. They say early admission is particularly risky if you need financial aid because the formal aid offers in the spring may fall short of the informal aid estimates in the fall.

Still, a recent survey of 360 high school counselors reports that three of four support early acceptance programs.

It's your call.

■ ■ ■ ■

The Last Summer

What should you do the summer between your junior and senior high school years: hang out, work in a routine job selling shoes, take a trip, or find an on-campus summer program to give you a taste of college?

With freshmen enrollments down and costs up, colleges have discovered that summer programs for high school students fill empty classrooms and dorms. The variety is dazzling, from the University of Alaska Fairbanks' kayak spin through the northern wilderness, to the University of Pennsylvania's sociological trek through drug-infested neighborhoods.

If you are edging toward a collegiate summer program, review your motives. If you merely think the program will help you get into a top school, it may or may not. That is, if you are a marginal student, it may tip the scales a bit in your favor, but if you have everything else going for you, it won't make much difference one way or the other. Nor, contrary to what many parents think, will a summer on campus put you at the head of the admissions line.

What about taking a challenging college-level course like advanced calculus? Yes, that adds a gloss to your application, unless of course you flunk the course. That's the risk you take.

Your counselor may have a library of summer offerings by both private and public colleges.

Or you can look in recent editions of *Summer on Campus* by Shirley Levin (The College Board) and *Summer Opportunities for Kids and Teenagers* (Peterson's).

We advise that you use the last summer in high school to preview your career choices, either in a job or in a study program. Suppose your career interest is in the food area. Whether you perfect your interpersonal skills in a food service job in your locale, or enroll in a one-week commercial cooking course at Johnson & Wales University in Providence, R.I., you are using your time beneficially. College admission officers like that.

■ ■ ■ ■

Turned Down? How To Get In Next Year

If your favorite college sends you a rejection letter, you may want to try again next year.

The usual problem is academic, either poor grades overall or even adequate grades in not-very-challenging courses.

Use the year wisely. Aim for an interim college where you can get excellent grades in core subjects. Use tutors if you must. At the most selective colleges, even one C may keep you out. Try for small classes where professors can get to know you personally and use their clout to recommend your acceptance as a transfer student.

If grades weren't the problem, ask an admission counselor why you were sorted out and think of ways to correct the deficiency.

■ ■ ■ ■

Paying for College

The cost of a four-year degree at a private, up-scale college can run to more than $100,000. At state schools, the total tab adds up to more than $30,000.

On top of that, yearly average tuition costs for an MBA range from $1,800 to $18,000; a law degree, $2,800 to $21,000; and a medical degree, $6,000 to $29,000.

Fortunately, bargain tuitions are available and you can cut the pain by an astute pursuit of student financial aid.

Paying college bills is far too complex a subject to discuss here in detail, but we offer several basic start-up tips.

◆ Learn how the student financial aid system works. The freshman year of high school is not too soon to begin. About $28 billion is awarded to students each year from the federal government, state governments, private organizations, and the colleges themselves.

◆ Three types of aid are available: grants and scholarships that do not have to be repaid; loans that do have to be repaid; and jobs.

◆ Although some scholarships are awarded on merit, most student financial aid is based on financial need. "Need" is the difference between what a particular student and the student's family can afford to pay and what it costs to attend a given college. Even if you think you won't qualify for aid but you need it, apply for it.

◆ Look for alternative sources of funds, such as the military. Investigate ROTC (Reserve Officers Training Program) and National Guard programs to see if you find their offers attractive.

◆ Education dollars do not always go to the student most entitled to receive them. They go to the student most expert at finding and applying for them.

◆ Apply to a favorite college even if it looks like it's too rich for your pocket. When there's a chance you'll stand in the upper 25 percent of the freshman class, you'll be seen as a valuable recruit and it is reasonable to assume you'll be offered generous aid. If it doesn't work out, at least you'll have the satisfaction of knowing you gave it your best shot.

◆ Be realistic but not intimidated in your expectations. Remember that student aid comes in packages—a mix of loan money, which you pay back, scholarship and grant money which you do not pay back, and student job opportunities.

If two schools of otherwise equal appeal offer differing financial aid packages, obviously you'll choose the most beneficial to you. If you really prefer the school with the lesser financial aid package, you might negotiate an improved offer—no school likes to lose a recruit to a direct competitor.

If you feel the aid offer is drastically under market and you want to attend the college, never hesitate to appeal the award to the school's director of financial aid. Many students think an award offer is set in concrete. It's not. It may be negotiable. Remember, higher education is a buyer's market.

Among the many student financial aid guides on the market, an inexpensive annual primer that provides an overview of the aid system is *The College Financial Aid Emergency Kit*, by Dr. Herm Davis and Joyce Lain Kennedy. It's available only by mail for $6.95 from Sun Features Inc., Box 368M, Cardiff, CA 92007.

Another inexpensive guide is *Need a Lift? To Educational Opportunities, Career Loans, Scholarships, Employment*. Published annually, it's available for $2 from the American Legion Education Program, Box 1050, Indianapolis, IN 46206.

For more comprehensive listings, see recent editions of such references as *The Scholarship Book: The Complete Guide to Private Sector Scholarships, Grants and Loans for Undergraduates*, by Daniel

Cassidy; *Chronicle Financial Aid Guide*; and *Peterson's Grants for Graduate Students*.

A growing number of high schools and colleges offer student financial aid search on computer databases. Ask at counseling centers and financial aid offices.

Two more useful resources:

Epsilon is our favorite need analysis software program for home computers. It helps you figure out the financial angles of attending college and is offered by National College Services Ltd., 600 S. Frederick Ave., Gaithersburg, MD 20877.

College Cost Explorer is a quality PC software program for helping plan college costs. It comes from The College Board, CB Publications, Box 886, New York, NY 10101.

Another resource published by the U.S. Department of Education is *Preparing Your Child for College: A Resource Book for Parents*. This book includes a financial preparation checklist for parents. The booklet is available in the On-line Library, and is also available at Web and Gopher sites: http://www.ed.gov/pubs/Prepare.

Of special interest to minorities is a series of modestly priced booklets updated regularly from Garrett Park Press, Box 190B, Garrett Park, MD 20896. A typical title is *Financial Aid for Minorities in Business and Law*. Ask about others.

■ ■ ■ ■

America's Colleges

From sea to shining sea there are about 3,500 higher education institutions.

How many are two-year colleges? At last count, 1,400.

How many are four-year colleges? Approximately 2,100, including 155 universities.

Now that you know the numerical shape of higher education, according to the National Center for Education Statistics, what direction will you pursue—liberal arts or vocationally oriented studies? Which environment will be best suit you—urban, suburban, or rural? Traditional, contemporary, or avant-garde? Coed or single-sex? Large or small? Public or private? Selective admission requirements or less selective? How far away from home are you willing to travel—20 miles or 2,000? North, east, south, or west?

It's a tough choice, all right. Later, we offer a step-by-step guide to help you make the right one. First, a few considerations as you explore options in a land rich with higher education opportunities.

Classifying the Colleges and Universities

Traditionally, the difference between colleges and universities has been that the latter provide graduate education. It's no longer easy to tell what's what. Bryn Mawr College in Pennsylvania offers doctorates; Miami University (Middletown Campus), a two-year college in Ohio, offers associate degrees.

Nevertheless, understanding the different categories and natures of institutions of higher education can be useful in determining which type best meets your needs.

Here is a representative cluster developed by the Carnegie Foundation for the Advancement of Teaching.

Four-year Institutions

(Graduate programs require one or more additional years of study.)

◆ *Research Universities*—oriented to research, receiving many government and private research grants; focus on graduate education; national in scope.

- *Doctoral-Granting Institutions*—focus also on graduate education, but less oriented to research; national or regional.

- *Comprehensive*—in addition to liberal arts, these institutions offer one or more occupational or professional programs; national or regional.

- *Liberal Arts*—colleges offering the classic broad education favored for fundamental knowledge; national or regional.

Two-year Institutions

Community Colleges, Junior Colleges, Technical Institutes—although termed two-year colleges for convenience, occupational programs may last from one year to three years; transfer programs are two years; regional or local.

Rating the Colleges

A frequent question is whether an Ivy League education is worth the price—or would it be better to spend four years at a quality state school and save $50,000 or $60,000?

Some business experts say you're buying prestige at a "brand name" school and that it's worth the money. Prestigious schools are prestigious for a reason, so the argument goes. The reasons include quality faculty, bright students, a powerful alumni network, and the self-confidence graduates feel. They know they're good because they keep hearing they're good.

The question is one of those that could be debated endlessly on TV talk shows. In drawing your own conclusions, research is your new best friend.

So which are the nation's best campuses for undergraduate study? Putting aside stock responses, the real answer begins with knowing who is doing the rating.

Is it academicians—faculty, deans, and college presidents? Or is it students, alumni, and employers?

Sometimes academicians recognize that a college has shot up in quality, passing longtime favorites. Employers, however, may not get the word for years. From a job market viewpoint, it obviously matters what employers think.

As you gather data on various colleges, jot down each institution's degree of difficulty for entrance. Here's a simple scale:

1. Highly selective (most difficult to enter)

2. Selective (choosy)

3. Traditional (most people can qualify)

4. Liberal (a minimal academic orientation is okay)

5. Open (anyone can enroll)

If you want to know the best schools, here are several places to look.

Two heavyweight comprehensive guidebooks with pounds of data on thousands of the nation's colleges are the *College Board's College Handbook* (annual) and *Barron's Profiles of American Colleges* (biannual). These books will help you get a general impression of schools, which you can expand by writing for the institutions' catalogs and other information. Selective guides are more subjective but can help you wade through mountains of data.

Ruggs Recommendations on the Colleges, by Frederick Rugg (5749 Colonial Oaks Blvd., Sarasota, FL 34232; 813–378–4324), is one of the most focused and easiest to use. It rates 650 colleges into three categories (most selective, very selective, and selective) for each career field or discipline. This unique reference is an ideal first place to start a college search.

Peterson's Competitive Colleges (annual) contains comparative data on more than 300 colleges that consistently attract a surplus of undergraduate applicants. Profiles indicate each school's degree of entrance difficulty.

The Money Guide to the Best College Buys in America is issued each September by *Money* magazine. It's available on newsstands or can be ordered through the magazine. An excellent source of financial tips, a recent issue featured the Cooper Union for the Advancement of Science and Art in New York City. More than a century old, the venerable institution charges only a few hundred dollars tuition per student annually but spends more than $15,000 a year on each of its 1,000 students, who are united by "career-mindedness and dedication to work, work, work."

America's Best Colleges is an annual guide published by U.S. *News & World Report* magazine. It is available on newsstands or can be ordered through the magazine. It is based on a survey of academicians; a summary report is published in the magazine in October. *America's Best Graduate Schools*, a separate report, is published in the magazine each March.

Barron's 300 Best Buys in College Education identifies 300 institutions that provide quality education at below average prices.

During the last few years a number of college guides have appeared that are more entertaining and humorous than factual and helpful. Although they do say where to find all-night drugstores and buy pizza, don't take them as gospel for the serious business of education. Ask yourself: Does the author have a background in education and did the author survey academicians, students, alumni, or employers?

Small or Large?

Some institutions are small—more than 700 colleges have fewer than 500 students. Others are huge—in excess of 100 institutions enroll 20,000 students or more.

The attraction of a large institution is fairly obvious: It's a shopping center of educational programs and offers name recognition, superior resources, and, often, famous faculty members.

A huge college can be a fast, somewhat impersonal track and best suits students who feel comfortable in a crowd.

By contrast, a small college can be bountiful to people who like to know their neighbors. The residential nature of a small campus, plus the intense focus on students, can nurture emotional as well as academic growth.

Attending an institution that boasts Nobel Prize winners is exciting, but do the winners teach or are instructional chores assigned to teaching assistants? At small colleges, professors are often more accessible, perhaps even inviting students majoring in their subjects home for tea and enlightenment.

Can you climb high and fast if you attend a small school that's not exactly a household word? A graduate of Eureka College in Illinois has done well. His name is Ronald Reagan.

Traditionally Black Colleges—To Attend or Not?

Large numbers of the best African-American students headed for Ivy League schools during the 1970s. Today many of the nation's 98 historically black institutions are enjoying a renaissance of popularity as African-American students rediscover the academic attentiveness and social support offered at these colleges and universities—an environment that mostly white campuses often cannot match.

Reasons why students choose a black college are varied. They include putting a primary emphasis on finding a nurturing atmosphere where black students, being the majority race, can feel at home. Professors are said to set high standards for their African-American students, while also giving struggling students the extra help needed to stay in school. Costs typically are less than at similar mixed schools.

Some African-American scholars argue against choosing a black college. They say that SAT and ACT scores are below the national average and so a superior student will be academically mismatched.

On the other hand, racial relations on college campuses are often troubled and a black college may still be the best choice whenever students are worried about the hassle of racism at a mixed school.

Advocates of attending a mixed school say making the transition to blended cultures has to come sooner or later and it may as well be on a college campus.

Checkpoints to determine an institution's racial environment: Talk to the head of the black students' union, read the campus newspaper, look in the cafeteria to see if racial and ethnic groups are glued together in little knots of people or if minorities are integrated around the room.

If you're wrestling with the black-or-mixed decision, a third option is to start at a black college and switch to a mixed institution in your sophomore or junior year. When you first leave home you'll likely benefit from a small, warm, college that affirms your values and culture. As you mature and gain confidence, you may want to try transferring to a mixed college.

Even if your decision is in the future, start batting it around in your head. A decision re-examined usually is better than one you grab for at the very last minute.

Schools That Are Different

Unorthodox courses are common at Evergreen State College in Olympia, Wash. A program on technology focuses on whether it helps or hin-

ders society. The school gives students narrative evaluations of their work rather than grades.

Berea College in Berea, Ky., charges no tuition. Each student must perform some of the labor required to maintain the institution, "thus gaining an appreciation of the worth and dignity of all the labor needed in a common enterprise."

St. Andrews Presbyterian College in Laurinburg, N.C., a private college of 750 students, offers an innovative curriculum and has such a commitment to people that its new campus was specifically built to attract and serve students with disabilities.

Armed with a $300 million endowment, Trinity University in San Antonio aggressively goes after top students with offers of generous scholarships and recruits renowned faculty with offers of superior pay. Quality is the name of the game at Trinity, which aims to become one of the strongest liberal arts schools in the Southwest.

Smith College in Northampton, Mass., offers dual degree programs in liberal arts and engineering. The purpose is to allow the strong math/science student the opportunity to obtain a Smith College liberal arts education, while pursuing an engineering discipline at the University of Massachusetts.

If you like marching to a different drummer, you can find compatible bandmates on a campus somewhere.

Cooperative Education: College Programs That Can Boost Your Career

Have you seen this bumper sticker on cars?

I owe, I owe, so off to work I go.

How true, how true. As a college student would you like to have a job that kicks in an average of $7,500 to your yearly budget? Would you like to have a job that has an excellent chance of leading to a permanent position after graduation?

About 275,000 students in 900 college co-op programs are saying "yes" to these questions.

Although there's money to be made, the economic benefits of co-op study are secondary to the educational aspect. In cooperative education, the objective is to *learn*—and earn while you're at it.

It is this objective that sets co-op education apart from campus work-study jobs, which emphasize earning over learning.

Co-op jobs can be highly responsible assignments. Students supervise production lines, manage customer accounts, write software instruction manuals, represent federal departments at meetings, or supervise architectural job sites, to give you an idea of the career-experience league you can expect.

In a four-year program, you usually spend the first year in school, after which you follow some pattern of study-work rotation based on the school's academic calendar. If attending a two-year college, you might work mornings or afternoons, or you might alternate semesters of study and work until you accumulate a year or more of work experience. Details vary among co-op programs.

On the downside, you may find you have limited time for studies outside your discipline, and, in several schools, it can take as long as five years to get a bachelor's degree. (If you want more of the academic spectrum, you can always take night classes after you're settled in a good job.)

All things considered, cooperative study is a superb approach to education; you bridge the gap from school to work more easily, and you may be more motivated to do your best in school because you better understand how what you learn can be applied to your entire life.

Studies show that 48 percent of co-op graduates turn their last student job into a permanent position; 40 percent find other jobs in the career field in which they prepared and most of the remaining number enter graduate school.

If you decide you want to try out a career field in advance, look for a cooperative education program that is well organized, well financed, well promoted, well filled, and well regarded. You may be disappointed if you are one of only a few co-op students on campus and the college administration treats the program with indifference.

Check, too, the job descriptions for students in your intended major. Do they sound educationally meaty or more like a very casual learning opportunity? Liberal arts co-op assignments may be difficult to assess, requiring the help of a seasoned co-op education professional to determine whether any real career exploration and development can take place.

Need more information? Two publications, *Co-op Education*, and the *Co-Op Education Undergraduate Program Directory* are free from the National Commission for Cooperative Education, Box 999, Boston, MA 02115. The directory of programs in colleges and universities shows where the programs are located and the disciplines involved.

Internet Degrees

The Western Interstate Commission for Higher Education has been awarded more than $700,000 to help expand the delivery of college-level certificate and degree programs to students in 15 western states by using existing elements of the Information Superhighway.

This program will bring higher education to students in rural areas, help integrate new technologies into teaching and learning, and allow students greater access to libraries, computer networks, and other modern technology resources. For more information, contact Mollie McGill at WICHE, P.O. Drawer P, Boulder, CO 80301-9752.

College Internships: Another Way to Test Career Goals

An internship is a short-term job that allows you to explore a career interest. You can try out work that interests you, make contacts, and acquire experience.

You may work for a famous journalist, a state governor's office, or a major corporation; internships are everywhere—private companies, public agencies, and non-profit organizations.

You may be asked to stay on the job when your internship ends. You may accept or, after the experience, decide that your interests are elsewhere.

Find out whether schools you're interested in have a strong track record in arranging student internships. While you can uncover or create them yourself, it is a time-consuming task.

Two guides of interest are:

The National Directory of Internships, published annually by the National Society for Internships and Experiential Education, 3509 Haworth Dr., Suite 207, Raleigh, NC 27609.

Internships, an annual directory of thousands of job training opportunities for many types of careers, published by Peterson's, 800–338–3282.

College Abroad

If you fancy crossing an ocean to study for a year or more, you can do it in one of two ways. You can enroll directly in a foreign university or, as most Americans do, go under the sponsorship of an American college.

Before becoming an American in Paris or elsewhere, be certain to compile all the pertinent facts. Will lectures be exclusively in the host country's language? If the university doesn't award credits or transcripts, how can your educational progress be documented for American credentials? Do you have to pay in American dollars or can you save by paying expenses in local currency?

American college-sponsored programs are abundant, and many are delighted to accept students from other schools. Nearly 2,000 programs, including those offered by foreign colleges, are listed in *Academic Year Abroad*, the annual catalog of the Institute of International Education, 809 United Nations Plaza, New York, NY 10017.

For anyone interested in overseas study, this publication is essential reading. It includes a great deal of wide-ranging information on how to plan for foreign study.

Military Academies Are Tuition-Free

If you're willing to serve your country for several years, you might attend college free and be paid while doing it.

Four U.S. military academies offer the option to complete a college degree with an officer's commission.

U.S. *Naval Academy*
117 Decatur Rd.
Annapolis, MD 21402

U.S. *Military Academy*
606 Thayer Road
West Point, NY 10996

U.S. *Air Force Academy*
Colorado Springs, CO 80840

U.S. *Coast Guard Academy*
15 Mohegan Ave.
New London, CT 06320

Each of the federal service academies—the U.S. Air Force, U.S. Military (Army), U.S. Naval, and U.S. Coast Guard—offer four years of college leading to a bachelor of science degree. Cadets and midshipmen receive tuition, medical care, and room and board, plus a monthly stipend to help pay for expenses.

If you think military academy education is all march, march, march, you've got a nice surprise coming. Academies have an incredible array of academic programs and physical and extracurricular activities.

Upon graduation, commissions are conferred for an active-duty period of no less than five or six years. Of course, the Pentagon brass hopes that after receiving a first-rate education on your fellow citizens, you'll choose the military for a lifetime career. If you decide that military life is not in your long-term game plan, however, you need not stay beyond your required duty period.

The academies look for evidence of character, scholarship, leadership, physical aptitude, medical fitness, goals, and motivation. In evaluating scholarship, they look closely at SAT and ACT scores, as well as school records.

Admission to the U.S. Air Force, U.S. Military, and U.S. Naval academies is by nomination. Most who win appointments do so through nominations from members of the U.S. Congress, although other sources of nomination are available through affiliations with the armed forces. In the fall of your junior year, contact the office of your U.S. representative or senators to obtain details about how you can be nominated. It is not necessary to know the congressional member personally to receive a nomination.

Appointments to the U.S. Coast Guard Academy are handled differently. Students who wish to attend the Coast Guard Academy must enter the nationwide competition held each year for the spaces in the freshman class. Write to the Coast Guard Academy for information.

Square one when you've got a military education on the mind is to contact the admission office of the military academies you wish to attend. Admission officers send out packets of information and link you with an academy liaison officer in your area.

Until recently in Palos Verdes, Calif., for example, Leon R. "Buzz" Busby, a Delta airline captain, was also an Air Force reserve officer who spent many hours identifying and encouraging outstanding students to consider the Air Force Academy. Because there have always been many more applications than openings, Lt. Col. Busby described his role as more like that of a college admission counselor than a military recruiter.

Competition for admission to the academies has been greater than ever since the Gulf War victory.

University-Affiliated Technology Parks

New business relationships are springing up between academia and industry—it's a trend that could ease your entry to a fast-moving technology career.

A number of universities are operating or developing technology parks, such as the Stanford Industrial Park in Palo Alto, Calif., the University Research Park operated by the University of Wisconsin-Madison, and the Texas A&M University Research Park.

If you're interested in science or engineering, these institutions should be high on your list of preferred colleges. Not only is the academic environment likely to be crisp with innovation, but the companies in residence are built-in employers.

Physically speaking, the technology parks are real estate developments usually adjacent to a campus. Corporations—most of which are research oriented—build facilities, hire staff that includes faculty and students, and sometimes fund research undertakings at the affiliated university.

The companies participate to obtain a steady labor pool of bright minds. The universities' motive for tying the knot with industry is to stop what they call "brain drains." University administrators have learned they must enhance income opportunities for faculty and students or risk losing their best people to the corporate world.

Before you enroll in one of these universities, ask the dean of the school of engineering or an appropriate science for an up-to-date list of the companies in residence, including the size of each company's workforce (does the company offer 20 jobs or 2,000 jobs?) and its product lines (you may be interested in computers when the company specializes in biogenetics).

Study the First Two Years at a Two-Year College and Save Money

Jennifer Turner says a funny thing happened on the way to a four-year degree. She became a community college student.

Turner opted to live at home and do her first two years of college at a nearby public community college. She saved a bundle, and she had the fun of a couple of extra years with her close-knit family. She now has her bachelor's degree from a four-year college and a good job in the computer industry. All her community college credits transferred. Turner was alert—she had confirmed with the four-year institution in advance the transferability of her credits before she enrolled in the two-year college.

At a time when tuition costs at baccalaureate institutions have zoomed upwards, it makes sense to consider the cost advantage of the community college. The average annual tuition of less than $1,000 is a fraction of the price charged by a full-fledged university.

Living at home helps keep the costs down even more, and most community college students do live at home.

The academic programs at community colleges are much like freshman and sophomore programs at four-year institutions and are designed to let you earn transferable credits.

To avoid annoying surprises—like repeating a year of study—make certain that courses will transfer to a senior institution. Most community colleges employ at least one counselor who specializes in credit transfer. Remember that four-year schools rarely accept credits for courses deemed purely remedial, or for certain general studies or vocational-track courses.

As soon as possible, decide where you'd like to finish your bachelor's degree.

Suppose you find that you want to transfer to an out-of-state college or university? Even when your credit transfer counselor is familar with the institution, it's prudent to meet (or call and write) the head of the department that, includes your chosen major—not just with a representative of the admission office. Supply the department head with a copy of your community college's course catalog and ask which courses you should take.

For example, a department head may say to an engineering transfer student, "You need to take calculus, which at your school is called MA 250." If you're smart enough to be an engineer, can't you figure that out for yourself? Perhaps, but it's easy to overlook the fact that some schools offer calculus for nonscience majors and calculus for science majors and the engineering school may only accept the latter credits.

There is a negative to attending a community college. With a little effort, you can overcome it. Students often build relationships with each other starting in the freshman year. You will miss establishing friendships from day one of your college career—friendships that can be of value later in life when you find the need to use contacts. The remedy: Make extra friends and contacts during your last two years.

If you plan to go to graduate school, does it matter that you began at a community college? A smidgen of stiff professors may cling to that old maxim: "If you didn't learn it here, you didn't learn it." But most graduate school faculty are more impressed with your last two years. Graduate school admission rests on grades, test scores, recommendations, and your statement of purpose. Some even say being a transfer student is a plus—it shows you have the flexibility to adjust to new settings and people. One more consideration—employers. Do they care where you spend your first two years of college? Not many give it a thought. What they want to know is from which college you graduated.

Besides public community colleges, there are public and private junior colleges. Public junior colleges are similar to community colleges. Private junior colleges are usually residential schools and sometimes are church-related. Their traditional purpose has been to prepare students for transfer to a senior institution, although many have switched their focus to career preparation. The cost of attending a private junior college is considerably higher than that of a public community or junior college (although often lower than a private four-year college).

In states like California where public four-year colleges are overcrowded, junior and senior students who, for whatever reason, failed to satisfy their core course requirements often can't get the classes they need to graduate because the classes are filled. The remedy in recent years has been to pick up those courses in a nearby community college and transfer them to the impacted four-year college the student attends.

You can read more about two-year colleges in Chapter 14.

■ ■ ■

Getting a Line on Four-Year Colleges

There are six basic ways to find out about particular colleges.

Reading. Comprehensive and selective college guides, such as those mentioned earlier in this section, are where most people begin their research.

After that they study college bulletins and catalogs. These may be available in your school media or career center, or you can write for those of particular interest. Don't expect an objective presentation—often you'll see a glamorized picture of smiling students standing in front of impressive buildings under a blue sky. Read the text with a critical eye.

Computer Search. Your high school may have the equipment to do a computerized search of colleges. Ask your counselor. You may prefer to buy software for a home computer.

Most software programs create an on-screen personal profile, allowing you to input criteria for your ideal college. You may be able to search by major, location, type of institution, degree requirements, costs, student body variety, enrollment size, campus setting, entrance difficulty, sports, student ethnic-geographic mix, and other factors. Instead of spending hours turning the pages of directories comparing schools, you confide to the computer what you want and tell it to get busy printing out a list of colleges that meet your requirements. List prices on software range from about $35 to $250. Most programs are available in software and book stores.

Among easy-to-use programs is this trio of winners:

College Probe (Carolina Programs) is the least expensive software on the spectrum. It describes 1,500 colleges by SAT scores, size, cost, location, and includes rankings. The program can print letters asking selected schools for more information. A bargain buy. IBMs/clones only.

Sold by mail for $35; order from Carolina Programs, 1904 Overland Drive, Chapel Hill, NC 27514.

College Selection (Peterson's) generates a letter that can be sent to admission directors, as well as summarize institutional data in the search. Comprehensive access to a vast college data base. IBM and Apple.

College Explorer (The College Board) can accomodate up to 600 criteria in the search and one handy why-not feature tells you instantly why a college didn't make your list. IBM and Apple.

Video Tours. Your high school may be in the armchair travel business, offering video tours of colleges across the nation.

The technology is usually videocassettes or CD-ROMs.

A word about video tours: The institutions of higher education are selling a lifestyle as well as an education. New England colleges are resplendently portrayed with autumn leaves while the Sun Belt colleges show the glamour of surfers and hang-gliders.

A video tour can help narrow your field of choice but should not be the basis of a final decision.

Asking Others. Alumni may remember—from the distance of time—their college days with overly fond memories, whereas present-day students, dealing with the here and now, give a more reflective picture of the campus. Business and family friends can give you an idea of a college's reputation.

College Fairs and Representatives. Most high schools are visited by a number of college representatives on recruiting tours. They may give solo presentations to an audience, or a dozen or more reps may gather in a gym, set up tables, unfurl banners, and hold a college fair.

You'll want to attend as many as possible of the presentations and fairs, bearing in mind that asking a college rep if he or she thinks the school is for you is like asking a barber if you need a haircut.

Campus Visits. Americans traditionally think of college as a promise of ivy-colored halls, rah-rah spirit, all-night fraternity parties, wisdom-infused profs, and winning football teams.

Many students, assuming this is how things will be, sign up and never lay eyes on the college of their choice until they report for freshman orientation week, a few short days before classes begin.

This is mistake. Your choice may work out, but then again, it may not. Would you buy a car sight unseen, or pick a mate by computer?

Even if the college is a good fit on paper, each institution is unique and has its own personality and environment. Only by being on the campus can you find out if a college is up your alley and down your street. Go there!

Perhaps you can combine a family vacation with visits to colleges, or join a tour of colleges conducted by a parent or paid guide.

Make an advance appointment with admission offices so there will be time for an adequate discussion. You may have to visit during the summer, but it is infinitely more rewarding to tour the school when classes are in session so that you can talk with students and get a feel for the "real thing."

If you need low-cost accommodations, ask about the possibility of booking rooms in the residence hall. Take along information about yourself—your high school record and test scores.

■ ■ ■ ■

A Word About Accreditation

Accreditation is a concept of potential significance to your career and you should know something about it.

Accreditation is a form of consumer protection. Experts who know how a school should be run, or what a program should be teaching, make judgments about the competence of an institution or curriculum.

The fact that a school or program is accredited does not mean it is top-notch. Accreditation means that evaluation experts believe it is providing the services it says it is providing.

Graduation from an accredited school or program is generally required for advanced study, or to qualify for professional practice.

How would you like to tunnel through four years of college work only to be refused admission to law school because your undergraduate degree is not from an accredited college?

Accredited institutions usually will not accept credits from non-accredited schools.

How would you like to transfer after one year from a non-accredited college to an accredited institution only to be told that none of your credits are acceptable and that you can look forward to spending an extra year in school?

Some employers, particularly those who employ technical personnel, will not hire new graduates of a non-accredited institution.

Still another benefit of attending accredited institutions is that you can be pretty sure the school is concerned about its reputation and product.

Broadly speaking, there are two basic types of accreditation:

1. Institutional, or regional accreditation, which applies to the entire institution. It is awarded by one of nine regional accrediting commissions. They are:

   ◆ Middle States Association of Colleges and Schools

   ◆ New England Association of Schools and Colleges (Commission on Institutions of Higher Education)

   ◆ New England Association of Schools and Colleges (Commission on Vocational, Technical, and Career Institutions)

   ◆ North Central Association of Colleges and Schools

   ◆ Northwest Association of Schools and Colleges

   ◆ Southern Association of Colleges and Schools (Commission on Colleges)

   ◆ Southern Association of Colleges and Schools (Commission on Occupational Education Institutions)

   ◆ Western Association of Schools and Colleges (Accrediting Commission for Community and Junior Colleges)

   ◆ Western Association of Schools and Colleges (Accrediting Commission for Senior Colleges and Universities)

   In addition, national associations accredit institutions that are single purpose in nature. These include:

   ◆ American Association of Bible Colleges

   ◆ Association of Advanced Rabbinical and Talmudic Schools

   ◆ Association of Theological Schools

   ◆ Association of Independent Colleges and Schools

   ◆ National Association of Trade and Technical Schools

   ◆ National Home Study Council

2. Specialized or program accreditation is given by national organizations that represent a specific career area. The organization usually accredits a particular program within an institution and not the entire institution. Examples are:

   ◆ American Dietetic Association

   ◆ Liaison Committee on Medical Education

   ◆ Society of American Foresters

When in Doubt, Check It Out

Two resources can aid in determining whether the school or program you are considering meets the standards of a recognized accrediting body.

1. COPA (Council on Postsecondary Accreditation) identifies and monitors accrediting bodies. A free list of its members can be obtained from COPA, Suite 305, One Dupont Circle NW, Washington, DC 20036.

2. The U.S. Department of Education also keeps a list of accrediting organizations. If you hope to receive educational grants or loans from the federal government, the institution or program you choose must be accredited by an organization recognized by the Department of Education. A free list of recognized accrediting bodies can be obtained by writing to the Accrediting Agency Evaluation Branch, Office of Postsecondary Education, U.S. Department of Education, Room 3036, 400 Maryland Ave. SW, Washington, DC 20202.

If an accrediting body is listed on either the COPA or the USDE list, you can write to the body asking for the roster of schools or programs that it has accredited.

Although the two resources overlap somewhat, COPA is chiefly concerned with the maintenance of educational quality, while the federal government's target is to make sure public funds are not squandered on substandard education.

What about the term "VA-approved" attached to the advertising of certain study courses? All it means is that eligible veterans can use their military educational benefits to pay for these courses. VA-*approved* certainly does not mean the course offers quality training.

In many states, a school or program must be state-approved to operate. To find out exactly what this means in your state, contact your state department of education.

If you don't want to waste time and money on questionable education, do your homework to determine what a school or program really means when it claims accreditation.

■ ■ ■ ■

College Prospecting Checklist

General Perspective

◆ Are you comfortable with the college's culture (emphasis on scholarly or social pursuits, religious affiliation, competitive or laid-back atmosphere, single sex or coed student body)?

◆ What is the school's reputation?

◆ By which associations is it accredited?

◆ What do you think of students you meet on campus? Will you feel at home there? (Student harassment of minorities and gays is up dramatically on some campuses.)

◆ Is public transportation available, or will you need a car?

◆ Do you prefer a specialized (such as engineering), liberal arts, or comprehensive (liberal arts and vocational studies) institution?

◆ If you plan to enter graduate or professional school, what percentage of the college's graduates enter advanced study (for instance, what percentage is accepted at a top-rated law school)?

◆ Is there a counseling center with qualified personnel to help you with school or personal problems?

◆ Is campus crime a concern? Is a security patrol available to escort students between night classes and library study? Is there night shuttle bus service on campus? Are dorms locked or guarded?

◆ Can you realistically expect to finish your degree in four years, or is the campus overcrowded? Are students forced into lotteries or on long waiting lists for popular courses?

◆ If you are a special-needs student, how barrier-free is the campus?

Career Perspective

◆ Does the college operate an aggressive career services center?

◆ Does the community offer adequate job opportunities for students?

◆ Does the school philosophy favor internships?

◆ Are co-op education programs available?

◆ Does the college have state-of-the-art computer equipment? Are computers readily available to students? What is the student/computer terminal ratio? Are students using computers in their work? Is your computer time limited?

◆ Have recent graduates in your future major found related jobs?

Academic Perspective

◆ Is the college a leader in the career fields that interest you? How many courses are regularly offered in areas in which you may wish to

major—do they thin out after survey courses, or are in-depth study opportunities such as senior seminars available?

◆ What courses are required? Is there a requirement you are unable or unwilling to meet?

◆ What's the typical student-teacher ratio? If some courses are given in auditoriums, what provision is made for giving special help if needed?

◆ How many faculty members actually teach? Is much of the teaching done by graduate students? Do superstars teach only graduate seminars or lecture in huge amphitheaters?

◆ How accessible are faculty members?

◆ How comprehensive is the library?

Location

◆ Do you want to stay close to home or handle the expense of travel several times a year?

◆ Is the slower pace of a college town or the hustle-bustle of a big city best for you?

◆ Is the locale saturated with people who majored in your field of interest (in case you want to stay in the area after graduation)?

◆ Does the locale offer the resources you prefer for leisure time activities (mountains, oceans, desert)?

◆ What is the weather like? Food?

Size

◆ Would you rather know everybody or be a face in the crowd?

- If you come from a large urban high school, would a small college bore you?

- If you come from a small high school, would a large, impersonal university intimidate you?

Expenses

- Can you, with student aid and working, afford a private college, or does a public college seem more practical?

- Have you counted in all of your expenses— books, social life, laundry, trips home?

- Will financial aid keep pace with rising costs or will you be forced into much heavier loans than you expected in your junior and senior years? (Ask the college student financial aid planner for an estimate.)

Campus Concerns

- What is the political atmosphere and does it agree with your views?

- Do you want to live in a dorm or in a private apartment? (You may not have the choice as a freshman.)

- Is there space in the dorms? Is off-campus housing plentiful and reasonably priced? (At overcrowded schools, the majority of entering students may be forced to live off campus.)

- Does it matter socially if most of the students live on campus and you live at home?

- Are there fraternities and sororities? Are they big deals? Do you have to be a "Greek" to be included in most social events?

- Do you want an athletic program in a particular sport?

Academic Requirements

- Do you have the academic track record to be accepted at competitive colleges?

- Would you prefer an easier school?

- How many hours a week will you have to study and is there a lot of pressure?

- Have you double-checked the application procedure, including deadlines, entrance exams, and fees?

■ ■ ■ ■

Pulling It All Together

Deciding on a college is a decision best shared between you and your parents. However the decision is made, try to cut through institutional rhetoric and see the college in the clear light of day.

When you're ready to ask the questions on the previous checklist, search out graduates and currently enrolled students and ask everything you want to know; ask department heads about the availability of classes and the employment demand for majors under their wings; ask administrators about total costs and things like campus security; ask high school counselors what they think of schools you like.

Once you begin to sag under the weight of relevant facts, devise a recordkeeping system to sort things out. Your counselor can suggest a commercial system or you can make your own along the lines of the following sample form.

■ ■ ■ ■

College Comparison Form

Name of College (address, phone, contact)	High School Grades Preferred	Class Rank Preferred	Freshman Average ACT or SAT	Majors of Interest	Cost/Tuition Fees, Room

Special Data (Note here all criteria of interest to you.)

Highlights of College Planning

Advance Calendar

9th Grade

❑ Start now to discuss your academic/career plans with your counselor. Completion of career exploration activities and aptitude tests will assist the counselor, yourself, and your parents to select appropriate colleges or vocational-technical schools.

❑ Become familiar with the resources available in your library and career center.

❑ Discuss your academic progress and plan your program for next year with your counselor. Remember, your GPA begins in 9th grade for some colleges. Others compute your GPA for 10th and 11th grades only, sometimes requesting the first semester of the 12th grade.

10th Grade

❑ In September, sign up for the P-ACT+. Consider taking practice PSAT/NMSQT if offered to 10th graders.

❑ In November/December, take interest survey if offered.

❑ In the spring, work out schedule of next two years with counselor.

❑ During summer, preliminary visits with parents to colleges.

❑ During summer, do something challenging: get a job, do volunteer work, take a learning program, travel.

11th Grade

❑ In September, sign up for the PSAT.

❑ October through May, meet with college admission representatives who visit your school.

❑ Attend college fair and school-sponsored programs. Confer with your counselor about college or vocational-technical programs.

❑ Explore college materials in the career center.

❑ In spring, register for college admission tests. Take appropriate achievement tests (for classes you are taking while knowledge is fresh in your mind).

❑ In spring, narrow priority list to five/six colleges.

❑ Early-decision candidates must take the SAT or ACT and achievement tests before June.

❑ During summer, write for college applications. Visit colleges with parents.

❑ During summer, do something challenging: get a job, do volunteer work, take a learning program, travel.

12th Grade Countdown

September

❑ If you have not already done so, register for college admission tests. (Arrange to have your scores sent to the colleges where you plan to apply.)

❑ Find out how your school's transcript procedure works.

October

❑ Continue to meet with admission representatives who are visiting your school. Update your college priority list.

❑ If needed, begin asking for letters of recommendation from teachers, employers, advisers.

❑ Correspond with the college admission and financial aid offices on your priority list to request admission, financial aid, and housing applications. Complete and submit forms as required. (Always select one or more fall-back colleges.)

❑ Take additional required achievement tests.

❑ Begin work on required application essays.

❑ If you are applying for early-decision admission, complete and submit your application now.

❑ If you have not already done so, set up tours of colleges or vocational-technical schools you are considering.

November

❑ Attend college fairs and financial aid nights.

❑ Reminder: If you have not already done so, find out which financial aid application is required by schools to which you are applying. Remind parents that financial aid application (need analysis form) is due after January 2, so they can start gathering financial records. Get the need analysis form (such as FAF or FFS) from your school guidance office.

December

❑ Reminder: Have you finished researching both private and public forms of student financial aid?

❑ Reminder: Have you mailed in your applications to the colleges to which you are applying?

January

❏ Mail need analysis documents (no later than March 15).

❏ Mail financial aid forms (even if you are using estimated income).

February

❏ Check with your guidance office to be sure your mid-year transcripts have been sent to the schools to which you have applied.

❏ Register for Advanced Placement exams.

March

❏ Begin looking for a summer job, if you have not already done so.

❏ Be certain you understand and have followed procedures for loan applications. Use certified mail to submit the loan forms to your school choices. (But only after deciding on which college you will attend should you submit the loan application to your bank.)

April

❏ Letters are coming in from colleges about your acceptance and financial aid packages. April 15 is usually the last day to receive decision letters. As well as career considerations, compare the financial aid offers. (If you are an outstanding student, you may be able to convince the financial aid officer at school A you want to attend to match the offer at school B you don't want to attend.)

❏ Wait to respond to an offer of admission and/or financial aid until you have heard from all the colleges and universities to which you have applied or until May 1, whichever comes earlier. Make your final decision on the school you want to attend and send in your deposit by the deadline. Notify schools you are not going to attend.

May

❏ Make sure all the loan paperwork is supplied to the financial aid office at the school you will be attending.

❏ Send thank-you notes to teachers and counselors who helped you begin your college journey.

❏ Double-check housing forms for on-campus and off-campus facilities.

June

❏ Be sure your guidance office has forwarded your final records to the school you'll be attending.

Narrowing the Field

Each application to a college costs a non-refundable fee of $10 to $30, and sometimes even more. A practical approach is to narrow your choices to six institutions.

Your first and second choices can be *long shots*—colleges you prefer but aren't sure of your chances.

Your third and fourth choices can be *probables*—colleges that offer you a solid chance of acceptance.

Your fifth and sixth choices can be *sure things*—colleges that offer excellent chances of acceptance.

Six isn't a magic number and, in many cases, you need not apply to that many.

Be sure you and your family agree about the amount they are willing to finance and how much you are expected to come up with. The College Talk is a ritual you can't ignore.

Want to apply as soon as possible? Early-decision admissions are becoming regular admissions in some competitive colleges. In these schools, the majority of freshmen are admitted on an early-decision basis.

✦   ✦   ✦

Your college choice is made and you're all set to enter school the next semester. This is a good time to glance over the glossary of educational terms in the Appendix. The next section looks at ways to make the most of your campus life.

■ ■ ■ ■

Making the Most of College

This chapter is devoted to the college experience and advanced study. It begins with advice on acclimating yourself to the college culture—getting along with the faculty and students, and learning to function within the institution's rules and regulations.

The topics include choosing advisers and professors, study tips, high-performance reading, writing research papers, and passing exams.

Next come career-related curricula considerations: the value of the liberal arts major in the job market, self-designed education programs, and double majors.

We then look at the importance of practicing power skills, making career contacts, and gaining work experience as an undergraduate.

The chapter concludes with a look ahead to graduate and professional education, concentrating on business administration, law, and medicine.

College: How to Make Sure Your Mind Never Returns to Its Original Size

Oliver Wendell Holmes said: "The mind, once expanded to the dimensions of larger ideas, never returns to its original size."

That's what will happen as a result of your college experience, assuming you don't fritter away these invaluable years.

■ ■ ■ ■

So Your First Choice Turns You Down

Contrary to popular thought, students who attend highly selective colleges do not learn more than students who attend less selective institutions. Nor, according to research, do students appear to develop fewer competencies because they do not attend a top-tier college.

Certainly you will be unhappy if your Number One college choice rejects you, but it is largely up to you whether you receive an excellent education wherever you enroll. Enthusiasm lights its own fire.

Second choice doesn't mean second class. It only means that's how the marbles rolled.

■ ■ ■ ■

Take Good Notes

◆ Use a loose-leaf notebook and date your notes.

◆ Condense what you hear or read. Do not write down every word. Jot down main ideas and flesh them out later.

◆ Review and revise your notes as soon as possible. Time is your enemy. Highlight key ideas. All this writing burns the data in your brain.

◆ Study your notes before the next assignment and class.

■ ■ ■ ■

Read Effectively

◆ Read the summary first—even if it's last in a chapter. This tells you what the chapter is about.

◆ Read headings.

◆ Read the entire text until the headings make sense. Write the major points of each heading in your notes.

■ ■ ■ ■

When the Grade Disappoints

When you receive a poor grade on a research paper, analyze what went wrong.

◆ You waited too long to start the paper and your research is so skimpy it's a laugh.

◆ Your organization of material is illogical. Again, time is the villain—three hours is the minimum period you need to organize materials.

◆ Your writing style suffered from poor planning and use of your time. You should spend at least 10 hours rendering your paper readable.

◆ Necessary corrections were not made because they were too much trouble. Arizona State University professor Claude Olney, creator of a seminar on smart study methods, says students who use computers for research papers score as much as a full point higher than do students who use typewriters. There's no mystery—it's easy to make corrections on computers and the finished paper looks neater.

When you honestly don't know why your grade was so disappointingly low, politely ask the professor to enlighten you, explaining that you are not challenging the grade, but trying to understand how you can do better in the future.

■ ■ ■ ■

Tips for Exams

◆ Go all the way through an exam, doing the easiest questions first; then return to the more difficult ones.

◆ If the test is in essay format, read the question carefully, make a quick outline of major points, then write on each one of the points in your outline.

◆ If the exam is oral, ask a friend to rehearse you with anticipated questions.

■ ■ ■ ■

Time Management

Although your semester grade depends on tomorrow morning's exam for which you feel ill-prepared, you don't know how to say "no" to friends who ask you to join them for the movies tonight.

Chris Laramore, the son of one of the authors, faced the situation as a college student. He says:

In the beginning I squandered time as though I had an unlimited supply. I had poor study habits, daydreamed a great deal, and got mixed up in unrewarding personal relationships. Then everything hit me at once. If I hadn't changed my way of living I would have flunked. A GPA is much harder to bring up than it is to lower. You need to sit down and organize. Find a time for study and stick to that time.

What Chris is recommending is the practice of time management.

In a simple form of time management, you first establish a semester calendar (months and weeks) and write in long-term assignments and final exams.

In addition, you prepare a weekly calendar for regular study and short-term assignments. Allot time for classes, relaxation and chores as well as study. A sample of a weekly calendar follows on page 298.

■ ■ ■ ■

The Freshman Blues

What's the remedy if, after several months on campus, you feel you've made a bad choice and want to transfer to another college?

In most cases, your best bet is to hang in and wait for your change-of-heart to change back again. The disenchantment is probably an adjustment problem that will pass. Alumni who did not throw in the towel during a siege of freshman blues tend to confirm they made the right decision in staying.

It's a different story for students whose expectations are at wide variance with the realities of the campus. They are misplaced students.

Misplacement usually comes about as a result of the student's inadequate research and preparation—both are key activities you need to master to be a successful college student. The selection of a college is a good place to begin developing investigative and planning skills.

If you believe you really are misplaced—rather than suffering the freshman blues—a long talk with your adviser and parents is in order. The best action may be to cut your losses and transfer elsewhere.

■ ■ ■ ■

Sample Time Management Weekly Calendar

	Monday	Tuesday	Wednesday	Thursday	Friday	Saturday	Sunday
8:00	Math	Economics	Math	Economics	Math	Clean Room	Sleep
9:00	Free	Economics	Free	Economics	Free	Clean Room	Sleep
10:00	Chemistry	Chemistry	Chemistry	Chemistry	Chemistry	Laundry	Church
11:00	Chem. Lab	Chem. Lab	Chem. Lab	Chem. Lab	Chem. Lab	Laundry	Church
Noon	Lunch	Lunch	Lunch	Lunch	Lunch	Lunch	Lunch
1:00	Study English	Study Math	Study English	Study Chemistry	Library	Free	Free
2:00	English	Study Math	English	Study Chemistry	English	Free	Free
3:00	Library	P.E.	Library	P.E.	Library	Free	Free
4:00	Free	Free	Free	Free	Free	Free	Free
5:00	Dinner	Dinner	Dinner	Dinner	Dinner	Dinner	Dinner
6:00	Study	Study	Library	Study	Free	Free	Study
7:00	Study	Study	Library	Study	Free	Free	Study
8:00	Study	Study	Library	Study	Free	Free	Study
9:00	Free	Study	Study	TV	Free	Free	Free
10:00	Free	Free	Study	Free	Free	Free	Free
11:00	Free	Free	Free	Free	Free	Free	Free
Midnight	Free	Free	Free	Free	Free	Free	Free

Reflections on Liberal Arts

Year after year, new graduates with technical majors dramatically outperform liberal arts majors in the job market, both in numbers of job offers and salaries.

Obviously, there are shades and nuances. Most technical programs, for example, are enriched by substantial doses of arts and humanities, social and behavioral sciences, and natural and mathematical sciences, collectively known as the liberal arts. Many liberal arts programs, on the other hand, boast strong vocationally relevant options.

Basically, a liberal education is preparation for the non-vocational aspects of life, including intellectual endeavor, aesthetic enjoyment, personal adjustment, and responsible citizenship.

You can make your liberal arts degree pay off *if you are willing to become a job hunting expert*, and if you enter a field for which there are no rigid entry requirements, such as banking, sales, insurance, human resources, fund-raising, and lobbying. Entrepreneurship is a possibility.

We recommend liberal arts graduates follow these steps to ease into the job market.

- Be sure you have at least one internship experience in the field you want to enter.
- Take a double major.
- Add specialized or even technical courses—accounting, computer science or statistics, for instance—to your liberal arts stew.

In the long term, in some work settings, liberal arts majors, especially those who have acquired further education, may be able to bypass vocationally oriented majors. In meritocracies, such as American Telephone and Telegraph, studies show that humanities and social science majors were promoted more rapidly than technical graduates.

If you decide to pursue a liberal arts major, consider vocationally oriented education at the graduate level. Some bachelor's degree graduates enroll in community colleges to acquire job-related skills.

For a glimpse of how you can apply your liberal arts education in the job market, turn to Chapter 15.

■ ■ ■ ■

What You Can Do With a Major in . . .

The following list shows how some graduates have applied their education to work. Observe that a number of jobs bear little relationship to the major, such as the biology major who became a computer programmer. Take into account, too, that some of the jobs listed require advanced education or additional training.

Accountancy	Art History	Biology
actuary	archaeological assistant	chiropractor
credit analyst	archivist	computer programmer
economist	artist	dentist
insurance claims examiner	art therapist	hospital administrator
market research analyst	cartographer	insurance claims examiner
real estate agent/broker	critic (art, drama, film)	laboratory technician
securities trader	curator	medical doctor
trust officer, bank	graphic designer	microbiologist
	private business owner	

Chemistry
chemical engineer
chemist
laboratory supervisor
marketing manager
medical technologist
production manager
systems analyst
toxicologist

Management and Marketing
brokerage house partner
cost accountant
credit and collection manager
financial planner
insurance underwriter
product distribution manager
public relations
purchasing agent

Physics
aerospace engineer
astronomer
business executive
oceanographer
patent attorney
physicist
private business
seismologist

Economics
administrative officer
auditor
bank officer
buyer, retailing
corporate lawyer
cost accountant
Internal Revenue Service agent
investment analyst
statistician

Mathematics
auditor
bank officer
industrial engineer
mission controller
real estate agent
special agent, FBI
tax administrator
writer, technical

Political Science
financial analyst
guidance counselor
investigator, criminal
lawyer
police officer
publisher
securities trader
writer

Education
audiovisual specialist
librarian
principal or superintendent
recreation director
rehabilitation counselor
speech pathologist
teacher
tutor

Modern Language
advertising manager
immigration inspector
musician
salesperson, wholesale
scientific linguist
stockbroker
systems analyst
teacher

Psychology
job analyst
occupational therapist
physician
probation officer
public survey worker
speech pathologist
statistician
travel agent

History
customs officer
foreign service officer
intelligence specialist
lawyer
public relations worker
research assistant
training specialist
writer

Philosophy
anthropologist
editor/journalist
foreign correspondent
hotel restaurant manager
museum guide
psychologist
research assistant
sales manager

Sociology
anthropologist
criminologist
management trainee
personnel manager
public health educator
recreation director
statistician
urban planner

■ ■ ■ ■

Doubling Your Chances With a Double Major

The chief reason to take a double major is marketability after you graduate.

In mathematics, for instance, a pure math major leads to teaching jobs, limiting your options. That's why it makes sense to do a double major (or a strong minor) in such fields as statistics, actuarial work, data processing, systems analysis, economics, or finance.

Other common combinations: history and economics, English and accounting, foreign language and education.

If you have a hunch you'll have trouble hitting employment targets with your present major (such as English literature or anthropology), consider adding another arrow to your quiver. Visit a counselor at your campus career services office. Ask for an opinion as to whether you should retool with a double major.

■ ■ ■ ■

The Real World: Working Part-Time

You have much to gain by working 10 to 20 hours a week as a college student. Whether it's an internship, co-op education stint, work-study employment, or something you lined up on your own, a job gives you money and experience, as well as career try-outs and contacts.

■ ■ ■ ■

Contacts: Your Partners in Success

Stretch out your hand often during the campus years. *The people you get to know through classes and extracurricular activities can be human bridges to the job market.* You never know who will open a door for you one day.

Many professional organizations have student divisions; join those in your interest area and attend meetings. Volunteer for projects. You'll be noticed. Your investment in contacts now will pay dividends after graduation.

■ ■ ■ ■

Get a Head Start on Power Skills

You hear a lot about team spirit making you a valued employee. You hear less about power skills that make you an influential leader. Maybe you won't use power skills your first day on the job, but you'll be in a better position to make the transition from team player to leader if you begin to raise your power consciousness now.

Real power is not ordering everybody out of the pool, or doing sneaky, manipulative things.

Real power is the clout to get things done. Power comes in different packages. Derivative power comes from your connection with an office or institution, or from association with a powerful person. Without the student governing office, the student council president is just another person on campus. You will not develop your own power skills if you rely too much on powerful campus friends to win stature and acceptance.

Gaining expertise in an area is a better basis for power. Becoming an expert frames you as influential in your own right.

Other avenues to power include making yourself stand out from the crowd. Offer to write your campus club's minutes, handle the public relations for a club event, or prepare the fraternity newsletter—all practical ways to be useful and, not coincidentally, gain power.

■ ■ ■ ■

Stop! Think About Graduate or Professional Study

The term *advanced study* describes both graduate and professional study.

Graduate study means post-baccalaureate education in a given academic field—such as history, chemistry, literature, or a foreign language. It is a time for in-depth education and for learning the style and method peculiar to a given discipline. The doctor of philosophy (PhD) is tops in the line of graduate academic degrees.

Professional study stresses the practical application of knowledge and skills—in business, law, architecture, and medicine, for instance. Examples of doctoral degrees in these fields are the doctor of business administration (DBA), doctor of architecture (D Arch), and doctor of medicine (MD or DO).

A doctorate usually is sought to teach at the college level or to do research.

Between the baccalaureate and the doctorate stands the master's degree. Generally, a master's requires two years of post-baccalaureate study,

although some programs can be finished in one year and others take three years to complete.

Many students obtain a master's degree and go on to earn a doctorate. Others skip the master's degree and head straight for the doctorate. Still others stop with a master's degree, either because they can't or don't want to continue on toward a doctorate, or because their chosen fields don't require it for employment. Examples of fields in which a master's is normally the highest degree of choice include the master's degree in business administration (MBA), master's degree in fine arts (MFA), master's degree in library science (MLS), and master's degree in social work (MSW).

The distinctions between traditional graduate academic programs and professional programs are not clear-cut. To get up to steam on the topic, thumb through a reference work like *Peterson's Graduate & Professional Programs*.

Review Your Reasons for Advanced Study

When you're scouting a career field requiring advanced academic or professional study, start exploring your options well before the time you hope to enter the hallowed halls of advanced learning.

Usually, an 18-month lead time is sufficient. But if you are applying for national scholarships—or your undergraduate school has an evaluation committee through which you are applying to the same institution's business administration program or law school—you'll need two years to prepare.

An advantage to planning for advanced study while you're a college sophomore or junior is that you'll have time for a course correction if your undergraduate education is not on the right track for the graduate/professional school of your choice. Determine the requirements of the programs you may want to enter, then double check that your undergraduate studies meet them. What a horrifying development it would be, at the last minute, to discover you are shy three hours of organic chemistry or statistics.

Not all paths leading to graduate/professional study are non-stop. Many students work for several years before picking up the books again. In some cases, this is a prudent idea. Educators say having a few years of work under the belt boosts motivation, commitment, and diligent pursuit of knowledge.

On the other hand, stepping out of school may make it very tough to pick up the study reins again, especially if you're trying to shuffle job, school, and, possibly, family obligations.

Whether you enter advanced study as a 21-year-old or later in life, be sure you're going onward and upward in academe for one of two reasons:

1. The career field you choose, such as medicine, librarianship, law, or college teaching, requires advanced education.

2. You plan to become an expert in a given field and you need more education in it either for career goals or personal rewards. Sometimes an advanced degree is added to an unrelated dicipline to open new vistas for professionals. Here are a few examples:

   ◆ *Physician*-MBA: This career coupling helps doctors manage private practices, or to work as administrators of health-care facilities.

   ◆ *Nurse-attorney*: Dual specialties prepare specialists in malpractice and personal injury law; practitioners may also find employment in insurance firms and government agencies.

   ◆ CPA-*lawyer*: These twin specialties are useful to tax and estate attorneys, as well as financial planners.

   ◆ *Engineer*-MBA: Technical know-how merged with business acumen is a powerful mix.

Do not—repeat, do not—pursue advanced study to please someone else; because you assume spiffy jobs with status and money will be your automatic rewards; because friends are headed for graduate school; or because you want another three-year ride on your parents' tab.

Remember, your values, goals, and decisions are what count.

Oh, Those Tests!

Colleges and universities usually require a specific graduate or professional admission test, and departments may have additional test requirements. The most frequently used tests for graduate school are the Graduate Record Examinations (GRE) and the Miller Analogies Test (MAT).

Professional schools may want you to take a specific discipline-related admission test, such as the Dental Admission Test (DAT).

Nearly all graduate and professional schools ask students whose first language is not English to take the Test of English as a Foreign Language (TOEFL).

Graduate Schools With National Reputations

Is graduate study on your agenda? If so, what should you look for in choosing a program? Here are three criteria suggested by Dr. Kenneth B. Hoyt, university distinguished professor at Kansas State University.

1. Where will you get the best assistantship package?

2. Will you receive individual help from at least one professor with academic interests and a national reputation in the chosen area of your specialization?

3. What happened to previous graduates of the program? Have they been successful in finding employment in the career fields for which they prepared?

What about the relative prestige of the nation's research universities? Here are some of the major-league institutions grouped by discipline. The list is not complete, but it will give you a starting point in finding a national quality graduate program.

Biological Sciences

Biochemistry
Massachusetts Institute of Technology
Stanford University
Harvard University
University of California, Berkeley
University of Wisconsin, Madison
Yale University
Rockefeller University
Brandeis University
University of California, San Francisco
Cornell University
University of California, San Diego
University of California, Los Angeles
Duke University

Botany
University of California, Davis
University of Texas, Austin
University of Wisconsin, Madison
University of California, Berkeley
Cornell University
University of Michigan, Ann Arbor

Cellular/Molecular Biology
Massachusetts Institute of Technology
California Institute of Technology

Yale University
Rockefeller University
University of Wisconsin, Madison
Harvard University
University of California, San Diego
University of California, Berkeley
University of Colorado
Columbia University
University of Washington, Seattle

Microbiology
Massachusetts Institute of Technology
Rockefeller University
University of California, San Diego
Johns Hopkins University
University of Washington, Seattle
Duke University
University of California, Los Angeles
University of Chicago
University of Illinois, Urbana-Champaign
University of Pennsylvania
University of California, Davis
University of Wisconsin, Madison
Columbia University
University of Michigan, Ann Arbor

Physiology
Rockefeller University
University of California, San Francisco
University of Washington, Seattle
Yale University
University of Pennsylvania
Harvard University
University of California, Los Angeles
Duke University
University of Michigan, Ann Arbor
Washington University, St. Louis

Zoology
Harvard University
University of California, Berkeley
University of Washington, Seattle
Yale University
Duke University
University of California, Los Angeles
University of Wisconsin, Madison

Engineering

Chemical Engineering
University of Minnesota
University of Wisconsin, Madison
University of California, Berkeley
California Institute of Technology
Stanford University
University of Delaware, Newark
Massachusetts Institute of Technology
University of Illinois, Urbana-Champaign

Civil Engineering
University of California, Berkeley
Massachusetts Institute of Technology
University of Illinois, Urbana-Champaign
California Institute of Technology
Stanford University
Cornell University
University of Texas, Austin

Electrical Engineering
Massachusetts Institute of Technology
University of California, Berkeley
Stanford University
University of Illinois, Urbana-Champaign
University of California, Los Angeles
Cornell University
University of Southern California
Purdue University
California Institute of Technology
Princeton University

Mechanical Engineering
Massachusetts Institute of Technology
Stanford University
University of California, Berkeley
California Institute of Technology
University of Minnesota
Princeton University
Purdue University
Brown University

Humanities

Art History
New York University
Harvard University

Yale University
Columbia University

Classics
Harvard University
University of California, Berkeley
Yale University
Princeton University

English Language and Literature
Yale University
University of California, Berkeley
Harvard University
University of Virginia
Cornell University
University of Chicago
Johns Hopkins University
Princeton University
Stanford University
Columbia University

French Language and Literature
Yale University
Princeton University
Columbia University
New York University
Cornell University
Indiana University, Bloomington

German Language and Literature
Yale University
University of Wisconsin, Madison
Princeton University
Indiana University, Bloomington
University of California, Berkeley

Linguistics
Massachusetts Institute of Technology
University of California, Los Angeles
University of Massachusetts
University of Texas, Austin

Music
University of California, Berkeley
University of Chicago
Princeton University
Yale University
Cornell University

Philosophy
Princeton University
University of Pittsburgh
Harvard University
University of California, Berkeley
University of California, Los Angeles
Stanford University
University of Chicago

Spanish Language and Literature
University of Pennsylvania
Harvard University
University of Texas, Austin
University of California, Berkeley
Yale University
University of Michigan, Ann Arbor
University of Wisconsin, Madison

Math and Physical Sciences

Chemistry
California Institute of Technology
University of California, Berkeley
Harvard University
Massachusetts Institute of Technology
Columbia University
University of Illinois, Urbana-Champaign
Stanford University
University of Chicago
University of California, Los Angeles
University of Wisconsin, Madison
Cornell University
Northwestern University
Princeton University
Yale University
Purdue University

Computer Science
Stanford University
Massachusetts Institute of Technology
Carnegie-Mellon University
University of California, Berkeley
Cornell University
University of Illinois, Urbana-Champaign

Geosciences
California Institute of Technology
Massachusetts Institute of Technology
University of California, Los Angeles
Columbia University
Stanford University
Harvard University
University of Chicago
Princeton University
Yale University

Mathematics
Princeton University
University of California, Berkeley
Harvard University
Massachusetts Institute of Technology
University of Chicago
Stanford University
New York University
Yale University
University of Wisconsin, Madison
Columbia University
University of Michigan, Ann Arbor
Brown University
Cornell University

Physics
Harvard University
California Institute of Technology
Cornell University
Princeton University
Massachusetts Institute of Technology
University of California, Berkeley
Stanford University
University of Chicago
University of Illinois, Urbana-Champaign
Columbia University
State University of New York, Stony Brook

Statistics/Biostatistics
Stanford University
University of California, Berkeley
University of Chicago
University of Wisconsin, Madison
Iowa State University, Ames
University of North Carolina, Chapel Hill

Social and Behavioral Sciences

Anthropology
University of Michigan, Ann Arbor
University of California, Berkeley
University of Chicago
University of Pennsylvania
University of Arizona, Tucson
Stanford University
Yale University

Economics
Massachusetts Institute of Technology
University of Chicago
Stanford University
Princeton University
Harvard University
Yale University
University of Minnesota
University of Pennsylvania
University of Wisconsin, Madison

Geography
University of Minnesota
Pennsylvania State University
University of Wisconsin, Madison
University of California, Berkeley
University of Chicago

History
Yale University
University of California, Berkeley
Princeton University
Harvard University
University of Michigan, Ann Arbor
Stanford University
Columbia University
University of Chicago
Johns Hopkins University
University of Wisconsin, Madison

Political Science
Yale University
University of Michigan, Ann Arbor
University of California, Berkeley
University of Chicago
Harvard University
Massachusetts Institute of Technology

Stanford University
University of Wisconsin, Madison

Psychology
Stanford University
Yale University
University of Pennsylvania
University of Michigan, Ann Arbor
University of Minnesota
University of California, Berkeley
Harvard University
University of Illinois, Urbana-Champaign
University of California, Los Angeles
Carnegie-Mellon University
University of California, San Diego
University of Chicago
University of Colorado
Indiana University, Bloomington
University of Oregon, Eugene
University of Wisconsin, Madison

Sociology
University of Wisconsin, Madison
University of Michigan, Ann Arbor
University of Chicago
University of North Carolina, Chapel Hill
University of California, Berkeley
Harvard University
Stanford University
University of Washington, Seattle
Columbia University
Indiana University, Bloomington
University of California, Los Angeles

■ ■ ■ ■

Windows On the World

Are foreign lands calling out to you? The U.S. Department of Education administers hundreds of fellowships related to foreign languages and international relations—the Foreign Language and Area Studies Fellowships and the Fulbright-Hays Doctoral Dissertation Awards.

Check out these and other funding possibilities with your institution's financial aid office.

Should you pack your bags for an overseas study tour?

Upside answer: Living in a foreign culture stimulates the senses, producing a heightened awareness of the world in which you live. It is a sophisticating experience and one which may be a high point in your life.

Downside answer: Living in less developed nations can be a culture shock that prevents you from maximizing your educational experience. If you make an unwise selection, the educational credential, such as degrees granted by certain foreign medical schools, may be of little value in the United States.

■■■■

Business School: Your Golden Passport?

The rocketing growth experienced by master's of business administration programs during the 1980s has leveled off, but the MBA mania is far from over.

About 750 MBA programs exist today, compared to 389 only 20 years ago. (But only one-third are accredited by the prestigious American Assembly of Collegiate Schools of Business.) Business schools grant nearly one-quarter of all master's degrees awarded in this country. There are now more than a million MBAs.

The MBA boom was originally driven by the needs in the 1960s and 1970s of large companies for astute executives to control their growing and diversified empires and to staff the management consulting firms that serviced them. The MBAs are smart, quick with numbers and can speak off the cuff with confidence. In the 1980s they invaded Wall Street.

"But the MBA boom has gone beyond its initial impetus and is now feeding on itself. Old MBAs hire new MBAs and the degree is often a de facto job requirement," observes *Newsweek* columnist Robert J. Samuelson.

An MBA has been widely thought to be embossed with magic—a reliable ticket to the executive suite and the riches and power that go with it. Other than medical school, it seems the quickest route to a six-figure income.

With this prologue, is it any wonder that many thousands of people annually head for business school after discovering their undergraduate educational backgrounds are not qualifying them for the kinds of jobs they want?

This translates each year to a record-breaking 75,000 newly minted MBAs bursting forth from campuses across the land, of which one-third are women.

What they are bursting forth to, however, has changed a bit since Wall Street's woes. Unless they are the best students from the most elegant B-schools, MBAs are waiting longer for fewer offers. The Wall Street shakeout caused many MBAs to end up in lower-paying finance or marketing jobs in industry.

And, as cost-conscious Corporate America strips away management layers, employers are shopping more carefully. Some executives have grown critical of MBAs' performance, saying the young marvels may know a lot of management theory, but not much about the realities of running a company. Critics charge them with being narrowly educated, arrogant, prone to job hopping—and say they expect to get ahead too fast.

The combination of a tidal wave of graduates and increasing disenchantment with MBAs' performance has made competition for good jobs a real scramble.

While the MBA no longer carries the cachet it once had, guess what executives recommend to their own children?

In a typical survey, 600 senior business leaders were asked: "If your son or daughter were planning a career in business, would you advise him or her to get an MBA, or not?" A whopping 78 percent said "yes."

MBAs: Dollars, Sense, and Sectors

Obviously not all employers rate the MBA as pampered and overpriced. Most new graduates are offered annual starting salaries in the low $30s, and some do even better. Among well-regarded business schools, $35,000 to $50,000 is the range of the average offer to new MBAs. Higher offers are in the $60,000 to the $85,000 span.

The knock-your-socks-off salaries generally go to MBAs who amassed working experience between their undergraduate and professional studies, have sought-after technical backgrounds, or were most successful in courting the glitter and gold of investment banking or consulting.

Apart from money, some people zero in on the degree for defensive reasons. They believe—with good reason—that when merit and abilities are equal, people with MBAs often get promoted faster than people without the degree. That's why someone with a master's degree in economics or banking may go back and finish an MBA program.

For women in particular, the degree may be seen as proof of commitment to career, and is probably the single best tool for getting ahead. Experts do not agree about the specific value of the MBA for women, but the weight of opinion seems to be that it's important for a woman to enter corporate employment with all the credentials she can get.

Many women who have been through business school say the experience has helped prepare them for the bias they faced in the business world after graduation. Some real world bias is obvious and comes early. Other bias is more subtle and comes later. It is referred to as the "glass ceiling" in corporations, and is an invisible barrier that prevents women from being promoted to the very top jobs.

Minorities also face bias and a lack of precedent. In an effort to attract more high quality minority students into business school doctoral programs and faculty careers, the Graduate Management Admission Council and the American Assembly of Collegiate Schools of Business each year jointly operate a six-week summer institute for 35 black, Latino, and Native American college students.

What jobs do MBAs take? The vast majority of all new MBAs work in finance or marketing. Others toil in general management and administration, information management, operations, and production.

They perform these functions in many industries—banking, data processing, accounting, consulting, insurance, food and beverage, automotive, financial services, and all types of consumer products.

A Report Card on Business Schools

The issue of who's Number One—Harvard or Stanford—has been hotly debated for years. Most employers perceive one or the other as being tops, although a prominent survey recently awarded the top spot to Northwestern.

There's far greater agreement on the general ranking of B-schools. Think of a pyramid. Approximately 25 institutions are at the apex. Another 25 or more rank on the second tier. Perhaps another 50 schools are on a third tier, and, at the base of the pyramid, are hundreds more schools flying the MBA banner.

Although some institutions slide in and out of lists of the top 25 B-schools, here's a recent U.S. *News & World Report* roundup in rank order.

1. Massachusetts Institute of Technology (Sloan)

2. University of Pennsylvania (Wharton)

3. Stanford University

4. Harvard University

5. Northwestern University (Kellogg)

6. Dartmouth College (Amos Tuck)

7. University of Chicago

8. Duke University (Fuqua)

9. University of Virginia (Darden)

10. University of California, Berkeley (Haas)

11. University of Michigan

12. Columbia University

13. University of California, Los Angeles (Anderson)

14. Carnegie Mellon University

15. Cornell University (Johnson)

16. Yale University

17. New York University (Stern)

18. University of North Carolina, Chapel Hill (Kenan/Flagler)

19. University of Texas, Austin

20. Purdue University

21. Indiana University

22. Georgetown University

23. Emory University (Goizueta)

24. University of Rochester (Simon)

25. The Ohio State University (Fisher)

(Source: "The Top 25 Business Schools," U.S. *News & World Report*, March 20, 1995.)

Which B-schools are in the second tier? Noting that Georgia Institute of Technology, Vanderbilt University, and the University of Southern California are poised for positioning in the top 25 in the near future, here's U.S. *News & World Report's* call on runners-up in alphabetical order:

American Graduate School of International Management (Thunderbird)

Arizona State University

Brigham Young University (Marriott)

Case Western Reserve University (Weatherhead)

Georgia Institute of Technology

Michigan State University (Broad)

Pennsylvania State University (Smeal)

Texas A & M University, College Station

Tulane University (Freeman)

University of Arizona

University of Florida

University of Georgia (Terry)

University of Illinois, Urbana-Champaign

University of Iowa

University of Maryland

University of Minnesota, Twin Cities (Carlson)

University of Notre Dame

University of Pittsburgh (Katz)

University of Southern California

University of Tennessee, Knoxville

University of Washington

University of Wisconsin, Madison

Vanderbilt University (Owen)

Wake Forest University (Babcock)

Washington University (Olin)

As you have probably deduced, not all MBAs are created equal. The B-school you attend not only affects how many job offers you get and how much you initially earn, but how you will go about running things down the road. Many of the leading schools teach the making of business decisions by quantitative (quantity, numbers) analysis and computer (mathematical) modeling. Others stress leadership skills and communications, or blend both approaches. In elite consulting firms, as in elite law firms, the clout of your alma mater shadows your career. But for other gilt-edge performers, it may not matter after five years where or how you got your MBA—experience is the crown that dazzles.

Beyond the differences in status and philosophy, there are other factors to consider when choosing a B-school. Let's say you do not enroll in a nationally known institution. Consider a highly regarded regional MBA program; its graduates often are first picks of neighboring businesses.

As a rule, MBA programs are spread out over two full-time academic years. Part-time B-school programs range from four or five years of evening school to 52 Saturdays, and from electronic study to two years' worth of alternate weekends plus overseas travel.

From off-campus study to night sessions, from weekend programs to electronic colleges, the rich diversity of ways to gain the degree has grown from pressures on B-schools to remain competitive. Some business educators fear the MBA market may be approaching saturation and speculate that a shakeout is ahead in which weak, unaccredited B-schools will close, perhaps hundreds of them. One observer remarked, "It may be a situation in which the stronger schools get fatter, and the marginal ones fail."

If you can't hack a total MBA program, often the prominent national and regional B-schools offer short-term, non-degree courses for practicing managers and executives, which can dress up a lackluster education.

Focus on The GMAT

The Graduate Management Admission Test (GMAT) is required by most schools of business. It's an exam with the same format as the SAT, but with harder questions. With a top possible score of 800, you need to nail more than 600 points to make it to a Top 25 school and at least 550 for the second tier. There are exceptions but that's the upshot.

Obtain modestly priced sample tests and software, and a free copy of the GMAT *Bulletin of Information* to register for the test, from the Graduate Management Admission Test/ETS, Box 6108, Princeton, NJ 08541; 609–771–7330.

Business School Action Steps

Of the 750 B-schools nationwide, some are quick make-overs of liberal arts schools and, like Rodney Dangerfield, their graduates get no respect. A safety check we recommend is accreditation by the Assembly of Collegiate Schools of Business, Suite 220, 605 Old Ballas Road, St. Louis, MO 63111. Write to the organization for a free list of accredited B-school programs.

Because a B-school education is expensive in cost and time invested, you won't want to make the decision lightly. Here are four books to study with the same intensity an MBA would attack a typical case study. The first book, *Business Week's*, is the definitive work you really must read and study. The others will add texture to your understanding.

Business Week's Guide to the Best Business Schools, second edition, by John A. Byrne (McGraw-Hill).

Admissions Guide to Selective Business Schools, by Matthew May (VGM Career Horizons).

The Insider's Guide to the Top Ten Business Schools, fourth edition, edited by Tom Fischgrund (Little, Brown).

Career Choices for the 90s for Students of M.B.A., by Career Associates (Walker Publishing).

Is Graduate Business Study For You?

Before exchanging two years of life for an MBA, reflect on your ultimate career goals.

If you want to be a corporate alpinist scaling the sheer cliffs of top management, an MBA is a must. If you want to rate as a management consultant or investment banker, get an MBA. If you seek powerful contacts, you can begin developing them in an MBA program. If you have a liberal arts degree and need marketability, an MBA will help. If you've got a technical undergraduate degree and you seek broadening managerial horizons, go MBA.

The ideal approach is to work hard to get into the best school you can and graduate near the top of the class. Warming up with a couple of years of working experience will help you understand the practical problems of applying what's taught in the classroom.

If you can't justify day school, you can get an MBA at night or on weekends. Try to find employment with a company that will pay for your studies.

A graduate school of business can help you acquire not only technical business skills, but communicate the lifestyle and values needed to move up in organizations that hire MBAs who would be kings—or queens.

■ ■ ■ ■

A Law Degree Can Lead Almost Anywhere

Lawyer bashing is nothing new.

"Can we bar lawyers from coming to the New World?" asked explorer Balboa of King Ferdinand in 1523.

"I would be loath to speak ill of any man, but I'm afraid this man is an attorney," said English author Dr. Samuel Johnson.

Attorneys have been under indictment from the public throughout history, but charges seem to be flying faster than ever before. In the past decade, an uncomfortable number of lawyers—a very small minority, true, but enough to tarnish regard for lawyers as a group—have been accused of everything from courtroom blunders and fee gouging to outright crookedness.

Sometimes critics are dead serious when blowing off lawyers; others take a droll swipe at a large target.

Michael Frasher, a West Virginian who will tongue-in-cheek call himself a "recovering attorney and former prosecutor," offers the "EXLEX" plan to cut down on the number of lawyers. Frasher says if farmers can be paid not to farm, why shouldn't lawyers be paid not to practice? Noting a University of Texas study indicating that each of the nation's lawyers costs the nation nearly $1 million a year through legal skirmishes, Frasher suggests the government pay each attorney $500,000 to turn in his or her license. The money would be used to steer would-be lawyers from law schools to what he terms "more socially useful" professions, such as teaching or nursing. We guess he's joking but a lot of people would say humorist Frasher has come up with a good idea.

Against this backdrop of modest public esteem for lawyers, it could be assumed that the profession has lost appeal for bright young minds.

A reasonable assumption, but a wrong one.

America is teeming with lawyers. Some people say there's a glut of them. Across the land, licensed lawyers total over 777,000, more than double the number only 20 years ago. (Don't confuse licensed lawyers with practicing lawyers. The numbers differ because some licensed lawyers do not practice but pursue careers other than law.)

Yet there's no end in sight. A sizable army of more than 90,000 young persons compete for half that number of places each year in the nation's 176 accredited law schools. Total enrollments, now in excess of 130,000, doubled over the past 20 years. In a recent year, 47,000 new lawyers sought domain in the professional marketplace.

Women have taken to law like judges to gavels; more than 40 percent of today's law students are female. Moreover, the U.S. Supreme Court has ruled that law firms must comply with federal employment discrimination laws when deciding who moves up from employee to partner, which is good news for women.

A small number of lawyers clerk for judges, but this is usually a short-term stop on career paths into other areas of the profession. The trend is away from one-lawyer firms, although many lawyers in private practice work alone. About 70 percent of all lawyers are in private practice, some as employees or partners in law firms. Other lawyers work for corporations or government agencies.

As we mentioned in Chapter 1, the legal profession does not guarantee affluence to its members. Legal aid lawyers often earn less than $25,000 yearly. Law clerks, solo practitioners, and young law firm associates may have to make do on less than $35,000 a year.

Most government lawyers are paid according to civil service scales, rarely earning more than $70,000 a year, even after decades of service. Corporate lawyers have earnings comparable to other company executives, which can top $150,000, or dip under $40,000.

The real money machines are found in prestige law firms, particularly in New York City, Washington, D.C., and other major cites. Partners in top firms can command $300,000 annually, or much, much more—better than a million dollars in a good year.

There is a down side even to being a successful lawyer. A 31-year-old Los Angeles defense lawyer earns $150,000 a year at a prestigious law firm, owns a home in an upscale neighborhood, and drives a sports car, but he is so unhappy with his profession that he is considering chucking his law career and doing something else. "I look around this firm and see so many people making very good money and being so miserable," he said.

Disenchantment with the legal life is so pervasive among lawyers that many were not surprised when prosecutor Christopher Darden recently questioned whether he wanted to try another case after the O.J. Simpson murder trial.

Lawyers tend to be more troubled by severe depression than other professionals. In California, one quarter of attorneys are on inactive status with the State Bar Association.

Some lawyers probably should not have entered the profession in the first place. Law schools became the "great dumping ground for liberal arts majors," who were not suited to the law profession, according to one insider.

A RAND study published in 1994 concluded that California attorneys were very pessimistic about the law, with only half of those surveyed indicating they would choose again to be a lawyer.

Law school applications peaked in 1990, and some statistics suggest lawyers may be leaving in greater numbers to become teachers, real estate agents, or psychologists, among many other professions.

What about starting out? If you do very well at a leading law school and go to work for a prestigious New York law firm, you will be paid about $85,000 a year to start. This happens to only a few lucky graduates. If you don't do so well at an obscure law school, you probably will have trouble finding your first job in law at a starting salary of $22,000 to $35,000. (*Student Lawyer Magazine*, published by the American Bar Association's Law Student Division, publishes an annual survey of law salaries by city and type of employer.)

Where you go to school is more important in law than it is in many other professions. Years after graduation, a lawyer looking for a job will be asked about his or her law school and rank in class.

Other than the hope of high earnings, what attracts hordes of people to the law? Sometimes it's idealism. Sometimes students decide that lawyers have special handles on the nation's power levers and they want to pull them. Other times they can't think of any other profession to enter. Sometimes training in the law seems useful whether it is to be practiced or not.

A law degree can lead to almost anything—the law, politics, business.

Howard Cosell, who was trained as an attorney, laid down the law to become a well-known figure in the sports world. Former International Ladies Garment Workers President Sol Chaikin used his law degree to look for and find the union label. Former CIA and FBI head William Webster began his illustrious career as a lawyer.

From the corridors of government power and the sky-hugging office buildings of New York, Houston, and cities everywhere, to the suburban shopping malls and the commercial districts of small towns, lawyers are everywhere, and into everything.

What Lawyers Do

Litigating, *negotiating*, *securing*, and *counseling* are the four broad categories of activities that lawyers can pursue.

The *litigators* are the courtroom warriors who parachute into the fray and blast away until a particular point of view has been pressed as vigorously as possible. The *negotiators* settle conflicts short of courtroom battle, reconciling divergent interests and opinions. *Securers* use communication skills to nail down contracts and other agreements that keep society running by a set of rules. *Counselors* advise clients on a broad spectrum of personal and business problems—they're in the "preventive litigation" business.

Not all lawyers do all of these things. Although most states prohibit lawyers from claiming a specialty, lawyers do say things like "focus on—" or "limit my practice to—." You can build a practice emphasizing any number of concerns such as tax, criminal, antitrust, immigration, high-tech, patent, personal-injury, divorce, employment, communications, and real estate law. It's a safe bet that as business goes global, international law will be among front runners in hot specialities for years to come. You may spot dozens of other law specialties by reading the telephone yellow page directories under "Attorneys Listed by Fields of Law."

Schools Where You Learn to Think Like a Lawyer

With lawyerly class, the degree you get after three years of law school—or four years in a part-time evening program—has been changed from the traditional LLB (bachelor of law) to JD for *juris doctor*.

Choosing a law school requires the same thought and research skills as choosing an undergraduate institution. You need to cross-examine the question with care because where you go to law school has much to do with where you will practice the profession and how successful you'll be in your legal career.

Some well-established firms recruit new lawyers only from law schools attended by the firms' present members or from law schools they consider their state's best. The toniest big-city firms often recruit new associates only from graduates of the nation's top law schools.

Schools often mentioned as being on the first tier are (in alphabetical order):

University of California, Berkeley

University of California (Hastings)

University of California, Los Angeles

University of Chicago

Columbia University

Cornell University

Duke University

Georgetown University

George Washington University

Harvard University

University of Illinois

University of Iowa

University of Michigan

University of Minnesota

New York University

University of North Carolina, Chapel Hill

Northwestern University

University of Pennsylvania

Stanford University

University of Texas, Austin

University of Notre Dame

University of Southern California

Vanderbilt University

University of Virginia

University of Wisconsin, Madison

Yale University

If you are accepted by more than one school, consider carefully before making your decision. It is an uphill battle to transfer from one law school to another.

Since the choice of a law school can have significant consequences, ask experienced lawyers and your college's prelaw adviser for guidance on which schools match your aspirations.

The only law schools you should consider attending are those approved by the American Bar Association. In nearly every state, graduation from an ABA-approved law school is required for admission to the bar. For all practical purposes, you can't become a lawyer in the United States without earning a degree from an approved law school.

Once you're in school, work hard. Employers put a lot of emphasis on a candidate's grades; being near the top of the class is more important than it is for graduates in many other fields. Everybody wants a "smart" lawyer.

How to Look Good to Your Favorite Law School

If you want to wear the school tie of a very selective institution, you must unwrap the mysteries of its admission process.

In general, the selection criteria are the same as those used by admission committees at professional schools of all types, with one notable difference: The standardized admission test may be taken more seriously by law schools than are standardized tests in other career fields, with the possible exception of medicine.

The importance of each selection factor depends on the law school's admission policy, but it is commonly believed that the Law School Admission Test (LSAT) is the single most significant element. The scoring scale is 120 to 180; you need a score of at least 165 to be considered a front-running candidate for the top law schools.

Grades are a close second on the academic measuring stick. Easy, pushover courses don't count as much as respectably difficult studies.

References and recommendations may be influential. A recommendation from one of the school's alumni benefactors could tip the scales in your favor if your qualifications are first-rate. Strong academic references from approving professors can help a lot, too. But if you've got a 1.5 grade point and a 135 LSAT score, you may be turned down even if you have a father who can contribute the west wing of a new library.

Extracurricular activities are frosting on the cake. The activities that reflect most favorably are those requiring communication skills, like public speaking, debating, and writing.

If you're a member of a minority group, be sure to mention the fact. There may be special programs available that work to your advantage.

To bask in the light of acceptance from your favorite law school(s), the appropriate strategy is obvious: Keep your grades up, and study for the LSAT. Yes, you can prepare for it.

Here's a Starter Law Library

The Law School Admission Council (Box 2000, Newtown, PA 18940) is a kind of one-stop shopping center specializing in materials that collectively tell you everything you ever wanted to know about law school. Three key publications are *The Information Book*, issued annually, *The Official Guide to U.S. Law Schools*, and *The Official LSAT Prep Test*. The Council also publishes smaller works on choosing the right law school and financing a law school education. Write for a catalog.

Running From the Law: Why Good Lawyers are Getting Out of the Legal Profession, by Deborah Arron (Ten Speed Press), gives you the downside of lawyering in a 200-page brief.

Full Disclosure: Do You Really Want to Be a Lawyer?, by Susan Bell/Young Lawyers Division of the American Bar Association (Peterson's), is a positive but penetrating look at the work.

Is a Law Career Really You?

To be an effective lawyer, you know you need strong communication abilities, but did you know you need a high tolerance for ambiguity?

Some students enter school thinking the law is filled with order. They are surprised to learn that law does not contain that kind of certainty. Lawyers must always take a judicial look at all sides of an issue. An individual with a rigid mind-set will be uneasy in an atmosphere of multisided disclosure.

Then there are real-life games of scruples. When you have tough calls to make—defending a confessed criminal, writing lopsided contracts for clients—you may be creating inner turmoil you can't handle.

How do you feel about generous participation in charitable, educational, and community activities as a way of attracting clients? In some communities, new lawyers regularly run for political office, not to win but to advertise their services.

Ambiguity, scruples, and public visibility are only a few of the factors you should consider before making a decision in favor of the law.

■ ■ ■ ■

Medical School: More Knocks on the Door

Despite high tuition and physicians' frustration with changes in the medical profession, applications to medical schools nationwide are at an all-time high.

Schools are hoping to attract healers rather than financially focused scientific learning machines. The nation is long on specialists but short on primary-care doctors.

Money continues to be a draw to the profession: The average practicing doctor earns about $155,000 annually. Here too, the imbalance between specialists and primary-care physicians continues. Surgeons average $220,000 and anesthesiologists can expect $185,000. But those in primary care are not as richly rewarded: Family practitioners average $96,000, pediatricians $105,000, and internists $147,000.

The excess of specialists and the shortage of primary-care doctors is not helped by the heavy-duty debt the average young physician accumulates by the end of medical school. The four-year cost of some private school medical educations has now outgrown the $100,000 category. Public medical schools cost half or less as much as private schools. The typical new doctor graduates with an average debt rapidly approaching $50,000.

After four stressful, hardball years in medical school, you're ready to move on to three or more grueling years of residency, where you are a doctor in training.

Now that you finally are earning money, how much will you get? The average resident earns $26,000 yearly.

If you still have med school in mind, the most important thing you can do right now is contact the premedical adviser in your college. Most colleges and universities have named a faculty member—usually in health sciences, chemistry or biology—as the adviser for pre-

medical students. The office of the dean of liberal arts and/or sciences usually can refer you to the premedical adviser. If your institution does not have such an adviser, contact the registrar or admission officer at a nearby medical school.

Examining the Medical Schools

Two types of physicians are trained in the United States. One has an MD (doctor of medicine) degree and the other has a DO (doctor of osteopathic medicine) degree. MDs outnumber DOs about 20 to 1.

The difference between the two is in their approach to medicine, but training for both MDs and DOs is similar in timing and professional requirements. MDs study in allopathic medical schools, DOs in osteopathic medical schools.

Of the nation's 127 allopathic medical schools, 126 are accredited by the Liaison Committee on Medical Education, the official accreditation group for MD programs. In addition, 16 Canadian programs are accredited.

All 15 osteopathic medical schools in the U.S. are accredited by the American Osteopathic Association, the official accrediting group for DO programs.

Accreditation, important to future licensure, is virtually universal among North American medical schools, which means you ought to obtain quality training in any one of them—after all, American physicians are the best in the world. Even so, certain institutions are more notable than others.

We asked numerous medical authorities which institutions they think rank in the highest tier of medical schools. Certain names came up consistently.

Among allopathic medical schools, in alphabetical order, the institutions most often mentioned include:

University of Alabama, Birmingham

University of Chicago

Columbia University

Cornell University

Duke University

Emory University

Harvard University

University of Iowa

Johns Hopkins University

University of California, Los Angeles

University of Michigan

University of North Carolina, Chapel Hill

University of Pennsylvania

University of Pittsburgh

University of California, San Francisco

University of California, San Diego

Stanford University

University of Texas, Dallas

Vanderbilt University

University of Washington

Washington University

Yale University

Among Osteopathic medical schools, these are notable:

Kirksville (Mo.) College of Osteopathic Medicine

Philadelphia College of Osteopathic Medicine

Chicago College of Osteopathic Medicine

Michigan State University

New Jersey School of Osteopathic Medicine

Texas College of Osteopathic Medicine

The big-name allopathic medical schools have far more clinical facilities and research capacity than do the best known osteopathic medical schools.

The book to read about allopathic medical schools is the *Medical School Admission Requirements*, published annually by the Association of American Medical Colleges, Suite 200, One Dupont Circle NW, Washington, DC 20036.

Information about osteopathic medical schools is available from the American Association of Colleges of Osteopathic Medicine, Suite 405, 6110 Executive Blvd., Rockville, MD 20852.

Because the majority of medical schools are state-related, restrictions will be placed on the number of out-of-state applicants who can be accepted. The University of Kansas School of Medicine, for example, will give preference to applicants who are graduates of undergraduate colleges in Kansas before considering applicants from other states.

In brief, you should apply to medical schools within your state, and to a reasonable number of private medical schools and a small number of state medical schools outside your state. Most students apply to an average of 10 medical schools.

Getting Into Medical School

If you knew before you entered college that you wanted to attend medical school, you probably chose your undergraduate institution with that goal in mind.

That's smart planning. Graduating from a college affiliated with a medical school can be advantageous. Medical schools tend to select graduates of particular colleges when they've been happy with past choices from those colleges. Attending a nationally known college maximizes the probabilities of your acceptance to a nationally known medical school.

But if you're already in college when the thought of becoming a physician enters your mind, make sure your curriculum meets all academic requirements for the premed track.

After you're into the routine of making good grades in the courses required for admission, you'll probably be debating with yourself whether you should apply to medical school as a three- or four-year applicant. If you try to speed up your education by entering medical school after three years of study, you will be the one out of ten who does so. More than 90 percent of students entering American medical schools have completed at least four years of college.

Preparing for the Medical College Admission Test (MCAT) makes good use of your spare time. With a few exceptions—the standardized admission test is one of the two big numbers medical schools' admission committees use for preliminary screening. Take the MCAT during the preceding spring, not the fall, of the year in which you plan to apply to medical schools. If you delay until the fall, you could be at a disadvantage at a school that uses a rolling admission process, because the longer you wait, the more individuals you must compete with for a place in the freshman class.

An essential and annually revised book to read on the topic of the admission test is the MCAT *Student Manual*, published by the Association of American Medical Colleges. You can buy it in most college bookstores or order it through your premedical adviser's office. The book contains helpful hints and practice tests.

New for the 1990s, also from the Association of American Medical Colleges, is a half-hour video on the MCAT which explains to medical school hopefuls what they face at test time. Using detailed graphics and narration, the video describes the four sections of the exam: verbal reasoning, biological sciences, physical sciences, and a writing sample of two 30-minute essay responses. It discusses specific topics the test may cover and recommends the undergraduate course work, study skills, supplementary reading, and exercises that will help examinees prepare for it. Premed advisers can make this new study tool available to you.

In still another strategy to beat out the competition, many premed students enroll in review courses, such as those offered by the Stanley H. Kaplan Educational Centers.

The other big number used by school admission committees for screening is the grade point average.

To have a reasonably good chance to get into an allopathic medical school that receives more applications than it can handle, you must have a good GPA and impressive scores on the MCAT. What's "good"? What's "impressive"? You want at least a 3.6 GPA in both science and non-science courses, and high MCAT scores. Some schools, particularly state institutions, will take into account an upward trend in the GPA; you may receive a nod of approval even if your GPA was sluggish for the first two years of college if it shoots up once a decision is made to pursue medicine.

Generally speaking, you will need better numbers at private and out-of-state schools than you will for your state medical schools. A student with a GPA of around 3.0 and MCAT scores in the 60 percentile who is accepted into an out-of-state school is a lucky person—it doesn't happen often. It can happen at in-state schools.

Osteopathic medical schools may not be interested unless you have a minimum 3.0 GPA and 50 percentile MCAT scores. Selection criteria vary somewhat from school to school, but usually the factors include interviews, references, faculty letters, minority goals, and political pressure from alumni.

Become wiser by reading these books. The first two relate to med school, the last to the profession.

Getting into Medical School: Strategies for the 90s, by Scott Plantz and others (Arco).

Medical School: Getting In, Staying In, Staying Human, by Keith R. Ablow (St. Martin's Press).

Careers in Medicine: Traditional and Alternative Opportunities, edited by T. Donald Rucker and Martin D. Keller (Garrett Park Press).

Not Getting In

It's a sad day when your last thin letter says, "Sorry, you didn't make it into our medical school." Weep a bit, then decide what you're going to do: reapply next year or make an alternative career choice. Foreign medical schools are no longer a good alternative, according to Dr. James G. Price, executive dean, University of Kansas School of Medicine. Their graduates have a poor track record passing medical licensure examinations and finding residency appointments. The challenge for graduates of foreign schools will be even greater now that the tough new *United States Medical Licensing Examination* has replaced two older tests. You won't be able to practice medicine here unless you have passed the USMLE.

Should There Be a Doctor in Your House?

In addition to wanting to help others, people are attracted to medicine for many reasons. Financial security and success are two of them. Add to the list of motivations intellectual challenge, the ability to exercise authority, independence, and social status.

But when it comes right down to it, we hope you'll be candid. Are you going into medicine for reasons that are right for you?

As Dr. Stuart Scott, a highly successful internist in Gaithersburg, Md., says:

Some people feel that doctors will always do well, that the money will take care of itself. That used to be true, and, to a degree, still is, but the real rewards, the daily uplifting satisfactions go to the sincere and diligent practitioner. Anyone who is focused on the bank statement should not be in the profession.

■ ■ ■ ■

An Educational Catalog: Pathways To Success

You don't have to pursue a traditional four-year college education to position yourself for the good things in life. You do have to develop job skills that are in demand and, with rare exceptions, the only way to get those skills is through comprehensive training.

This chapter describes the spectacular array of specialty training and skill-learning options you can choose from—both now and later as you update your competencies to remain competitive throughout your career years. Included are vocational-technical schools and community colleges, as well as opportunities in distance learning, external degree programs, continuing education, work-based learning, and military training programs.

You will find information on programs offered by professional societies, trade organizations, community organizations, churches and synagogues, libraries, museums, seminar sponsors, and summer institutes.

Apprenticeships, formal and informal, are also described. The chapter concludes with suggestions on how to choose a skill-learning option.

Feast on a Banquet of Job-Training Programs

A young friend says she chose between two vocational programs—cosmetology and medical assisting—by tossing a coin. Before we could close our astonished mouths, she explained:

"When you flip a coin in the air, that's when the truth hits you of how you hope it will come out."

Fortunately, from our friend's point of view, the coin landed right side up. She likes her work. But there's a better way. Do the necessary homework on yourself and on the job market before signing up to learn specific job skills.

Ask yourself: Am I really interested in this work? Will there be demand for the kind of work I want? Are there more people training for my kind of work than there are jobs? Do potential employers say there is a local need for workers in the career field I'm considering? If prospects are poor for working locally but are better elsewhere, am I willing to move to where the jobs are?

Think about these kinds of things as you choose from an appetizing feast of skill-learning options.

Heads or tails—can you believe that?!

According to 1995 edition of *The Tech Prep Marketing Guide*, published by the American Vocational Association, 80 percent of the best jobs in the next century will be in the field of technology—and they won't require a four-year college degree.

However, a student who wants to go this route is well-advised to make up his or her mind by the end of the 10th grade, since it is best to start courses in this field the last two years of high school and then go on for two additional years of training in a community college or technical institute.

Since business and industry leaders help to write the curriculum, they make sure that graduates who come to work for them will have the preparation they need.

Following are a list of some technical and trade careers that don't require a four-year degree:

Career	Percent of growth by 2005	Training after high school	Average salary
Paralegal	85%	2 to 4 years	$24,900
Radiological technician	70%	1 to 4 years	$29,200
EEG technologist	57%	1 to 2 years or OJT*	$22,250
Computer programmer	56%	2 to 4 years	$34,000
Surgical technologist	55%	1 to 2 years	$20,850
Medical records technologist	54%	2 years	$20,175
Nuclear medical technologist	52%	1 to 4 years	$28,500
Respiratory therapist	52%	2 to 4 years	$26,200
Licensed practical nurse	42%	1 years	$19,600
Dental hygienist	41%	1 to 2 years	$36,400
Computer repairer	38%	1 to 2 years	$28,200
Dispensing optician	37%	2 to 4 year or OJT	$25,000
Emergency medical technician	30%	1 to 2 years	$27,300
Electrician	29%	4 to 5 years apprenticeship	$27,250
Engineering technician	28%	2 years or OJT	$24,350
Aircraft mechanic	24%	2 to 3 years	$30,000

*OJT = on-job-training

Science technician	24%	2 years	$24,700
Numerical-control machine tool operator	23%	OJT	$33,000
Sheet metal worker	22%	4 to 5 years apprenticeship	$54,000
Auto body repairer	22%	OJT	$38,000
Auto mechanic	22%	1 to 2 years and OJT	$38,700
Barber cosmetologist	22%	1 to 2 years	$21,850
Diesel mechanic	22%	1 to 2 years and OJT	$29,900
Glazier	22%	3 to 4 years apprenticeship	$49,900
Heating and A/C mechanic	21%	1 to 2 years apprenticeship	$23,250
Plumber	21%	4 to 5 years apprenticeship	$26,400
Structural reinforcing iron worker	21%	3 years apprenticeship	$29,600
Elevator installer	17%	OJT	$36,150
Carpenter	14%	3 to 4 years apprenticeship	$21,400

■ ■ ■ ■

Schools Where Students Pay to Learn Paying Jobs

If you're the sort of person who likes to get straight to the point, you may be a candidate for vocational-technical (vo-tech) education. One option: the nation's network of 5,500 private profit-making vo-tech schools that send graduates into the world with a marketable set of work skills.

Another 1,000 vo-tech schools in the private sector are set up as non-profit institutions that have the same mission and operate in ways similar to the profit makers.

Together, they compose about 92 percent of the nation's 7,100 or so postsecondary vo-tech schools.

The private schools offer pure and lean training programs that usually can get you into a paying job within a year, although some programs last two years. Private courses skip over academic subjects, unless they are necessary to do the work. They emphasize solving everyday work problems similar to those found on the job.

Most private vo-tech institutions aren't cheap. Costs run from about $600 for a four-week manicuring program, to more than $9,000 for a one-year program in aviation mechanics. A three-week floral design program costs about $700, while a computer technology program costs more than $7,000 for 39 weeks of study. If the school is accredited by an agency recognized by the U.S. Department of Education, you can apply for federal and state student aid—loans, grants, and work-study programs—just as college students do.

Who attends private vo-tech schools? The typical enrollment mix might include these fictional but representative people: Kevin, a high school graduate who is fed up with conventional education; Marsha, a college graduate who finds her academic credentials aren't helping her obtain a well-paying job; Jonathan, a mid-career switcher who wants to change his line of work; Tiffany, a homemaker who wishes to return to the job market but needs skills quickly, Rob, who lost his job in an auto plant and is forced to find a new way of earning a living.

Logically you may ask why spend the money for a private school when you can learn the same job skills in a less expensive public vo-tech school or a community college? Good question. Here are the pluses of private vo-tech training.

know the material. Such a school is said to have an open exit philosophy. If you can pass the test—for instance, tune an engine—you can leave immediately as a graduate, rather than wait out the full term.

◆ Classes are usually small. The teachers may give extra attention, doing their best to see that a student doesn't drop out, because for them a drop-out is a lost sale.

◆ Private vo-tech schools usually are very concerned about their placement records and business reputations. They must satisfy their customers, or eventually they will go out of business. Staffs tend to work hard to place graduates and to cultivate the esteem of local employers.

Advantages of Private Vo-Tech Schools

◆ Some students choose the private route for a basic reason: job first, culture later. They just want job training, not academic enlightenment. They don't see themselves as college oriented, but feel they need additional training to land jobs.

◆ Students can usually enroll any time in a private vo-tech school; they need not wait until the semester or quarter break. Because these schools offer short-course units—with nearly instant intervals of completion and success—students who did not do too well in high school often get their first sweet taste of accomplishment in a private vo-tech school classroom. This feeling of success may help them as much as the content of the course in preparing to work in skilled jobs.

◆ An attractive feature at some private vocational schools is a performance evaluation policy that permits you to leave when you

Disadvantages of Private Vo-Tech Schools

◆ A drawback to private vo-tech study is that the school may not have the extensive classroom, laboratory, and recreational facilities that a government-supported school does. If you are considering a private vo-tech course requiring hands-on experience with various tools, such as auto mechanics, be sure you are learning on up-to-date equipment.

◆ Beware of the "dream schools," institutions that feed on individuals chasing unlikely dreams in glamour careers.

The never-ending stream of would-be stars has spawned an industry of dream merchants who operate schools for actors, artists, authors, baseball and basketball players, comedians, disc jockeys, models, musicians, race car drivers, and songwriters.

No matter how well-intentioned the dream merchants, the fact is that very, very few of their students reach the crests they seek. As one psychiatrist says, "Many people set themselves up for failure by training all year for the next football camp or the next movie tryout and avoid getting on with their lives."

◆ Very, very few courses at a private vo-tech school will transfer for academic college credit. You may eventually want a college degree; don't be surprised when you can't apply vocational studies to an academic degree program and have to start at the beginning.

◆ The best private vo-tech schools can provide skills necessary to get good jobs and to advance more quickly. Unfortunately, some schools are operated by "Fast Eddies" who promise high-paying jobs and rosy futures they cannot deliver. If you don't want to be fleeced by a scan operator, do your homework in checking out the school. How do you find a good school? Follow this guide.

Choosing a Private Vo-Tech School

◆ Check the advertising. A school's advertising should communicate that *students* are sought, not employees. Ads recruiting "trainees for immediate openings" are not straightforward.

◆ Watch out for guarantees. Steer clear of a school that guarantees you a job, or insists that there's "a place for you in ____ field." Avoid schools that suggest you'll be anything other than a trainee after graduation.

◆ Don't fall for hype. Resist pressure to sign an enrollment agreement quickly in return for a discount. You're looking for quality training, not a bargain. In many instances, the so-called discount is a myth. Most states have a cooling-off period of several days that allows

you to cancel a contract without financial penalty.

◆ Be very clear about the fine print in the enrollment agreement regarding payments and tuition refunds if you drop out. For instance, if the agreement says you'll get a refund if you withdraw because of an emergency, will you get it if a parent becomes ill and you must quit to work full time, or is an emergency refund given only if you become ill? Ignore verbal assurances from a school's representative. Get clarifications or modifications to the agreement in writing.

◆ Request placement figures. What percentage of graduates find jobs related to their studies? The average is said to be about 80 percent.

   As a practical matter, you have no way to verify the school's placement rate. That's why contacting recent graduates is important. Ask for the names of a dozen and get in touch with four or five. Try to reach graduates who live in your geographic area so you can talk face to face.

◆ Determine employer views. Ask employers such key questions as: Would you hire this school's graduates? Have you hired any during the past year? Were they hired because of school training? Did that training make any difference in starting salary?

◆ Talk to students privately. Find out if there's a time when you can visit the school and speak to them on a random basis. See how they evaluate the training they're receiving.

◆ Verify licensing. Most states require licensing by the state's postsecondary school licensing body. Your state's department of education can confirm whether a particular school is licensed.

◆ Verify graduation credentials. Because they specialize in specific job fields, vo-tech schools usually do not give academic degrees. When you complete the program the school will give you a certificate or diploma attesting to your newly learned skills. Find out if completion of the program qualifies you to take the state certification examination, if there is one for your field, such as cosmetology, real estate, or certain medical technologies.

◆ Ask whether the school is accredited and, if so, by what group? Accreditation should be given by an agency recognized by the U.S. Office of Education. A school can be a fine institution without being accredited, but if you're considering attending an unaccredited school, you should do extensive research on it before signing up. For a quick check on accreditation, obtain free guidebooks from these two groups: *National Association of Trade and Technical Schools*, Box 10429, Rockville, MD 20850; *Association of Independent Colleges and Schools*, Suite 350, One Dupont Circle NW, Washington, DC 20036.

◆ Get catalogs from at least three institutions and compare them. You can look up names and addresses of vo-tech schools in a library copy of *Vocational School Manual*, issued annually by Chronicle Guidance Publications, or the *Directory of Postsecondary Institutions*, Part 2 (*Occupational Programs*), published annually by the National Center for Education Statistics; U.S. Office of Education.

■ ■ ■ ■

Public Schools Where Students Train for Jobs

"Dear Mom and Dad," the letter from the college student began. "It's been a whole month since I've heard from you. Why not drop me a check so I'll know you're okay?"

Does this sound like something you might come up with? We heard it from a college student's parents, but the student is at a special kind of college—a *job college*.

Just as some students go away to academic colleges, others go away to state-supported residential vocational-technical schools, also called residential technical colleges or residential technical institutes.

In the following pages we tell you more about live-in job schools, as well as other types of public vo-tech schools.

"Stop right here!" you say? You're all set to be a philosophy major at Old Ivy U. and you may as well skip this portion because it doesn't apply to your immediate plans. Please keep reading. You won't be wasting your time learning something about public vo-tech education.

Point 1: Higher education costs today run somewhere between extraordinary and impossible. You may face a choice between a skyscraper of debt and working your way through college. Without work skills, you likely qualify only for minimum-wage jobs. With skills, such as hairdressing or automotive technology, you can earn far more.

Point 2: A changing world is sending more and more adults into vo-tech classrooms for retraining. You may not be interested in vo-tech education now, but you could be very interested later.

Point 3: Your plans may change. Roughly half the students who enter college don't cross the finish line four years later. Moreover, college grads sometimes decide they'd rather chuck office jobs to do such things as cabinetmaking or running swimming pool services.

From any angle, you're ahead of the game when you know where to find inexpensive schools that teach marketable job skills.

What You Can Learn in Vocational-Technical Schools

Look over this abbreviated list of programs offered by both private and public vocational schools to get an idea of career fields you can learn.

- accounting
- administrative assistant training, health
- advertising art /design
- agricultural management
- air conditioning, heating, refrigeration service
- aircraft maintenance technology
- airline and travel career training
- audio and recording technology
- automated office administration
- automated system service technology
- automotive body repair
- automotive mechanics

- baking
- barbering
- bartending
- biomedical equipment technology
- blood bank technology
- blueprint reading
- bricklaying
- broadcast technician training
- building maintenance
- burglar and fire alarm technology
- business administration
- business communications
- business computer systems
- business machines maintenance

- cardiovascular perfusionist training
- carpentry
- cartooning/animation
- cat grooming
- charm training
- chemical technology
- child care
- coin-operated machine repair
- communications electronics
- computer graphics
- computer information systems

- culinary arts

- data processing
- dental assisting
- dental laboratory technology
- diagnostic medical sonography
- diamond and gem cutting
- diesel technology
- digital electronics
- distributive education
- dog grooming
- drafting, computer-aided design
- dressmaking and design
- driver education

- electricity, construction
- EKG technology
- electrolysis
- electromechanical technology
- electronic technician training
- electronics technology
- engineering technology
- equestrian studies
- esthetics (cosmetics and skin care)

- farrier training (horseshoeing)
- fashion design
- fashion illustration
- fashion merchandising
- fiber-optic technology
- finance
- fine arts
- floristry
- fluid power technology
- food service technology (includes catering)
- forestry technology

- gemology
- geriatric assisting

(continued)

- golf instruction
- graphic arts
- greenhouse management
- gunsmithing

- heavy equipment operation
- hematology
- histological technology
- home furnishings sales
- home health aide training
- horticulture
- hotel and motel management

- illustration
- income tax
- industrial electronics
- information processing
- institutional management
- instrument repair
- interior decoration
- international trade

- jewelry design
- jewelry repair

- kennel management

- landscaping/gardening
- laser technology
- legal assisting
- locksmithing

- machine tool operations
- manicuring
- manufacturing technology
- marine mechanics
- marketing
- massage therapy
- medical assistant training
- medical records technology
- microcomputer repair
- mobile communications
- modeling
- multi-image production

- nuclear medicine technology
- nurse aide training
- nursing, registered

- office assistant training
- office machines operations
- optical technology
- orthotics

- paperhanging
- paralegal assisting
- patternmaking
- photography, commercial
- plastics technology
- plumbing, construction
- private investigation

- radiation therapy technology
- radio and TV broadcasting
- radio and TV repair
- radiologic (x-ray) technology
- real estate sales and management
- receptionist training
- record engineer training
- records management
- recreation and tourism
- respiratory care
- robotics
- roofing, construction

- sales management
- secretarial studies
- security management
- sheet-metal trades
- shipbuilding
- sign painting
- small business management
- small engine repair
- solar energy technology
- stenography
- supermarket management
- surveying and mapping

- tailoring
- telecommunications electronics

- ◆ textile design
- ◆ tool and die design
- ◆ toxicology
- ◆ travel personnel training
- ◆ truckdriving
- ◆ turf management
- ◆ typing
- ◆ upholstering

- ◆ veterinarian assisting
- ◆ VCR repair
- ◆ violin making
- ◆ water technologies
- ◆ welding
- ◆ woodworking/cabinetmaking
- ◆ word processing
- ◆ yacht design

Secondary Public Vo-Tech Schools

Most high school districts operate job training programs that are open to adults. These vo-tech programs and courses are designed to provide skills, knowledge, and techniques that prepare you for employment immediately upon leaving school.

A large number of programs operate elaborate skill centers that boast the latest equipment and industrial techniques.

AVTSs are area vocational-technical schools that teach technical skills ranging from "soft" specialties such as floristry, to "hard" technology like electronics. The schools' prime purpose is to deliver vo-tech education in a wide range of occupations to students in the areas' high schools, but most also offer adult education programs at night. Study requirements for these programs range from several weeks to two years.

Comprehensive high schools offer vocational-technical programs in a variety of areas, such as agriculture, technology, marketing, and health technologies education, as well as home economics. Programs vary widely in length, but two years is common.

Technical high schools are found most often in large cities. Their programs, usually lasting three or four years for high school students,

may be condensed to a year or two for adults. Studies tend to be on the technological side, such as computer science and plastics molding, but programs are offered in such traditional trades as cosmetology.

You may have noticed there's an overlapping of skill-learning options among secondary institutions. Don't worry about whether the school is called an AVTS, a comprehensive high school, or a technical high school. If you want vo-tech education at the secondary level, just call the board of education in your community and ask about available opportunities wherever they may be.

Postsecondary Public Vo-Tech Schools

Actor Jack Lemmon says the best advice he ever received was from his father, an executive of a company that manufactures bakery goods. In encouraging Lemmon to follow his heart, his father said: "The day I don't find romance in a loaf of bread, I'm going to quit."

What the father meant was that what you are doing is not as important as loving it.

Loving the idea of practical versus theoretical work is one of the reasons—probably the best reason—that students enroll in the 2,000 postsecondary public institutions across the nation that ready people for jobs.

The institutions offer programs ranging in length from one to four years, most often two years. Typically, they have institutional titles like *technical institutes, vocational-technical institutes, area vocational-technical institutes* and *technical colleges*.

To add a note of confusion, a number of postsecondary public vocational-technical education institutions are known as—are you ready for this?—*community colleges* or *state colleges*.

Some are regionally based, like the Lake Washington Vocational Technical Institute in Kirkland, Wash., serving the northwestern portion of the state, while others are state oriented, like the North Dakota State College of Science at Wahpeton.

By any name or area, public postsecondary vocational-technical schools are designed to provide relevant, effective, and efficient job training at nominal cost to students. A $3,000 course at a private vocational school might cost one-fourth that—or less—at a public vocational school.

Collectively, public institutions offer the full range of occupational programs listed earlier in this section. No school offers all fields any more than all colleges offer all majors. Whether you're interested in business machines or photography, culinary arts or truckdriving, you'll have to look around for schools offering appropriate training programs.

You can ask a school counselor, career center specialist, or reference librarian for the names of vo-tech schools appropriate to your needs. You also can write to the postsecondary education specialist in your state's education department to request a list of vo-tech programs within your state.

Do students ever make education and career selections the other way around—hearing about an excellent vo-tech school and then selecting one of the career fields the school offers? Yes. Sometimes the reverse method of decision making works out, sometimes it doesn't.

Earlier we mentioned that the vast majority of vo-tech programs offer certificates and diplomas, not academic degrees. There are exceptions. Institutions that include a general education component in a program lasting two years or more may award associate degrees similar to those offered by community colleges.

If you are going for training, rather than for retraining, it's wise to consider a program that contains some general education. Technologies die; knowledge remains.

In describing the need for students to be flexible throughout their careers, Larry W. Johnson, a former chief executive officer of the Vocational Industrial Club of America, argues against education that is sliced too thin.

We need to educate our young people broadly enough that they have the ability to cope with changing requirements in the workplace. This means we need to be teaching them not only job skills they can use immediately, we also need to be teaching them to learn—they will need to continue learning all their lives to live in our new world.

Let's look now at a special group of exciting postsecondary public vocational schools—the job colleges we mentioned earlier.

Live-In Job Colleges

A parent writes:

Dear Registrar: Our son, Rob, is the kind who can find 50 uses for a paper clip, has helped his dad build and wire three houses, works on his sports car constantly, and will be captain of the football team his senior year. But he has no interest in four long years in a college. Please rush a brochure on your school to Rob.

The letter is typical of the thousands received each year by the registrar of Oklahoma State University/Okmulgee, the nation's largest residential technical college campus. Housed in an impressive spread of modern buildings, the institution provides a learning experience that places equal importance on educating hand and mind.

OSU/Okmulgee looks and operates much like most state colleges, except that its graduates emerge with immediately marketable skills and are inundated with job offers in such fields as computer-integrated systems service, automotive technology, electronics, air conditioning, visual communications, and other technologies.

The live-in job college, as represented by OSU/Okmulgee, is not a second-best choice for second-best students. On the contrary, it is the very best choice for thousands of very fine students.

OSU/Okmulgee, for example, has a 160-acre, multimillion-dollar campus, more than 4,000 full-time students each year who come not only from Oklahoma, but every other state and several foreign countries, nearly 200 full-time, industry-experienced instructors, many millions of dollars in instructional equipment for student use, and a national reputation for excellence.

Like academic colleges, the school has dorms, clubs, intramural sports, a student union, medical facilities, and other familiar college attractions.

Programs are divided into trimesters and may be completed in two years. Students can enter in early January, mid-April or late August. The programs are open to male and female high school graduates; non-graduates who are at least 17.5 years old are admitted as special students.

All coursework is offered for college credit, and all five- and six-trimester programs lead to the associate in applied science degree.

Costs are equivalent to many state-supported schools; in-state students pay less than $600 tuition a trimester, out-of-state students pay more, but are eligible for tuition waivers under certain conditions.

At OSU/Okmulgee, students can choose from more than 40 career programs. A catalog is available from Oklahoma State University, 1801 E. Fourth St., Okmulgee, OK 74447.

Our research turned up a mere handful of residential vo-tech institutions that, like OSU/Okmulgee, are considered on a par with state colleges where you live on campus and receive comprehensive training in job skills. Here is the list we developed:

North Georgia Vocational-Technical School
Clarkesville, GA 30523

South Georgia Technical Institute
Americus, GA 31709

Ferris State College
Big Rapids, MI 49307

Southeast Community College
Milford, NB 68405

North Dakota State College of Science
Wahpeton, ND 58075

Texas State Technical Institute
Waco, TX 76705

In choosing a public postsecondary vo-tech school, use some of the same guidelines recommended for selecting a proprietary institution. You want to know if the instruction and equipment are up to date, whether the faculty is first-rate, and if there's a demand for the occupational skills you will learn. To find out, query employers, students, graduates, and counselors.

We've never heard anyone speak of vo-tech education in terms of skylarking poetry, presumably because it is, after all, a practical pursuit leading to practical career skills. Remember, though, that in choosing this option, you make a real contribution to others as well as to your own career prospects.

A vision without skills is a dream;
Skills without vision is a grind;
A vision and skills is achievement.

■ ■ ■ ■

The Two-Year College: Opportunity With Excellence

More people are getting more education in our country than at any time in the past, and growing numbers of them are getting it at community, technical, and junior colleges.

Freshman class size has shot up an average of 10 percent at two-year colleges recently, but fallen about 1 percent at four-year colleges. In the last decade and a half, average undergraduate enrollment grew 17 percent at two-year colleges, but only 7 percent at four-year colleges.

Why the disparity? Probably it's the practical, economical, and convenient offerings of community colleges. These factors attract students who want to save money during the first two years of college, or who need to pick up entry-level job skills in a hurry. Where can you join the two-year crowd?

Some 1,200 community colleges have sprung up throughout the United States during the last 35 years, putting one of them within commuting distance of almost every citizen.

Terms, Those Pesky Terms

For convenience, we use the term *community college* to mean all associate-degree-awarding institutions offering programs lasting two years or more, but less than four years, regardless of whether the institution's name includes the title *technical institute*, *technical college*, or *junior college*.

Technical institutes, you'll remember, are included in the previous pages on vocational education because most originated as vo-tech schools. As increasing numbers of technical institutes award associate degrees, rather than diplomas and certificates, they may be classified under the community college banner.

Technical institutes teach many of the same subjects as other vo-tech schools, but the training tends to be more intense, and to require advanced math and scientific theory courses. Graduates are considered technicians and usually have a potentially higher level of responsibility on the job than do graduates of some vo-tech schools. Technical institute programs typically run from one to three years, most often two years.

According to the American Association of Community and Junior Colleges, the term *technical college* refers to an institution that primarily offers associate in science or associate in applied science degrees aimed at employment after graduation. A *junior college* primarily offers associate in arts or associate in science degrees aimed at transfer to a baccalaureate-degree-granting institution after graduation. The term *community college*, in AACJC usage, denotes a comprehensive institution that primarily grants associate degrees in technical (work related) or academic (transfer oriented) areas.

You've figured it out—there are no absolutes in educational terminology.

Each year about six million students, part-time and full-time, teenagers to octogenarians, attend community colleges. They pay an average annual tuition of less than $1,000, a fraction of study costs at four-year colleges and universities. Living at home helps keep the costs down, too, and most community college students do commute to classes.

More than half the students who attend community colleges have a specific purpose: They want to learn job skills that lead to employment in a specific career field. Are you interested in acquiring specific job skills? Depending on the course, you can graduate with a two-year associate degree, or a certificate in a specialty area, which usually is awarded for a program lasting one year or less. In either case, you will be prepared to start working at the technician or paraprofessional level, assisting or reporting to a professional-level worker.

In many states, associate degrees reflecting technical training come in two forms. They are: the associate in applied science (AAS) and the associate in occupational studies (AOS). The AOS generally requires fewer liberal arts courses.

Either the AOS or the AAS may stand alone or may reflect specific studies in the title, such as AAS in computer technology, or AOS in scientific data processing. Other titles used in technically focused programs include associate in business, associate in a specific occupation, and associate in applied arts and sciences.

The choice of skills you can learn is vast, from automotive technology to word processing. Among popular programs are business and management, health occupations, electronics, and police work.

A community college can also teach you advertising, agricultural technologies, art education, drafting and design, recreation and leisure services, wildlife management, and more.

Another large group of students attend community colleges with the plan to switch later to a four-year college. The core programs at community colleges are much like freshman and sophomore programs at four-year institutions and are designed to let you earn transferable credits.

The appropriate degrees for transfer students often are the associate in arts (AA) and associate in science (AS). The AA degree is appropriate to those majoring in the social sciences, humanities, arts, and like subjects. The AS is for students who want to major in engineering, agriculture, or the sciences with heavy undergraduate requirements in math and science.

Whether you have an associate degree in arts or in science, you should be accepted as a junior-level transfer student in baccalaureate degree-granting institutions. Associate in applied science and associate in occupational studies programs are another matter; because the programs are planned as complete units of study, many of the credits you earn in them will not transfer to a four-year college.

If you think you can stand one more perplexing point, hundreds of four-year colleges offer associate degrees. Credits from your associate degree years theoretically should be valid for a bachelor's degree at the same college, but don't take chances—ask about baccalaureate degree requirements in advance of your first day as a freshman.

The community college, being a uniquely American creation, has felt free to invent itself. Instead of fielding a rigid curriculum during working hours on weekdays on a quadrangled campus, the community colleges operate at all hours in all kinds of places, from storefronts and movie theaters to office buildings and modern classrooms. As writer Jeremy Main has said, "Students in search of ivied halls or a boozy fraternity social life won't find them at community college."

What they will find is opportunity with excellent teaching in many colleges. In study after study, students report they experienced the best teaching of their college careers in a community college. If strong teaching matters to you, include community colleges on your list of best bets for education.

To recap, you have many choices in a community college. You can take a couple of courses for personal satisfaction in subjects like scuba diving or gourmet cooking. You can take a two-year academic program that ends with an associate degree or credits that can be transferred to a four-year school. You can enroll in a technical program leading to a certificate or associate degree.

When you've got a caviar taste for knowledge and are on a casserole budget, check out your community college.

■ ■ ■ ■

New Opportunities: Work-Based Learning

Do you know the story of the professor who visits a Japanese Zen master? According to the parable, the wise teacher suspects the professor is set in his ways and may be unable to learn new ways of doing things.

Picking up a pot of tea, the master begins pouring liquid into the professor's cup. He keeps on pouring. Soon the cup is overflowing and spilling out of the saucer onto the table and floor.

"Master," shouts the professor. "What are you doing? My cup is filled to the brim. There is no room for more tea in it."

"Just like your brain," replies the master. "Until you empty your head of old notions, you will have no room for new ideas."

Like the professor in the story, we sometimes lock onto ideas that may be quite wonderful but, as times change, need to be broadened to allow new variations on a theme. New variations on the theme of traditional apprenticeship are beginning to stir throughout the land.

These "new style apprenticeships" offer good futures for students who choose not to follow the college path for four years but who would like to have a skill to be proud of and who want to earn high pay.

From the perspective of a high-school student, the important thing to know about work-based learning is that the *accent is on learning*, rather than on *earning*.

The major reason for the working part is not so that students can earn a few bucks to buy cars or clothing, but to prepare them for jobs that have a future.

Many students who leave high school without job skills wind up in minimum-wage jobs for a decade or more. Work-based learning is an attempt to help students start out in front-line jobs that have career ladders.

From the perspective of employers, the current revival of interest in how front-line workers are prepared for work came about in the last decade. It happened when they noticed that other nations are giving us a run for the money. If we're going to hang onto our standard of living, the United States must staff a complex workplace, one filled with computers and other high-tech equipment.

Students coming out of high school, employers now complain, can't handle the math or basic language needed to compete in world markets. We don't have enough *skilled* workers, employment recruiters say. Too many untrained people—or bozos who have bad attitudes, they complain. This concern is sparking a host of efforts to find better ways not only to help young people become skilled, but to help them make a seamless move from high school into the job market.

Everybody has joined the act—leaders in business, education and government. They started out with the age-old plan of an apprenticeship—the process that allows you to earn while you learn. Then they began giving apprenticeship new faces. Creative minds are producing a new generation of learning/work ideas that are being tried out as you read these words. A very short list of pilot programs illustrates.

What You Can Learn in Community Colleges

Here is a sampling of the programs available in community colleges throughout the nation. Not all schools offer all programs.

- accounting
- advertising
- aerospace sciences
- African studies
- agricultural business
- agronomy
- aircraft maintenance
- American studies
- animal hospital technology
- animal sciences
- anthropology
- archaeology
- architectural technologies
- art/fine arts
- astronomy
- automotive technologies
- aviation administration

- behavioral sciences
- biological sciences
- biomedical technologies
- black studies
- botany
- broadcasting
- business administartion
- business education
- business machine technologies

- carpentry
- cartography
- ceramic art
- chemical engineering technology
- chemistry
- child care studies
- child psychology
- city planning
- civil engineering technology
- communication equipment technology
- community services
- computer information systems

- computer programming
- computer science
- computer science
- computer technologies
- conservation
- construction management
- consumer services
- corrections/prison management
- cosmetology
- court reporting
- creating writing
- criminal justice
- culinary arts
- cytotechnology

- dance
- data processing
- deaf interpreter training
- dental services
- dietetics
- drafting/design
- drama theraphy

- early childhood education
- ecology/environment studies
- economics
- educational media
- electrical/electronics technologies
- electrical engineering technology
- emergency medical technology
- energy management technologies
- English
- environmental health sciences
- ethnic studies
- equestrian studies

- family services
- farm/ranch management
- fashion design
- fashion merchandising

(continued)

- film studies
- finance/banking
- fire science
- fish/game management
- flight training
- food marketing
- food sciences
- food services management
- forensic sciences
- forestry
- French
- funeral services

- geography
- geology
- German
- gerontology
- graphic arts
- Greek

- health education
- heating, refrigeration/air conditioning
- Hebrew
- Hispanic studies
- history
- home economics
- horticulture
- hospitality service
- human services
- humanities

- illustration
- Industrial administration
- industrial arts
- industrial design
- industrial engineering technology
- industrial equipment maintenance
- instrumentation technology
- insurance
- interior design
- Italian

- Japanese
- jewelry/metalsmithing

- journalism

- labor relations
- laboratory technologies
- landscape architecture
- law enforcement
- library science

- marriage counseling
- materials sciences
- mathematics
- mechanical engineering technology
- medical assistant technologies
- medical illustration
- medical laboratory technology
- medical records services
- medical secretarial studies
- metallurgical technology
- meteorology
- Mexican-American studies
- military science
- mining technology
- museum studies
- music

- Native American studies
- natural resource management
- natural sciences
- nuclear medical technology
- nursing
- nutrition

- occupational safety/health
- occupational therapy
- oceanography
- operating room technology
- optometric technologies
- ornamental horiticulture
- painting/drawing
- paper/pulp sciences
- paralegal studies
- parks management
- photography

- physical education
- physical theraphy
- plumbing
- practical nursing
- printing technologies
- public adninystration
- public relations
- publishing

- quality control technology

- radio/TV studies
- radiological technology
- real estate
- recreation/leisure services
- rehabilitation theraphy
- religious studies
- respiratory theraphy
- retail management
- robotics
- Russian

- safety/security technologies
- sanitation technologies
- science education
- sculpture
- secretarial studies
- social work

- soil conservation
- solar technologies
- Spanish
- speech/public address
- sport administration
- sports medicine
- statistics
- surveying technology

- taxation
- technical writing
- telecommunications
- textile arts
- theater arts
- tourism and travel
- transportation technologies

- urban studies

- veterinary sciences
- vocational education

- water resources
- welding
- wildlife management
- women's studies
- wood sciences

- zoology

The German Model

In Germany, apprentices are found not only in major skill trades (such as plumbing and electrical work), but in such service fields as banking, retailing, and food service. Often starting at age 16, apprentices study at a vo-tech school one or two days a week and spend the remainder of time being taught by the employer offering the apprentice contract. In many cases, by age 18, the student is certified as proficient in a given occupation.

European firms with offices in America already are beginning to establish German-style apprenticeship programs.

Company-Specific Apprenticeship Model

In Ft. Wayne, Ind., the Cole Pattern and Engineering Corporation couldn't find the patternmaking people it wanted through area vocational-technical schools so it started its own apprenticeship program to train pattern makers. To operate the apprenticeship-style program, the firm brought in a consultant who tailored company requirements into the paid training program.

The 2 + 2 Model

This program stretches from the junior year of high school through the first two years of course work and job training at a community college. In Oregon, the state works with business and industrial leaders as well as educators to operate 2 + 2 programs in construction and manufacturing—sheet-metal work, welding, and machining, for instance. The programs incorporate the apprenticeship concept.

Apprenticeship-style programs may lead to an associate degree or to a technical certificate in a specific career field or occupation.

These and similar new training ideas are collectively called *work-based learning*. Although the revitalized movement to increase opportunities for American youth to learn by doing is still in the embryonic stage, it already has resulted in the establishment of a new federal agency, the Office of Work-Based Learning, in the U.S. Department of Labor. The Office of Work-Based Learning encourages school systems and companies to create apprenticeship-style programs.

We call them "apprenticeship-style" because these programs in reality are traineeships. But they are based on and expand the essential concept of traditional apprenticeship (described more fully below).

If you are not college-bound, these programs may be coming along in the nick of time to save you from a bleak economic future. Focus on this point:

More than 70 percent of the jobs in America will not require a college education by the year 2000.

Most companies organize work in ways that do not require high skills so that workers do the same narrow tasks over and over. This is not good news. A direct connection exists between skills and pay. High pay goes with high skills. Low pay goes with low skills.

At this point, four-year college graduates are earning almost twice as much as high school graduates.

Moreover, students who do not graduate from a vo-technical school or other training course that grants a certificate or associate degree are thrown haphazardly into the world of

work. Students who know few adults to help them get their first jobs are left to sink or swim.

In the future, programs based on the concept of apprenticeship—those that combine work and learning—will come in all shapes and sizes. Some will be short—a year or so. Others will take a couple of years to complete. Still others will require four or five years of training prior to final certification of competency in specific occupations or career fields.

Because the renaissance of work-based learning is so recent and varied, we can't give you concise directions on how to find a program in your community if your school system doesn't offer one.

But if you are thinking you just want to get away from school—maybe even without a diploma—don't leave without asking your school counselor to help you find a work-based learning program that will help you beat minimum wage pay for many of your young years.

How to Learn and Earn Through Traditional Apprenticeships

As the carpenter said to the yardstick, let's get a couple of things straight up front.

1. In everyday conversation, you may hear someone say he or she is an *apprentice*, when, in fact, the correct term is *trainee*. Being an apprentice means you are enrolled in a formally structured program designed to give you A-to-Z knowledge of a particular occupation.

2. Apprentices are hired by employers, not by labor unions. Some apprenticeship programs are operated by employers and labor unions in partnership, but it's the employer partner who signs the paychecks. Employers run some apprentice programs without the participation of labor unions.

Now that we have these two points squared away, picture yourself with an apprenticeship opportunity.

Apprenticeship programs allow you to earn while you learn. You usually start a job at about 50 percent or more of journeyworkers' pay and move progressively up the wage scale to as much as 95 percent of journeyworkers' pay during your last six months of training. Time frames and percentages differ by occupation and program, but here is a sample wage schedule.

Three-year Apprenticeship Program

1st six months—50% of journeyworkers' wages
2nd six months—60% of journeyworkers' wages
3rd six months—70% of journeyworkers' wages
4th six months—80% of journeyworkers' wages
5th six months—90% of journeyworkers' wages
6th six months—95% of journeyworkers' wages

An apprenticeship combines on-job training under the supervision of certified journeyworkers, plus 144 hours of related technical instruction per year, usually in a classroom setting. The training can be as short as one year or as long as six years, with most trades requiring four to six years.

Apprenticeship programs may be registered with the U.S. Department of Labor's Bureau of Apprenticeship and Training (BAT) or with a federally approved state apprenticeship agency.

Registration is somewhat like accreditation for schools in that it indicates the program meets minimum standards of quality and fair admission practices.

Conditions are spelled out in writing in the apprenticeship agreement. Pay, training, and supervision are all clearly described, along with other particulars of employment. The apprentice and the employer sign the agreement. The employer promises to make every effort to keep the apprentice employed and to comply with standards established for the program; the apprentice promises to work faithfully and to complete the required study. Laws to protect the rights of minority groups are part of the apprenticeship agreement.

Apprentices who complete registered programs receive certificates of completion from the U.S. Department of Labor or a federally approved state apprenticeship agency.

Registered programs offer apprenticeships in more than 830 occupations. New programs include such occupations as electronic imaging systems operator, health care sanitary technician, gas utility worker, and telecommunications technician.

When an employer and a union work together to run a training program, a joint apprenticeship committee is formed to oversee the program's progress. An apprentice who participates in a joint apprenticeship program is accepted for membership in the co-sponsoring union. The vast majority of programs registered with BAT are operated by employers without the participation of a trade union.

What's best—getting into a union apprenticeship or getting a non-union apprenticeship? It depends on where you live and how heavily the state is unionized. The money, benefits, and retirement security are likely to be superior for journeyworkers who are members of trade unions. The opposite side of the coin reflects the preference of many employers to hire less costly non-union journeyworkers whenever they can. If you live in a state without a strong union presence, you'll find more openings without a union card, but the opposite is true in states where organized labor is strong. The question becomes moot where there are few apprenticeship opportunities open—you may want to grab whatever you can get.

Sometimes special opportunities arise to enter apprenticeship, or to get credit for what you know because of linkages with other institutions. You may receive apprenticeship credit for the skills you learn in the military. Some community colleges sponsor programs that award academic credits as well as apprenticeship credits to apprentices. Skills acquired in a vo-tech school can count for apprenticeship credit. High school seniors in many states can apply to participate in school-apprenticeship linkage programs as part-time apprentices, assuming full-time apprentice status after graduation.

Jobs You Can Learn Through Apprenticeship

Registered programs offer apprenticeship in more than 830 occupations. The following list—by no means all-inclusive—indicates the range of jobs. Over half of all apprentices are in construction trades.

- aircraft mechanic
- airframe mechanic
- automobile body repairer
- automobile mechanic
- baker
- biomedical equipment technician
- blacksmith
- bookbinder
- bricklayer
- cabinetmaker
- carpenter
- cement mason
- chemical laboratory technician
- coin machine service repairer
- cook
- cosmetologist
- custom tailor
- dairy equipment repairer
- dental laboratory technician
- drafter, mechanical
- dry cleaner
- electrical repairer
- embalmer
- engraver
- farm equipment mechanic
- firefighter
- floorlayer
- glazier
- instrumentation technician
- jeweler

- laboratory technician
- landscape gardener
- leather stamper
- locksmith
- machinist
- millwright
- model maker
- operating engineer
- optician
- orthotist
- painter
- patternmaker
- photoengraver
- plasterer
- plumber
- prosthetics technician
- roofer
- sheet-metal worker
- shipwright
- sign writer
- silversmith
- stationary engineer
- stonemason
- TV and radio repairer
- tile setter
- tool-and-die maker
- transmission mechanic
- upholsterer
- welding technician
- X-ray equipment tester

Women face unique obstacles to apprenticeship, a traditionally male preserve. Not infrequently they are hassled and harassed. Why are women willing to suffer hostility from earlier settlers in the world of journeyworkers? For the money, of course. As a journeyworker, a woman can earn triple what she gets as an unskilled worker.

Even if you decide apprenticeship is an ideal learning option, it may not be all smooth sailing. The competition for an apprentice opening can be intense. After you take an aptitude test, produce a high school diploma or equivalent, meet an age requirement, pass occupationally essential physical requirements, show acceptable school grades, and come through an interview with flying colors, you may still have to go on a register, or waiting list. The wait on the register can last months or even years.

The flood of qualified applicants for some trades has reached discouraging numbers on many registers of local apprentice programs. Although about 100,000 openings occur across the nation each year, hundreds of thousands of people want them.

Once you're in, you could face unemployment if the sponsoring employer runs out of work temporarily. Beginning apprentices may feel their work is menial or boring, and advanced apprentices may feel their pay is less than what they could earn elsewhere with their skills.

Other than above-average earnings, what's the incentive for the crowds of people who clamor to climb aboard the apprenticeship system? Mastery of a skilled trade sets you apart from other workers, is often satisfying and rewarding, and is a marketable asset.

Apprenticeship bestows versatility by giving you exposure to all aspects of a trade, and transforms you from inexperienced outsider to experienced insider.

A study of construction apprenticeship graduates and other construction workers in six cities concludes that apprenticeship training provides construction workers considerable advantage over those trained by informal means. Apprenticeship grads in the study were more educated, worked more steadily, learned their trades faster, and were more likely to be supervisors than were those who picked up their know-how here and there.

Interestingly enough, the current number of apprentices, about 300,000, has remained steady for the past decade because most new jobs are in the services sector. And most apprentices still are found in construction and skilled trades, such as carpentry, plumbing, bricklaying, and cabinetmaking.

Another reason traditional apprenticeship has not grown is because in America, people who do manual labor aren't looked up to as much as people in white-collar and managerial jobs.

That's too bad. Skilled workers can earn large incomes in certain jobs and even larger incomes if they open their own contracting companies.

It is said that "learning is better worth than house or land." If so, apprenticeship is especially valuable, because you get paid while you're learning.

The formal apprenticeship gets an A in our grading system.

Where To Go For Help

1. *Your School.* Look for information in your school library, guidance office, career center, or vo-tech department.

2. *Public Employment Service or Job Service.* Ask about local apprenticeship programs and any available literature.

3. *Bureau of Apprenticeship and Training.* There are BAT offices in every state. If you can't find one in your city (look in the telephone book under U.S. Government, Department of Labor), ask at a library or public employment service

office. If you're still stuck for information, contact the headquarters office: Bureau of Apprenticeship and Training, U.S. Department of Labor, 200 Constitution Ave. NW, Washington, DC 20210.

4. *State Apprenticeship Agencies.* Offices are located in about half the states, the District of Columbia, and Puerto Rico. A BAT office can tell you if there is one for your state.

5. *Labor Unions.* If you are interested in a particular trade, contact the union to see if there is a joint apprenticeship committee in the trade that reviews applications for apprenticeships and interviews applicants.

■ ■ ■ ■

Education and Training: Employer Style

OJT is the Number One source of training for obtaining jobs and improving skills. OJT is the *on-job training* you obtain by working. It's like the young bank officer who rushed into his supervisor's office, and sputtered in desperation:

"I have lent a foxy businessman $100,000 and he has not given me a receipt. What can I do?"

"Something like that happened to me once," his boss nodded in sympathy. "Here's what to do. Write and firmly demand a receipt for $200,000."

"I guess you didn't hear me," objected the troubled bank officer. "I told you it was only $100,000."

"I know," agreed the boss, "and your borrower will indignantly write and tell you so. Then you will have your receipt."

When experienced supervisors and co-workers share know-how with newcomers, that's

OJT! They teach individuals with lesser experience how to do things. They explain the tricks of the trade and the best way to handle the job. Many people are surprised to find that OJT is the most common source of training for qualifying skills to get a job, and for improving skills to move up in the ranks. The U.S. Department of Labor says OJT dominance is a fact.

Not wanting to be a passenger in an airliner where the pilot is learning to fly, you understand that some jobs lend themselves more readily than others to OJT; see the accompanying list of occupations commonly learned on the job.

Jobs You Can Learn on the Job

Here are some of the most popular occupations you may be able to enter without prior training.

auto mechanic
bookkeeper
busdriver
carpenter
cashier
computer operator
cook
electrician
insurance sales worker
machine operator
machinist
nursing aide and orderly
plumber
police officer
production supervisor
secretary
telephone installer
truckdriver
typist
waiter and waitress
welder

Employer training programs come in many stripes.

◆ The job training may be informal, where you pick up knowledge as best you can. It may come in a formal package, inside the workplace or at a school.

◆ The training may be *qualifying*—the type you need to do the job. It may be *skills improvement*—what you need to move up in the ranks.

◆ Some courses may carry no academic credit, or may carry academic credit for a bachelor's, master's, or doctoral degree. Some employer-sponsored training earns continuing education units, or CEUs. Basically, one CEU is awarded for every 10 classroom hours of participation in systematic, supervised learning. In the job market, it's helpful to have your course work summed up in CEU terms.

Business Educates Workers

American business spends an estimated $60 billion each year to train workers, slightly more than one-third the amount spent by all colleges and universities. Some of the money goes to cooperating colleges. Sometimes the training is comprehensive, such as the previous example of the Cole Pattern & Engineering Corporation's patternmaking apprenticeship program.

Most typically, business education funds are spent inside the companies themselves on courses tailored to build specific skills companies need.

High school equivalent courses for employees include such basics as arithmetic, effective listening, grammar-spelling-punctuation, statistical typing, letter- and report-writing skills for technical staff, algebra, effective reading, and English for the foreign educated.

Management and executive courses usually fit into four categories: managing people, time, money, or production and operations. Student workers learn how to motivate employees who don't want to be motivated; how to manage time and get the important tasks done; how to handle the old bugaboo, budgeting; and how to keep the executive's operation profitable. Courses may be taught in-house, or executives may travel to executive seminars, sometimes located in beautiful conference centers in scenic places like Aspen, Colorado, and Harper's Ferry, West Virginia. Some companies work directly with universities to custom design courses for their employees.

Some companies buy prepackaged programs. Others create their own.

Postsecondary formal corporate education has become so sophisticated that a few businesses and professional associations have set up institutions accredited to award the bachelor's, master's, and doctoral degrees once viewed as the sole prerogative of traditional universities.

The degree-granting institutions spawned as an effort to train employees or upgrade their skills commonly are called *corporate colleges*.

Examples include the RAND Graduate School operated by the RAND Corporation in Santa Monica, California, the College of Insurance in New York City, and National Technological University (NTU is described more fully later in this section under "Telecourses and Beyond.")

Many of these companies are not aiming to replace traditional institutions of learning, but to continue education where the schools leave off.

■ ■ ■ ■

Career Training in the Armed Forces

If your values do not conflict with military service, the excellent and free career training you get in the Armed Forces might be the way to go.

But make no mistake, when you join Uncle Sam's Armed Forces, you are first a defender of your country, and secondarily a government employee perfecting career skills.

The families of some servicemembers apparently were surprised when their loved ones were called to arms during the Gulf War. When you join a military service you are obligated to carry out military operations as directed by the chain of command, at the top of which is the commander-in-chief, the President of the United States.

If you do not want to risk finding yourself in combat boots, don't join the military no matter how attractive the career options.

Even in peacetime, you face long periods away from your family and friends. You follow orders with no backtalk. You go to boot camp, where you run miles with a full backpack, crawl through slimy mud, wade through icy streams, and, in general, show that you can take the physical stress of battle training.

Other than that, military life provides you with room, board, paycheck, and training that can be superb, simply superb.

It begins with basic fitness and the military regime. After that, you begin learning the skills and acquiring the knowledge you need to do your assigned job. You study in classrooms and on the job in programs that last from a few weeks to more than a year, depending on the skills needed for the occupation.

You'll probably receive additional training as you move on to new responsibilities. Whatever you study, you can be assured you are the beneficiary of state-of-the-art training. Each military service spends hundreds of millions of dollars making sure personnel get the best instruction.

Armed Forces ABCs

The Army, Navy, Air Force, and Marines are part of the U.S. Department of Defense.

The Coast Guard is part of the Department of Transportation.

During time of war, the Coast Guard may be placed under command of the Navy—within the Department of Defense.

All five services offer employment and training opportunities. But not all services offer every kind of occupational training. Determine if the service you prefer offers the job training of your choice.

About three military jobs in four relate to a similar job in civilian life. The fourth job is specifically combat-related.

You'll be given a duty assignment—a job—when you finish your training. All services make an effort to fulfill the enlistment contract, but understand clearly that you may not get the job or the place you want. As in the civilian world, you may or may not get the job, even when there is an opening, if someone else has better qualifications. Further, your test scores and educational history will be used in determining whether you are suited for a particular opening.

Test scores? You'll have to take an aptitude test—the Armed Services Vocational Aptitude Battery, or ASVAB for short—that classifies you according to the career areas for which you qualify.

Here's a key point: *You don't have to enlist until you find out which occupational training programs you may be assigned to.* If you're not happy with the fields that are available to you by virtue of your ASVAB scores, don't join the service.

Remember, though, there are *no guarantees.* Even if your ASVAB scores qualify you for the training program of your choice, there are *no assurances* that an opening will occur at the time you need it.

It's true that most military service slots can equip you with transferable *employability* skills—such as self-discipline, perseverance, and development of leadership traits—that are useful in most jobs.

But our advocacy is based on the opportunities for career training. That's why we recommend you try for a job that has a civilian counterpart. The only transferable technical skill you acquire as a tank driver is the ability to steer a float in the Rose Bowl Parade. By contrast, the technical experience you acquire as a military air traffic controller rolls over into a civilian air traffic controller's position.

Beyond getting you ready to do the job, the training you receive in the military may count toward academic credit at a civilian college. Each college makes its own decision, but the American Council on Education has recommended that about 10,000 military courses be considered for conversion to academic credit.

Navy Recruiting Goes Online

The U.S. Navy Recruiting Command has an Internet site on the World Wide Web. Although the Navy has been present on the Web since 1989, the new recruiting home page incorporates a more sophisticated level of content, multimedia, and interactivity.

The purpose of the Navy Web site is to provide Web users with the chance to learn more about the many job opportunities offered by today's Navy. The site can be accessed at (http://www.navyjobs.com).

Once in the site, users can browse through a number of selected topics, including "Jobs in the Fleet," "Medical Jobs," "Money for College," "Worldwide Travel," and "Benefits." In addition to providing comprehensive information on each topic, the site offers a catalog of downloadable photos of Navy hardware. Additional information can be received by filling out an electronic business reply card.

Use a Web search engine to find Web sites for the other branches of the armed services.

A Sampling of Enlisted Military Jobs

Each year the five Armed Forces hire tens of thousands of of young men and women. High school graduates are preferred. Collectively the services offer training and jobs in hundreds of military occupations. We clustered selected occupations into the 12 groups listed below with samples of the civilian-related jobs found in each.

Administrative
court reporter
computer operator

Construction
building electrician
plumber and pipefitter

Electronic and Electrical
aircraft electrician
data processing equipment repairer

Engineering, Science, Technical
air traffic controller
computer systems analyst

Health Care
operating room technician
physical therapy specialist

Human Services
caseworker and counselor
recreation specialist

Machine Operation and Precision Work
printing specialist
water and sewage treatment plant operator

Media and Public Affairs
graphic designer and illustrator
TV camera operator

Personal/Public Service
firefighter
detective

Transportation and Materials Handling
flight engineer
truckdriver

Vehicle and Machinery Mechanics
automotive body repairer
office machine repairer

*Combat Specialty**
artillery crew member
tank crew member

The Officer Route

You can become a military officer in a number of ways. One is by graduation from one of the four service academies described in section 12.

You can also consider preparation through an ROTC program.

If you are a senior in high school—or are already in college—and know you want to enter the military as an officer, you may be eligible to receive financial assistance while still in school. Scholarships are offered through Reserve Officers Training Corps programs to cover tuition, fees and books. Campus ROTC officers can give you the particulars.

Another route to becoming an officer is graduation from an officer candidate school (OCS) operated by the military service you select. People enter an OCS in various ways. Briefly stated, you may be able to enter an OCS directly as a college graduate. Even if you do not have a college degree, you may qualify for an OCS after

*For jobs in this category, there are no matching jobs in civilian work life.

you gain experience in the enlisted ranks and pass an OCS exam.

Once commissioned as an officer, the outstanding training will continue. The courses you attend are determined by your assignment.

Off-Duty Study Bonanza

Education is the "golden handcuffs" of the military services. No other employer can match the educational fringe benefits they offer.

Here's an example of how you could cut college costs by enlisting to serve on active duty for three or four years: Take college courses during off-duty hours. The military may pay 75 percent of tuition costs. Make sure all the courses will transfer to a four-year college degree program. Accumulate college funds through the G.I. Bill. At discharge you may have credit for two years of college and a tuition fund of about $9,000 to help pay for the last two years of college. Get a job during your last two years and you'll graduate debt free. Yes, you'll be two years or so older than the traditional college student, but you'll have greater maturity and work experience— two attributes employers prize.

The variations of military educational benefits are beyond the scope of this book, but recruiting officers will be tickled red, white, and blue to tell you all you want to know. Start with the Army—it has the most generous education benefits.

■ ■ ■ ■

Distance Learning

It seems almost too marvelous. Students are sitting in their kitchens and living rooms and basements going to vo-tech school or college.

But that's what's happening as educational technology crosses a threshold to a new generation. Rather than transport people to information, technology is transporting information to people.

Distances—sometimes thousands of miles—between teachers and students are being bridged with both familiar methods (printed and recorded material sent through the postal service) and fantastic new delivery systems parented by cross-continental television and computer networks.

What makes today's distance learning different from earlier attempts is interactive capacity.

Now learners and teachers can talk back and forth, ask questions, clarify points, and evaluate how well students are learning.

Distance learning in elementary and high school classrooms has increased dramatically over the past few years according to Dr. Mel Chastain, director of the Educational Communications Center at Kansas State University, Manhattan. But for purposes of career preparation, we'll focus on college by electronics (computer networks), telecourses (television), and adult home study.

The new technology sometimes overlaps. Written course material may be sent by fax machine rather than the postal service. Video cassettes may be combined with computer networks. Telecourses may be configured with audio cassettes. The mix is exciting.

College by Electronics

Computer services now bring college education to the comfort of your own home or workplace. Instead of hauling yourself to class every morning or evening, you need traipse only as far as your computer.

The Internet's success has spawned an explosion in online studies. Two outstanding books explaining online study and identifying institutions that offer it are *The Virtual University*, by Pam Dixon, and *The Electronic University*, by the National University Continuing Education Association. Both are published by Peterson's.

Telecourses and Points Beyond

Educational Telecommunications—ET—creates glorious learning opportunities not bound by time and space. A leading ET player, the Public Broadcasting Service's Adult Learning Service, built on the efforts of pioneer educational television broadcasters and began demonstrating ET's technological potential in 1981. ALS distributes more than 45 different telecourses produced by academic experts, colleges and universities, instructional designers, and experienced producers. Already ALS productions are a smash hit for the more than 260,000 tuition-paying students who watch each year.

ALS telecourses—often as visually lush as a major motion picture—instruct students in topics of wide appeal: *Eyes On the Prize*, *Computer-Works*, *Economics USA*, *The Civil War*, and many more. Each course includes integrated video and print materials (texts and study guides), and sometimes audio and computer components.

Colleges and universities work with their public television stations to broadcast courses in many fields of learning. If you want to earn college credit through television viewing, enroll in a local college, pay tuition, study under the guidance of an instructor, probably attend several class meetings, communicate more frequently with the instructor by phone, watch the programs at home or at work, read the print material, complete assignments and exams, and receive grades.

The easiest way to find out what's available locally is to call the education/adult learning department of the public television station and ask which telecourses will be offered for the coming semester and which colleges/universities are participating.

If the idea of becoming a "multimedia megalearner" is appealing, give a wave to The Annenberg/CPB Project. It was created in 1981 by a gift of $150 million from The Annenberg School of Communications to the Corporation for Public Broadcasting to develop college-level instructional materials and to demonstrate the power of technology applied to higher education.

Going beyond quality-rich telecourses, The Annenberg/CPB Project funds educational innovations that can make it easier for students learning via television to communicate with professors and even with other students.

Among the innovations are an awesome array of electronic aids that can be fused with various telecourses. You might say it's a case of "electrolearning meets teleteaching." The goal is to make learning interactive—a two-way street—as it is in the best classrooms. Examples of electrolearning aids are videodiscs and electronic mail, as well as computer simulations, networking, and conferencing.

Non-traditional students—over 25 and often employed while going to school—now make up about 40 percent of all college enrollments.

Their need for flexible educational scheduling to accommodate busy lives suggests a growing reliance on educational telecommunications. A variation of telecourses is the opportunity to earn a master's degree in one of seven programs at National Technological University in Fort Collins, Colorado.

NTU began in 1984. It has no ivy-covered walls. In fact, it doesn't have walls. Its classroom basically is the facility beaming out courses 24 hours a day, six and one-half days a week to employees of participating companies, government agencies, and other organizations that hire technical people.

Some students view the video presentations on company hours, while others tune in on their own time. In most cases, the employer pays the costs. Students respond by computer conferencing, E-mail (computer mail), fax machines, the telephone, and the postal service.

Examinations are proctored on the work sites. Two or three years of study are required to qualify for a master's degree in materials science/engineering, management of technology, computer science, computer engineering, electrical engineering, engineering management, and manufacturing systems engineering.

Even without ivy, NTU now has 1,100 master's students and is one of the fastest growing graduate institutions in America.

Can any ambitious engineer sign up? No. The unique requirement is that applicants must be sponsored by their employers.

Prediction: The decade of the 1990s could mark the emergence of telelearning as an important force in the changing educational order.

The recession of the early 1990s caused millions of working adults to live in fear of future layoffs. While they still may have their well-paying jobs, many will prepare for a rainy day by acquiring new educational credentials at night and on weekends. For a large number of adult students, the answer will be telelearning and online learning.

Home Study Schools: You Ring the Classroom Bell

Captain Patricia A. Brown is a Florida Army National Guard helicopter pilot who successfully navigated through required communications electronics courses, thanks to correspondence study programs. Louisiana insurance executive James Moye III earned his professional credential, the prestigious Chartered Life Underwriter, with knowledge acquired in a home study program.

Why does home study appeal to Brown and Moye? Why might it appeal to you? Control and convenience are two cardinal reasons.

When you learn at a distance from the campus, you learn at your own pace in your own home. You determine the time when you will use textbooks, workbooks, audiotapes, videotapes, exercises, projects, and the other materials supplied by the institution. You determine when you will complete and return lesson assignments for grading and credit by the institution's faculty. Within reasonable limits, you control the clock and you control the calendar of when and how fast you learn.

As Pat Brown says, "I feel that correspondence courses have greatly helped my educational efforts. I always keep a course segment in my car, one in my briefcase, and one in my flight bag. You never know when the opportunity will present itself to enrich your education."

Home study is different from self-study in that you receive responses from a faculty member who provides information, advice, and explanations of points that aren't immediately clear to you. You can write or telephone your instructor to receive answers to your questions.

The range of courses available is similar to an exotic bazaar teeming with colorful items, heady fragrances, and interesting activities. In the more than 2,000 courses offered through correspondence schools, some are not available at most conventional institutions—diamond grading, doll repair, yacht design, catering management, exercise studio management, and outdoor sporting goods repair.

Are home study courses really helpful in starting a career such as income tax counseling or business management? While we don't advocate learning brain surgery by mail, home study can be a highly desirable way to acquire skills for many kinds of business, trade, and industry occupations. In a study of 1,800 correspondence school graduates, 54 percent said they won jobs related to their courses, and when asked if they would take a correspondence school course again, 85 percent said "yes."

Every major research study on correspondence education in the past half century has shown that home study students achieve and perform as well as, if not better than, resident-trained students who studied the same subject. How can this be? Various reasons are suggested, ranging from greater personal discipline to selection of courses by home study students in which they have a special interest and aptitude.

Despite the fact that home study does work, how do employers feel about skills you acquire in this manner? No definitive studies probe employer attitudes, but the proliferation of correspondence courses by colleges and universities, corporations, labor unions, professional groups, and government agencies suggests a wider acceptance that the point is what one knows—not where or how one learned it.

A U.S. Navy study says the cost of home study is 10 percent to 25 percent of the cost of resident systems. Home study courses, running from four weeks to four years, range in price from about $300 for a basic electronics course to $3,400 for a travel career course.

Can you get college credit, or even degrees by mail? Yes, although most degrees available exclusively through home study are associate degrees; baccalaureate degrees more often are awarded through the broader concept of external degrees, discussed later in this section.

More than three million people enroll in correspondence courses each year. Since 1900, approximately 80 million Americans have taken courses by mail, including U.S. President Franklin D. Roosevelt, "Peanuts" cartoonist Charles Schulz, and newscaster Walter Cronkite.

Home study can be a fine way to learn, but this method isn't for everyone. Ask yourself these questions:

◆ Do I have strong motivation in whatever I do?

◆ Do I learn most easily by reading and trying to understand by myself?

◆ Do I have an excellent ability to concentrate?

◆ When working by myself, can I set up and follow my own schedule?

◆ Do I have a quiet place at home where I can read?

◆ Am I able to understand most subjects that interest me?

◆ Do I prefer to learn things on my own?

It your answers are "yes," you probably would be a successful home study student. If you decide there's a school in your mailbox, match your needs with the right institution.

How to Select a Home Study School

1. Write to schools that teach the subject you want to study and ask for catalogs and brochures. Examine them closely. Be certain you understand exactly what you are buying. Compare learning objectives, subjects taught, length of the course, materials provided, tuition, and various services.

2. Many excellent schools are not accredited, but the single best assurance of product reliability is accreditation. The Accrediting Commission of the Distance Education and Training Council, recognized by the U.S. Department of Education, accredits home study schools. This organization checks to see if a school advertises truthfully, has a quality staff and a sound curriculum, and shows evidence of student success.

   All of the colleges and universities offering correspondence study that are members of the National University Continuing Education Association are accredited appropriately.

3. Evaluate the institution's refund policy. Accredited institutions offering correspondence

courses have a liberal refund policy. Understand your obligations when you sign the enrollment contract.

4. Get an estimate of how long it takes for the course to be completed by a typical student. Before you enroll, decide how much time you're willing to devote.

5. For vocational courses, find out if the training really qualifies you for the job you want. Contact employers who hire in the industry for which you are preparing. Would they recognize training from specific home study schools? Ask if they would hire someone who acquired their skills in a correspondence school.

6. Make sure that the school is properly licensed. The state department of education where the school is located will know whether the school complies with appropriate laws and regulations. Check the school's reputation through your area's better business bureau.

7. If you're taking the course to transfer credits to a local college or to an external degree program, check with the registrar (and/or the head of the department that includes your chosen major) at the degree-granting institution to be sure it will accept the credits and that the credits will apply toward the specific degree you seek. College policies on acceptance of credits differ.

How to Find a Home Study School

Two guides will help you locate home study courses.

◆ The *Directory of Accredited Home Study Schools* is available free from the Distance Education and Training Council, 1601 18th St. NW Washington, DC 20009.

◆ *The Independent Study Catalog* is updated every few years by Peterson's, Box 2123, Princeton, NJ 08543. The book lists 10,000 distance education courses offered by the 70-plus colleges and universities that are members of the National University Continuing Education Association.

Examples of new courses (from the University of California Extension) are *hazardous materials management, artificial neural networks, second-year Chinese, community responses to alcohol and other drug problems,* and *mathematics for electronics.*

■ ■ ■ ■

More Avenues of Education

Educana strikes us as a word the language needs. Were there such a word, it would mean the seemingly endless variations of learning opportunities inherent in education. The ones we've mentioned thus far, from colleges to employee training programs, are the options most likely to be chosen by large numbers of young adults.

Countless other learning options exist in educana, many of which are used more often by adults in the work force than by young people starting out. Here are some of them.

External and Non-Traditional Degrees

Higher education used to be *four-square and five-five.* Society chiefly recognized the kind that takes place in colleges with four walls and two five-month semesters.

All that changed in the early 1970s when college lecture halls began spinning off brightly colored pinwheels of fresh ideas. The innovations whirl from conducting college classes on commuter trains to academic credit for life experience learning. For simplicity, the new ideas can be described as *external degree programs* or *non-traditional degree programs,* and their similarities stand out more than do their differences.

Both types of programs require little, or even none, of your three-dimensional presence on campus to obtain credits toward a degree. In fact, there may not be a campus, only an administrative office. There is one major difference: Institutions that offer external degrees usually provide instruction for off-campus learning, while institutions that offer non-traditional degrees may accept credits from a variety of unrelated sources.

Degree requirements can be met through a combination of proficiency exams, college course work, military service schools, courses sponsored by professional societies, and home study, to mention only a few of the vibrant vanes in the pinwheel of innovative ideas. Be certain to select an accredited institution if you pursue an external or non-traditional degree program.

One of the nation's top authorities on this type of study is Dr. John Bear who tells all in *College Degrees by Mail* (Ten Speed Press).

Another reference is Eugene Sullivan's *The Adult Student's Guide to Alternative and External Degree Programs* (American Council on Education, One Dupont Circle, Washington, DC 20036).

Continuing Education

In the context of careers, continuing education is learning that prepares you for entry into new fields or for advancement in present fields. Continuing education takes place in many of the settings noted in this section and it covers the gamut of career interests.

Two types of credit are available in continuing education. *Certificate/degree credit* is used as a measure of terminal programs for which formal credit may be awarded. If you complete the program, you receive either a certificate or an academic degree in the discipline you studied.

CEU *(continuing education unit) credit* is, as mentioned earlier, a nationally recognized, standard unit of measurement awarded by colleges and other institutions for participation in qualified continuing education programs. It also is a means by which professional organizations measure and keep track of required continuing education of their members. Upon completion of a program, you might receive two CEUs, for example. CEUs do not lead to a certificate or academic degree, but you might obtain a transcript of your CEU credits. Some professional associations record members' CEU credits in the ACT National Registry Service, a continuing education record-keeping service operated by the American College Testing Program. A number of colleges and other accredited institutions also use the ACT National Registry Service.

Tip: Programs that award neither a certificate or degree nor CEU credit will do little to romance your resume in the job market. That's because employers want to know—in measurable terms—your educational qualifications. Take a non-credit course for pleasure or professional improvement, if you wish, but don't expect it to enhance your marketability.

Adult Education Programs

The teaching of adults didn't begin yesterday. Aristotle, Plato, Socrates, and the other great historical teachers taught adults, not children. The lessons of the ancient teachers spread ideas and values. Now, in industrialized nations, a renaissance of lifelong learning has sent adults scurrying for training. Many people choose the learning options offered through evening programs at high schools, vo-tech institutions or community colleges. Libraries often compile listings of local educational offerings.

P.S. The term *adult education* usually refers to basic and secondary education; on the other hand, *continuing education* usually refers to post-secondary education.

College/University Extension Centers

Most colleges and universities have both day and evening classes or divisions. College/university extension centers may provide courses outside the main campus.

A laudable example is Purdue University's statewide technology program, given in a number of Indiana communities apart from the main and regional campuses. It is designed to aid adults who feel their jobs are becoming obsolete, who want to upgrade skills, or who want to assume a leadership role without giving up their jobs to move to a college town. The program offers an associate or bachelor's degree in specific technologies, such as electrical, computer-integrated manufacturing, industrial, and mechanical. This ultra-extension center approach provides valuable and tangible help to workers whose jobs are sliding into history.

Extension centers often reach out to the adult market, establishing programs in community centers, storefronts, libraries, and school buildings that have been closed.

In considering flexplace education, be alert to a number of factors. Will up-to-date instructional aids and equipment be on hand? Is parking adequate and safe? Can the required books be purchased at the extension center? Do library facilities exist?

When centers are operated by a high-quality institution like Purdue, they can be passports to better jobs. But be certain you get all the facts. Some students are disappointed to find that their extension center gives them inferior instruction for only part of a curriculum, the rest of which must be taken on the main campus several states away.

Professional Societies

Membership organizations are an important part of educana. The Air Pollution Control Association offers correspondence instruction for professionals in the field. The American Institute of Chemists sponsors lectures and symposia for members. The American Federation of Police offers conferences, courses, and seminars to police officers. The American Society of Pension Actuaries holds workshops for members at various locations. The Society of Real Estate Appraisers fields a full schedule of conferences, courses, seminars, and workshops for those who assess land and building values. These examples illustrate the incredible variety of training available from peers once you've entered a career field.

Other Places to Learn

The treasures of educana go on and on:

◆ *Seminars.* Short programs are offered in every community to help adults enhance their job knowledge or skills. They may be sponsored by trade associations, professional societies, universities, profit-making companies, or other entities. At least two companies help seminar users locate, compare, and select appropriate offerings of professional education opportunities across the country: Seminar Clearinghouse International (P.O. Box 1757,

St. Paul, MN 55101-0757) and The First Seminar Services (600 Suffolk Street, Lowell, MA 01854).

◆ *Summer Institutes.* Many colleges and universities offer special short-term summer institutes that focus on topics ranging from the University of Denver's renowned Publishing Institute to the University of Chicago's wide variety of summer workshops for professionals in social work and other helping fields. Locate them through professional or trade associations.

◆ *Public Libraries, City Recreation Departments, Churches, Synagogues, Community Centers, Y's, Museums.* With a telephone call, you can find out about the special classes or courses these institutions offer. Newspapers and radio and television stations report educational offerings.

After seeing much of what's available in educana, you'll have to agree—if you want to learn, there's no shortage of opportunities.

■ ■ ■ ■

Ways to Make Good Decisions

Having a clear purpose in mind makes it easier to select the right training. If you're muddled, try writing down your reasons for seeking studies and course work.

Choose a program that meets your needs. Maybe you need college. Maybe you need a vocational-technical program. Maybe the training you need is available through employer-sponsored schooling. If the occupation you're considering requires licensure, such as nursing or architecture, find out from its professional organization what kind of program would be best.

Compare the job market outcomes for those who approach an occupation in different ways. For instance, you may find that a private vocational school is so superior that it's worth every dime, or you may find it makes little difference which program—private or public—you attend as far as employability is concerned.

Most important, don't make the poor decision of thinking you can bumble your way through high school and catch up later in advanced technology such as robotics. If you can't read and you can't do math, you can't make it in the emerging workplace.

One final thought: Never give up trying to learn in some way. Unlike stupidity, ignorance is curable.

■ ■ ■ ■

Looking For Your First Full-Time Job

Like learning to dance or to drive or to cook, learning to find a good full-time job is a specific area of knowledge you must master. This know-how is especially important for new graduates, including any:

◆ College graduate

◆ Vocational graduate

◆ High school graduate

◆ Military service graduate.

The following chapter discusses the basics of what you must know to become an expert job seeker. It examines the job search skills you need, building on insights you acquired about student jobs in Chapter 11. As a student, you did not need to learn the complex or subtle concepts of a successful job search. Now you do.

Your First Full-Time Job: The Art of Getting Hired

Just as you learned the complexities of freshman English composition, you can learn the nuances of job search skills. A sterling performance in school is rewarded with grades. In the job hunt market, it's rewarded with dollars.

Learning to market yourself now will pay off handsomely throughout your career. Here are several reasons why:

1. Expert job seekers often snare the best jobs, beating out competitors who may actually have superior technical skills. This is because expert job seekers know the mechanics of making good contacts, and they know how to present themselves in the best possible light. Individuals who have only technical skills and little job search savvy may not be in the right place at the right time, or if they are, may not know the right things to say.

2. Expert job seekers are confident of their ability to reach out for a more important position. They are not glued to a job merely because they do not know how to find another. On the contrary, they have mobility. Possessing job search skills is like owning a car: You can travel further when you have wheels.

3. Expert job seekers are their own best unemployment insurance policies. Should sudden joblessness strike, they don't go to pieces—they go out and find another position as good as or better than the one that folded.

Even in a good economy, finding that first job can be tough. As one young man who graduated from California State University at San Francisco with a degree in marketing says, "No one can be sure of getting a job anymore, but getting depressed and giving up is the worst thing you can do."

If experience is a problem, joining a temporary employment agency may be a solution. Temp agencies send you on short-term assignments, which may allow you to get a feel for what really happens inside a business. Temp agencies are a good idea for those who are not sure about what they want to do, because they give you a chance to get a sense of different industries.

By choosing to become an expert job seeker, you gain a clear understanding of job search skills.

■ ■ ■ ■

Three Broad Categories of Job Search Skills

While there are many ways to view these skills, they can be grouped into three broad categories:

1. Knowing *what you have to sell*, which means self-assessment reflected in resumes

2. Knowing *where to make the sale*, which means job market strategies and sources.

3. Knowing *how to make the sale*, which means job interviewing and follow-up.

What follows is a streamlined course on getting hired. The information is organized into the three broad categories we just described.

Take control of your career by becoming an expert job seeker.

■ ■ ■ ■

Knowing What You Have to Sell

Think of yourself as a product. You have special features—particularly skills—that people are willing to pay money to acquire.

Are You Who Your Resume Says You Are?

Now it can be told. When we discussed the techniques of composing a resume for student jobs in Chapter 11, we may have gone into more detail than you needed.

We confess we had ulterior motives. For the same reason that champion athletes begin their training young, we wanted you to get a head start in thinking about your strengths and how to verbalize them.

We wanted you to form the habit of thinking about your accomplishments in the measurable terms that impress employers.

We wanted you to become comfortable thinking about how to create a paper document that reflects the very best you.

Look again at the principles explained in Chapter 11. Building on that foundation, you can create new resumes reflecting your growth and maturity.

Examples can be instructive. Two follow on the next two pages. The first is incredibly weak, the second is powerful.

A Losing Resume

The resume on the next page was sent to one of the authors. The writer's name and certain facts have been changed to protect the job hunter's identity. The young man who wrote this resume said he had "not had very good luck finding a job using my education." Why do you think he's having problems? Would you invite him for an interview?

A Powerful Resume

By contrast, the hypothetical resume on page 359 is a powerful advertisement of a young man's qualifications. In fact, the resume's creator, Richard Lathrop, prefers to call it a *qualifications brief*—to focus attention on the need to stress your qualifications for the job. It is adapted from Lathrop's outstanding book, *Who's Hiring Who* (Ten Speed Press).

Special Tips for New Graduates

◆ Don't date your resume. If you don't find a job quickly, a dated resume will make you look as though nobody wants to hire you—as though you are a leftover.

◆ You'll be using your resume to line up job interviews. Target it to the person who has the power to hire you. Usually that's the head of the department where you want to work. But new graduates often enter through the doors of the director of college relations or another manager in the company's human resources (personnel) department. Research!

◆ As a new graduate, your education counts more than your work experience. List it first, after your objective.

Write the name of your educational institution; the type of degree, diploma, or certificate you received; the date of your graduation; and courses relevant to the type of work you want.

ROBERT J. GLUM

2626 Memory Lane, Highpoint, Florida 78787
101/884-1818

Education:	Bachelor of Science in Mathematics (with a minor in Economics), from South State College, South Fork, Florida, December 1991.
Career Objective:	To find a challenging position in which I can use my education and work experience.
Work Experience:	February 1992 to August 1992—Computer Operator at Haig Foodservice in South Attleboro, Mass. February 1993 to August 1994—Computer Operator at Happy Farmer Corporation in Bedford, Mass. December 1994 to Present—Assistant Manager for Tastee Fried Chicken Corporation, Framingham, Mass.
Work Skills:	Extensive knowledge of the Hewlett-Packard 3000 Series III Computer System
Programming Courses Taken:	Basic I, II Fortran I, II Cobol I, II Statistical Packages—SPSS, BMPD
Hobbies:	Participate in most sports, especially basketball and golf.

References/Placement Papers will be furnished upon request from South State College Placement Office in South Fork, FL.

JOHN BROWN

2923 Clink Street, Ajax, Washington 92361
206/555-5777

Objective	EDITORIAL, MANAGEMENT OR RESEARCH ASSISTANT in an organization concerned with public affairs—especially where analytical approach, broad writing ability and a major in human factors are needed to assure strong development of articles, studies, or programs.
Education	Bachelor of Arts, University of Washington, Seattle, 1995. Major: history and government. English minor. Edited campus newspaper. Swim team captain. Graduated in top 10 percent. Earned all expenses.
	Served as clerk with the Gulf, Colorado & Santa Fe Railroad. Handled all routine functions of a RR disbursing office—office machine operation, voucher recording, routing. (Summer, 1994)
Analysis of office experience	PRIMARY GAIN: Obtained practical experience in handling large volumes of routine office work. Observed factors that contribute to high operating costs and resistance to improved methods. Chief clerk's comment on our parting handshake: "Best yet."
	During previous summer vacations, served as a counselor in a seashore camp for 100 teenagers. After the first year served as a senior counselor. Directed the staff (most of whom were senior in age) in all recreational activities. Supervised 10-member crews in construction, maintenance and deactivation of all camp and waterfront facilities. One result: Returning campers increased 45 percent from season to season. (Summers, 1990–1993)
Successful work-crew supervision and public relations	PRIMARY GAIN: Learned how to elicit strong cooperation from others (including an occasional irate parent) and how to schedule work crews for best results. According to the director, the strong reputation of the camp during these years was largely based on my performance.
Personal data	Enjoy good music, all aquatic sports.
Other facts	Aiming for employment that will enable me to create my own opportunities and accept responsibility for results . . . energy and drive . . . successful in relationships with others . . . strong interest in national and international affairs.

Mention—as primary education—only the most advanced institution from which you graduated.

An exception to the rule is when you have an advanced (master's or doctoral) degree, or a professional (such as medical or law) degree. In this case, record all your degrees—professional, graduate and undergraduate.

All pertinent special courses, seminars, workshops, and vocational-technical training can be listed under "Other Education."

◆ Emphasize a strong overall grade point average. Despite efforts of some researchers showing only a modest correlation between GPA and job performance, recruiters still head first for the academic stars.

If your overall GPA isn't anything to brag about, highlight the grade point average in your major.

If you barely squeaked by, omit on your resume any mention of grades. (And begin now to practice your sales pitch about the value of judging the *whole candidate* and other criteria such as job-related experience, leadership activities, and progress in improving your grades over time.)

In fact, a negative factor of any sort has no place on your resume. When you must admit to anything that weakens your chances of being hired, save it for the job interview where you can interpret the sticky wicket in the least damaging way.

Remember: On your resume you are advertising yourself, not letting it all hang out.

◆ Mention any scholarships you received and briefly state the criteria on which they were awarded.

◆ Because you have little experience, you should compress your resume onto a single page, but two pages are acceptable. Personnel executives tend to declare one-page resumes obligatory because they can be scanned in a wink. While you should try to be accommodating, remember this important point:

You and company recruiters do not share the same goal. Their goal is to effectively screen applicants as quickly as possible. Your goal is to make the strongest possible sales presentation of yourself.

If it takes two pages to get the job done, so be it.

Electronic and Internet Resumes

Job computers are used by growing numbers of companies to read resumes. Computers see resumes in a different light than do human eyes. If the right words—called keywords—aren't on your resume, job computers will pass you by.

What are the right words? The keywords to use are those each employer requests—usually nouns that define what you have to offer an employer—*engineering degree, associate in arts degree, word processing skills,* and so forth. The keywords that make your resume computer-friendly (scannable) describe your skills, your education, your accomplishments, and other basic facts about your qualifications to do a given job.

Action verbs—*consulted, directed, improved*—which have been favorite components for paper resumes are rarely powerful on electronic resumes.

Design factors are also important to make your resume scannable—use no underlining, graphics, or unusual or arty typefaces, for example. These design elements make computers stumble and your resume will remain buried in a resume database where no one can see you. Computers like plain "vanilla" resumes.

In addition to making a resume that computers can read, many job seekers are sending resumes over e-mail or posting them on the Internet.

For more information on how to write and distribute the new style resumes, see *Electronic Resume Revolution* by Joyce Lain Kennedy (John Wiley & Sons). Most Internet Web sites contain information on how to build a resume that will sweep effortlessly across the Net. For example, see the directions offered for free by the Online Career Center (www.occ.com).

Want an Interview? Write a Cover Letter with Snap

Along with your resume, you will need to send a cover letter that calls attention to specific reasons why you should be interviewed.

Include four sections in your cover letter: why you are writing, what you want, why your qualifications might interest the employer, and how you plan to follow up.

Since employers may receive many resumes for a specific job, it may be up to a clerk in the human resources department to determine which of the many resumes should be considered by the manager, who will make the final decision.

This clerk will make this selection based on whether the resume matches the job description or ad. Therefore, while working on your resume, keep the job description or ad in front of you, with all the keywords high-lighted. If your cover letter includes these words, you will look like a winner and your resume will be sent on—rather than go straight into the circular file.

Responding to Recruitment Ads

Hundreds of hopefuls send resumes for an advertised position, but only a handful receive an interview.

A major reason why many who answer ads do not receive invitations for interviews is that they fail to include an appropriate cover letter with their resumes. When cover letters *are* included, many are overblown or, conversely, reminiscent of the adolescent thank-you notes you wrote to Aunt Margaret for birthday gifts.

Take as much care with a cover letter as you do with your resume, advises John D. Erdlen, president of the Erdlen Bograd Group, a human resources consulting firm in Wellesley, Mass.

Cover letters that boil down to "I saw your ad and I'm looking for a job and here's my resume" are duds.

The objective of a cover letter is to highlight your credentials. The cover letter should always supplement and support your resume. Because a resume is seldom aimed specifically at any ad, the cover letter must be individualized and tailored to the job advertised.

Here are tips from Erdlen on writing cover letters:

1. Type on white bond business-letter size paper. Use correct grammar and spelling. Be brief and succinct.

2. Save the best information for the interview. Write just enough to entice the person designated in the ad.

3. You may gain more attention by not being in the first wave of responses. Don't feel compelled to mail your package the day the ad appears.

In general, open enthusiastically, mentioning the advertiser's need and how you meet it.

Use industry jargon when possible. Close with the action step—a suggestion of an interview. The sample cover letter on page 363 serves as an example.

An Unsolicited Cover Letter

You follow the same principles, but phrase your letter differently, when you are writing to an employer who has not advertised a job opening.

The key is to attract the reader's attention immediately by a personal tie-in. Perhaps you read a professional article the employer wrote, or met the employer through a campus activity or—best of all—have a mutual friend. An example of an unsolicited cover letter appears on page 364.

As you portray the most favorable version of yourself on paper or electronic screen, never lose sight of the central resume idea mentioned in the student jobs section. It bears repeating:

The central resume idea is to create a document saying you and the job are a good match. A good match means that you know the job's requirements, and that you can do the work, that you will do the work, and that you will behave pleasantly while doing it.

■ ■ ■ ■

Knowing Where to Make the Sale

How often have you seen the job market depicted as a maze with frustrating twists and turns, or as a roadway with crazy signs pointing in all directions, or as a jungle with scary animals lurking in the bushes waiting to pounce on the unsuspecting traveller?

There's a certain truth behind these visualizations, but as an expert job seeker, you will not attempt a job hunt without drawing up a plan of attack. Let's talk strategy.

Choose a Strategy

Three strategies cover the basics of looking for a job.

1. The *target approach* is by far the best strategy. You go after selected jobs that fit into your overall career plan. You learn the jobs' requirements and set a course destined to prove to specific employers that you and the jobs are a good match.

   The pure target approach works most easily for job seekers who are graduates of vocationally focused education, or who have a pretty good idea of what they want to do.

   The target strategy is superior because you take greater control of your future. As outplacement counselor Roderick Deighen observes, "Why let your career drift down the river like a log? Put a motor on it. Steer it. Be in charge of it."

Sample Cover Letter Responding To An Ad

Ms. Vi Bradley Felton
Manager
Revenue & Treasury Systems
NDJ Telephone Company
3000 Goodview Blvd.
Rockville, MD 20857

Dear Ms. Felton:

Your ad asking for a production analyst trainee with a background in marketing and finance made my day. It seems to be exactly what I am looking for in the telecommunications industry.

In several weeks I'll have my MBA from George Washington University; my concentration is in marketing and finance. I may be exactly what you are looking for and I'd like to meet with you to talk about my qualifications.

I've had mainframe and microcomputer experience, both in my classwork and as a graduate research assistant to a senior professor of marketing. My resume more fully describes how I might fit into your department.

I will call you next week to see when we can meet.

Sincerely,

Ryan R. Bodman

Sample Unsolicited Cover Letter

Mr. Clayton Byers
Manager
La Ritzy Country Club
4321 Pacific Palisades Road
Bel Air, California 90088

Dear Mr. Byers:

You may remember my mother, Irene Lark, who worked as your secretary 20 years ago. You were her all-time favorite employer, a fact which encourages me to contact you now.

As a new graduate of the Dana Point, Calif. Community College hotel and restaurant management program, I am very much interested in working in the club management industry, perhaps starting as an assistant club manager. Would it be possible to arrange an interview with you to discuss this? Obviously, I would be delighted to have the opportunity of working at a prestigious club like yours, but if there isn't a job opening at the present time, perhaps you could refer me to a colleague.

I am not a beginner. Prior to my graduation from Dana Point, I worked for three years in food-and-beverage management in the Army, serving the non-com clubs. I am energetic and do not have family duties so my hours can fit the needs of a club. People say I inherited my mother's cheerful disposition. I have enclosed my resume, which provides specifics.

I will call you later this week to see if an interview can be arranged.

Sincerely,

Georgina Lark

2. The second strategy can be called the *oyster approach*, as in "the world is my oyster." The premise is that the job seeker can do anything. An underlying belief is, "I can think and so I can learn to do any job."

To operate by this strategy, you locate and apply for all job openings that are vaguely in your ball park. Who knows what lucrative hidden job might turn up?

Many liberal arts graduates opt to pursue this strategy.

The advantage to oyster advocates: This strategy maximizes your opportunities. You cast a wide net. The disadvantage: Not all oysters contain pearls.

3. The third strategy is the *combination approach*. In it, you join the best elements of both the target and oyster approaches.

Our advice is to place primary emphasis on the target approach, spending maybe 80 percent to 90 percent of your time tracking jobs that fit into your career plan. Use the remainder of your time to look at anything and everything that comes your way.

Hire Yourself to Look for a Job

Some unfortunate people start off in the wrong job and, after establishing a pattern, keep repeating the same unhappy choice job after job.

Make an effort to avoid a false start. Do this by spending an absolute minimum of 35 hours a week on your search (assuming you're out of school and unemployed). Anything less and your efforts are recreational.

The chief mistake most people make is to throw out a few hooks, read a few ads, sign up with an employment agency or two—and then go home and wait. Unfortunately, the wait can

be a long one. The better plan is to take the offensive in the job market.

Plan to see at least five employers a week. Be prepared to interview time and time again. If you have 50 interviews, certainly you have a much better chance than if you have only a few. It's a matter of numbers. Like the ads for the lotteries say, "You gotta play to win."

Commit enough of your personal resources to do the job of getting the job you want. If time drags by and nothing much seems to be happening, don't throw in the towel. Remember the words of Winston Churchill: "There are two kinds of success: immediate and ultimate."

Keep Track of the Jobs You Apply For

Even when there are plenty of jobs available, the better a particular job, the stiffer the competition. Don't allow opportunities to slip from your memory.

Keep detailed records of all your job search moves. Write down the name of the person or organization you apply to, who interviews you, the name of the interviewer's secretary, who referred you, what was discussed, what follow-up action you took, and to whom the interviewer referred you. Include phone numbers, addresses, job titles, and comments. Immediately after an interview, jot down pertinent details before you forget.

Summary to Maximize Your Chances

Know yourself. Identify your strength and weaknesses, your work interests, and what matters to you in a job.

Do your homework. Research the companies and fields that interest you.

Follow the business news, especially the papers that cover areas where you want to live. Call the chambers of commerce in your target cities for information, too.

Start a file on companies. Gather information on firms that interest you and are growing. Check to see if there is a trade or professional society in your fields of interest, then call your area's chapter and ask if you can attend a meeting. At the meeting, introduce yourself to the officers and ask to be introduced to other members.

Try to get some work experience. Internships and temporary jobs can help you make up your mind about the fields that interest you. If you're a high school graduate, consider applying to small businesses in your area or register with a temporary employment service. Be sure your resume highlights previous part-time and volunteer work, as well as computer and other skills.

Be professional. Job candidates should always be well-dressed and should provide employers with a well-organized, concise, and error-free resume.

Make a List of Employers

Who is going to be the lucky recipient of your talents? Make a list of employers worthy of that honor.

Your list of prospects can be as elaborate as you like, but at minimum it must contain the name, address, and telephone number of the prospective employer, and the name of the person who can hire you, or at least get you through the door.

Where will you get good leads for your prospects list? From looking at all available sources, of course.

The Bushes to Beat for Jobs

Here are the sources (and resources) to turn to when you look for job openings.

School Sources

High school graduates should check in the work experience or career center office for possible job openings.

Vocational-technical schools usually help place graduates in their first jobs.

Colleges and Universities

If you're a graduate of a two- or four-year college or university, your school's career services center can offer specific knowledge of job openings. Typical job openings include those for engineers, accountants, and management trainees in insurance and retailing.

Even if you find nothing to your taste in the current openings file, you could still benefit from it. Call the contacts listed for jobs you don't want, say you are interested in another type of position, and ask if you could drop by for a talk.

Your alumni office is another job-hunting ally. Its directory of past graduates can be an excellent source of contacts. You need not overdo the school spirit routine—just call to say you are about to graduate from the alum's school, need help breaking into the job market, and would appreciate a chance to talk. Leave several copies of your resume with alumni you meet.

The career services office and the alumni office may work together for your benefit; find out what services they offer jointly, as well as individually.

Campus organizations and senior classes may sponsor lectures and workshops with business people; this is a fine chance to meet individuals who can brighten your future. Some campus groups produce books containing resumes of prospective graduates that are distributed to employers.

Professors often work as consultants to business organizations; frequently they are asked to recommend appropriate students, or you can take the initiative by asking them for suggestions of whom you might contact.

Campus recruiters are looking for graduates who are the cream of the crop. Because it's too costly for small companies to send professionals to college campuses around the country, the recruiters usually represent major corporations and local employers.

Recruiters are selective. They are interested only in graduates of high-demand fields: engineering, computer science, math, accounting, and other technical majors. Liberal arts students get the nod from banks, insurance companies, retailers, fast-food chains, and utilities.

Do not put all your chips on the campus recruiting crew because you may miss a whiz of a job in a medium-size company in another city.

You may be interested in a glamour or competitive field that virtually never recruits (media, films, travel, and fashion design, for example).

You may be left on the shelf until the unemployment plague is upon you.

Go forth and seek on your own initiative after you and the recruiters have talked things over.

Networking

Networking is meeting people, asking around for information you need, and being referred to others. It's making and using contacts. It's

developing to a fine art whom you know, even if it's knowing someone who knows someone who has an uncle.

Perhaps you're having lunch with a friend who happens to mention that his uncle is looking for someone to be his construction assistant for a new luxury apartment complex. This someone has to be willing to live for a year in Paris.

Or perhaps you're having lunch with a friend who happens to mention that her aunt will soon have openings for entry-level employees at her firm.

Maybe we got carried away with the examples, but our point should not be missed: Networking brings you insider's news to act on.

You have a head start. Do you remember back in Chapter 5 when we asked you to begin keeping a personal contacts log? We hope you followed our advice because this is payday. Dig out your log and list the people who you already know can play a role in your job search. Consider them your varsity team for networking.

Build on that base by adding others to your networking team. Make systematic contacts with people who can give you a break.

Even when an interview fails, ask to be referred from one manager to another, always with a recommendation, until you and your job meet.

There's no doubt about it: The coattails of contacts are a powerful way to travel in the job market.

Direct Application

When your strategy is the target or combination approach, you'll spend a lot of time making unsolicited approaches to employers.

Many jobs are won by just asking. Sometimes a job has not been advertised or sent to the personnel department because it is still on management's drawing boards—this is what is meant by the term *hidden job market*.

You learn about the hidden job market either by networking or by direct application.

What's the best way to make a cold call on an employer—make an appointment by letter or telephone, or just pop by and hope you can get in to see the boss?

We suggest you write or call for an appointment; whether you use the mails or telephone depends on which one best fits your style.

If you can't seem to wrangle an appointment, and you really want to see someone, you might try getting past the receptionist. Here's how to handle it:

You are making a cold call on a company. By research, you've learned that Julian H. Miller is hiring applicants with your kinds of skills. You ask the receptionist to see Mr. Miller.

The receptionist asks if he is expecting you. When you admit that he is not, the receptionist says that Mr. Miller never sees anyone without an appointment and that he's busy all week. The receptionist asks that you leave your resume.

Don't do it. The resume could make a round trip to China before you'll receive a response.

Instead, reply pleasantly that you'd rather give it to Mr. Miller yourself because there are items you need to explain. Moreover, you have some questions of your own. Say you need only a few minutes of his time.

At this point offer to come back tomorrow to find out when Mr. Miller can see you. Be tactful but firm—you are coming back tomorrow. Be generous with your appreciation to the receptionist for helping to set the appointment.

This tactic shows you value the receptionist as an important person and a potential fellow employee. You are trying to create an ally and an advocate.

A further point: We mentioned that the misuse of informational interviewing by people who saw it as a gimmick to get a job ruined the technique with many employers. Here are excerpts from a letter to one of the authors from a young man seeking a job in microbiology. For confidentiality, several names are changed:

I have read and done most of the exercises in several contemporary career guides. While they were thoughtful, interesting, and fun to read, I do not think they helped me very much in finding a job. Perhaps it is just the highly competitive nature of the scientific-technical job market, but when I have approached a potential employer with an unsolicited inquiry or attempted "interviewing for information only," I get nowhere.

If you are lucky enough to talk with the person with the power to hire, he or she is extremely rushed, will not want to talk to a stranger for more than five minutes or in any detail about what they are doing, and will not hire anyone until an opening occurs.

Several years ago I spent my one-week vacation in the Philadelphia area doing informational interviewing. Company X's secretaries would not let me speak to anyone, Company Y's secretaries would let me speak only to the personnel staff, and so on.

After these experiences, I decided to sneak into the back door of a pharmaceutical company and act like I worked there. Unfortunately, I did not know whom to speak to and had to approach a secretary for information. She asked who I was, how I got in, and there was a big uproar, with a guard eventually seeing me out.

Another example of impractical advice is that one should thoroughly research a company, uncover their problems, and show how you might solve them. Most high-tech or scientific companies are as secret as the CIA and as accessible as Ft. Knox. Except for the financial statements and stockholder information that exists for larger companies, virtually no printed information exists on these companies, research activities or problems.

Advice on this order really is not that practical, at least for science majors.

We agree that no one approach works for every one and that's why we're giving you the whole spectrum of job search.

Direct Mail

In days of old, circa 1960, job market experts commonly advised sending out *broadcast letters*. The idea was to compile huge lists of prospective employers—as many as 1,000—and write to them outlining your qualifications and asking for an interview.

The letters were expensive and usually didn't work, critics say.

Today most job market experts view direct mail buckshots as being wasteful of time and money.

We think direct mail is worth considering under certain conditions:

1. Your strategy is the target or combination approach and you are highly selective about whom you write. You obtain the name and title of the decision-maker.

2. You write a persuasive cover letter for your resume; or, you write a broadcast letter, which combines the highlights of your cover letter and resume.

Still, your chances of getting a job this way are slim. One man tells us that he sent out more than 2,000 broadcast letters, received 13 replies, four job interviews, and no offers.

Newspapers

In addition to leads picked up by reading the news sections of daily papers, follow the recruitment ads. Many appear in classified sections, others are found on sports or business pages, and still others are collected in special career groupings. Read the ads daily, not just on Sundays, because many ads first appear during the week.

Ads are useful because they tell you about jobs that somebody wants to fill immediately. Are they effective for professional jobs? You bet.

Most professionals are hired through recruitment advertisements, according to a survey conducted by the Employment Management Association (EMA), a professional organization for personnel executives. The response indicated that an average of 30 percent of their total of new experienced hires were recruited through advertising in newspapers, trade journals, and other media.

The other major sources of recruitment were employee referrals, 27 percent; employment agencies, 24 percent; and direct contact, 8 percent.

Although you aren't in the experienced category of potential new hires, you see why ads are near the front of the job market parade.

Here are tips on answering recruitment ads, as suggested by EMA officials.

1. Put yourself in the position of the person who receives your letter and resume. Ask yourself: What information about someone's background would induce me to invite that person for an interview? Be sure that your reply sparks the reader's interest.

2. Tailor your response to fit the ad. Highlight experiences and accomplishments that directly relate to the specific opening.

3. Limit yourself to a single page. Keep your correspondence brief and use the resume to spell out your qualifications. The reviewer cannot be expected to examine your credentials in depth.

4. Should you answer the ad immediately or wait a few days before responding? Employment experts have trouble agreeing which timing has the best chance of receiving interest— the early response or the resume arriving after the deluge of replies has diminished. (The authors favor waiting two or three days before replying to a help-wanted ad.)

5. Avoid references to salary requirements. This point is controversial, but at this stage it is advisable to indicate that your requirements are open. A compensation figure that is either too high or too low can eliminate you from consideration despite your experience or attractive credentials.

6. Address the reply exactly as it appears in the advertisement. These ads are usually coded, so they can be handled promptly.

7. Indicate why you have an interest in the company whenever the employer is identified in the ad. Including this information will require that you do some homework to learn about the organization, its products, and its services.

8. Send in a second reply if you have not heard from the company after two weeks. Resumes are often lost, misplaced, or misread. A follow-up telephone call is recommended.

Although EMA reports that 8 out of 10 employers use ads, the large response they attract can drown the individual in a sea of applicants. Your replies to ads should be the strongest you can produce.

Associations and Trade Journals

Most job fields are covered by at least one trade journal. Some are published by private firms, while others are products of trade associations and professional societies.

Trade journals may carry ads for jobs. Some trade associations and societies operate a job clearinghouse, in addition to staging meetings where you can find jobs through formal employment booths or through chance meetings. Ask whether a trade organization offers a directory or list of its members who are working in the job field that interests you.

Employment Services

You have several different types of employment services to consider.

Private employment agencies

Placement firms—commonly known as employment agencies—are matchmakers. Their purpose is to find people for the job openings of client employers.

When a firm makes a match it is entitled to a fee. Usually the employer pays; occasionally, the newly hired employee pays.

The choice is yours. You can tell the firm that you will consider (a) only fee-paid jobs; (b) that you are willing to pay the total fee for the right job; (c) that you will split the fee with the employer; or (d) that you will pay the fee, or a portion of it, provided the employer agrees to reimburse you after you've been on the job a year or so.

Even if you sign a contract agreeing to pay for a job, you owe nothing unless you accept one the firm finds for you. And if you do pay a fee, find out what the placement firm's policy is on refunds if you should be laid off before a year has passed.

The fact that it is the employer who most often pays the fee is at the bottom of many misunderstandings.

What job seekers don't focus on is that the placement firm is primarily responsive to the bill payer and provider of repeat business—the employer. The firm is usually recruiting good people for listed job openings, not scouting openings for job seekers.

The slant changes somewhat if you agree to pay a fee. It then is reasonable to expect the firm to develop job leads for you. But whether a firm's consultant actively markets you by canvassing employers depends largely on how busy and how motivated the consultant is.

Once you realize that you have no grounds to insist that a firm act as your personal representative, your expectations will be more realistic.

When choosing employment agencies, keep in mind the following suggestions.

♦ Determine whether the firm is a member of a state employment agency association (names vary from state to state) or of the National Association of Personnel Consultants (3133 Mt. Vernon Ave., Alexandria, VA 22305). Members agree to abide by specific business ethics.

It's a bonus if your consultant has passed rigid exams and met experience requirements to become certified by a state or national association. The national credential is *Certified Personnel Consultant.*

♦ Call placement firms to ask which specialize in your field. Unless there's only one in your community that handles the kinds of jobs you want, sign up with several firms. No one employment agency is in touch with all possible employers.

If you're highly marketable, let each firm know it has competition for your placement; each consultant will want to be the first to put you before employers.

If you're not so marketable, you need all the help you can get, but, unless you are asked outright, keep it to yourself that you are registered with a dozen placement firms.

Your strategy is to make each consultant feel prime responsibility for your employment status.

It is the agency's *consultant working directly with you* who counts most. Good employment consultants draw out your background, work record, and career goals before rushing you to specific jobs.

Contingency recruiters

A close relative of the private employment agency is the contingency firm. Sometimes called *technical recruiters* and sometimes *headhunters*,

these recruiters tend to specialize in engineers and other technical personnel. Their fee is always paid by the employer. Increasingly, the lines are blurred between employment agencies and private contingency firms. Traditionally, employment agencies advertise to fill job openings, while contingency recruiting firms use networking techniques to track down candidates for job openings. But contingency recruiters sometimes advertise and employment agencies may use networking techniques.

Executive recruiters

A recruiter or executive-search firm does not work on a contingency basis. Executive recruiters are paid in advance to search for middle and senior managers with specific credentials and experience. They also are known as headhunters. Don't bother contacting executive recruiters until you've got a track record.

Public employment service

Tax dollars support the public employment service, in some states called the Job Service. Run by the state employment security agencies under the direction of the Labor Department's U.S. Employment Service, the 1,700 local public employment service offices offer a range of services without charge.

The exact mix of services offered from office to office varies. You may be sent on job interviews, be invited to inspect the *Job Bank*—a computerized list of job openings in both private industry and government agencies—or offered counseling and testing services.

Veterans, by law, get priority in interviewing, counseling, testing, and job placement. If you're a vet, ask to see the veterans' employment representative.

If you decide to try the public employment service, here are three suggestions.

1. While many of the jobs in the files are positioned on the low end of the career scale, only you can decide whether this source is worth your time. A couple of visits to look over Job Bank listings will give you an idea of whether your kind of work is included.

2. Critics often charge public employment service personnel with being bureaucratic and inept. We don't agree. Like private employment services, the quality of help you receive depends on the person with whom you deal. Many public employment service counselors are talented and dedicated.

3. Be assertive. If you don't feel you are getting good service, don't hesitate to ask the public employment service office manager to reassign your search to another staffer.

Books

Bookstores and libraries are stacked high with job search guides; for more suggestions, turn back to Chapter 8.

Among the authors' favorites are:

◆ A trio of books by Jeffrey G. Allen. They are *Jeff Allen's Best: The Resume*, *Jeff Allen's Best: Get the Interview*; and *Jeff Allen's Best: Win the Job* (John Wiley)

◆ Two books by Martin John Yate. They are *Resumes that Knock 'Em Dead* and *Knock 'Em Dead with Great Answers to Tough Interview Questions* (Bob Adams)

◆ *The Guide to Basic Resume Writing* by the Job and Career Information Services Committee of the Adult Lifelong Learning Section, Public Library Association/American Library Association (VGM Career Horizons)

◆ A *Young Person's Guide to Getting & Keeping a Good Job* (for high school graduates) by J. Michael Farr and Marie Pavlicko (JIST Works Inc.)

◆ *Resumes for Dummies*, *Cover Letters for Dummies*, and *Job Interviews for Dummies*, all by Joyce Lain Kennedy (IDG Books Worldwide).

Summing Up on Sources

We've reviewed the most frequently used sources for finding beginning employment. Which should you pursue first?

We recommend:

1. School and college career services offices; employers list immediately available openings with them.

2. Recruitment ads in newspapers and trade journals; they contain news of immediate openings.

3. Employment services; they offer immediate openings.

4. Networking; contacts, while extremely effective, may take longer than you can wait to find a job. Start early.

5. Direct application; you may have to market yourself longer than you can comfortably wait to obtain employment.

How much emphasis you should place on each of these five channels depends on your strategy and goals.

If you want to work in films, don't waste your time on recruitment ads or employment services. Filmmakers don't have to recruit.

If you're in one of the business fields, recruitment ads and employment services are key sources. Think about it.

Let's look now at several special concerns and what to do about them.

■ ■ ■ ■

How To Break Into Competitive Industries

Some job fields seem to be surrounded by insurmountably high fences.

These are the fields that drip with glamor, pay big money, or both. You probably have thought about one or two of them yourself.

How do you become a television talk show host? A film producer? A recording engineer? A sports team publicist? A literary agent? An auto designer? A travel tour packager? A fashion photographer? A rock star?

While particulars change from field to field, all share certain characteristics. Here are tips for climbing over the fences that shut you out of competitive industries.

1. When you can't lasso your immediate job target, try to snare the most closely related job you can while continuing to move toward your goal. Even film producers need people to act as housekeepers, baby sitters, and gofers.

2. While you are gaining related experience, change your status from outsider to insider. You do this by becoming a regular in the circles in which you'd like to work. Make friends with people who can give you advance word of job openings. Read the field's trade press regularly. Join pertinent associations and attend their meetings and annual conventions. Volunteer for committee work to gain exposure and contacts. Go wherever the people you want to join gather.

"Persistence pays" is a cliché, but clichés usually have a basis in truth. Keep calling on employers even when they say there won't be an opening for the next five years. Employers have no idea who might walk out tomorrow—and there you are, waiting in the wings, ready to step on stage.

■ ■ ■ ■

Liberal Arts Majors: What Can You Do?

Year after year, technical majors dramatically outperform liberal arts majors in the job market, both in offers and salary.

This is why it is essential for liberal arts graduates to become expert job seekers and to concentrate on fields in which there are many jobs that do not have precise entry requirements. Such fields include banking, telecommunications, sales, insurance, human resources, fund-raising, and entrepreneurship.

When you need a friendly push to liberal arts employment, a couple of books do a nice job of shoving. Their titles say it all: *Liberal Arts Jobs—What They Are and How to Get Them* and *Liberal Arts Power! What It Is and How to Sell It on Your Resume*. Both are by Burton Jay Nadler (Peterson's).

■ ■ ■ ■

Looking for a Job Far Away

Whether you intend to return to your home base or relocate to a completely new locale, a little planning can ease your long-distance search.

Before you are hired, you'll have to be present for interviews. Set a time at least two months away when you will be in the distant city.

Network to find the names of decision-makers or influential people who can refer you to decision-makers. Among those this group might include are business executives, civic leaders, religious leaders, bankers, stock-brokers, and other professionals.

If you don't know a soul in your target city, you may have to develop contacts in two phases:

1. Obtain the names of reputable residents of the city and ask for a referral to decision-makers.

2. Write to the decision-makers or influential people and ask for an appointment.

Your request letters should not put pressure on recipients. Communicate that you are a new graduate, that you want to take the business pulse of the city, and that you would appreciate a 10-minute meeting. During interviews ask about the business climate, job market, and the community as a place for young adults. Mention your chief skills and abilities, too. Ask, "Can you recommend where I might find (a job, a place to live, who's hiring in my field, and so forth)?" People like to recommend.

■ ■ ■ ■

Disorganized? Discouraged? Try the Buddy System

Sometimes you just can't seem to pull your job-hunting head together. You mean to get organi-zed, but before you know it the clock is striking four and another day is shot.

When you can't be your own best career friend, find a buddy. Use the mutual support system.

In tandem with another new graduate, share leads, review each other's resumes, do practice interviews, boost each other's morale and, most important, keep each other on your collective 20 toes.

Want to give it a try? There are only two rules: Communicate daily, and agree that the buddyship doesn't break up until both partners have a job.

During the times when nothing seems to be clicking and nobody seems to want to hire you, remember that rejection doesn't mean failure; it means try harder.

■ ■ ■ ■

Knowing How to Make the Sale

Selling is persuading people to act—convincing the customer to buy.

Selling yourself is convincing employers to buy your skills.

Happily, you've got a running start on your sales effort. Now that you've finished your re-sume and mapped out your search, there's only one more function to master before you can call yourself an expert job seeker: interviewing.

Facing the Interview

No matter how superb your resume and how organized your campaign, the interview is the magic moment when you sink or swim.

Actually, the magic moment is more like 30 minutes, although some interviews may stretch out to more than an hour. Knowing that your future's on the line during these crucial periods is likely to produce anxiety and psychological blips. That's the downside.

Here's the upside: The interviewing experience need not give you a rash if you take the time to learn the ropes. Once you understand interviewing and its methods and madnesses, you'll know that you're not dealing with normal, everyday behavior.

All *the face-to-face chats you must survive to get a job are about* 10 *percent reality and* 90 *percent theater.*

Interviewing is drama, so shape your performance to fit the role. Knowing what's expected and what you should say will make everything much, much easier.

Despite your best efforts, suppose the worst happens and you blow an interview for a job you really want? Unless you are touched by angels, interviewing disasters will happen in your life. To keep the right perspective, call a failed interview a learning experience and vow to do better the next time.

Remember that while flubbing interviews can make you want to pound sand, events far more upsetting can happen in your career. As former Montreal Canadian hockey goaltender Jacques Plante once said: "How would you like a job, where if you make a mistake, a big red light comes on and 18,000 people boo?"

Okay? Now we'll show you how to bypass the big red lights and the roar of boos on your way to making interviewers choose you.

is important for applicants to demonstrate that they have made an effort to learn something about the company prior to the interview.

The research gives you something in common with the interviewer. Don't you like best those friends with whom you have the most in common? Interviewers react in the same manner.

The key reason, however, for finding out what's happening at a potential employer's organization is that it gives you the basis of information to suggest how you might fit into the organization.

When you are unprepared, you tend to talk about you and what you want. When you are prepared, the talk can focus on the employer's needs and how your skills match them.

No one expects a new graduate to be a walking encyclopedia, but your school's placement office will usually have literature available about companies that are recruiting on campus.

You may also obtain a copy of the company's annual report at the career services office or a business library. Read the president's message and the financial figures. You'll get an indication of the company's priorities.

Whenever you want to be a cut above the crowd, research your target to the hilt. Try to chat with the company's employees, read the industry's trade press and check for clippings at a large library.

After you gather the information, use it judiciously. Don't walk in and discuss reorganizing the company. Coming across as a know-it-all and attempting to tell the employer how to run the business are deadly sins.

Preparation is the Great Relaxer

Is it important to research a company before the interview?

In a recent survey of personnel directors of 100 large companies, 84 percent said they feel it

Save the Best for Last

A common mistake is to arrange interviews with your best prospects before you have had enough practice at interviewing to do well. You can't control campus recruiting schedules, but you can work out some of the bugs by mock interviewing with friends.

Use the Truth Rule

Bogus information is everywhere.

A woman's magazine advises its job hunting readers to "fudge facts" when necessary.

A men's magazine says that job hunters "sometimes should lie," and implied that advice to the contrary is hopelessly naive.

A professional resume writer suggests in a newsletter to fellow professionals that they should change a client's job titles to "more accurately reflect what the client did for an organization."

A headhunter in the Seattle area says he can't recall a single recruiting search in the last five years where he didn't uncover at least one education falsification.

What about it? Has the code of ethics in the American job market changed that much? Are you likely to be caught and punished by the deceived employer if you take liberties with the truth?

The answer to the first question is "no." Mainstream ethics have not changed; it's still wrong to obtain employment under false colors.

The answer to the second question is "maybe." You may get away with lies, or you may be discovered in a fabrication that could seriously damage your career.

If your lie is revealed during a reference check before an offer is made, you can forget that job.

Suppose your breach of integrity isn't discovered and you are hired. In that case, you live with a time bomb that could go off at a bad time in your career. If it does, what then?

Many companies will let you keep your job if you are doing it well. Here are typical comments from employers reflecting this philosophy:

"When we find falsification, we confront, not dismiss."

"Dismissal would result only if it were to be a serious lie."

The problem is you can never be sure what will happen. In opposition to the "fess-up-and-forgive" view is the personnel chief of another company who says:

"When we want to terminate a problem employee, we go through the legal application form looking for lies."

An executive for another large company sees matters in a similar vein:

"We were about to transfer the guy when we found out he claimed two phony doctorates and we dismissed him."

If you lie, you take your chances. In our opinion, lying siphons your concentration by making you nervous trying to remember exactly which lie you told.

As we see it, claiming fake job titles or unearned educational degrees is dumb. Be wise enough to tell the intelligent truth. Here is the truth-in-telling rule for all interviews that we recommend.

When it helps your cause to reveal a fact, do so in glowing detail.

Keep negative information in your pocket unless you are concealing an impediment that would prevent you from doing a fine job.

What Employers Look For

Which factors turn an employer's head? Here are several that employers say are high on their lists of hiring criteria.

Enthusiasm. You don't show enthusiasm by responding with a steady stream of "oh, wows" in the interview, but by paying close attention, smiling, maintaining eye contact, asking appropriate questions, and stating your interest in the job.

Grades. They're important, but if grades were everything, you could mail them in and recruiters wouldn't have to spend vast amounts of time and money traveling from campus to campus. People who hire want to see the three-dimensional you in the flesh.

Having said that, you know that grade point averages will open or close certain doors. Stand-out grades indicate to many employers that you are motivated and swift of mind.

Communications Skills. Information has to pass with clarity between you and others or the job will suffer.

Interpersonal Skills. Employers want to be sure you will fit into their organizations so they watch for clues that you get along well with others.

High Energy Level. Your physical behavior during an interview—a spring in your step, sitting up straight—leads employers to speculate whether you have the physical stamina to work quickly and hard.

Judgment. Employers want employees who behave in an adult manner. They want people whose suggestions reflect judgment, not just mere opinion.

Which Self Should You Be?

Many job hunt experts tell you the way to behave in an interview is to "be yourself" and "act naturally."

Which self? What's natural?

Don't you behave differently in differing circumstances? Are your shiny shoes natural? Combed hair? Clean fingernails?

Earlier we stressed that an interview is mostly theater. There's nothing real about compressing a lifetime in a 30-minute conversation. The best role to play is one that most closely matches what you understand the requirements of the job to be. Your behavior would be different when applying for a job as a bank loan officer than when auditioning for a job as a television quiz show host.

The best self at any interview exudes self-confidence, even if you don't feel it. When you have no confidence in yourself, others won't either.

Echo Your Interviewer

Try to get a handle on the interviewer's style. If the interviewer speaks in short clips, don't rattle on and on. If the interviewer seems laid back, don't come on like gangbusters. If the interviewer is formal, don't be casual. Once more, the point is: It's human nature to like people who are like ourselves.

Within the framework of your true personality, hum the interviewer's tune.

Reinvent Yourself: The Miracle of Videotape

Before you set off on interviews, study your image in living color and if you don't like the picture, improve it.

Videotaping with a friend makes it easy to evaluate and upgrade your performance in a job interview. Camcorders are dropping in price, but you don't need to own the equipment—many school media centers maintain videotaping equipment students can use.

When you see yourself on tape, you may be surprised at how often you scratch your head, pop chewing gum, crack all 10 knuckles, swing your eyeglasses like a New Year's Eve noise-maker, or commit other interviewing errors. By seeing and eliminating irritating mannerisms, you dramatically boost your chances of being hired.

How You Look

Image is a business tool. Image is how you walk, talk, present yourself, and behave. Definitely, it's what you wear and how you look.

When your appearance is contemporary and attractive, the interviewer is likely to credit you with better-than-average awareness of the world at work.

The opposite is true, too. If you appear as though you never notice what others are wearing, the interviewer may very well question your awareness.

You do not have to project the image of a fashion plate if you are not in a fashion industry, but it is important to be perceived as someone tuned into today's tempo. Aware people are smart enough to know what's happening and care enough to be a part of it.

Magazines regularly include articles on the latest ways to dress for business. Read them. In brief, there are only two basic principles to bear in mind.

1. *Dress appropriately for the job you seek.*

2. *For most jobs, project a conservative, businesslike image.*

In non-conservative companies, business clothing means costuming, according to image consultant Jane Segerstrom.

If you are an artist, writer, photographer, musician, or other creative type, or one who sells to the youth market, your office wear could be quite different from the three-piece suit.

♦ Men may opt for Western, ivy league, sport, or turtleneck shirts. Vests or jackets may top jeans, cords, slacks, or drawstring pants.

♦ Women may choose overblouses, shawls, sweaters, wide and wild belts, scarves, vests, pants or skirts of all descriptions. Jewelry can be bold. Extreme hairstyles complete costuming at its height.

In hands-on and service industries, such as construction or health work, the dress of the day appropriately could be clean jeans, sweat shirt, or uniform.

Shaping your image can be one of the major rewards—and investments—of your career.

Body Language Can't Keep a Secret

Body language sometimes reveals true feelings that may be contrary to what a person says.

Gain a secret weapon. Learn the basics of non-verbal signals and always use them to your advantage.

A number of books on non-verbal communication are available. From them you can learn such things as how to know when an interviewer is bored and that it's time to change the subject of your conversation.

How can you tell when an interviewer is bored? Among the clues: playing with an object on the desk or tapping fingers. If this happens, stop and simply ask for direction. Say something like this: "Would you like to hear more about my minerals economics studies or about my computer lab work?"

Another sign that an interview may not be going well is when the interviewer crosses arms in front of the body and leans away from you.

A positive sign that you're coming across well is when an interviewer leans forward in the chair.

Once you learn to read body language, you'll be more aware that non-verbal movements, mannerisms, and gestures reveal what's on your mind, too.

Tugging at your skirt or jiggling your keys makes you look nervous and short on self-confidence.

Reaching up and touching the back of your head when an interviewer asks if you have a given skill may suggest you really don't—that you are disturbed or startled by the idea.

Looking at the ceiling as you collect your thoughts may cause an interviewer to view you as vague or even insincere. If you have trouble keeping eye contact, look at the bridge of an interviewer's nose. It will appear that you are looking the interviewer straight in the eyes.

As a child, somebody probably told you never to point at anyone. Even kidding around, never point at an interviewer—it's rude.

The combination of attentive listening, thoughtful speaking, and the ability to interpret non-verbal signals is a step toward power.

In every interview, try to show a pleasing temperament and a high energy level. Lethargy is the quicksand of job hunting.

On paper, the issues are straightforward. In practice, they become fuzzy. Discrimination law is complex.

In addition to federal discrimination laws, many states and some cities or counties have fair employment practices laws. They vary widely. Some of them flatly prohibit employers from asking certain questions. You can get a list of suspect questions from state or local labor and human rights agencies that administer anti-discrimination laws in your area.

Contrary to popular belief, there is no such thing as a list of illegal questions forbidden by federal law. Other than questions about arrests and (prior to an unqualified job offer) whether you have a disability and its severity, employers can ask anything they wish to know. *The key is what use the employer makes of the information. If it is used to discriminate against you, the question becomes illegal.*

Which set of laws takes precedence in employment rights cases? When the federal law is stronger, it prevails; state and local statutes prevail when they are stronger than the federal versions.

One thing you should know: Questions that might be judged discriminatory in pre-hire situations may be valid once you're employed. Employers often are required to collect personal information for affirmative action programs and insurance plans.

Job Bias: What to Do if It Happens to You

It's the law: When you apply for employment, if you can do the job, you can't be discriminated against because of your race, color, national origin, religion, sex, age, or disabilities. The point is to give everyone an equal chance at jobs.

Thin-Ice Questions

Interviewers usually stay up-to-date on employment laws and avoid sensitive topics, but some may be so busy juggling a variety of duties that they ask risky questions out of ignorance. Here are examples of questions to look out for.

Race or color. Neither should be commented on in any way during an interview, nor should you be asked for a picture when you apply for a job.

National origin. If fluency in another language is relevant to the job, the interviewer shouldn't ask whether the language is your native tongue or even how you acquired your fluency if that might reveal information about your national origin.

It is okay to ask if you are a U.S. citizen; if you are not, it is acceptable to ask if you have the legal right to remain and work in the United States.

Sex and marital status. You should not be asked about your marital status, whether or where your spouse works, or even whom you'd like an employer to notify in case of an emergency. Other risky questions are those about children, child care arrangements, the probability of pregnancy, and your views about birth control.

Disabilities. Under the *Americans With Disabilities Act of* 1990, employers are not to ask if you have a disability and are not to inquire as to the nature or severity of any disability. These questions should not be on application forms and should not be asked in interviews. *What is permitted is for employers to inquire about your ability to perform the essential functions of the job.*

A rule of thumb. What basic compass can you use to assess whether employers are getting too nosey? Just ask yourself:

Is this information relevant to my doing the job?

All pre-hire questions should be relevant to a given job. And the questions—the same questions—must be asked of all applicants, regardless of sex, age, race, religion, or national origin.

Good Answers to Poor Questions

Pretend you are in the interviewer's office, ready to begin the interview and prove you're the best qualified for the job.

The interview starts and suddenly the interviewer shoots you a question that seems irrelevant. Your indignation is soaring. How will you handle the situation?

You have three basic choices.

1. Answer the question and don't make waves.

2. Finesse the issue or politely explain that the question doesn't seem related to your ability to do the job.

3. Tell the interviewer you understand laws prohibit employers from considering potentially illegal information in evaluating job applicants.

The last option is not advisable if you want the job. The first option may be acceptable to you if the interviewer's questions seem to come from ignorance rather than bias.

The second option is our preference. The moderate response shows not only that you are accommodating, but that you also are an aware, thinking person.

Here are a few sample answers using the second option.

Q. *Do you plan to be married?*

A. That decision is still in my future. I haven't made it yet.

Q. *I see that you speak Spanish. Where did you learn it?*

A. I studied Spanish in school. What opportunity would I have to use it in this position?

Q. *What does your father do?*

A. I would appreciate it if you would clarify for me how this question relates to my ability to do the job. Then I would have a better idea of the type of information you're looking for.

Q. *What's your credit rating?*

A. I haven't been out of school long enough to establish one. But . . . I didn't know I'd be handling money.

Q. *Do you want to be addressed as Ms., Miss or Mrs. Smith ?*

A. Joan Smith is fine, thanks.

If Discrimination Threatens You

Should you find yourself involved in a blatant case of discrimination, you may want to get advice from your state or local labor or human rights agencies, or from an office of the Equal Employment Opportunity Commission.

What About Employment Tests?

Many people think equal opportunity and affirmative action laws made employment tests illegal. Not so. These tests become illegal only when they are used to discriminate on the basis of race, color, national origin, religion, sex, age, or disabilities.

The upshot is that when you're asked to take an employment test, agree to do so if you want the job. Make the best of the situation and greet the test-giver, often a psychologist, as an alert, well-adjusted, happy person.

Here are several tips on selling yourself in employment tests.

◆ On timed tests, attempt to answer all questions. On some tests, you may be limited to several choices and find that none describe the action you would take in a hypothetical situation. Choose the option closest to your way of thinking. Try to be consistent in your approach.

◆ Should you guess? Guess answers to anything you don't know when there is no penalty for wrong answers. Guessing may pay off even if there is a penalty. Typically, you will receive a full credit for every right answer and be docked only a fraction of a credit for every wrong answer. Figure your odds.

◆ Sentence completion should be upbeat. You know better than to end the sentence, "Work is . . ." with "the pits." Another illustration revolves around the notion of mice playing when the cat's away. The right ending to "When the boss came in . . ." is not "everyone worked harder." A better answer is "everyone smiled."

The integrity test is a recent wrinkle. In 1988, when the polygraph test was virtually outlawed, paper-and-pencil "son of polygraph" tests grew in popularity. Usually they are not tricky but ask about theft or dishonesty straight out. The amazing thing is how people will incriminate themselves on "impersonal" written tests.

Here's a tip: Avoid absolutes such as "always" or "never." These are red flags to psychologists who then try to determine if you are straying from the truth. The reasoning is that anyone who "never stole anything" probably pinched cookies as a kid.

Two studies have been made which fail to hang winner's wreaths on the integrity tests. The first, by the U.S. Congress' Office of Technology Assessment, concludes there isn't enough research to give integrity tests a passing mark. The other, by the American Psychological Association, is a shade more positive, saying there's adequate research to affirm that some of the tests are good, but some are bad or lack verification research and that the whole issue needs more study.

Critics say that honesty tests are genuinely predictive only when big numbers of people are involved—that companies play the percentages. This means innocent people may be misclassified and wrongly denied jobs.

When you are asked to take an integrity test, ask how the results will be used. After the interviewer answers, you may want to add something like this:

I hear there's some disagreement about the reliability of integrity tests. Would you let me know if something negative turns up on mine so I can have the opportunity to look at it and respond? I'm really interested in this job and I wouldn't want a statistical fluke to knock me out of it. That's fair, isn't it?

If the employer asks where you got such an idea, quote the authors of this book.

If you're worried about taking tests, your library may have sample tests for practice.

Screening and Selection Interviews

In organizations large enough to operate a personnel department, interviewing usually is a two-stage process.

A representative of the personnel department conducts screening interviews designed to weed out all but the best-qualified candidates. Survivors are passed to the person who has the hiring authority, often a department head. The recommended behavior at a screening interview is simple: Be pleasant, be bland.

You have nothing to gain by risking strong opinions that may conflict with those of the screener.

It is the screener's job to check that your credentials are satisfactory—that you can do the job and that you will do the job.

The screener does not make the decision on how you'll fit in with the rest of the team. If your credentials are acceptable and you don't make waves, you probably will be passed on to the hiring authority. (Campus recruiters usually are conducting screening interviews.)

At the selection interview, you'll be dealing with the decision-maker, and, perhaps, one or more colleagues. The decision-maker probably is the person you will be working for, so now is the time to express your best personality.

You've got to hit it off with the decision-maker, but if you rub each other the wrong way, it's better to discover the fact up front and continue your search.

Please Come In . . .

The moment has arrived. Your interview is about to begin. You smile, make eye contact, shake hands, and introduce yourself, "Hello, I'm_____."

Be ready with initial pleasantries and safe small talk—"What an interesting painting on your wall," or "What a handsome view from this office." Avoid all personal references, such as comments about the interviewer's appearance or family photographs.

Try to project businesslike warmth and friendliness. Your aim is to make the interviewer like you. Many recruiters say far more people are turned away for personality factors than for lack of capability.

By personality factors, we mean "vibes"—the non-verbal communication and other under-the-surface factors that make people like or dislike you.

In the final analysis—assuming your qualifications are adequate for the position—what convinces an employer to hire you over someone else can be boiled down to two words: liking you.

If things go well in the first few minutes, you'll create the halo effect, which means if you shine in one area, it is assumed you shine in others. When you like a person, you tend to see everything the person does in a favorable light.

The Most Important Question in the Interview

As early as possible, ask the interviewer to describe the scope of the job and the qualifications of the ideal person for it. Keep your antennae up and your headlights on. The information you receive will be the key to the entire interview.

Listen carefully. Take notes if you wish. If an ideal qualification is "careful attention to detail," give the interviewer examples of how carefully you pay attention to detail. If an ideal qualification is "to organize massive projects," give the interviewer examples of what a great organizer you are. If an ideal qualification is "the ability to solve problems," give the interviewer examples of your problem-solving skills.

Throughout the meeting take every opportunity to remind the interviewer of the link-up between your qualifications and the ideal person the interviewer described.

To be blunt, you will feed back what you have been fed. You will show how your qualifications match what the interviewer wants.

Do not interpret this basic strategy to mean that it's okay to fabricate information. Cynical parroting might work—but not for long.

A Special Tip for Minority Applicants

Minority students often wonder how much should be said about minority-oriented extra-curricular activities.

As an example, a young woman asked whether she could mention her participation in African-American organizations when she graduated and applied for accounting jobs.

Our answer: If the activities support your objective of being hired, mention them.

If they do not add anything to making you look good for the job, why clutter your image?

In seeking an accounting job, there's not much value in pushing the point that you played on an all-black basketball team, or on any basketball team, for that matter, because basketball is unrelated to accounting. The exception would be if it is the only activity that shows teamwork experience and the ability to get along with others.

But suppose you were president of the state African-American studies club. Play up the experience. It suggests you possess leadership potential and are academically minded.

Do bring up any topic that strengthens the relationship between your background and the job's requirements.

Basic Reminders

Try to use the interviewer's name several times during the meeting. Don't smoke even if the interviewer lights up; if you're a non-smoker, don't imply criticism of the habit. Gum chewing is out of place. Stand until you're invited to sit.

You may run into an oldtimer who uses what is called the *stress interviewing* method. You're asked to sit in a chair with uneven legs, or placed so that you face the sun or are subjected to similar childish gambits to see "how well you stand up to stressful situations." Leave these people to their own amusement and look for work elsewhere.

Questions You May Hear

Most questions can be slotted into one of three categories. They are:

A. Questions that show you can do the job; these relate to skills, education, and experience. Examples:

Why should I hire you?
Why do you want to work here?
Which subject in school did you like best and why?

B. Questions that show you will do the job; these relate to positive work attitudes, ability to cope, and motivation for success. Examples:

What would you like to accomplish in the next 10 years?
What is it that you want to do ?
Why did you major in _____?

C. Questions that show you can get along with others; these relate to interpersonal relationships, focus, flexibility, and personality. Examples:

Can you describe an ideal working place in terms of your coworkers?
If I called your former adviser, how do you think you would be described?
What three people in public life do you admire most?

50 Questions Recruiters Ask College Seniors

Here are 50 questions asked by employers during interviews with college seniors.

A job interview is not the best place for surprises. That's why it would be time well spent to go over these questions, placing them in one of the three above categories. *Some questions you may want to place in two—or even all three categories.* It's a matter of individual interpretation. This is not a right-or-wrong quiz, but merely a device to help you consider each question in turn.

Category (A,B or C)	Questions
_____	1. What are your long-range and short-range goals and objectives; when and why did you establish these goals and how are you preparing yourself to achieve them?
_____	2. What specific goals, other than those related to your occupation, have you established for the next 10 years?
_____	3. What do you see yourself doing five years from now?
_____	4. What do you really want to do in life?
_____	5. What are your long-range career objectives?
_____	6. How do you plan to achieve your career goals?
_____	7. What are the most important rewards you expect in your business career?
_____	8. What do you expect to be earning in five years?
_____	9. Why did you choose the career for which you are preparing?
_____	10. Which is more important to you, the money or the type of job?
_____	11. What do you consider to be your greatest strengths and weaknesses?
_____	12. How would you describe yourself?
_____	13. How do you think a friend or professor who knows you well would describe you?

14. What motivates you to put forth your greatest effort?

15. How has your college experience prepared you for a business career?

16. Why should I hire you?

17. What qualifications do you have that make you think that you will be successful in business?

18. How do you determine or evaluate success?

19. What do you think it takes to be successful in a company like ours?

20. In what ways do you think you can make a contribution to our company?

21. What qualities should a successful manager possess?

22. Describe the relationship that should exist between a supervisor and subordinates.

23. What two or three accomplishments have given you the most satisfaction? Why?

24. Describe your most rewarding college experience.

25. If you were hiring a graduate for this position, what qualities would you look for?

26. Why did you select your college?

27. What led you to choose your field of major study?

28. What college subjects did you like best? Why?

29. What college subjects did you like least? Why?

30. If you could do so, how would you plan your academic study differently? Why?

31. What changes would you make in your college or university?

32. Do you have plans for continued study? An advanced degree?

33. Do you think your grades are a good indication of your academic achievement?

34. What have you learned from extracurricular activities?

35. In what kind of work environment are you most comfortable?

36. How do you work under pressure?

37. In what part-time work are you interested? Why?

38. How would you describe the ideal job for you following graduation?

39. Why did you decide to seek a position with this company?

40. What do you know about our company?

41. What two or three things are most important to you in your job?

42. Are you seeking employment in a company of a certain size? Why?

43. What criteria are you using to evaluate our company?

44. Do you have a geographical preference? Why?

45. Will you relocate? Does relocation bother you?

46. Are you willing to travel?

47. Are you willing to spend at least six months as a trainee?

48. Why do you think you might like to live in the community in which our company is located?

49. What major problem have you encountered and how did you deal with it?

50. What have you learned from your mistakes?

How to Answer Major Questions

You can bet that several of these questions are going to be asked at most interviews. Here are illustrations of good responses.

"What Can You Tell Me About Yourself?"

This is the bone crusher of all interview questions. Memorize a short answer. Summarize your background quickly and then narrow the focus to discuss your qualifications for the job at hand. Here's an answer for a marketing trainee position:

I graduated from the University of Southern California last June with a major in marketing. I was in the top 10 percent of my class. I was on the tennis team. I was elected treasurer of the marketing club. Through student jobs, I earned 60 percent of my school expenses. I'm a self-motivater and generally a pretty happy person. I like people.

"How Much Money Do You Want?"

As a beginner, you'll have little control over the salary you command, but you have a shot at negotiating if you don't name a figure. Respond to the question with a question of your own. That is: "What do you think would be fair pay for this job at the starting level, and what do you see as the long-term compensation potential?" Ask for a hair more than the offered figure to show you're an above-average candidate.

"What Are Some of Your Strengths and Weaknesses?"

Try to present strengths without seeming to brag:

Other people tell me I am effective at getting the job done.

I pride myself on meeting deadlines. I work well under pressure.

I enjoy working with others and have good relationships.

I am told I am a person who can come up with creative solutions to hard problems. I am a team worker.

Present a weakness as a strength:

Although I try to do everything assigned to me in a professional manner, I would get bored if I did nothing but routine work everyday.

Some people say I should allot more time to social activities.

People tell me I'm too thorough.

I become impatient in non-productive meetings.

(Never say anything like, "I'm not too well-organized.")

"Why Should We Hire You?"

If you haven't researched the company, you're going to have a hard time with this one. After research, you can say this:

I've checked out your company and it appears to be a good match with my qualifications and would probably result in a long-term relationship.

"What Kind of Job Are You Looking For?"

Don't unburden your soul. Employers have no time to explain banking to one who really wants to be a filmmaker.

Questions You Should Ask

One of the least understood parts of the interview is the type of questions you should ask. Categorize your questions into two broad groups: *employer agenda* and *personal agenda*.

A. *Employer Agenda*

These are questions that sell you to an employer. Because you are focused on employer benefits, you are selling without selling. These are questions you ask before the offer of employment is made to you. Your focus is on work, tasks, functions, duties, and challenges. Within the employer benefit group, your questions can be thought of in three categories. They are:

1. *Questions that demonstrate knowledge of the field.*

Will company expansion occur more rapidly in the Ohio or Texas divisions?

In the researcher-writer position, would I have the opportunity to use my history knowledge by working on the forthcoming Civil War series?

2. *Questions that show you are paying close attention.*

Could you explain a bit more about the new department you mentioned?

In connection with the sealing process, what is the time allotted between design and manufacture?

3. *Questions that show you are work focused.*

As I understand the position, the title is _____, the duties are _____, and the department is called _____. I would report directly to _____. Is that right? (You are making sure your facts are straight.)

Can you describe a typical day?

Would you describe the atmosphere here as formal and traditional, or informal and progressive, or what?

What became of the last person who held this job? (You are trying to find out if it's a steppingstone to bigger things or a road to nowhere.)

You mentioned company training. Would that be formal or informal and how long does it last? What skills would I learn ?

Is travel involved? If so, approximately what percent of my time would be spent traveling?

What do you see as opportunities for advancement in this job? (You are double-checking advancement potential.)

How is job performance evaluated? (You are trying to find out if performance evaluations, and hence raises and promotions, are based on objective criteria that employees know and understand.)

B. *Personal Agenda*

Save questions that are important only to you until after you have received a job offer or a close facsimile. To ask personal agenda questions before the offer clouds the employer's mind with nagging suspicions that you only care about what's in the job for you. But once the offer has been made, the employer has decided in your favor and has a wide open mind for thinking about what it will take to bring you aboard.

Now you need the information necessary to make an intelligent decision. Here are questions for this purpose.

What is the compensation level for this job? Does that figure include employee benefits? (If you are offered the job and nothing is said about salary.)

What sort of health insurance benefits do you offer?

What about other benefits, such as leave time and vacation?

What is this company like as a place to work? Has the company had to lay off groups of people? If so, what sort of severance package did they receive?

If relocation is involved, how much will the company help? Will I receive a written job offer spelling out the basics? (The basics include job description, title, pay, employee benefits, relocation expenses, starting date, and incentive awards, if any.)

May I talk to someone who is doing what I will be doing (or will work closely with?) (Find out if your prospective boss is a good person to work for, the pluses and minuses of the company and the job, and the factors needed to be a success in the position.)

As a new graduate, be careful how you ask personal agenda questions so you don't come across as too self-important. Lace your conversation with your interest in making a good, long-term match for both employer and employee and that's why you want to do a thoughtful job of gathering information.

Never ask sensitive questions that may put the hiring manager on the defensive before you receive an offer, such as "Have you had any organizational downsizing lately?"

Don't use questions to make a speech or be a show-off about your research: "I understand that product QQQ has a subzero component dating back to minus quimbies; could you give me the upquotient on that?"

And don't ask naive questions research would have answered. To IBM: "Do you make laptop computers?"

Even though you are new in the job market, learning to make questions work for you in selling yourself will help you get job offers and to acquire the information to know when you should say "I accept with pleasure."

Ask for the Job— Or at Least Leave the Door Open

When it's time to go, the interviewer may stand up or inquire whether you have any further questions about the job. This is your cue to close with an approach that encourages an offer, or at least leaves the door open. In marketing circles, this is called *asking for the order* or *closing the sale*.

Use the following script as a guide in choosing your own words.

I'm very excited about this job. My qualifications seem to fit very well.

Follow this assertion with a summary of your qualifications. Although you've mentioned them throughout the interview, people forget what they hear. Next, attempt to draw objections out in the open.

Do you see any gaps between my qualifications and the requirements for the job?

If any shortcomings are mentioned, try to overcome them. If the objection is that you have no experience, say you learn fast and will work as hard as it takes to get the job done. Continue to show interest by asking if you've missed any points.

Do you have any further questions or concerns about my background, qualifications, or anything

else? I'm very interested in this job and I'd like to be sure you have all the information you need to assess how I might fit in here.

You may even have the opportunity to ask the brass-ring question: "Do I get the job?" Opinion is divided on whether experienced people should ask to be hired. After you've held a couple of full-time jobs and established a track record, you may not find it advantageous to look too available. Enthusiasm is irresistible in beginners, however, and you may as well make it work for you by being straightforward if you want the job.

In any event, don't leave without asking when a hiring decision will be made. Remember, if the answer is fuzzy, ask if you may call back to check on the status of the job.

Be certain to express your appreciation for the time the interviewer spent with you.

Interview Thanks: Is It an Outdated Idea?

In a competitive situation, anything you use as a tactic to call attention to why you should be hired is never out of date. In the best book on the subject, *The Perfect Follow-Up Method to Get the Job* (Wiley), author Jeff Allen says a follow-up letter makes you stand out from the crowd. And that it "restates the areas you want to emphasize" and permits you to actually "re-interview" over mistakes.

Here are the viewpoints of two executives who evaluate many applicants:

From a supervisor of professional employment for a manufacturer in Cleveland, Ohio:

Having recruited for positions at the entry—as well as upper-level, I favor notes of appreciation from individuals interviewing for lower-level jobs. Competition for these jobs can be fierce and a thank-you letter will often help me remember a person.

For higher-level positions, a thank-you note might be viewed as unprofessional or unnecessary.

Thank-you letters should be sent promptly, within 24 hours of the interview, and should be brief, concise, and sincere. Flowery or verbose letters tend to signal oversell.

From a manager of human resources for a defense contractor in Carlsbad, Calif.:

Thank-you notes are an excellent means for reminding the interviewer of the person applying. A grateful, warm, personal note is a plus in the process. In addition, a reminder of skills and qualities and a suggestion as to where the person could fit in is helpful.

Both personnel executives are suggesting that at the professional level, you should use a follow-up letter for more than a thank you.

You can (1) impart a sense of urgency, (2) offer new information, or (3) restate your benefits.

Urgency

I've had other interesting discussions, but your organization is tops on my list. I've got to make a decision within two weeks. May I have the opportunity of seeing you again next week to provide any additional information you may find useful in making your final decision?

New Information

After reflecting on our meeting, I realize there is a strong linkage between the areas of specialized knowledge you need and the technology I have studied. You mentioned that the company intends to enter the fiber optics market. Although I mentioned that I have completed six courses specific to fiber optics, it occurs to me that I did not elaborate on their content as it relates to your needs. I'm enclosing a brief statement of my fiber optics education and would be glad to meet with you again this week to amplify my qualifications.

Restate Benefits

The description of the work your organization is doing was helpful in reviewing my qualifications in light of your requirement . . . (restate your benefits) . . . I'm sure we could work together profitably and productively. Can we meet this week and finalize matters?

If you miss out on a job, you can still bank on the future when you write.

I was disappointed that I did not get the job but I appreciate your time and consideration. If you again find a similar position open, I would be grateful for a chance to compete for it.

View thank-you letters not as an exercise in good manners, but as an effective follow-up tactic; the higher the job level, the more sophisticated your communication should be.

■ ■ ■ ■

Senior Year Job Search Countdown

September

Check in with your college career services center. Many offer daily or weekly orientation sessions.

If you don't have a good idea of the career direction in which you want to travel, ask at the career services center for tests to take and books to read. (A review of earlier sections of this work will help clear the fog.) Try to get a handle on job functions and what people actually do in marketing, personnel, transportation, finance, and other options.

Sign up for job search seminars.

See if internships are available.

Join student organizations whose students share your career interests.

Find out about career days and job fairs.

Begin to make lists of places you'd like to work; begin gathering research on them. (Review Chapter 7 on how to make future files.)

Establish a credentials file at the career services center. This file typically contains your resume, transcript, and reference letters. Employers use it to evaluate your candidacy.

Talk with a placement specialist responsible for on-campus recruitment; get a copy of the recruiting schedule and register for preferred employers.

Write your resume and ask a specialist at the career services center to review it.

October

Identify references and ask them to respond with comments that support your career goal.

Schedule a practice interview with a career specialist to polish your interviewing techniques.

Invest in good interviewing clothes; you never know when an opportunity will turn up.

Consciously expand your network of contacts to reach your target employers; don't forget your professors—many have good contacts outside campus.

Devise forms to manage your job search. Use index cards for reminder messages, calendars, and sheets to record whom you contacted, what was said, and what follow-up action is needed. Your career services center may have forms, so why reinvent the wheel?

November

Keep researching and making future files of career areas and companies that interest you.

Make contact with employers to schedule informational interviews during holiday break.

December

Campus interviewing slows down. Use the time to research employers and plan your spring semester job search campaign.

About now you may begin to receive call-backs to second interviews. Get tips about plant visits and second interviews from books, workshops, and career center advisers. How you handle yourself, including your deftness with business etiquette, can make or break your chances for an offer. If your eating habits are a tad unrefined, get help quick!

At holiday break time, keep the appointments scheduled in November. Make the rounds of contacts for information and for job leads.

January

It's The Get-Serious Hour. Your job hunt should be in full swing as you continue doing all the job-producing activities described in this book. If you haven't yet begun to practice interviewing techniques in a job search seminar, start now.

February

The campus recruiting program is in peak operation now after having started last fall. But recruiter ranks are thinning out and you may have to press harder than ever to get interviews.

Pause to take stock of how you're doing. Are you happy with your progress? Do you need to reassess your career direction? Are employers responding to you? You should have a fairly good feel of whether you need extra help in reaching your goals. If so, go back to the career services center and ask for it.

March

All flags should be flying. If you haven't been tapped by on-campus recruiters, step up your outside job search. Spend at least 15 hours a week—more if possible—calling contacts, writing letters, researching, and trying to interview.

April

Ditto.

May

Check to see if the career services center offers summer interviewing schedules. With finals and graduation looming, you may have to back off a bit on job search time.

If you don't yet have a job, there are two schools of thought about your next move. Should you take the summer off and start hard-charging again when there's less competition in September? Or should you maintain momentum and continue your search right now? We advise maintaining momentum, but we can't make that decision for you. We don't know how tired you are.

(*Drema Howard and Diane Kohler, of the University of Kentucky Career Center, are the kind professionals who helped us with this calendar.*)

Interviewing is a Numbers Game

So you didn't get an offer of a dream job in a garden spot of the world. So your only offer is to join the oil workers in Deadhorse, Alaska, where it's so cold that people wear gloves 10 months a year, snow falls on the fourth of July, and contact lenses can freeze to the eyes. Don't let depression drag you down.

Liberal arts graduates, in particular, should not be discouraged if they go through dozens of interviews without receiving a single good offer.

The main thing is not to lose heart. The more interviews you experience, the better you'll become at talking about who you are and what benefits you can bring to an employer. You might have to suffer through 100 "no's" before getting one good "yes."

■ ■ ■ ■

Choosing and Succeeding on Your First Full-Time Job

After putting forth a herculean effort in your job search campaign, let's assume you made all the right moves and earned your reward—one or more job offers. Now that employers have said they want you, it's your turn to be selective.

This chapter tells you how to recognize the offers you should refuse and the one you should grab. It discusses what employers expect of you, the importance of hitting it off with your boss, and techniques you can use to win recognition, promotion, and raises. We also offer information for dealing with sexual harassment.

The discussion concludes with a consideration of knowing when it's time to find greener pastures, and how to look good to the boss you leave behind.

Stick to Your Career Plan

If a job doesn't boost your career aims, let someone else have it.

There are major exceptions: Any job is better than no job when you need rent money, your car requires an engine overhaul, your education loans are coming due, your roommate is threatening to stop paying the food bill, or your parents are about to throw you out of the house.

As a guideline, don't take a job in supermarket operations when you really want to be a leader in travel and tourism. Stay close to your field and watch where you step.

Ask yourself: "Will this job *position me* for future advancement in my field?"

Position you? What's that? Positioning is an important ingredient in career success, and it means putting yourself into a situation where opportunity may salute you. It means gaining exposure to various types of work in your field. It means being visible to higher-ups who have the power to single you out for advancement.

Here is a brief example of career positioning.

Imagine you have a degree in business, emphasizing marketing and finance. You have two job offers. One is with the accounting department of a solar energy equipment manufacturer where you would be assigned to a regional office. In the other job, you would be a traveling consultant working for an association of mortgage bankers.

The solar job would qualify you to do other financial work in the solar industry, and probably qualify you for financial work in other industries. Not being at the headquarters office, you would be away from top management and have less chance of being noticed by higher-ups. Unless you make a concerted effort to read industry news and attend industry meetings, you'll not be exposed to other areas of work in the solar field. It's possible you eventually could become the vice president of finance for the solar maker. It's also possible you could be locked into a career closet.

The traveling consultant job would position you to learn about many opportunities in financial marketing. You would see and be seen by influential bankers who could offer you a good job. Two years on the road could provide your lucky break.

A less obvious situation in positioning analysis is the offer that on the surface seems distant from your goals but in reality can set you up for better things. An example is: "I-don't-wanna-sell insurance." Maybe not. But maybe you do want to be in the public relations field. Insurance companies have sizable public relations staffs. Positioning could help your goals see daylight.

Be sure the job you accept is in the right ball park even if you have to push back the fences a bit, and be sure the position you play offers benefits.

As we mentioned in earlier sections, temporary employment agencies are a good way to experience a variety of jobs, and if you do an outstanding job, this could work out to be a permanent position in your field with a company you feel comfortable with.

■ ■ ■ ■

Big Company, Small Company: Which Is Best for Your First Job?

True, you gain professional breadth more quickly by wearing several hats at a small firm than by specializing at a large company, but we suggest that you *think big*.

Large corporations may offer excellent training programs for career development. Small firms can't afford them.

Large corporations may be willing to move you around, giving you a chance to try out work or at least observe various tasks at close range. Rotating assignments can give you access to a wide range of ideas and people outside the company.

Moreover, it's easy to move from prestige large to obscure small, but not as easily done the other way.

Generally speaking, the larger the company, the larger your training opportunity; the greater the company's reputation, the greater your career clout.

What often happens is that new graduates take the expensive training offered by a giant and run, frequently to a more responsible job at higher pay in a smaller company.

If a large company doesn't book your maiden career voyage, look on the bright side of working for smaller organization. Small businesses employ about half the non-government workers in the country and small firms have provided virtually all new jobs in the U.S. recently.

By working for a small company, you get greater exposure to senior management, faster advancement and more opportunities to become involved in corporate goals and directions.

Don't Overlook Work in Non-Profit Organizations

There appears to be a greater demand for many management, marketing, fund raising, and public relations positions in the non-profit sector.

According to Michael O'Neill, director of the Institute for Non-Profit Organization Management at the University of San Francisco, the latest growth phase of the non-profit sector began in the mid-1960s and has continued at

enormous rate. The number of people who are in need of social or other services has jumped dramatically, creating a tremendous demand for highly trained professionals.

■ ■ ■ ■

Job Offer Evaluation Checklist

Miracles never cease. You have a job offer. What a relief. You were beginning to wonder if anyone would ever invite you aboard. You may be tempted to snatch the first job offered, but slow down. As with anything else done in haste, the results can be disappointing.

Instead of saying "yes" or "no" on the spot to a job offer, express your gratitude in a warm and friendly manner and then ask for a day or two to consider the opportunity.

You will make your own decisions, but we think the most important criteria in evaluating a job offer are, in this order: your new boss, the work content of your job, the positioning opportunities, the company, and, lastly, the salary.

Use the following checklist to explore what you think about a job offer. Remember to focus on the items most important to you.

The Job

_____ In my best guess, will I get along well with my boss?

_____ How will I be managed? Will I have more than one boss?

_____ Do I clearly understand the nature of the work?

_____ Do I know specifically what I will be doing? Are my responsibilities reflected in my job title?

_____ Is the position itself interesting and challenging?

_____ Can I make final decisions affecting my work?

_____ Do I have the feeling that I will get along well with co-workers?

_____ Will I need more training? Will the company pay for it?

_____ Will overtime be necessary or available? Night work? Weekends?

_____ Will I travel? How much? Where?

_____ Will I relocate? Where? Will the company pay moving expenses?

_____ Is there reasonable job security?

_____ Will I be proud to tell my friends what I do?

Positioning

_____ Could this job result in a significant promotion?

_____ Is the background I'm building too narrow to be of interest to most other employers?

_____ In contrast, will this job help broaden my experience and build a saleable background?

_____ If this isn't my dream job, can it be a springboard to something better as I acquire experience and skills for advancement?

_____ Does this job give me exposure to other opportunities in my field?

_____ Will I be visible to decision-makers?

_____ How frequent are my performance reviews? (Important for improving your performance and being rewarded for a good one.)

The Company

_____ Is the organization too large and rigidly structured for my personality?

_____ Is the organization too small to offer room for advancement or impressive credentials for a future resume?

_____ Is a written personnel statement available that describes vacations, sick leave, cause for dismissal, and so on?

_____ Is the company growing faster than its competitors? Is its financial position healthy?

_____ Is there a high turnover of personnel? If so, why?

_____ Is the company's location convenient?

_____ Is the commuting time acceptable?

_____ Is the physical setting acceptable? (Enough light, ventilation, cleanliness.)

_____ If I relocate, do I like the lifestyle the company's location offers? Are desirable community, cultural, religious, shopping, and recreational facilities available?

_____ What is the firm's reputation for fair treatment of employees?

_____ Is the organization in a growth industry? If it's in a shrinking industry, do I have reason to believe the industry can still offer good opportunities over my working lifetime?

Financial Rewards

_____ Is the salary competitive? (Does it pay the market rate or more?)

_____ If it is not competitive, is it possible to get an early review and an increase before one year?

_____ Do I clearly understand the method of payment—salary, hourly wage, commission, wage and tips, by the piece, fee?

_____ Are raises based on merit, length of service, formal exams?

_____ Are employee benefits competitive? Do I receive any of these common benefits?

- ◆ Insurance: health, dental, life.
- ◆ Memberships: professional societies, trade associations, health clubs.
- ◆ Free parking.
- ◆ Time off: vacation days, holidays, sick days, maternity leave.
- ◆ Retirement plan. How much does the company pay and how much do I pay?

_____ Do I receive any of these less common employee benefits?

- ◆ Company car.
- ◆ Clothing allowance for special uniforms required but not provided by employer.
- ◆ Expense account.
- ◆ Employer-paid tuition for college.
- ◆ Travel to conferences, conventions.
- ◆ Subscriptions to professional and trade journals.
- ◆ Profit sharing or stock purchase program.

career commitment to the position. For that reason, you have to be sure there are no loose ends.

Not having adequate facts on which to weigh a job offer the moment you receive it is another reason to ask for time to reflect. Once you accept an offer, renegotiating is difficult, often impossible.

But some gains may be possible before you accept a job. Once all the data are in, compare the offer with your job objective.

Unless you enjoy complex computations, keep it simple. A scale of 1 to 10 works well for many people.

If the offer rates less than 6 on your scale, the job probably isn't for you. You want to do better than break even, don't you?

If the offer scores above 6 points, a majority of its factors appear to meet your requirements. What's missing in the offer? What would bring it closer to the top of your scale—a little more money, a bit more visibility? Although you won't have much leverage as a beginner, you might negotiate minor concessions.

In our observation, there is no such thing as a perfect 10 job. If you find one, tell the employer you'd be as happy as a clam at a shellfish singing contest to come aboard. Is yesterday too soon?

■ ■ ■ ■

Rate the Offer

You may find you lack enough information to even guess at some of these questions.

In that case, telephone the person who made the hiring offer, saying you have several questions and would appreciate a chance to clear them up. Ask when you can drop by for a brief meeting.

Once in the employer's office, take the curse off your hesitancy by saying that while you're 99 percent sure the job is perfect for you, as a conscientious person you intend to make a serious

Discover the Best Companies to Work For

What makes a company good to work for? Surveys of executive recruiters and studies by business writers show common characteristics.

Excellence. A study by *Money* magazine says the quality of excellence seems to be what sets the best companies above others. The term refers to all-around excellence in products, research, marketing, management, and people. A company that operates on sound values and gives good value seems to spur the enthusiasm of its employees to conquer the marketplace.

Somewhat Higher Pay and Employee Benefits. Compensation is often a bit higher at the best companies. They appreciate good employees and want to keep them.

Sensitivity to Human Problems. The top companies pay more than lip service to the fact that human resources are as important as capital and products. Doors are open, and promotions are made from within. Management builds team loyalty by being fair and competent.

Among the leaders, the Xerox Corporation is a vivid example of caring about people. In 1971, Xerox announced that each year it would let about 20 employees have up to one year off with full pay and benefits to pursue social projects in their communities. Employees work in concerns of their own choosing, such as drug addiction, civil rights, literacy, and penal reform. Hundreds of people have had leaves since 1972 at an average annual cost of up to $500,000 in replacement salaries.

Want to know about other corporate standard bearers? A ready reference is *The 100 Best Companies to Work for in America*, by Robert Levering, Milton Moskowitz, and Michael Katz (New American Library).

Steelcase Inc. is one of the companies highlighted in the book. The office furniture manufacturer's benefits are extensive: from an innovative child-care referral program to an eight-week program for spouses and employ-

ees soon to retire; from a 1,100-acre employee campground to company-sponsored recreation programs in sports, hobbies, and wellness.

Not only do husbands and wives often both work at Steelcase, but the company offers employees' children student loans, summer jobs, and priority status on full-time work.

That's not all: Steelcase offers high quality dining-room food at cost, superior pay, and profit sharing. A flextime policy allows employees to structure their own working hours. If you like a family atmosphere, you can't beat Steelcase, Inc. in Grand Rapids, Mich.

Other companies frequently named in the top group are such well-known giants as IBM, Procter & Gamble, Eastman Kodak, 3M, General Electric, Weyerhauser, Cummins Engine, DuPont, Hallmark Cards, Hewlett-Packard, Northwestern Mutual Life, and Citicorp. This listing is by no means complete, but it gives you some idea of enlightened corporations and how they operate.

By contrast, what makes a company not so attractive to work for? Always make your own judgments based on individual assessments, but, as a general rule, executive recruiters warn against companies with a high turnover, a rigid management unsure of itself, or a management with many layers. Recruiters also advise you to carefully check companies that are family-owned, and companies that are run by an autocrat. While such companies often pay better than average, they may offer little satisfaction or security.

Right about now you may be thinking, "Oh, yeah, sure . . . it would be great to go with the pennant winners but there isn't room for everyone in the best companies. I might not get in the door."

That's true. Neither is there room for everyone in the worst companies.

It's good to know the difference.

■ ■ ■ ■

Government Jobs: A Spectrum of Career Opportunities

Government jobs are found at the federal, state, and local levels. Each level has its own hiring process.

The most visible government workers are elected officials and appointed high-level advisers—the people you see on news programs.

Although they're in the spotlight, such people are a small portion of the 17 million employees throughout all levels of government.

About one worker in seven has a government job. There are hordes of engineers, secretaries, health specialists, journalists, law enforcement officers, firefighters, teachers, historians, biologists, labor economists, hydrologists, foresters, social insurance representatives, artists, lawyers, food service workers, intelligence agents, diplomats, accountants, laborers, bankers, and more.

Virtually all occupations that flourish in private enterprise exist in the government sphere.

The money is adequate and the benefits are excellent, but don't count on buying a yacht if you opt for the public sector.

Our general advice is to choose the business world for your first job, unless you intend to spend your entire career in government service. If you begin in government, you may find it difficult to switch later to a corporate position. The reason is that many business executives are reluctant to hire former government workers, feeling that they care too little about making money for commercial establishments.

Beginning in January, 1995, a new process was established that made it easier for applicants to find out about federal jobs and how to apply for them.

The most welcome change implemented in 1995 is the end of the Standard Form 171, which had caused many applicants to tear out their hair. Job applicants may now use a resume, the new Optional Application for Federal Employment, or any other written format they choose.

Career Entry Group's deputy associate director Donna Beecher stresses that applicants should look at the vacancy announcement carefully to see what skills and abilities the job require. They should then make sure that the resume, optional application form, or other written documents that are submitted specifically address those needs.

Anyone with a computer and a moderm can now access the Federal Jobs Opportunity Board from home. The electronic bulletin board lists thousands of vacancy announcements worldwide. Callers can download any listing within minutes, allowing greater access to the federal hiring process.

It is now possible to apply for federal vacancies without ever having to leave home. The applicant can use a telephone application process, using the telephone key pad to "tap" information directly into the Office of Personnel Management (OPM).

In addition to electronic bulletin boards and telephone application systems, the Internet makes it easy to find out about government jobs. Find government jobs at any of these Web sites: Federal Jobs Digest (http://www.jobsfed.com/-fedjob4.html); Federal Jobs Central (http://www.-fedjobs.com/); JobWeb (http://www.jobweb.org/fedjobsr.-htm).

Entry-level job seekers no longer need to have their names added to a central job listing with little hope of being referred for a position. Now, when job seekers find a specific job of interest to them, they complete a computer-scannable questionnaire highlighting their qualifications and job-related experience. OPM scores the responses and sends a list of the best qualified applicants to hiring agencies.

If you prefer books, Neale Baxter's *Opportunities in Federal Government Careers* (VGM Career Horizons) gives you a quick fill-in. You are introduced to the kinds of jobs available and offered excellent suggestions on how to obtain them.

Additional rich resources are a pair of books by Dr. Ronald L. Krannich and Dr. Caryl Rae Krannich (both by Impact Publications): *Find a Federal Job Fast*; and *The Complete Guide to Public Employment*, which also covers state and local jobs.

Government Job Finder, by Daniel Lauber (Planning/Communications, 7215 Oak Ave., River Forest, IL 60305; 708–366–5200), is the most complete compendium of resources for government jobs at federal, state, and local levels.

■ ■ ■ ■

It's Attitude Adjustment Time

As a high-school senior, you were at the top of your profession (of student). Now you're starting over. It's back to square one—you're a freshman, a beginner, a rookie. Entering the working world is almost like being a newcomer in a foreign land. You'll have to adjust to a new culture, different behavior, unfamiliar customs, and, if technical jargon is spoken where you work, a new language.

Change your perspective. While your intellectual floor may be the average person's ceiling, don't give in to the temptation to behave in ways that cause co-workers to see you as elitist, superior, or overbearing. Adopt the attitude that you are bright enough to know you have much to learn, but you can do it with time and effort.

Reliability is another area that may require an adjustment in your attitude. In school, when you didn't feel like going to class, you may have stayed at home. It's different at work because others depend on you. The consequences can be severe if you continue to exercise the independence that was yours as a student.

Another difference between school and work is the weight of your responsibilities. In class, a partially right answer may have brought you partial credit; if you flubbed an exam, usually you could make it up by scoring a higher grade next time.

An employee doesn't have a similar latitude. Being half-right or flubbing a question can result in horrendous costs or downright disaster. Suppose, for example, you take a job as an engineer who makes recommendations for evaluating the catalyst in a nuclear reactor, or a quality assurance technician who checks pacemakers for human hearts, or a mutual fund analyst who researches million-dollar transactions in the stock market. The outcome of "oops" could be overwhelming.

The attitude adjustments you'll have to make are many, but simply recognizing this fact can smooth the transition.

According to a 1994 survey conducted by the Career Development and Placement Services at Michigan State University, employers are continuing to hire new college graduates in increasing numbers, but they are also advising graduates to reexamine their attitudes and expectations of initial high-paying positions and quick climbs up the corporate ladder.

Patrick Scheetz, director of the Collegiate Employment Research Institute, who conducted the study says, "Employers are reminding students that they still have some learning to do and that they need to show positive performance on the job. Students are thinking advancement when they should be thinking job performance. There's a whole new awakening; students proved themselves in college, now they have to prove themselves all over again."

Scheetz adds: "The attitudes and expectations of new college graduates are higher than their value on the market."

The students who generally do better on the job are those with significant work-related experiences, as well as computer proficiency, and good interpersonal, public speaking, writing, reasoning and teamwork skills, and strong customer relations abilities.

A misstep at school usually was repairable and forgivable. At work, the end result could be much different, depending on the severity of the goof. The following warning, posted in offices across the nation, is exaggerated, but it gives you the general idea:

To err is human, to forgive is not company policy.

■ ■ ■ ■

The Boss: Gatekeeper to Your Future

Many people don't fully comprehend that the person they call "boss" has make-it-or-break-it power over their work life.

Your boss can be a friend or enemy, mentor or tormentor. Your boss evaluates your performance and recommends you for promotion or good riddance. You won't get a raise unless your boss agrees.

Even after you leave the organization, your boss's power reaches out from the past in the form of references.

We know it is impossible to maintain a good relationship with some supervisors, but if ever you see a rift developing, act quickly and try your best to mend it.

■ ■ ■ ■

First Days on a New Job

Yes, every newcomer is as nervous as you are at starting a job. Here are tips to help relieve the tension and create a good beginning impression.

♦ Personality is a powerful influencer of career success. No longer is it safe to wallow in grouchy days as you may have at school, to exhibit coolness, abrasiveness or insensitivity to others. Positive traits, such as enthusiasm, cooperativeness, and self-confidence will ease your way.

♦ Give top performance on the job. One of the shortest routes to success is to show your boss you can get things done and that you place company concerns before personal pleasures.

♦ Ask questions until you know what you're doing. For small, routine questions, ask the boss to name a "shepherd," or "buddy," for you. When you want to know how to order supplies or where the files are, you can say to your shepherd, "The boss said to ask you my newcomer's questions." The shepherd is doubly flattered at being asked by the boss and you.

♦ Watch the use of first names. Simply ask your boss, "Shall I call you Mr./Ms. _____?" If the boss wants you to use first names, you'll be told.

♦ Ask your boss how an assignment is to be handled—with regular progress reports or contact only when you're stumped. You need to know how much responsibility and authority the boss is willing to delegate to you.

♦ Remember that people like other people who are like them. If your boss's office looks like a garbage can, yours can be neater but not pin-perfect. If your boss shows up a half hour early each morning, you make the great sacrifice and do so too.

♦ Follow office etiquette. A sharp listener will soon pick up on the special office language that's used to answer telephones, in office memos, and to address co-workers personally.

♦ In dress, take an employer's lead. When you're in doubt, dress conservatively until you know what's accepted.

♦ Arrive at work on time. Staying late does not make up for a tardy arrival. Your morning absence may play havoc with the work schedule of others.

It's just as important to arrive at work ready to work. Be sure grooming and eating are finished before you cross the office threshold. Eating lunch at your desk can create an image of dedication while eating breakfast at your desk makes you look disorganized and uncommitted.

♦ Lunch with different groups. You want to avoid being linked with an inappropriate group before you've had time to figure out who's who.

♦ Chances are you'll be introduced around. But if not, take advantage of naturally occurring meeting opportunities—in the elevator or at the water fountain—to introduce yourself.

♦ Learn the artful use of the memo. You may have to write a memo as a proposal to persuade someone to take an action, to report on an assigned project, or simply to protect yourself by getting an incident on paper and in the files. Remember to ask yourself, "Why am I writing? What is the problem? Why is it important? What do I want done about it? Who will decide?"

Your memo must answer those questions, and the fewer words it takes, the more likely it will be read and acted upon.

If your memo is not addressed to your boss, be certain he or she knows what you are doing and approves it. Don't ever appear to be side-stepping your boss's authority.

♦ Be alert to rank. Despite widespread talk about "the flattening of hierarchies," change in organizational structure is a slow process. Most people work in a hierarchy, not too different from the military in its ranking system—except in business rank-holders don't wear insignia.

When an outsider who is higher in the hierarchy comes to your work station, give the civilian equivalent of a salute. That is, graciously stand up and greet your higher-level visitor. Smile. Be ready to shake hands if the executive offers.

Fading into the woodwork as though you don't know a person of authority is in your space shows a lack of respect for the rank.

♦ Be cautious about socializing after hours. As journalist Wes Smith has observed, "Going out for a drink with the boys after work every night is a bad idea. Notice that the boss doesn't go. That's why he's the boss and they're still the boys."

■ ■ ■ ■

Dealing With Sexual Harassment

Sexual harassment exploded into the national consciousness like a giant stink bomb in late 1991. Although harassment has been a problem working women, and some men, have faced for decades, it took the televised hearings for Clarence Thomas' Supreme Court confirmation to make the topic a household word.

A spotlight of attention shows that public opinion and the law have changed radically in recent years. Although retaliation is still possible for speaking out, media focus has helped women realize they need not accept harassing behavior in the workplace. Federal law now permits recovery of punitive damages as well as recovery of lost wages.

What is harassment? When you need an in-depth understanding of the issue, contact the National Organization for Women, or 9 to 5, a working woman's advocacy group. (A library can supply addresses and telephone numbers.)

Briefly, sexual harassment is at the core of sex discrimination. When it is between employer and employee, it turns victims into second-class citizens because of the disparity of power in the professional relationship.

Sexual harassment includes unwelcome sexual advances, requests for sexual favors, and other conduct of a sexual nature—verbal or physical.

Harassment can take place before employment or after employment, and can be the basis for employment decisions affecting the worker's status. It is sexual harassment when the aggressor's conduct unreasonably interferes with a worker's job performance or creates an intimidating, hostile, threatening, or offensive working environment.

The 9 to 5 organization gives several examples of what is harassment and what is OK.

HARASSMENT: "Hey, great legs."
OK: "You look very nice today."

HARASSMENT: Pornography on bulletin boards or lockers, especially with comments about fellow employees.
OK: Keeping pornography at home.

HARASSMENT: Staring up and down someone's body; a pat on the behind.
OK: Making eye contact while speaking; a friendly pat on the shoulder.

HARASSMENT: Repeatedly pressuring someone who refuses for dates.
OK: Asking a colleague with whom you're on good terms to a company-sponsored social event.

What can you do if an employer or co-worker harasses you?

These are several suggestions from various sources:

◆ Seek advice and counsel from friends and co-workers. Don't ignore the harassment.

◆ Keep a log or diary in a safe place, not your desk. You will need the data to file a complaint with your company or with a government agency.

◆ Carry a small tape recorder to document evidence.

◆ Take advantage of company internal complaint procedures.

◆ Write a letter, and send it certified with return receipt requested to the harasser, keeping a copy for your files. State every instance of harassment and say you want the relationship to be totally professional from that point on. The tone of the letter should be rational, not angry.

◆ To contact the appropriate government agencies for information or to file a complaint, look in your telephone directory under "U.S. Government Offices" for a local office of the Equal Employment Opportunity Commission. Look under state and city government listings for state and local human rights agencies.

■ ■ ■ ■

How to Get a Raise

You may receive a raise without asking for one after you've been on the job for a year. Then again, you may not.

If this is confusing, a little background will help you better understand today's pay trends.

For the past several decades, the typical compensation policy of American corporations has been for managers to conduct annual performance reviews of each staff member and, as night follows day, conclude the reviews by awarding salary increases.

The review-raise process has been such an established routine that unless you had bombed the CEO with water balloons at the company picnic, you were sure to be rewarded for time served and loyalty rendered.

Automatic raises that are tied to performance evaluations continue to be the norm in many corporations, but growing numbers of large employers are becoming cost-conscious, especially in service industries where payroll expense is the biggest financial drain.

The cost-containers are looking at the relationship between productivity and pay. Their recommendations can boil down to giving no automatic raises, or more frequently, to stretching them out to 18 or 24 months, rather than the former 12-month review.

More large employers are relying on merit raises—increases given only to the most productive employees.

Find out what the compensation policy is at your company. If it has dropped automatic increases in favor of merit rewards, prepare to actively campaign for regular and generous raises. That is, be your own advocate.

How much should you expect? Compensation specialists say typical annual increases are about 5 percent when inflation is in the 5 percent range. If you change jobs, look for a boost in pay between 15 percent and 20 percent.

How can you prepare? As we said before: Maintain records. From the first month on the job, keep a journal of your achievements. Write down any contribution to the employer's success that can be used to win a raise. Spend 5 or 10 minutes of your own time every Friday jotting down your ammunition; summarize it every six months.

Rehearse your negotiations with a friend. Tape record the practice sessions. If your arguments seem weak, devise more persuasive points.

What if you are turned down on the basis of performance? Ask what you need to do to be rated as outstanding and make sure your manager sees you writing down the advice. Request another review in three months. Improve your performance and at the second review, refer to your notes to explain how you have met the standards set by your manager. Ask if you now can be rated as an outstanding worker (and, not incidentally, qualify for a merit increase).

Large corporations aren't the only places where automatic increases are under attack. A growing number of small companies are basing salary increases on achievement of goals and ability to pay, rather than on pure seniority.

Charles King, senior compensation consultant with William M. Mercer Inc. in San Francisco gives these tips for getting a bigger paycheck:

Do

Prepare a plan before you ask. Familiarize yourself with basic negotiation strategies and tactics. Identify potential objections and devise ways to overcome them.

Research. Find out how your company's compensation policy is structured and where you fit within it. Determine whether your salary is higher or lower than comparable positions both inside and outside your company.

Set your goals. Define a range of what is acceptable to you, leaving yourself some latitude to negotiate the exact amount. Consider alternatives, such as seeking a promotion, better hours, better benefits, or a performance-based bonus.

Gather information that supports your request. Maintain a log of your accomplishments, focusing on what you've done to improve the company's bottom line. Quantify your contributions if possible, either in dollar or productivity terms.

Tell your boss about projects or ideas. Demonstrate that you want to pursue innovative ideas that will boost profits or save money for the company.

Don't

Expect a raise for satisfactory work. For more than a cost-of-living increase, outstanding performance is required.

Bring up personal needs or financial problems. You won't get a raise simply because you need more money to pay the bills.

Get defensive or argumentative. Attempt to make the negotiations a "win-win" situation for you *and* your employer.

Be unrealistic in your request. You should have a good idea of the range of pay for your job and the ability of your company to pay you more.

Threaten to leave the company unless you are serious. An ultimatum may land you in the unemployment line.

For additional strategies to increase your compensation, two books are outstanding: *How to Make $1,000 a Minute Negotiating Your Salaries and Raises,* by Jack Chapman (Ten Speed Press), and *Salary Success: Know What You're Worth and Get It!,* by Dr. Caryl Rae Krannich and Dr. Ronald L. Krannich (Impact Publications).

■ ■ ■ ■

When You've Chosen the Wrong Job, Quit

Sometimes a job goes sour and you wonder what happened. Where did you go wrong? You thought you did everything you were supposed to do. You researched the company. You filled out the job-offer evaluation checklist. You felt you were on the same wavelength as your boss.

Despite everything, the job turned out to be a huge disappointment. After only three months, you are certain you have made a monumental false start.

How long do you have to stick with such a job? *Stay only as long as it takes you to find a better job.*

Cut your losses and try again. One or two years of your life is too stiff a price to pay for a miscalculation.

Analyze what went wrong. Somewhere there's a gap in your prior planning. Be more careful about which job offer you accept next time. You don't want to build a reputation as a quick-change artist.

■ ■ ■ ■

If You Bow Out, Do It Gracefully

All things eventually end, even a satisfying first job. Either you'll be selected for promotion in your company, or you'll move on. If your career is in a holding pattern, about two years is a benchmark for knowing when it's time to pack up and get out.

When you go, depart in style, leaving behind an image of you as a classy person.

Tell your immediate supervisor first; follow up with a letter of resignation. Then tell subordinates because they will be affected by your leaving. Next, notify higher-ups in writing. Last, share the news with your associates and clients.

How much notice should you give? Two weeks to one month is appropriate.

About your leaving, explain that you have mixed feelings. You're pleased to be tackling a new challenge, but you'll miss the people with whom you currently work.

The exit-interview can be a booby trap. A manager asks you to be frank and let your hair down about your views toward the company and why you're leaving. It's a mistake to assume you're finished with this company and attempt to clear the air with your gripes. Limit your remarks to positive reasons—you liked your job and the company, but you received an offer you couldn't pass up. You can never tell when negative words will haunt you. People talk— sometimes to other people with whom you will be dealing. In addition, you might be invited down the road to rejoin the company at a higher level if your file is filled with kind words.

Try to finish projects and establish a line of transition with co-workers for tasks you can't conclude. Offer to serve as a resource for your successor and to do everything possible to make the changeover go smoothly.

On departure day, thank everyone for opportunities, loyalty, support, courtesies, and favors. Put your appreciation in writing to your boss and top management.

It is not unheard of for employers who can't handle rejection to fire you once you resign. The day you give notice becomes your last day.

Reputable companies don't behave in such a second-rate manner, but if you have any hint that it could happen, here's a tip to protect yourself.

When accepting a new job, prepare the way with your future employer. Say, "I will, of course, offer two weeks' notice, but it's possible that my boss will be willing to release me sooner than that. Would it be okay if I let you know in a few days the exact date I can start with you?"

Should it turn out that your boss demands you leave the moment you resign, you're covered. With dignity, call your new employer to say you were able to work it out so that you can start work immediately. Offer no explanations, and never refer to the jerk who didn't play by the rules. Doing so would reflect unfavorably on you.

■ ■ ■ ■

You Can Own the 21st Century

In the 21st century, career paths will not be as clearly marked as they were for previous generations.

Expect to encounter twists and turns along the way, some pleasant, some unpleasant. Once you get a toehold in the success market, there's still a great deal you'll need to know about getting ahead and staying out in front of the crowd.

Of course, we can't lead you through all the minefields in your first job, but we can point out some important basics of career success.

One way to achieve that success is to give your career regular checkups. This chapter tells how to do this and continues with a treasury of success pointers gathered from respected sources.

A Regular Career Checkup Keeps You on Course

A lot of hard work went into finding your first job. It wouldn't be surprising if after getting it under control, you feel that it's time to relax, to lighten up. After all, it will be several years before anyone trusts you with managerial responsibility. Right?

Wrong. This kind of thinking will keep you from wanting to show up at your class reunion a decade from now.

There is never a time in your career when you can just coast. This is true on your first job, your second job, and every job thereafter.

While there is a legal age for certain things— voting and registering for the draft, for instance—there is no legal age for seizing opportunities. Good career chances could come your way at any time of your life, starting now. If you're busy taking it easy, you may miss some humdingers.

Beginning with your first full-time job and continuing throughout the course of your working years, devote a corner of your life to the management of your career.

Set aside a regular time—say, a half-dozen times a year—for this purpose. Use the time to review where you've been, how you're doing and where you're headed. It's useful to map out a plan, one that includes:

♦ Goals

♦ Objectives

♦ Obstacles to be overcome

♦ Activities to achieve objectives

♦ A timetable

(To refresh your memory about goal-setting, turn back to Chapter 9.)

Because career and life planning is not a one-time proposition, view your plan as flexible. Be ready to amend it if you get wind of changing situations, developing disasters, or unexpected opportunities.

You may ask, "Why write a plan that isn't set in stone?" The mere act of planning puts structure and substance into your career management. Planning makes you *think*.

During your career checkup, assess your progress and make revisions to your plan, when needed. Here's a list of questions you might ask yourself.

Career Checkup Questions

1. Am I meeting my objectives on the timetable I set for myself? If not, why not? What am I going to do about it?

   _____

   _____

   _____

2. Do I have enough experience to advance in my field? If not, what can I do to get more? Would I gain by asking for a transfer to another department within the company? Would it be possible to work on an interdepartmental task force?

   _____

   _____

   _____

3. Do I have enough education to continue to advance in my field? If not, what specific additional education do I need? Can I get it without quitting my job? Will my company pay for it? If not, can I afford to pay for it?

_____

_____

_____

4. Am I satisfied with this job? Do I enjoy the daily functions and responsibilities? Does this job meet my personal values requirements? If not, is it time to start looking for another job?

_____

_____

_____

5. Does this job have a future? Can I expand my responsibilities (with a promotion in mind)? Is the company growing and is it financially stable? Is the industry stable or expanding? If negatives exist, can I reasonably expect the situation to improve within the next year, or should I look for other opportunities?

_____

_____

_____

6. Is my career on the right course? Are my earnings what they should be compared to others at my level in the field? Are my benefits up to par? Do I enjoy good interpersonal relationships with my boss and co-workers? If there are problems, what can I do to resolve them?

_____

_____

_____

Points to Check

1. If your career is not moving along at the right pace, reconsider whether your goals and ob-

jectives are realistic. Perhaps your timetable is too ambitious. Maybe you need to take a hard, objective look at your qualifications for the job.

2. Do you need more on-job training? To illustrate, assume you sell personal computers to computer stores and often can't answer the technical questions. You worry that you don't have credibility with your customers. A candid discussion with your supervisor, asking for advice, is a good place to start overcoming your experience deficiency.

3. Do you need more education? Assume you are employed as a case worker for a public social agency. You have a bachelor's degree. You want to be the agency director one day. You will need at least a master's degree and perhaps a doctorate.

4. If a job is personally unfulfilling, be sure the trouble isn't really within yourself. Many people who believe the clouds will float away and the sun will shine again once they have a new job need to take a closer look at the sources of their unhappiness.

5. Anticipate which way the highway you are following will branch and branch again in the distance. Some jobs provide 10 years of experience. Other jobs provide one year of experience 10 times. Read business publications and trade journals for your industry to help you look around corners.

6. When you don't know what you should be earning (your market value), do research. Contact executive recruiters, private employment agencies, college career offices, and the public employment service.

Study recruitment ads in newspapers and trade journals. Professional societies and trade associations often have local salary figures or know where to get them.

The reference librarian at a major library can direct you to private salary studies such as those conducted by the Administrative Management Society, the American Management Association, or books about what people earn, such as *American Almanac of Jobs & Salaries*, by John W. Wright (Avon/Hearst).

As for employee benefits, compare your employer's package with that offered by most other companies, as given in the table on the next page.

Keeping track of how you're doing places you on a career trampoline to spring higher and higher.

■ ■ ■ ■

today, and that you'll be working in an era of space travel between planets, living in a time when machines think like humans, and experiencing years in which the science of biotechnology changes life itself, you can see that your future is not going to be business as usual.

Even so, there are enduring and anchoring wisdoms that can light your way today, next year, and through a million galaxies tomorrow. Here are some of them.

■ ■ ■ ■

The Success Market

We hope that by now you've developed a fascination for career ambition.

Be as ambitious as you like. As Mark Twain once said: "I'm against millionaires but it would be dangerous to offer me the position."

We can't be sure what lies beyond the year 2000, but it is customary for authors and commencement speakers to solemnly inform each new crop of graduates that the challenges they face are greater than any since the Ice Age. In your case, it's true. That's because of the technological speedup that is occurring as you read this page.

You are going where no generation has gone before. But isn't that the same for everyone? Yes, but what's different for you, and why your challenge is greater than that of, say, your parents, is that your crystal ball is almost fogged over as a result of the *rate* of change: It's happening in fast-forward motion.

When you consider that about 90 percent of all scientists and engineers ever born are alive

Time and You

Besides the noble art of getting things done, there is the noble art of leaving things undone. The wisdom of life contsists in the elimination of non-essentials.

Lin Yutang

Time is a non-renewable resource. We cannot stockpile it; the best we can do is manage it well.

Start each day with a list of things you want to do. Separate the list into "must do today" and "can wait." Chances are you will have "can waits" left over each day. If a "can wait" gets pushed to the next day five times, consider whether you need to do it at all.

A good expenditure of your time is to spend several hours pursuing a time management course or a book on the subject. You'll learn about such things as the "80/20 trap," which holds that the majority of people spend 80 percent of their time on activities that produce only 20 percent of their results.

For one week, keep a log of how you spend your time. You will be amazed at how many precious moments you can save

■ ■ ■ ■

Build Power Alliances

In virtually every organization, there are two kinds of power systems—*formal*, which appears on the organization chart, and *informal*, which is a system of alliances.

Even as a new employee, begin to build power by participating in alliances. If there's a problem or opportunity in the wind, you'll probably hear about it through your alliances. If the change could affect you, the advance notice buys time to plan a strategy in response.

■ ■ ■ ■

Fired!

One day you may be fired from a job. Before going to pieces, remember that you lost only a *job*. You didn't lose your intrinsic worth. The sun will rise tomorrow.

Many people are fired at least once during the course of their careers. They just don't tell you about it. You are young. You are resilient. You will find a better job.

■ ■ ■ ■

Line vs. Staff Jobs

Line jobs are those that earn income for an organization. Often they involve the making or selling of a product or service. In banks, loan officers hold line jobs; in manufacturing, plant managers are line personnel; in newspapers, reporters are in line slots. In one way or another,

they fatten company coffers. Line jobs generally are viewed as being on the fast track.

Staff jobs are support positions that spend money rather than earn it. Staff expenses are necessary to keep the business afloat or to promote the general profitability of the enterprise. You'll find staff people in human resources departments, recruiting and devising benefits; in communications, writing and lobbying; in management information systems, analyzing data and preparing reports.

Support staff provide an organization's accounting and legal services, advertising, and administration. Many people view staff jobs as being on the slow track.

Historically, the top executive suite jobs have gone to line people who "knew the business." In recent years, several studies have come along to claim aides-de-camp can become heirs to their bosses' jobs. Moreover, lawyers and financial specialists not infrequently rise to the Number One job in their companies. Still, the weight of opinion appears not to have changed dramatically. Business school wisdom still says that if you want to fly an airplane, get a job in the cockpit, not in the maintenance hangar.

The type of company also affects how far you can go. In an accounting firm, accountancy is line work; in a corporate internal communications department, a reporter holds a staff job.

Being a staff worker is not without luster. In a large corporation, the top of the staff ladder is a department or division head, and, upon occasion, an executive in the upper echelon of management. The vice-presidential level of staff jobs can be impressive in money (six figures), power, status, and recognition. A human resources or communications VP might, for instance, direct the activities of hundreds of people. The scope can be wide enough to prevent a hint of boredom; an administrative vice-president might oversee food services, security, facilities, purchasing, and information management. The limit to advancement in some staff jobs is at a lofty level.

In small firms, a staff worker can rise to owner, partner, or head.

One problem about staff jobs is that when times turn lean-and-mean, they are more likely to be cut back than are line jobs.

Staff skies can be friendly, but if you are determined to become a high-flying captain, line jobs are the safest choice.

■ ■ ■ ■

Getting Noticed

Many young people assume that if they work hard and are loyal, they'll be rewarded. That's not necessarily true. Your management may be so involved with its own concerns that you remain merely a face in the crowd.

Don't make a mistake and keep your professional qualifications a secret. If you are ambitious, execute a personal image-building campaign.

Here are tips on acceptable horn-tooting from public relations expert David Drobis:

1. Get your name in the newspaper, perhaps as a consultant to an editor on topics involving your specialty.

2. Speak on radio and television talk shows as an expert on some topic.

3. Garner magazine publicity with by-lined articles. (Try writing a piece for your company publication.)

4. Join a club and contribute visibly.

5. Give a speech and arrange for your organization's public relations department to publicize it.

6. Give a presentation to management showing your department's problem-solving capabilities.

7. Use written internal communications to publicize your accomplishments. (But be careful not to sound like a braggart.)

8. At work, plug into the interpersonal communications grapevine, join committees and speak at luncheons.

9. Win an award and see that it is publicized.

■ ■ ■ ■

How to Be Lucky

Keep your personal contacts log up to date. Contacts are not a substitute for competence, but the fact remains that the more well-placed people you know, the greater the number of opportunities that will come your way.

In *The Luck Factor* (Macmillan), journalist Max Gunther, who has interviewed more than 1,000 people about what made them lucky or unlucky, says you can exercise a degree of control.

The basic difference between lucky and unlucky people, he says, is that "lucky people have a spider web network of friends and contacts, and unlucky people tend to be loners. Most of the big lucky breaks in life come through knowing people. The more people you know, the more chances you have to get lucky."

Professional societies and trade associations are excellent places to begin. Find out what groups operate in your field and join today.

■ ■ ■ ■

Learn the Art of Compensatory Responding

Answer questions and requests from strength. Never answer an employer's query with a naked "no" and let it end at that. Build your answer on a "yes."

For example, if an interviewer should ask whether you ever worked in the hotel field and you reply, "No, I haven't," add something like this: "but I've worked in the restaurant field and I know a good deal that is common to both of these related industries."

If your boss should inquire if you are willing to take a stab at preparing next year's budget and the thought petrifies you, never say so. Instead tell the boss that while the budget drafting is new to you, you're willing to give it your best shot and would appreciate guidelines.

For a young person, the art of compensatory responding means finding ways to overcome a lack of experience. Compensate by focusing on your high energy, your fine education, your flexibility, your willingness to work hard, and your ability to learn fast.

When you apply the art of compensatory responding to your answers, you let others know you are a "can-do" person.

■ ■ ■ ■

Handle Money, Manage Technology

If you're a private who wants to be a field marshal in the 21st century, learn to handle money and to manage technology. This is a high-performance team of talents.

This is the MBA who is comfortable with computers. This is the electrical engineer who understands high finance. This is the accountant who is clear on the mechanics of water resource management.

Perhaps you learned about money or technology your first time through school. Why not pick up the other half during evening or weekend studies?

Money and technology are an unbeatable combination.

■ ■ ■ ■

Getting More Money

What is the single most important thing you can do to receive a higher salary when you start a new job as an experienced worker?

Delay talking about money until you've been offered a specific position. Before that time, you are the seller and the employer is the buyer. After the offer, you negotiate as equals settling the price of a commodity. You are discussing value for value.

If you're asked too soon in a job interview how much money you want, say you're sure salary will not be a problem once you both understand the dimensions of the position and the quality of the contributions you'll be expected to make.

Can you imagine an interviewer saying the job is trivial? That an idiot could do it? No, you're likely to hear it is an important assignment and that a superior performer is required.

Once you show you are a superior performer for an important job, your value is up. And your price is up.

■ ■ ■ ■

Support Your Local Boss

Being at war with your immediate boss is like turning cartwheels on an ice floe: Dangerous with a capital **D**.

If you and your boss don't see eye to eye, maybe you can escape to a new job. Otherwise, act unilaterally to solve the problem.

Why? Because the boss holds the power. The boss controls the quality of your daily life. The boss can keep you from passing through the gate to praise, a raise, promotion, or glowing reference. Unfair, perhaps, but true.

One reason people flub boss relationships is a fear of authority carried over from childhood. This tends to make us treat the boss as a kind of god rather than as another adult who has needs and problems, fears and values.

If there's tension on the job, make a research project out of the boss and analyze the conflict with as little emotion as you can manage.

Note body language. Listen for hidden meanings. Read between the lines. Once you get a glimmer of why the boss acts in a particular manner, you gain a measure of control over the situation.

■ ■ ■ ■

Look for a Job When You Have a Job

One of the big "never's" in the success market is "never quit a job until you have another job." Or, looking at it another way: The best time to look for a good job is when you have a good job.

With the exception of new graduates, employers like to hire people who already are on somebody else's payroll. This is assurance that

somebody wants you. It is much harder to find employment when you're jobless.

This means you often have to keep your job hunt a secret.

When you need to make a quiet search, bear in mind these tips from Robert Half, the author of *Robert Half on Hiring* (Crown Publishers):

♦ Don't take longer lunch hours than usual.

♦ Keep personal phone calls to a minimum.

♦ Maintain your normal level of communication with management—staying out of sight is a clue that you're ready to move.

♦ Don't start coming to work dressed noticeably better than usual.

♦ Don't clear your desk of personal effects.

♦ Don't make a sudden change in your vacation pattern.

♦ Don't be less aggressive than normal.

Robert Half says that usually as soon as your company suspects that you're getting ready to leave, you can consider yourself as good as fired.

But in some cases, employers will make you a buy-back offer—that is, make you an offer that will induce you to stay. The career management skills come in knowing whether it is to your advantage to keep your search quiet or to let it be known.

■ ■ ■ ■

Coping With Crisis

One of the best rules I know is, when a crisis occurs or is in the process of occurring, don't react. Just say you'd like to think about it.

Once you have analyzed the crisis in terms of its potential for disaster, then you can respond. This at least allows for clearheadedness in dealing with the problem, and if you're savvy about what's going on and haven't become caught up in crisis yourself, it may present a very interesting edge.

This advice comes from Mark H. McCormack in his book *What They Don't Teach You at Harvard Business School* (Bantam Books).

When McCormack says "don't react," he does not mean you should stand still and let the office burn down.

He does mean keeping your cool in an emergency. Have you noticed that movie heroes never seem to be out of control even in a disaster film? In reality, you may be panic-stricken when a crisis occurs, but do your best to maintain a calm facade. The more unflappable you appear, the more people will follow you.

■ ■ ■ ■

Learn to Follow Money

To find jobs, find industries, businesses, private insitutions, and government agencies that are expanding. To find these organizations, follow money.

Bankers and investment counselors know about money. Ask one of them who is spending it. Or ask two.

John L. Munschauer, who wrote those words in *Jobs for English Majors and Other Smart People* (Peterson's Guides), is right. Even in recessions, the turnover rate for American corporations is around 15 percent.

As Munschauer says:

Prospering and growing organizations need money to finance growth. Bankers, who make money by lending it, make it a point to find organizations that are growing and need to borrow. Organizations that are growing need talent . . . You can't ask bankers to discuss their business, but you can ask them to nominate employers that are generally regarded . . . as progressive and growing.

■ ■ ■ ■

Make Yourself Obsolescence-Proof

The pupfish is a sort of quick-change artist that makes evolutionary modifications in response to environmental changes.

For 40,000 years, the pupfish has lived in the Death Valley area, where—although it is only an inch long—the piscatorial creature has amazed scientists with its ability to adapt and survive in desert waterholes.

The pupfish reconciles itself to rigorous conditions of wide extremes, and you can learn from its example: Expect inevitable change and minimize the risk of your own job-market obsolescence.

Accept the idea of continuing education as a way of life for all your life.

You need not take formal course work each year, but make it your style to read, watch educational programs on the tube, and attend industry meetings where new trends surface.

Just as you work out to keep fit, get into the habit of doing an information workout on a regular basis.

The dogged pupfish survived by moving with the times; you can too.

■ ■ ■ ■

Five Strategies For Moving Up

How can one move up in managerial circles? While there's no certain pathway of progress, the chairman of one of the world's largest executive recruiting firms notes five strategies that can put rockets under your heels.

Korn/Ferry International Chairman Lester B. Korn says:

1. *Get profit-center responsibility.* This means reach for positions that make money for the company and where your contribution can be clearly measured.

2. *Know how and when to take risks.* "Bidding for a risky assignment can propel you to the top, or become a suicide mission," says Korn.

3. *Internationalize your career.* "In an overseas management position, a competent executive can often achieve dramatic gains and impressive results more spectacularly than in the U.S.," the top recruiter explains. "But make sure your company has a proven U.S. re-entry program which recognizes your overseas experience," Korn adds.

4. *Learn to communicate effectively*—speaking and listening, reading and writing.

5. *Use career mobility selectively.* "Unless your company is in danger of disappearing, never move unless you'll be getting a sizable increase in growth and responsibility. If you can't negotiate a higher recognition level in the new position, your chances for success are diminished."

■ ■ ■ ■

In the Race to the Top, Who Wins—Scramblers or Stabilizers?

Getting to the top used to be a straight path. You worked for 30 years with the same company, showed unswerving loyalty, and were promoted. You stabilized.

"No more. Today large numbers of men and women at the top have gotten there by working for five businesses in 10 years, dedicating themselves totally to their own advancement and to getting a better and better job. These corporate zigzaggers are scramblers," says career consultant and educator Dr. Elwood N. Chapman. In his book *Scrambling—Zigzagging Your Way to the Top* (J.P. Tarcher/Houghton Mifflin Co.), Chapman concludes that scrambling is the wave of the future for career advancement.

Not everyone agrees. Some advisers say that today's chief executive officers (CEOs) are the type of people who have long-term time horizons.

Both viewpoints have merit. You'll have to choose the path that best fits your personal temperament—scrambling or stabilizing.

The scrambler places self above organizational interest. The stabilizer is devoted to the organization for which he or she is working.

In the past, traits exhibited by scramblers caused critics to label them as opportunists, job hoppers, and hustlers, but it is a mistake to assume that scrambling techniques are something nice people don't do.

Suppose you decide on the scrambling route. If you are challenged by an interviewer who suggests you've been job hopping, turn a negative to a positive and speak enthusiastically of the advantages of your *diversified* experience.

■ ■ ■ ■

Become an Expert

How can you become a person who makes things happen?

A key suggestion, offered by management consultant Dennis J. Kravetz, is to become an expert. In his book, *Getting Noticed—A Manager's Success Kit* (Wiley Press), he advises:

Become highly knowledgeable in your specialty. Be the most expert accountant, programmer, mechanical engineer, or middle manager. Others will seek your advice when they want to do things correctly, because they know you are the best source of information they have.

When you've mastered your own specialty area, keep going. Master another area, then a third and a fourth, until you know all the ins and outs of the company, including areas you're not responsible for. Get to know the people in other departments, divisions, and even regions. Learn how their operations run. More and more people will seek your counsel, and the reputation you build will increase your control over your future.

■ ■ ■ ■

No Job Gives You Everything

While you're not expecting too much if you want a great career, you are going to be disappointed if you expect any occupation to fill all your needs.

There's always a glitch, always something you wish were not a part of the job. A letter from a 40-year-old electrical engineer working in the aerospace industry illustrates:

I have always found engineering to be personally satisfying and stimulating, but the only defense against career frustration seems to be well-nourished cynicism and a bit of plain resignation.

This apparently negative attitude isn't unusual, but rather more the norm. Believe me. I've been in the trenches a long time, and I've met a lot of other guys shoveling alongside me that feel the same way.

There really isn't any such thing as the "corporate advancement ladder" for engineers. As you get older and smarter, you get more responsible job assignments, your title changes occasionally, but one is still an engineer. Okay, fine. That's what I wanted. The rewards, to get to the bottom line, are ultimately financial—the paycheck.

Which way is up? Supervision? No thanks. I've worked for a lot of people, and I wouldn't trade jobs with any of them. Private consulting? Ask the Small Business Administration what the failure rate is. Besides, I'm no businessman. I'm an engineer. Transfer within the company? Different frying pan, same fire. Quit, and work for another large company? Same pattern after the initial hire-in inducements. Small company? I've tried it. Aside from having to be a jack-of-all-trades, work man-killing hours, and hope the outfit doesn't fold up, it's all right. There is the one advantage of being close to where money decisions are made.

Get out of engineering? Many have. My choice?

Stick it out. I like engineering and besides, I'm probably too stubborn for my own good.

Thanks for letting me sound off.

Don't anticipate getting everything you want from work. Total safisfaction is no more assured in your career than in any other area of life. There are days, weeks, even months, when things go well—or badly.

Many jobs have great moments, but they are not eternal. Most jobs have bad times, but they pass.

For instance, Americans continue to lose free time and they're not happy about it. Indeed, Harvard economist Juliet Schor has predicted in her book, *The Overworked American*, that if present trends continue to the end of the century, Americans will be spending more time at work than they did back in the 1920s.

The Bureau of Labor Statistics reports that workers are averaging more than four hours of overtime a week. This may well be why people are beginning to say, "Money isn't everything. We want time with our families."

White collar workers are also putting in more hours. Corporate downsizing is partly to blame, as fewer people must perform the same amount of work.

This concentration on longer hours is an American phenomenon. Where Americans are finding their two-week vacations threatened, workers in Austria, France, Germany, and Sweden are guaranted five weeks of paid leisure a year.

Interestingly, a national study by the University of Pennsylvania's Wharton Business School found higher earnings among students who in high school told researchers that they rated a good marriage as very important.

The researchers analyzed the responses of 4,268 students originally polled in the National Longitudinal Survey of the Class of 1972, a research project that questioned high-school seniors on a variety of issues.

In a follow-up study 14 years later, the students who rated family as a major goal were earning more than those who had rated having a lot of money and finding a steady job as more important than a stable marriage.

Married woman had 4 percent higher earnings, and married men had 7 percent higher earnings.

This study indicates what economists have known for some time, that married men earn considerably better pay—from 10 to 50 percent more—than their single peers.

"Paying attention to family early on is going to pay off," said Peter Capelli, lead researcher in the study and co-director of Wharton's Center for Human Resources.

The message here is to develop satisfying leisure time activities and attempt to keep your life balanced. Include leisure time in your goals.

■ ■ ■ ■

Increase Your Intellect, Improve Your Memory

Marilyn Vos Savant, arguably the smartest woman in the world (listed in the *Guinness Book of World Records* under "Highest IQ") once was asked what one could do to increase intellectual level and memory.

Vos Savant's answer is deceptively simple:

Read more. It is far easier to understand and remember in context, and reading gives you that background.

As Vos Savant points out, it's quite hard to recall six simple Chinese characters when you don't know a thing about Chinese. Can you disagree? Isn't it, for example, much easier to understand and remember what happened in Washington today when you know a bit about how our federal government works? Read. Grow.

■ ■ ■ ■

Keep Your Ears Up

Employment experts John D. Erdlen and Donald H. Sweet say you are not expected to know everything, and that you cannot learn without asking. That's one of the reasons you have supervisors. It's always better to ask questions than to risk making a costly mistake.

And you'd better learn to listen carefully. In their book *Job Hunting for the College Graduate* (D.C. Heath and Co.), the authors report:

The biggest problem most people have in whatever they do is the failure to listen. This is compounded when, in an effort to demonstrate ability and effectiveness, the new employee rushes to get a job done without knowing fully what has to be done or how it is to be accomplished.

■ ■ ■ ■

By the way, if you should find yourself with a job that has few real duties, first try volunteering for extra assignments; if that fails, get out of there before you yawn yourself to death.

Some observers argue that image (how you appear to do the job) is more important than your technical skills (how you actually do the job). We're not willing to go that far (witness the brilliant professor who walks around wearing socks of two different colors), but there is no question that a high-performance image is jet fuel for moving up.

■ ■ ■ ■

The Success Image

You may need coaching in the status-behavior perception area.

In *Market Yourself for Success* (Prentice-Hall/A Spectrum Book), career counselor Richard A. Payne says many people get ahead in large measure because they give the appearance of being successful.

These people may not [be] the quickest, the brightest, or more importantly, the greatest contributors in their jobs. But they sure knew how to play the role inherent in their job title. And whammo, they were promoted ahead of others who offered more long-term benefits.

As for behavior, never let others think you are loafing. If you have a job you could finish daily by 10 a.m., be resourceful about looking busy. Write letters, create projects, attend meetings. Don't be seen as one who reads personal magazines on company time, takes long coffee breaks, lingers in the hallways, or makes lengthy personal phone calls. Act as though somebody were videotaping your day to play it back before your company's board of directors.

Manners Matter

Maybe you won't listen to your parents or your teachers about manners, but hear this from a best-selling business author, active corporate CEO, internationally renowned speaker, marathoner, and a Number One ranked tennis player in Minnesota. Harvey Mackay, in *Beware the Naked Man Who Offers You His Shirt* (William Morrow & Co.), says:

Rudimentary etiquette, particularly table manners, probably ranks Number One as the most totally abandoned tradition in American life, but it can matter hugely to your career. . . . They don't teach etiquette much anymore, but if you ever have to choose between Incredibly Advanced Accounting for Overachievers and Remedial Knife and Fork, head for the silverware.

Somewhere along the line, someone who can do you a lot of good is going to invite you to join him at the table instead of the office. He or she may have already seen how you handle your pocket calculator. Now, the person wants to see how you handle yourself. Don't expect to fake it. If you haven't had much practice, it's going to show. Sissy manners stuff? Don't kid yourself.

It's the seemingly unimportant stuff like this that separates the people at the peak from those in the pack.

■ ■ ■ ■

Extend Your Range

When you can't find a job you want in your home town, consider relocating.

When your company offers a promotion but it's in a faraway community where you don't know a soul, consider relocating.

When you have close personal ties to your college town and you'd like to stay on after graduation, consider relocating.

Sometimes you've got to be courageous and push yourself out into the world. To continue with our aeronautical metaphor, if you want to build airplanes, you have to go to the place they build airplanes.

There is no getting around the fact that if you stubbornly refuse to consider relocating to greener pastures, you drastically cut back the number of jobs you could get—perhaps by as many as 90 percent of job openings.

How can you evaluate whether it's worthwhile to change scenery? You weigh advantages against disadvantages, including income against expenses. You review your priorities and values, as well.

If, after reading this advice, you still intend to spend eternity right where you are, reflect on the admirable little coyote, a strong example of the benefits of following the brisk winds of opportunity.

In this country some years ago, the coyote was found only in the western states. When humankind began building houses and shopping centers on enormous sections of rural land the small wolf called home, the long-time canine resident was squeezed out. It had to make a move or perish. The coyote solved the immediate problem by extending its range and fanning out to all of the 48 contiguous states.

Although a spouse's job or other family considerations will eliminate some relocation options, your basic stance should be a willingness to consider a change of geography when the change is a stepping-stone to your goals.

Think about it: How wide-ranging is *your* habitat?

■ ■ ■ ■

Of Pride and Criticism

One of the toughest things in life is to objectively assess criticism—and if it's fair and constructive, to learn from it.

That's because we all hate criticism, valid or not. We'd much rather hear that we're Heaven's gift to Earth.

The inability to see criticism as something we can learn from rather than as an assault on our competence is harmful to successful careers. Sometimes, for crying out loud, we even cry when criticized.

Promise yourself you won't let pride stand in the way of benefiting from constructive criticism. Remember the axiom:

Today a peacock, tomorrow a feather duster.

■ ■ ■ ■

The Myth of Company Loyalty

Business has become much more impersonal during the past decade.

In the old days, you graduated and tried to find a fine company wanting a few good men and women that would keep you happily employed, through thick and thin. Those days, by and large, are history. No longer can you expect to work for a caring company for a lifetime.

Companies are bought and sold, restructured and downsized, staffed and de-staffed—all with troubling frequency.

In case you've been so busy studying that you haven't noticed, a new lean-and-mean mentality is streaking through most U.S. industries. If you complacently figure that a company will take care of you if you take care of it, you may one day wake up to discover you have been "set free" before you want to go.

Companies are loyal to their own survival, not to employees no longer seen as essential, whether those employees are young or old.

The reality of the myth of company loyalty is that your career is happening on your watch. You have the responsibility of monitoring what is happening in your world of work. You have the responsibility of maintaining a state of readiness (like keeping your resume up to date) so that you can move quickly if you see storms ahead.

To repeat an important point: Company loyalty is a myth. Reality is that your career is happening on your watch.

■ ■ ■ ■

The More Mentors The Merrier

A mentor is someone who teaches you, advises you, or promotes your career.

The mentor who teaches you is likely to be your immediate boss. The mentor who advises you may be your boss or a co-worker—or even someone outside your company. Some people develop relationships only with those who can enhance their careers.

The mentor who promotes your career is in the sponsor or "godfather" category and is likely to be a highter-up in your company, or someone connected with your company or industry who is powerful and influential.

Although you need at least one mentor, gratefully take as many as you can get. The more people you have pulling for you, so much the better.

■ ■ ■ ■

Getting the Golden Worm

Perhaps the most important tip is the one at the heart of this book: *Think early about your career goals.*

When he was 35, multimillionaire entrepreneur and co-founder of Apple Computer Steve Wozniak advised job market beginners to:

Realize that you have more energy now than you will later, and that you'll lose that after a while. If you want to really move up, this is the time to put in a few more hours. Make your job Number One, and work it like a pyramid, building on a strong base.

Start by gaining a little acknowledgement for yourself. That's what's remembered the next time around. It's like the kids in class who put in extra. hours and distinguish themselves. The teacher pegs them as smart, and the label sticks.

Another youngster—just as intelligent but lacking in initiative—gets just as strong a label the other way, and it sticks, too.

That's exactly how it works in the corporate world, so don't slack off in your early career years.

■ ■ ■ ■

This Is Goodbye

After reading this book, you are better equipped than most of your friends to plan how your dreams and serious ambitions will fit into the maze of life's choices.

While you may not have a completely clear idea of everything your dreams encompass, chances are they involve love, respect, happy days, enough money to live the kind of life you want, and good health.

As you prepare to make your dreams real, we ask you once again to remember that whatever your choice, it's not always the salary or stature or security that counts most *for you*.

A healthy regard for the future and a rainy day is basic. Beyond that, your work must give you personal rewards—excitement and involvement and purpose. In other words—

Do something you'd do for nothing.

■ ■ ■ ■

Study Terms Beyond the High School Level

As you move higher in your education, you'll hear terms with which you may be vaguely familiar, but are not positive about their meaning. Here's a glossary so you'll be sure.

Acceptance   Candidate is admitted. Colleges notify students in early April. Students should reply as soon as possible whether they will or will not attend the college. (For details see "admission programs.")

Accreditation   The process by which a nongovernmental accrediting association or professional organization grants public recognition to an institution or particular course of study. Generally, accreditation guarantees that certain minimal educational standards are met. Periodic evaluations are carried out to ensure the standards are maintained.

Admission Programs

Early Action   A plan allowing students to know the decision on their admission application before the standard April notification date. It differs from "early decision" in that students are not required to accept admission immediately.

Early Admission   A program in which a college accepts enrollments of high school students before they graduate from high school. Admission standards are more stringent for early admission.

Early Decision   A plan in which students apply in November or December and learn of the decision on their application during December or January. This plan is suggested only for students who are academically strong and know where they want to attend college. If accepted, early-decision students are often required to withdraw their applications to other colleges and must agree to matriculate at the college accepting them.

Early Notification   A program in which applicants must file their papers by December 1 in order to receive an admission decision by Feburary 1.

Midyear Admission   An option allowing applicants who were placed on the waiting list for fall admission and not admitted to allow them to start classes in the second semester.

Rolling Admission   A program in which admission applications are evaluated upon receipt and applicants are immediately notified of the decision.

Many colleges employ more than one of the admission programs described above.

Admissions Testing Program (ATP)   A program of College Board entrance tests that includes the Scholastic Aptitude Test, Test of Standard Written English, Achievement Tests, and the Student Descriptive Questionnaire.

Admit-Deny   Candidate is accepted but denied financial aid.

Advanced Degree   A degree beyond the associate or bachelor's degree. First professional, master's, and doctor's degrees are usually considered advanced degrees.

Advanced Placement   Admission or assignment of a freshman to an advanced course in a certain subject based on evidence that the student has completed the equivalent of the college's freshman course in that subject.

Advanced Placement Program (APP) A College Board service that provides high schools with course descriptions of college subjects and the Advanced Placement Examinations in those subjects. High schools implement the courses and administer the examinations on the basis of satisfactory grades. Students are then eligible for advanced placement, college credit, or both.

Advanced Standing Advanced status accorded to students who score high on Advanced Placement tests or who have taken "advanced" or "college level" courses in high school. If qualified, a student may gain credit for a semester or a full year of collegiate study, or a student may be allowed to skip certain introductory courses.

American College Testing Program A non-profit membership organization headquartered in Iowa City, Iowa, that provides tests and other educational services for students, schools and colleges.

American College Testing (ACT) Program Assessment Test battery of the American College Testing Program, given at test centers throughout the year. It includes tests in English usage, mathematics usage, social studies reading, and natural sciences reading. The composite score referred to in some colleges' descriptions is the average of a student's scores on these four tests.

Application A document submitted by a student who wants to be admitted to the college.

Approval The process by which a governmental or non-governmental agency or association gives official recognition to an educational program. Usually, approval does not include standards or inspections as rigid as those in accreditation, although approved programs or schools may or may not be superior to those with full accreditation.

Associate Degree The degree given for finishing a two- or three-year program of college work (most often a two-year program). In some colleges, associate degrees are given for partial completion of work in a bachelor's degree program.

Bachelor's Degree The degree given for finishing a college program of at least four but not more than five years of academic work. Usually this degree is either a BA (bachelor of arts) or BS (bachelor of science). There are also a number of specialized bachelor's degrees for certain fields such as BArch (bachelor of architecture).

Certificate An award for finishing a one- or two-year postsecondary school program. It usually certifies competency in a specific job field. Example: certified welder.

College Board A non-profit membership organization, headquartered in New York City, that provides tests and other educational services for students, schools, and colleges.

College Fair A large gathering of college recruitment officers to provide information about admissions to their respective institutions. Some public schools have college nights which are similar to college fairs, but on a smaller scale. Usually, the college night is restricted to an area of a county or region.

College-Level Examination Program (CLEP) A program of examinations in undergraduate college subjects and courses that provides students and other adults with an opportunity to show college-level achievement for which they have not previously received credit. The examinations are used by colleges to evaluate the entering freshmen and the status of students transferring from other colleges.

Common Application An admission application that, when completed, can be sent to several institutions.

Community College A two-year college offering courses to fit the needs of the local community. Occupational, adult, and general education courses are included along with liberal arts transfer courses. Though the terms *junior* and *community* colleges are often used interchangeably, junior colleges are more often limited to liberal arts transfer courses.

Cooperative Education A combination of classroom study and work experience directly related to the classroom study.

Curriculum A planned sequence of activities that helps students gain special skills or a certain body of knowledge. Most curricula also lead to a degree, diploma, or certificate in the particular field of study.

Deferral A term used by the college to handle early-decision candidates who were not accepted in December but have a chance in regular admission.

Degree A title given as official recognition for satisfactorily completing a curriculum. This is an "earned" degree. ("Honorary" or "unearned" degrees don't count as academic achievement, but rather as a school's recognition of people with special achievement, or who have donated money to the school.)

Diploma A document that states a person has satisfactorily completed a curriculum.

Doctoral Degree (Doctorate) The highest degree in a field of study or profession. The doctoral degree usually requires three or more years of work beyond the bachelor's degree and a dissertation (lengthy written work based on original research). PhD (doctor of philosophy) and LLD (doctor of laws) are two examples of doctoral degrees. Do not confuse this degree with MD (doctor of medicine), which is a first professional degree in medicine.

First Professional Degree The degree that shows all academic requirements have been completed for practicing a profession. A first professional degree requires five, or more often, six years of college work, sometimes seven or eight. Examples: MD (doctor of medicine), PodD (doctor of podiatry).

Grade-point Average or Ratio A system used by many colleges to evaluate the overall scholastic performance of students. GPA is found by first determining the number of grade points a student has earned in each course completed and then dividing the sum of all grade points by the number of hours of course work carried. Grade points are found by multiplying the number of hours given for a course by the student's grade in the course. The most common system of numerical values for grades is A = 4, B = 3, C = 2, D = 1, and E or F = 0.

Graduate School The part of a university that offers programs for advanced degrees.

Liberal Arts College A college in which the emphasis is on a program of liberal arts and basic sciences, usually leading to a bachelor's degree. Some pre-professional programs such as prelaw and premedicine may also be offered.

Major A student's main field of study.

Master's Degree The degree given for finishing one year (sometimes two) of academic work beyond the bachelor's degree. Some master's degrees are MA (master of arts), MS (master of sciences), MBA (master of business administration).

Matriculation Admission to, and attendance at, a post-secondary institution working toward a degree.

Open Admission The college admission policy of admitting high school graduates and other adults generally without regard to conventional academic qualifications, such as high school subjects, high school grades, and admission tests scores. Virtually all applicants with high school diplomas or their equivalent are accepted.

Pass-fail Grading System Some colleges rate students' academic performance in their courses as either passing or failing instead of giving grades to indicate various levels of passing work. The college's entire grading system may follow this pattern, or it may be an optional one for individual students in specific courses.

Rejection   The rejection letter usually starts: "There are a large number of well-qualified candidates for the few places in next year's freshman class. . . ." If rejected by a school, you may want to apply there later as a "transfer" or a prospective graduate student.

Reply Date   Date that an accepted student must indicate desire to attend. Failure to reply means acceptance will be withdrawn by the college.

Student-designed Major   An academic program that allows a student to construct a major field of study not formally offered by the college. Often non-traditional and interdisciplinary in nature, the major is developed by the student with the approval of a designated college officer or committee.

Undergraduate School   The part of a university offering programs leading to the bachelor's degree.

University   An institution of post-high school education that has these main aims: (1) teaching graduate and undergraduate programs; (2) conducting research to find new knowledge and more ways to use old knowledge; (3) making its findings and teachings available to society. The university grants advanced degrees as well as bachelor's degrees in many fields including liberal arts, sciences, and professions.

Waiting List   A kind of limbo that leans closer to rejection than acceptance. If placed on such a list for a school that still appeals to you, let the school know of your interest. It may sway a decision when openings appear.

Matching Yourself With the World of Work

The following guide was designed to help you compare job characteristics with your interests and skills. Listed and defined are 14 occupational characteristics and requirements that are matched with 200 occupations.

The table can be used in at least three ways. First, if you already have some idea of which occupation you wish to enter, you can use the table to find out the general characteristics of that occupation. Second, if you've decided on a general field of work—such as health or sales— but not on a particular occupation, the table can help you learn about the different jobs in that field. Third, if you haven't thought much about occupations, but you do know what skills you have, the table can introduce you to several occupations you might be good at.

One note of caution: The chart can be helpful in organizing occupational information, but it is intended only as a general exploratory tool.

Before you eliminate an occupation from consideration because of a single characteristic, you should realize that the job characteristics presented in the table refer only to a typical job in the occupation.

All jobs in an occupation are not alike. Most accountants, for example, work alone, but accountants who are auditors or investigators may work with others. Therefore, if you have an interest in an occupation, you should not disregard that career simply because one or two of its characteristics do not appeal to you. You should check further into the occupation— either through reading or by talking to your counselor—to find out how particular jobs in the occupation or occupational cluster might match up with your personality, interests, and abilities.

* This appendix is excerpted from the *Occupational Outlook Quarterly*. It was written by Melvin Fountain, editor of the *Occupational Outlook Quarterly*, U.S. Department of Labor, Bureau of Labor Statistics.

Key to Letter Codes in Column 14

Column 14—Entry requirements:
Three categories of education and training requirements are shown:

L = high school or less education is sufficient, and the basics of the job can usually be learned in a few months of on-the-job training

M = post-high school training, such as apprenticeship or junior college, or many months or years of experience are required to be fully qualified

H = 4 or more years of college usually required

	Job requirements								Work enviroment			Occupational characteristics		
	1. Leadership/persuasion	2. Helping/instructing others	3. Problem-solving/creativity	4. Initiative	5. Work as part of a team	6. Frequent public contact	7. Manual dexterity	8. Physical stamina	9. Hazardous	10. Outdoors	11. Confined	12. Geographically concentrated	13. Part-time	14. Entry requirements
Executive, Administrative, and Managerial Occupations														
Managers and Administrators														
Bank officers and managers	•	•	•	•	•	•						•		H
Health services managers	•	•	•	•	•	•								H
Hotel managers and assistants	•	•	•	•	•	•								M
School principals and assistant principals	•	•	•	•	•	•								H
Management Support Occupations														
Accountants and auditors		•	•		•	•						•		H
Construction and building inspectors		•	•	•	•		•			•				M
Inspectors and compliance officers, except construction		•	•	•	•		•			•				M
Personnel, training, and labor relations specialists	•	•	•	•	•	•								H
Purchasing agents	•		•		•	•								H
Underwriters			•											H
Wholesale and retail buyers	•	•	•	•	•									H
Engineers, Surveyors, and Architects														
Architects			•	•	•	•	•							H
Surveyors	•				•		•	•		•				M
Engineers														
Aerospace engineers			•	•	•							•		H
Chemical engineers			•	•	•									H
Civil engineers			•	•	•									H
Electrical and electronics engineers			•	•	•									H
Industrial engineers			•	•	•									H
Mechanical engineers			•	•	•									H
Metallurgical, ceramics, and materials engineers			•	•	•									H
Mining engineers			•	•	•									H
Nuclear engineers			•	•	•									H
Petroleum engineers			•	•	•							•		H

	Job requirements								Work environment			Occupational characteristics		
	1. Leadership/persuasion	2. Helping/instructing others	3. Problem-solving/creativity	4. Initiative	5. Work as part of a team	6. Frequent public contact	7. Manual dexterity	8. Physical stamina	9. Hazardous	10. Outdoors	11. Confined	12. Geographically concentrated	13. Part-time	14. Entry requirements
Natural Scientists and Mathematicians														
Computer and Mathematical Occupations														
Actuaries			•	•								•	•	H
Computer systems analysts	•	•	•	•	•							•		H
Mathematicians			•	•										H
Statisticians			•	•										H
Physical Scientists														
Chemists			•	•										H
Geologists and geophysicists			•	•	•					•		•		H
Meteorologists			•	•	•									H
Physicists and astronomers			•	•										H
Life Scientists														
Agricultural scientists			•	•										H
Biological scientists			•	•										H
Foresters and conservation scientists		•	•	•	•			•	•	•				H
Social Scientists, Social Workers, Religious Workers, and Lawyers														
Lawyers	•	•	•	•	•	•								H
Social Scientists and Urban Planners														
Economists			•	•										H
Psychologists		•	•	•		•								H
Sociologists			•	•		•								H
Urban and regional planners	•		•	•	•	•								H
Social and Recreation Workers														
Social workers	•	•	•	•	•	•								H
Recreation workers	•	•	•	•	•	•	•	•		•			•	M
Religious Workers														
Protestant ministers	•	•	•	•	•	•								H
Rabbis	•	•	•	•	•	•								H
Roman Catholic priests	•	•	•	•	•	•								H

| | Job requirements | | | | | | | | Work enviroment | | | Occupational characteristics | | |
	1. Leadership/persuasion	2. Helping/instructing others	3. Problem-solving/creativity	4. Initiative	5. Work as part of a team	6. Frequent public contact	7. Manual dexterity	8. Physical stamina	9. Hazardous	10. Outdoors	11. Confined	12. Geographically concentrated	13. Part-time	14. Entry requirements
Teachers, Counselors, Librarians, and Archivists														
Kindergarten and elementary school teachers	●	●	●	●	●	●	●	●						H
Secondary school teachers	●	●	●	●	●	●		●						H
Adult and vocational education teachers	●	●	●	●	●	●	●	●					●	H
College and university faculty	●	●	●	●	●	●		●					●	H
Counselors	●	●	●	●	●	●								H
Librarians	●	●	●	●	●	●		●					●	H
Archivists and curators		●	●	●										H
Health Diagnosing and Treating Practitioners														
Chiropractors	●	●	●	●	●	●	●							H
Dentists	●	●	●	●	●	●	●							H
Optometrists	●	●	●	●	●	●	●							H
Physicians	●	●	●	●	●	●	●						●	H
Podiatrists	●	●	●	●	●	●	●							H
Veterinarians	●	●	●	●	●	●	●	●	●	●				H
Registered Nurses, Pharmacists, Dietitians, Therapists, and Physician Assistants														
Dietitians and nutritionists	●	●	●	●	●	●								H
Occupational therapists	●	●	●	●	●	●	●	●						H
Pharmacists	●	●	●	●	●	●						●		H
Physical therapists	●	●	●	●	●	●	●	●						H
Physician assistants	●	●	●	●	●	●	●							M
Recreational therapists	●	●	●	●	●	●	●	●		●				M
Registered nurses	●	●	●	●	●	●	●	●	●				●	M
Respiratory therapists	●	●	●	●	●	●	●							L
Speech pathologists and audiologists	●	●	●	●	●	●								H
Health Technologists and Technicians														
Clinical laboratory technologists and technicians			●		●		●					●		
Dental hygienists		●			●	●	●	●					●	M

	1. Leadership/persuasion	2. Helping/instructing others	3. Problem-solving/creativity	4. Initiative	5. Work as part of a team	6. Frequent public contact	7. Manual dexterity	8. Physical stamina	9. Hazardous	10. Outdoors	11. Confined	12. Geographically concentrated	13. Part-time	14. Entry requirements
								Job requirements				**Work enviroment**	**Occupational characteristics**	
Dispensing opticians		•	•	•	•	•	•							M
Electrocardiograph technicians		•	•		•	•	•							M
Electroencephalographic technologists and technicians		•	•		•	•	•							M
Emergency medical technicians	•	•	•	•	•	•	•	•	•	•	•			M
Licensed practical nurses		•			•	•	•	•	•				•	M
Medical record technicians					•							•		M
Radiologic technologists		•			•	•	•		•					M
Surgical technicians		•			•	•	•							M
Writers, Artists, and Entertainers														
Communications Occupations														
Public relations specialists	•		•	•	•	•								H
Radio and television announcers and newscasters	•	•		•	•	•						•		H
Reporters and correspondents	•		•	•	•	•								H
Writers and editors	•		•	•	•							•	•	H
Visual Arts Occupations														
Designers			•	•	•	•	•							H
Graphic and fine artists			•	•			•							
Photographers and camera operators			•	•		•	•						•	M
Performing Arts Occupations														
Actors, directors, and producers			•	•	•	•	•	•				•	•	M
Dancers and choreographers			•	•	•	•	•	•				•	•	M
Musicians			•	•	•	•	•	•				•	•	M
Technologists and Technicians Except Health														
Engineering and Science Technicians														
Drafters					•		•					•		M
Electrical and electronics technicians			•		•		•							M
Engineering technicians			•		•		•							M
Science technicians			•		•		•							M
Other technicians														
Air traffic controllers		•	•	•	•		•					•		H
Broadcast technicians			•		•		•					•		M

| | Job requirements | | | | | | | | Work enviroment | | | Occupational characteristics | | |
	1. Leadership/persuasion	2. Helping/instructing others	3. Problem-solving/creativity	4. Initiative	5. Work as part of a team	6. Frequent public contact	7. Manual dexterity	8. Physical stamina	9. Hazardous	10. Outdoors	11. Confined	12. Geographically concentrated	13. Part-time	14. Entry requirements
Computer programmers			•		•							•		H
Legal assistants					•									L
Library technicians		•			•	•	•						•	L
Tool programmers, numerical control			•				•		•					M
Marketing and Sales Occupations														
Cashiers		•				•	•					•	•	L
Insurance sales workers	•	•	•	•		•							•	M
Manufacturers' sales workers	•	•	•	•		•								H
Real estate agents and brokers	•	•	•	•		•					•		•	M
Retail sales workers	•	•				•							•	L
Securities and financial services sales workers	•	•	•	•		•							•	H
Travel agents	•	•	•	•		•								M
Wholesale trade sales workers	•	•	•	•		•								M
Administrative Support Occupations, Including Clerical														
Bank tellers					•	•						•	•	L
Bookkeepers and accounting clerks					•							•	•	L
Computer and peripheral equipment operators			•		•		•					•		M
Data entry keyers					•		•					•		L
Mail carriers					•	•	•			•				L
Postal clerks					•	•	•	•				•		L
Receptionists and information clerks		•			•	•						•	•	L
Reservation and transportation ticket agents and travel clerks		•	•		•	•						•		L
Secretaries				•	•	•	•							L
Statistical clerks					•							•		L
Stenographers				•	•	•	•							L
Teacher aides	•	•			•	•	•	•					•	L
Telephone operators		•				•						•		L
Traffic, shipping, and receiving clerks			•	•	•									L
Typists							•					•	•	L

	Job requirements								Work enviroment			Occupational characteristics		
	1. Leadership/persuasion	2. Helping/instructing others	3. Problem-solving/creativity	4. Initiative	5. Work as part of a team	6. Frequent public contact	7. Manual dexterity	8. Physical stamina	9. Hazardous	10. Outdoors	11. Confined	12. Geographically concentrated	13. Part-time	14. Entry requirements
Service Occupations														
Protective Service Occupations														
Correction officers	•	•				•		•	•			•		L
Firefighting occupations		•	•			•	•	•	•	•			•	L
Guards							•	•	•	•		•	•	L
Police and detectives	•	•	•	•	•	•	•	•	•	•	•			L
Food and Beverage Preparation and Service Occupations														
Bartenders			•			•	•	•				•	•	M
Chefs and cooks except short order			•				•	•				•	•	M
Waiters and waitresses			•			•	•	•					•	L
Health Service Occupations														
Dental assistants		•				•	•	•	•				•	L
Medical assistants		•				•	•	•	•					L
Nursing aides		•				•	•	•	•	•			•	L
Psychiatric aides		•				•	•		•	•				L
Cleaning Service Occupations														
Janitors and cleaners								•					•	L
Personal Service Occupations														
Barbers						•	•	•				•	•	M
Childcare workers	•	•		•		•		•					•	L
Cosmetologists and related workers						•	•	•	•			•	•	M
Flight attendants		•				•	•	•	•					L
Agricultural, Forestry, and Fishing Occupations														
Farm operators and managers	•	•	•	•	•			•	•		•			L
Mechanics and Repairers														
Vehicle and Mobile Equipment Mechanics and Repairers														
Aircraft mechanics and engine specialists			•		•			•	•	•	•		•	M
Automative and motorcycle mechanics			•			•		•	•	•		•		M
Automotive body repairers			•					•	•	•		•		M
Diesel mechanics			•			•		•	•	•		•		M
Farm equipment mechanics			•					•	•	•	•			M
Mobile heavy equipment mechanics			•					•	•	•		•		M

| | 1. Leadership/persuasion | 2. Helping/instructing others | 3. Problem-solving/creativity | 4. Initiative | 5. Work as part of a team | 6. Frequent public contact | 7. Manual dexterity | 8. Physical stamina | Job requirements | Work environment | Occupational characteristics | | | |
									9. Hazardous	10. Outdoors	11. Confined	12. Geographically concentrated	13. Part-time	14. Entry requirements
Electrical and Electronic Equipment Repairers														
Commercial and electronic equipment repairers			•	•		•	•							M
Communications equipment mechanics			•	•		•	•							M
Computer service technicians			•	•		•	•							M
Electronic home entertainment equipment repairers			•	•		•	•		•				•	M
Home appliance and power tool repairers			•	•		•	•							M
Line installers and cable splicers			•		•		•	•	•	•				L
Telephone installers and repairers			•		•	•	•	•	•					L
Other Mechanics and Repairers														
General maintenance mechanics			•				•		•					M
Heating, air-conditioning, and refrigeration mechanics			•				•		•					M
Industrial machinery repairers			•				•	•	•					M
Millwrights			•				•		•					M
Musical instrument repairers and tuners							•							M
Office machine and cash register servicers			•	•	•		•							M
Vending machine servicers and repairers			•	•			•							M
Construction and Extractive Occupations														
Construction Occupations														
Bricklayers and stonemasons			•		•		•	•	•	•				M
Carpenters			•		•		•	•	•	•				M
Carpet installers			•		•	•	•	•	•					M
Concrete masons and terrazzo workers			•		•		•	•	•	•				M
Drywall workers and lathers			•		•		•	•	•					M
Electricians			•		•		•	•	•	•				M
Glaziers			•		•		•	•	•	•				M
Insulation workers			•		•		•	•	•					A
Painters and paperhangers			•		•	•	•	•	•	•				M
Plasterers			•		•		•	•	•			•		M
Plumbers and pipefitters			•		•	•	•	•	•	•				M
Roofers			•		•		•	•	•	•				M
Sheet-metal workers			•		•		•	•	•					M
Structural and reinforcing metal workers			•		•		•	•	•	•				M

	Job requirements								Work enviroment			Occupational characteristics		
	1. Leadership/persuasion	2. Helping/instructing others	3. Problem-solving/creativity	4. Initiative	5. Work as part of a team	6. Frequent public contact	7. Manual dexterity	8. Physical stamina	9. Hazardous	10. Outdoors	11. Confined	12. Geographically concentrated	13. Part-time	14. Entry requirements
Tilesetters		•		•			•	•						M
Extractive Occupations														
Roustabouts				•			•	•	•	•		•		L
Production Occupations														
Blue-collar supervisors	•	•	•	•	•		•		•					M
Precision Production Occupations														
Boilermakers		•					•		•					M
Bookbinding workers		•			•		•	•	•			•		M
Butchers and meatcutters						•	•	•	•			•		M
Compositors and typesetters							•	•	•			•		M
Dental laboratory technicians								•				•		M
Jewelers	•	•	•	•	•	•	•					•	•	M
Lithographic and photoengraving workers		•	•		•		•	•				•		M
Machinists		•					•	•	•			•		M
Photographic process workers								•				•		L
Shoe and leather workers and repairers		•			•	•	•							M
Tool-and-die makers		•					•	•	•			•	•	M
Upholsterers							•	•				•		M
Plant and System Operators														
Stationary engineers		•					•	•	•					M
Water and sewage treatment plant operators		•	•				•		•	•				M
Machine Operators, Tenders, and Setup Workers														
Metalworking and plastic-working machine operators							•	•	•			•	•	L
Numerical-control machine-tool operators		•					•	•	•			•		M
Printing press operators		•	•		•		•	•	•			•		M
Fabricators, Assemblers, and Handworking Occupations														
Precision assemblers					•		•	•				•		L
Transportation equipment painters							•	•	•			•		M
Welders and cutters							•	•	•	•				M

	1. Leadership/persuasion	2. Helping/instructing others	3. Problem-solving/creativity	4. Initiative	5. Work as part of a team	6. Frequent public contact	7. Manual dexterity	8. Physical stamina	9. Hazardous	10. Outdoors	11. Confined	12. Geographically concentrated	13. Part-time	14. Entry requirements
Transportation and Material Moving Occupations														
Aircraft pilots			•	•	•		•					•		M
Busdrivers				•		•	•	•				•	•	M
Construction machinery operators				•			•	•	•	•		•		M
Industrial truck and tractor operators				•			•	•				•		M
Truckdrivers				•			•	•				•		M
Handlers, Equipment Cleaners, Helpers, and Laborers														
Construction trades helpers					•		•	•	•	•				L

Index

VGM CAREER BOOKS

BUSINESS PORTRAITS
Boeing
Coca-Cola
Ford
McDonald's

CAREER DIRECTORIES
Careers Encyclopedia
Dictionary of Occupational Titles
Occupational Outlook Handbook

CAREERS FOR
Animal Lovers; Bookworms; Caring
People; Computer Buffs; Crafty
People; Culture Lovers;
Environmental Types; Fashion Plates;
Film Buffs; Foreign Language
Aficionados; Good Samaritans;
Gourmets; Health Nuts; History
Buffs; Kids at Heart; Music Lovers;
Mystery Buffs; Nature Lovers; Night
Owls; Number Crunchers; Plant
Lovers; Shutterbugs; Sports Nuts;
Travel Buffs; Writers

CAREERS IN
Accounting; Advertising; Business;
Child Care; Communications;
Computers; Education; Engineering;
the Environment; Finance;
Government; Health Care; High
Tech; Horticulture & Botany;
International Business; Journalism;
Law; Marketing; Medicine; Science;
Social & Rehabilitation Services

CAREER PLANNING
Beating Job Burnout
Beginning Entrepreneur
Big Book of Jobs
Career Planning & Development for
    College Students &
    Recent Graduates
Career Change
Career Success for People with
    Physical Disabilities
Careers Checklists
College and Career Success for Students
    with Learning Disabilities
Complete Guide to Career Etiquette
Cover Letters They Don't Forget
Dr. Job's Complete Career Guide
Executive Job Search Strategies
Guide to Basic Cover Letter Writing
Guide to Basic Résumé Writing
Guide to Internet Job Searching
Guide to Temporary Employment
Job Interviewing for College Students
Joyce Lain Kennedy's Career Book

Out of Uniform
Parent's Crash Course in Career
    Planning
Slame Dunk Résumés
Up Your Grades: Proven Strategies
    for Academic Success

CAREER PORTRAITS
Animals; Cars; Computers;
Electronics; Fashion; Firefighting;
Music; Nature; Nursing; Science;
Sports; Teaching; Travel; Writing

GREAT JOBS FOR
Business Majors
Communications Majors
Engineering Majors
English Majors
Foreign Language Majors
History Majors
Psychology Majors
Sociology Majors

HOW TO
Apply to American Colleges and
    Universities
Approach an Advertising Agency and
    Walk Away with the Job You Want
Be a Super Sitter
Bounce Back Quickly After
    Losing Your Job
Change Your Career
Choose the Right Career
Cómo escribir un currículum vitae en
    inglés que tenga éxito
Find Your New Career Upon
    Retirement
Get & Keep Your First Job
Get Hired Today
Get into the Right Business School
Get into the Right Law School
Get into the Right Medical School
Get People to Do Things Your Way
Have a Winning Job Interview
Hit the Ground Running in Your
    New Job
Hold It All Together When You've
    Lost Your Job
Improve Your Study Skills
Jumpstart a Stalled Career
Land a Better Job
Launch Your Career in TV News
Make the Right Career Moves
Market Your College Degree
Move from College into a
    Secure Job
Negotiate the Raise You Deserve
Prepare Your Curriculum Vitae

Prepare for College
Run Your Own Home Business
Succeed in Advertising When all You
Succeed in College
Succeed in High School
Take Charge of Your Child's Early
    Education
Write a Winning Résumé
Write Successful Cover Letters
Write Term Papers & Reports
Write Your College Application Essay

MADE EASY
College Applications
Cover Letters
Getting a Raise
Job Hunting
Job Interviews
Résumés

ON THE JOB: REAL PEOPLE WORKING IN...
Communications
Health Care
Sales & Marketing
Service Businesses

OPPORTUNITIES IN
This extensive series provides detailed
    information on more than 150
    individual career fields.

RÉSUMÉS FOR
Advertising Careers
Architecture and Related Careers
Banking and Financial Careers
Business Management Careers
College Students &
    Recent Graduates
Communications Careers
Computer Careers
Education Careers
Engineering Careers
Environmental Careers
Ex-Military Personnel
50+ Job Hunters
Government Careers
Health and Medical Careers
High School Graduates
High Tech Careers
Law Careers
Midcareer Job Changes
Nursing Careers
Re-Entering the Job Market
Sales and Marketing Careers
Scientific and Technical Careers
Social Service Careers
The First-Time Job Hunter

VGM Career Horizons
a division of *NTC Publishing Group*
4255 West Touhy Avenue
Lincolnwood, Illinois 60646–1975